CHE GUEVARA ■ READER ■

SECOND, EXPANDED EDITION

Edited by David Deutschmann and María del Carmen Ariet

ocean

Centro de Estudios
CHE GUEVARA

ISBN 978-1-876175-69-6
Library of Congress Catalog Card No: 2003102876

Second edition 2003
Fourth printing 2007
Fifth printing 2013
Printed by Asia Pacific Offset Ltd., China

Available from Ocean Sur in Spanish as *Che Guevara Presente*, ISBN 978-1-876175-93-1

PUBLISHED BY OCEAN PRESS
PO Box 1015, North Melbourne, VIC 3051, Australia
E-mail: info@oceanbooks.com.au

OCEAN PRESS TRADE DISTRIBUTORS
United States: Consortium Book Sales and Distribution
        Tel: 1-800-283-3572   www.cbsd.com

Canada: Publishers Group Canada
        Tel: 1-800-663-5714   E-mail: customerservice@raincoast.com

Australia and New Zealand: Palgrave Macmillan
        Tel: 1-300-135 113   E-mail: customer.service@macmillan.com.au

UK and Europe: Turnaround Publisher Services
        Tel: (44) 020-8829 3000 E-mail: orders@turnaround-uk.com

Cuba and Latin America: Ocean Sur
        E-mail: info@oceansur.com

ocean

www.oceanbooks.com.au
info@oceanbooks.com.au

■ CHE GUEVARA READER ■

CHE GUEVARA PUBLISHING PROJECT

THE DIARIES:

The Motorcycle Diaries (1952)

Latin America Diaries (1953–55)

Reminiscences of the Cuban Revolutionary War (1956–58)

Diary of a Combatant (1956–58)

Congo Diary (1965)

The Bolivian Diary (1966–67)

Che: The Diaries of Ernesto Che Guevara

ALSO AVAILABLE:

Che Guevara Reader

The Awakening of Latin America

Global Justice: Liberation and Socialism

Self-Portrait: A Photographic and Literary Memoir

Marx & Engels: A Biographical Introduction

Guerrilla Warfare

Our America and Theirs

■ CONTENTS ■

PART 3: INTERNATIONAL SOLIDARITY

PART 4: LETTERS

"We are realists...
We dream the
impossible."

Che Guevara

Ernesto Che Guevara

Ernesto Guevara de la Serna was born in Rosario, Argentina on June 14, 1928. As a medical student in Buenos Aires and after earning his degree as doctor, he traveled throughout Latin America. Living in Guatemala during 1954 — then under the elected government of Jacobo Arbenz — he became involved in political activity there and was an eyewitness to the overthrow of that government in a CIA-organized military operation.

Forced to leave Guatemala under threat of death, Guevara went to Mexico City. There he linked up with exiled Cuban revolutionaries seeking to overthrow dictator Fulgencio Batista. In July 1955 he met Fidel Castro and immediately enlisted in the guerrilla expedition Castro was organizing. The Cubans nick-named him "Che," a popular form of address in Argentina.

From November 25 to December 2, 1956, Guevara was part of the expedition that sailed to Cuba aboard the cabin cruiser *Granma* to begin the revolutionary armed struggle in the Sierra Maestra mountains. Originally the troop doctor, he became the first Rebel Army commander in July 1957.

In September 1958, Guevara and Camilo Cienfuegos each led guerrilla columns westward from the Sierra Maestra to the center of the island. Through fierce fighting they successfully extended the Rebel Army's operations to much of Cuba. At the end of December 1958, Guevara led the Rebel Army forces to victory in the battle of Santa Clara, one of the decisive engagements of the war.

Following the rebels' victory on January 1, 1959, Guevara became a key leader of the new revolutionary government. In September 1959 he began serving as head of the Department of Industry of the National Institute of Agrarian Reform; in November 1959 he became President of the National Bank; and in February 1961 he became Minister of Industry. He was also a central leader of the political organization that in 1965 became the Communist Party of Cuba.

Guevara was a leading Cuban representative around the world, heading numerous delegations and speaking at the United Nations and other international forums.

In April 1965 Guevara left Cuba to participate directly in revolutionary struggles abroad. He spent several months in the Congo in Africa, returning to Cuba secretly in December 1965. In November 1966 he arrived in Bolivia where he led a guerrilla detachment fighting that country's military dictatorship. Wounded and captured by U.S.-trained and supervised Bolivian counterinsurgency troops on October 8, 1967, he was murdered the following day.

Introduction

his expanded edition of a book first published in 1997 on the 30th anniversary of Che Guevara's death has a simple purpose: to make available to an English-reading audience a selection of articles, speeches and letters by Ernesto Che Guevara. It is not a biography nor a book of reminiscences by others — it is Che Guevara in his own words.

In the almost four decades since his death, the world's image of Che Guevara has become increasingly distorted and somewhat one-dimensional. The romanticized portrait known to many is that of the individual guerrilla fighter — heroic to some, to others an adventurer. His organic connection to the Cuban revolution fades in this picture. His work side by side with Fidel Castro for nearly a decade; his contributions to Marxist theory; his efforts as a government minister in the first years of the new Cuba after the overthrow of the Batista dictatorship; his tireless labor grappling with the problems of guiding the economic development of a backward country besieged and attacked by U.S. imperialism; his championing the interests of the people of Asia, Africa and Latin America — all this is missing from most popular portrayals of Che Guevara outside of Cuba.

This is reflected in the fact that for two decades or more after his death his writings were largely unavailable in English. Several collections of speeches by Che were published in the 1960s, but most were long out of print. The 30th anniversary of his death saw several new biographies and many commentaries on his life and death, but still few efforts to publish the ideas of Che himself, in his own words.

This book presents the political lessons drawn by Che Guevara from his experiences and the many tasks that he took on: as Rebel Army commander and strategist of guerrilla warfare; as a leader of the July 26 Movement, which played a central role in the overthrow of the U.S.-backed Batista dictatorship; as head of the National Bank and Ministry of Industry in the new government; as a forger of Cuba's close ties with liberation movements throughout the African continent; and as a representative of the Cuban government on platforms throughout the world.

In a speech given before one million people in Havana on October 18, 1967, at a memorial service for Che Guevara, Cuba's Fidel Castro placed significant emphasis on the breadth of Guevara's political contribution:

> Those who attach significance to the lucky blow that struck Che down try in vain to deny his experience and his capacity as a leader. Che was an extraordinarily able military leader. But when we remember Che, when we think of Che, we do not think fundamentally of his military virtues. No! Warfare is a means and not an end. Warfare is a tool of revolutionaries. The important thing is the revolution. The important thing is the revolutionary cause, revolutionary ideas, revolutionary objectives, revolutionary sentiments, revolutionary virtues!
>
> And it is in that field, in the field of ideas, in the field of sentiments, in the field of revolutionary virtues, in the field of intelligence, that — apart from his military virtues — we feel the tremendous loss that his death means to the revolutionary movement.
>
> Che's extraordinary character was made up of virtues that are rarely found together. He stood out as an unsurpassed person of action, but Che was not only that — he was also a person of visionary intelligence and broad culture, a profound thinker. That is, the man of ideas and the man of action were combined within him.
>
> But it is not only that Che possessed the double characteristic of the man of ideas — of profound ideas — and the man of action, but that Che as a revolutionary united in himself the virtues that can be defined as the fullest expression of the virtues of a revolutionary: a person of total integrity, a person of supreme sense of honor, of absolute sincerity, a person of stoic and Spartan living habits, a person in whose conduct not one stain can be found. He constituted, through his virtues, what can be called a truly model revolutionary.
>
> Because of this, he has left to the future generations not only his experience, his knowledge as an outstanding soldier, but also, at the same time, the fruits of his intelligence. He wrote with the virtuosity of a master of our language. His narratives of the war are incomparable. The depth of his thinking is impressive. He never wrote about anything with less than extraordinary seriousness, with less than extraordinary profundity — and we have no doubt that some of his writings will pass on to posterity as classic documents of revolutionary thought.

Thus, as fruits of that vigorous and profound intelligence, he left us countless memories, countless narratives that, without his work, without his efforts, might have been lost forever.

An indefatigable worker, during the years that he served our country he did not know a single day of rest. Many were the responsibilities assigned to him: as President of the National Bank, as director of the Central Planning Board, as Minister of Industry, as commander of military regions, as the head of political or economic or fraternal delegations.

His versatile intelligence was able to undertake with maximum assurance any task of any kind. Thus he brilliantly represented our country in numerous international conferences, just as he brilliantly led soldiers in combat, just as he was a model worker in charge of any of the institutions he was assigned to. And for him there were no days of rest; for him there were no hours of rest!

If we looked through the windows of his offices, he had the lights on all hours of the night, studying, or rather, working or studying. For he was a student of all problems; he was a tireless reader. His thirst for learning was practically insatiable, and the hours he stole from sleep he devoted to study.

He devoted his scheduled days off to voluntary work. He was the inspiration and provided the greatest incentive for the work that is today carried out by hundreds of thousands of people throughout the country. He stimulated that activity in which our people are making greater and greater efforts.

As a revolutionary, as a communist revolutionary, a true communist, he had a boundless faith in moral values. He had a boundless faith in the consciousness of human beings. And we should say that he saw, with absolute clarity, the moral impulse as the fundamental lever in the construction of communism in human society.

He thought, developed, and wrote many things. And on a day like today it should be stated that Che's writings, Che's political and revolutionary thought, will be of permanent value to the Cuban revolutionary process and to the Latin American revolutionary process. And we do not doubt that his ideas — as a man of action, as a man of thought, as a person of untarnished moral virtues, as a person of unexcelled human sensitivity, as a person of spotless conduct — have and will continue to have universal value.

The imperialists boast of their triumph at having killed this guerrilla fighter in action. The imperialists boast of a triumphant stroke of luck that led to the elimination of such a formidable man of action. But perhaps the imperialists do not know or pretend not to know that the man of action was only one of the many facets of the personality of that combatant. And if we speak of sorrow, we are saddened not only at having lost a person of action. We are saddened at having lost a person of virtue. We are saddened at having lost a person of unsurpassed human sensitivity. We are saddened at having lost such a mind. We are saddened to think that he was only 39 years old at the time of his death. We are saddened at missing the additional fruits that we would have received from that intelligence and that ever richer experience.

Che Guevara first left Cuba in April 1965. From that time rumors began to circulate as to his whereabouts. He was "spotted" in almost every country of Latin America while speculation grew that Fidel Castro had eliminated his "rival." A campaign began — which has managed to survive these past four decades — to separate Guevara from both the Cuban revolution and Fidel Castro. The most powerful and convincing rebuttal to this calumny is provided by Guevara himself in the words of the speeches and writings contained in this selection.

A companion volume to *Che Guevara Reader* which takes up this theme is *Che: A memoir by Fidel Castro*. In the closest thing to a biography of Guevara to yet emerge from Cuba, Fidel Castro writes with candor and affection of his relationship with Guevara. In particular, Castro describes his last days with Che in Cuba, giving a remarkably frank assessment of the Bolivian mission of 1966-67, which resulted in Guevara's death in October 1967 at the hands of the Bolivian Army acting under the instructions of the Central Intelligence Agency.

■ ■ ■

This wide-ranging selection of Guevara's speeches and writings includes four parts: the Cuban guerrilla war (1956-58); the years in government in Cuba (1959-65); Guevara's views on the major international issues of the time, including documents written from Africa and Latin America after his departure from Cuba in 1965; and a selection of letters written by Guevara, including his farewell letters to Fidel Castro and his children and family.

The first work on this book was the result of an editorial collaboration in 1987 between the editor and the José Martí Publishing House in Havana, Cuba. Subsequently, the participation of the Havana-based Centro de Estudios Che Guevara [Che Guevara Studies Center] has led to a major expansion of the first edition of this anthology.

An invaluable aid in the preparation of the first edition of this volume were two comprehensive Spanish-language selections of Che Guevara's works: the nine-volume *Ernesto Che Guevara: Escritos y discursos* [Writings and Speeches] (Havana: Ciencias Sociales, 1977) and the two-volume *Ernesto Che Guevara: Obras Escogidas 1956-67* [Selected Works] (Havana: Casa de las Américas, 1970).

As an aid to the reader, the book contains:

■ A chronology of significant events in the life of Ernesto Che Guevara and of the Cuban revolution during his lifetime.

■ A bibliography of Guevara's published writings and speeches, which provides an overview of his broad political responsibilities, interests and activities in the years 1958-67.

■ A glossary of the names of many individuals, organizations and publications referred to in the text.

These annotations will help readers to place Guevara's writings in the appropriate political and historical context.

The new, expanded edition includes several new chapters that among other goals seeks to highlight Che Guevara's vision toward Latin America. Readers of this volume will want to explore this further in the anthology of Che's writings on Latin America contained in *Latin America: Awakening of a Continent* (an editorial project of Ocean Press and the Che Guevara Studies Center).

In coming years, the principal writings of Che Guevara will be published in a series of books prepared by the Che Guevara Studies Center of Havana and Ocean Press. Although perhaps best known as a guerrilla fighter, this multi-volume series will show Che Guevara as a profound thinker with a radical world view that still strikes a chord with young rebels in every country today. Eager readers will be introduced to Che the political economist and philosopher, Che the revolutionary humanist.

Some of these works have never before been published, such as Che's *Critical Notes on Political Economy*. Other works have only recently been uncovered, while many have been overlooked or available intermittently. A number of the books will be thematic anthologies.

■　■　■

It is necessary to acknowledge the support given to the preparation of this volume by the Che Guevara Studies Center. Special gratitude needs to be given to the Center's director, Aleida March, and its research coordinator, Maria del Carmen Ariet García. They made suggestions on how the selection could be expanded as well as alerted us to various errors. Although this is a joint editorial project with the Che Guevara Studies Center, full responsibility for annotation is taken by Ocean Press.

David Deutschmann
2003

Chronology

June 14, 1928 Ernesto Guevara is born in Rosario, Argentina, of parents Ernesto Guevara Lynch and Celia de la Serna; he will be the oldest of five children.

1947 Guevara family moves to Buenos Aires.

1947–53 Ernesto Guevara is enrolled at medical school in Buenos Aires.

December 1951–July 1952 Guevara visits Chile, Peru, Colombia and Venezuela. While in Peru he works in a leper colony treating patients.

March 10, 1952 Fulgencio Batista carries out coup d'état in Cuba.

March 1953 Guevara graduates as a doctor.

July 6, 1953 After graduating, Guevara travels throughout Latin America. He visits Bolivia, observing the impact of the 1952 revolution.

July 26, 1953 Fidel Castro leads an armed attack on the Moncada army garrison in Santiago de Cuba, launching the revolutionary struggle to overthrow the Batista regime. The attack fails and Batista's troops massacre more than 50 captured combatants. Castro and other survivors are soon captured and imprisoned.

December 1953 Guevara has first contact with a group of survivors of the Moncada attack in San José, Costa Rica.

December 24, 1953 Guevara arrives in Guatemala, then under the elected government of Jacobo Arbenz.

January 4, 1954 Guevara meets Ñico López, a veteran of the Moncada attack, in Guatemala City.

January–June 1954 Unable to find a medical position in Guatemala, Guevara obtains various odd jobs. He studies Marxism and becomes involved in political activities, meeting exiled Cuban revolutionaries.

June 17, 1954 Mercenary forces backed by the CIA invade Guatemala. Guevara volunteers to fight.

June 27, 1954 Arbenz resigns.

August 1954 Mercenary troops enter Guatemala City and begin massacring supporters of the Arbenz regime.

September 21, 1954 Guevara arrives in Mexico City after fleeing Guatemala; subsequently gets job as doctor at Central Hospital.

May 15, 1955 Fidel Castro and other Moncada survivors are freed from prison in Cuba due to a massive public campaign in defense of their civil rights.

June 1955 Guevara encounters Ñico López, who is also in Mexico City. Several days later López arranges a meeting for him with Raúl Castro.

July 7, 1955 Fidel Castro arrives in Mexico with the goal of organizing an armed expedition to Cuba.

July 1955 Guevara meets Fidel Castro and immediately enrolls as the third confirmed member of the future guerrilla expedition. Guevara subsequently becomes involved in training combatants, with the Cubans giving him the nickname "Che," an Argentine term of greeting.

June 24, 1956 Guevara is arrested as part of a roundup by Mexican police of 28 expeditionaries, including Fidel Castro; Guevara is detained for 57 days.

November 25, 1956 Eighty-two combatants, including Guevara as doctor, sail for Cuba aboard the small cabin cruiser *Granma*, leaving from Tuxpan in Mexico.

November 30, 1956 Frank País leads uprising in Santiago de Cuba, timed to coincide with scheduled arrival of *Granma* expeditionaries.

December 2, 1956 *Granma* reaches Cuba at Las Coloradas beach in Oriente Province.

December 5, 1956 The rebel combatants are surprised by Batista's troops at Alegría de Pío and dispersed. A majority of the guerrillas are either murdered or captured; Guevara is wounded.

December 21, 1956 Guevara's group reunites with Fidel Castro; at this point there are 15 fighters in the Rebel Army.

January 17, 1957 Rebel Army overruns an army outpost in the battle of La Plata.

January 22, 1957 Rebel Army ambushes government column at Arroyo del Infierno.

March 13, 1957 Fighters from the Revolutionary Directorate attack the Presidential Palace in Havana; attack fails and a number of students are killed, including José Antonio Echeverría.

May 27–28, 1957 Battle of El Uvero takes place in the Sierra Maestra, with a major victory for the Rebel Army as it captures a well-fortified army garrison.

July 1957 Rebel Army organizes a second column. Guevara is selected to lead it and is promoted to the rank of commander.

April 9, 1958 July 26 Movement calls for a general strike throughout Cuba; strike fails.

May 24, 1958 Batista launches an all-out military offensive against the Rebel Army in the Sierra Maestra. The offensive eventually fails.

July 1958 Battle of El Jigüe; decisive Rebel Army victory marks beginning of Rebel counteroffensive.

August 31, 1958 Guevara leads an invasion column from the Sierra Maestra toward Las Villas Province in central Cuba, and days later signs the Pedrero Pact with the March 13 Revolutionary Directorate, which had a strong guerrilla base there. Several days earlier Camilo Cienfuegos had been ordered to lead another column toward Pinar del Río Province on the western end of Cuba.

October 16, 1958 The Rebel Army column led by Guevara arrives in the Escambray Mountains.

December 1958 Rebel columns of Guevara and the March 13 Revolutionary Directorate, and Cienfuegos with a small guerrilla troop of the Popular Socialist Party, capture a number of towns in Las Villas Province and effectively cut the island in half.

December 28, 1958 Guevara's column begins the battle of Santa Clara, the capital of Las Villas.

January 1, 1959 Batista flees Cuba. A military junta takes over. Fidel Castro opposes the new junta and calls for the revolutionary struggle to continue. Santa Clara falls to the Rebel Army. Guevara and Cienfuegos are ordered immediately to Havana.

January 2, 1959 Cuban workers respond to Fidel Castro's call for a general strike and the country is paralyzed. The Rebel Army columns of Guevara and Cienfuegos arrive in Havana. Guevara's column occupies La Cabaña fortress, a former bastion of Batista's army.

January 5, 1959 Manuel Urrutia, the designated choice of the July 26 Movement, assumes presidency.

January 8, 1959 Fidel Castro arrives in Havana, greeted by hundreds of thousands of people.

February 9, 1959 Guevara is declared a Cuban citizen in recognition of his contribution to Cuba's liberation.

February 16, 1959 Fidel Castro becomes prime minister.

February 27, 1959 Revolutionary government approves law reducing electricity rates.

March 6, 1959 Revolutionary government approves law reducing rents by 30–50 percent.

March 1959 Revolutionary government outlaws racial discrimination.

May 17, 1959 Proclamation of the first agrarian reform law, fixing legal holdings at a maximum of 1,000 acres and distributing land to peasants.

June 12–September 8, 1959 Guevara travels through Europe, Africa and Asia; signs a number of commercial, technical and cultural agreements. A central objective of this trip is to visit the countries leading the Bandung Pact.

July 16–17, 1959 Castro resigns as prime minister because of government crisis stemming from Urrutia's opposition to revolution's measures; in response, a massive popular outpouring forces Urrutia to resign from presidency and he is replaced by Osvaldo Dorticós.

July 26, 1959 Castro returns to post as prime minister.

October 7, 1959 Guevara is designated head of the Department of Industry of the National Institute of Agrarian Reform (INRA).

October 21, 1959 Following an attempt to initiate a counterrevolutionary uprising, Huber Matos, military commander of Camagüey Province, is arrested by army chief of staff Camilo Cienfuegos.

October 26, 1959 Announcement of creation of National Revolutionary Militias, to incorporate thousands of workers and peasants into the fight against counterrevolution.

October 28, 1959 Camilo Cienfuegos's plane goes down over sea. Cienfuegos is lost at sea.

November 26, 1959 Guevara is appointed president of the National Bank of Cuba.

March 4, 1960 *La Coubre,* a French ship carrying Belgian arms, explodes in Havana harbor as a result of sabotage, killing 81 people; at a mass rally the following day, Fidel Castro proclaims the slogan of the Cuban Revolution: "Patria or muerte!"

March 17, 1960 President Eisenhower orders the CIA to begin preparation of Cuban exile army to invade Cuba.

May 8, 1960 Cuba and the Soviet Union establish diplomatic relations.

June 29–July 1, 1960 Revolutionary government nationalizes Texaco, Esso and Shell refineries following their refusal to refine petroleum purchased by Cuba from the Soviet Union.

July 6, 1960 Eisenhower orders reduction by 700,000 tons of sugar that the United States has agreed to purchase from Cuba.

July 9, 1960 Soviet Union announces that it will purchase all Cuban sugar that the United States refuses to buy.

August 6, 1960 In response to U.S. economic aggression, the Cuban Government decrees the nationalization of major U.S. companies in Cuba.

October 13, 1960 Revolutionary government nationalizes Cuban and foreign-owned banks as well as 382 large Cuban-owned industries.

October 14, 1960 Urban reform law approved, nationalizing housing; Cubans are guaranteed the right to their dwellings.

October 19, 1960 U.S. Government decrees a partial embargo of trade with Cuba.

October 21, 1960 Fusion of revolutionary youth movements into Association of Young Rebels. Guevara leaves on extended visit to Soviet Union, German Democratic Republic, Czechoslovakia, China and North Korea.

October 24, 1960 Cuban Government nationalizes remaining U.S. companies in Cuba.

January 3, 1961 Washington breaks diplomatic relations with Cuba.

January 6, 1961 Guevara reports to Cuban people on economic agreements signed with Soviet Union and other countries.

January 17, 1961 U.S. Government imposes ban on travel by U.S. citizens to Cuba.

February 23, 1961 Ministry of Industry established, headed by Guevara.

March 31, 1961 President Kennedy abolishes Cuba's sugar quota.

April 15, 1961 As a prelude to planned invasion by U.S.-organized mercenary army, planes attack Santiago de Cuba and Havana.

April 16, 1961 At a mass rally to honor the victims of the previous day's attacks, Fidel Castro proclaims socialist character of the Cuban Revolution; Cuba is put on alert in anticipation of the impending attack.

April 17–19, 1961 1,500 Cuban-born mercenaries, organized and backed by the United States, invade Cuba at the Bay of Pigs on the southern coast. The aim was to establish a "provisional government" to appeal for direct U.S. intervention. They are defeated within 72 hours, with the last ones surrendering at Playa Girón (Girón Beach), which has come to be the name used by the Cubans for the battle. Guevara is sent to command troops in Pinar del Río Province.

August 8, 1961 Guevara delivers speech to Organization of American States (OAS) Economic and Social Conference in Punta del Este, Uruguay, as head of Cuba's delegation.

December 22, 1961 Cuba completes year-long nationwide literacy campaign.

January 31, 1962 OAS votes to expel Cuba.

February 3, 1962 President Kennedy orders total embargo on U.S. trade with Cuba.

March 8, 1962 National Directorate of the Integrated Revolutionary Organizations (ORI) is established, based on fusion of the July 26 Movement, Popular Socialist Party and Revolutionary Directorate; Guevara is a member of the National Directorate.

August 27–September 7, 1962 Guevara makes second visit to the Soviet Union.

October 22, 1962 President Kennedy initiates the "Cuban Missile Crisis," denouncing Cuba's acquisition of missiles capable of carrying nuclear warheads for defense against U.S. attack. Washington imposes a naval blockade on Cuba. Cuba responds by mobilizing its population for defense. Guevara is assigned to lead forces in Pinar del Río Province in preparation for an imminent U.S. invasion.

October 28, 1962 Soviet Premier Khrushchev agrees to remove Soviet missiles in exchange for U.S. pledge not to invade Cuba.

1963 United Party of Socialist Revolution (PURS) is formed; Guevara is a member of its National Directorate.

July 3–17, 1963 Guevara visits Algeria, then recently independent under the government of Ahmed Ben Bella.

March 1964 Guevara meets with Tamara Bunke (Tania) and discusses her mission to move to Bolivia in anticipation of a future guerrilla expedition.

March 25, 1964 Guevara addresses UN Conference on Trade and Development in Geneva, Switzerland.

November 4–9, 1964 Guevara visits the Soviet Union.

December 9, 1964 Guevara leaves Cuba on a three-month state visit.

December 11, 1964 Guevara addresses the United Nations General Assembly.

December 17, 1964 Guevara leaves New York for Africa, where until March 1965 he visits Algeria, Mali, Congo (Brazzaville), Guinea, Ghana, Tanzania and Egypt.

February 24, 1965 Guevara addresses the Second Economic Seminar of the Organization of Afro-Asian Solidarity in Algiers.

March 14, 1965 Guevara returns to Cuba and shortly afterwards drops from public view.

April 1, 1965 Guevara delivers a farewell letter to Fidel Castro. He subsequently leaves Cuba on an internationalist mission in the Congo (subsequently Zaire, and now the Democratic Republic of the Congo), entering through Tanzania. Guevara operates under the name Tatú.

April 18, 1965 In answer to questions about Guevara's whereabouts, Castro tells foreign reporters that Guevara "will always be where he is most useful to the revolution."

June 16, 1965 Castro announces Guevara's whereabouts will be revealed "when Commander Guevara wants it known."

October 1, 1965 Communist Party of Cuba officially formed.

October 3, 1965 Castro publicly reads Guevara's letter of farewell at a meeting to announce the Central Committee of the newly formed Communist Party of Cuba.

December 1965 Guevara returns to Cuba in secret, and prepares for an expedition to Bolivia.

January 3–14, 1966 Tricontinental Conference of Solidarity of the Peoples of Asia, Africa and Latin America is held in Havana.

March 1966 Arrival in Bolivia of the first Cuban combatants to begin advance preparations for a guerrilla detachment.

July 1966 Guevara meets with Cuban volunteers selected for the mission to Bolivia at a training camp in Cuba's Pinar del Río Province.

November 3, 1966 Guevara arrives in Bolivia in disguise and using an assumed name.

November 7, 1966 Guevara arrives at site where Bolivian guerrilla movement will be based; first entry in Bolivian diary.

November–December 1966 More guerrilla combatants arrive and base camps are established.

December 31, 1966 Guevara meets with Bolivian Communist Party secretary Mario Monje. There is disagreement over perspectives for the planned guerrilla expedition.

February 1–March 20, 1967 Guerrilla detachment leaves the base camp to explore the region.

March–April 1967 U.S. Special Forces arrive in Bolivia to train counterinsurgency troops of the Bolivian Army.

March 23, 1967 First guerrilla military action takes place with combatants successfully ambushing a Bolivian Army column.

April 10, 1967 Guerrilla column conducts a successful ambush of Bolivian troops.

April 16, 1967 Publication of Guevara's Message to the Tricontinental with his call for the creation of "two, three, many Vietnams."

April 17, 1967 Guerrilla detachment led by Joaquín is separated from the rest of the unit. The separation is supposed to last only three days but the two groups are unable to reunite.

April 20, 1967 Régis Debray is arrested after having spent several weeks with a guerrilla unit. He is subsequently tried and sentenced to 30 years' imprisonment.

July 6, 1967 Guerrillas occupy the town of Sumaipata.

July 26, 1967 Guevara gives a speech to guerrillas on the significance of the July 26, 1953, attack on the Moncada garrison.

July 31–August 10, 1967 Organization of Latin American Solidarity (OLAS) conference is held in Havana. The conference supports guerrilla movements throughout Latin America. Che Guevara is elected honorary chair.

August 4, 1967 Deserter leads the Bolivian Army to the guerrillas' main supply cache; documents seized lead to arrest of key urban contacts.

August 31, 1967 Joaquín's detachment is ambushed and annihilated while crossing a river after an informer leads government troops to the site.

September 26, 1967 Guerrillas walk into an ambush. Three are killed and government forces encircle the remaining guerrilla forces.

October 8, 1967 Remaining 17 guerrillas are trapped by Bolivian troops and conduct a desperate battle. Guevara is seriously wounded and captured.

October 9, 1967 Guevara and two other captured guerrillas are murdered following instructions from the Bolivian Government and Washington.

October 15, 1967 In a television appearance Fidel Castro confirms news of Guevara's death and declares three days of official mourning in Cuba. October 8 is designated Day of the Heroic Guerrilla.

October 18, 1967 Castro delivers memorial speech for Guevara in Havana's Revolution Plaza before an audience of almost one million people.

February 22, 1968 Three Cuban survivors cross border into Chile, after having traveled across the Andes on foot to elude Bolivian Army. They later return to Cuba.

Mid–March 1968 Microfilm of Guevara's Bolivian diary arrives in Cuba.

July 1, 1968 Guevara's Bolivian diary published in Cuba is distributed free of charge to the Cuban people. The introduction is by Fidel Castro.

June 28, 1997 Guevara's remains are discovered in Bolivia, almost three decades after being hidden.

October 1997 Guevara's remains are returned to Cuba and buried in Santa Clara along with others located in Bolivia.

PART 1

THE CUBAN REVOLUTIONARY WAR

"We are now in a position in which we are much more than simple instruments of one nation. We are now the hope of the unredeemed Americas."

Episodes of the revolutionary war

On December 2, 1956, Fidel Castro and 81 other combatants, including Che Guevara, landed in Cuba to begin the revolutionary war against the U.S.-backed regime of Fulgencio Batista. Over the next two years, the Rebel Army conducted an ever-widening guerrilla struggle that won increasing popular support in the countryside and the cities, culminating in the revolution's victory on January 1, 1959. Between 1959 and 1964 Guevara wrote a number of articles describing some of his experiences as a guerrilla combatant and comman-der. These were later published in Cuba as a book entitled Pasajes de la guerra revolucionaria *[Episodes of the revolutionary war]. These are several articles selected from that account.*

A revolution begins

The history of the military takeover on March 10, 1952 — the bloodless coup led by Fulgencio Batista — does not of course begin on the day of that barracks revolt. Its antecedents must be sought far back in Cuban history: much farther back than the intervention of U.S. Ambassador Sumner Welles in 1933; much farther back still than the Platt Amendment in 1901; much farther back than the landing of the hero Narciso López, direct envoy of the U.S. annexationists. We would have to go back to the times of John Quincy Adams, who at the beginning of the 19th century announced his country's consistent policy toward Cuba: it was to be like an apple that, torn away from Spain, was destined to fall into the hands of Uncle Sam. These are all links in a long chain of continental aggression that has not been aimed solely at Cuba.[1]

This tide, this ebb and flow of the imperial wave, is marked by the fall of democratic governments and the rise of new ones in the face of the uncontainable pressure of the multitudes. History exhibits similar characteristics in all of Latin America: dictatorial governments represent a small minority and come to power through a coup d'état; democratic governments with a broad popular base arise laboriously, and, frequently, even before coming to power, are already compromised by a series of concessions they have had to make beforehand to survive. Although in this sense the Cuban Revolution marks an exception in all the Americas, it is necessary to point out the antecedents of this whole process. It was due to these causes that the author of these lines, tossed here and there by the waves of the social movements convulsing the Americas, had the opportunity to meet another Latin American exile: Fidel Castro.

I met him on one of those cold Mexican nights, and I remember that our first discussion was about international politics. Within a few hours — by dawn — I was one of the future expeditionaries. But I would like to clarify how and why it was in Mexico that I met Cuba's current head of state.

It was during the ebb of the democratic governments in 1954, when the last Latin American revolutionary democracy still standing in the area — that of Jacobo Arbenz Guzmán — succumbed to the cold, premeditated aggression carried out by the United States of America behind the smoke-screen of its continental propaganda. The visible head of that aggression was Secretary of State John Foster Dulles, who by a strange coincidence was also the lawyer for and a stockholder of the United Fruit Company, the main imperialist enterprise in Guatemala.

I was returning from there, defeated, united with all Guatemalans by the pain; hoping, searching for a way to rebuild a future for that anguished country.

And Fidel came to Mexico looking for neutral ground on which to prepare his men for the big effort. An internal split had already occurred after the assault on the Moncada military garrison in Santiago de Cuba.[2] All the weak-spirited had split away, all those who for one reason or another joined the political parties or revolutionary groups that demanded less sacrifice. The new recruits were already joining the freshly formed ranks of what was called the July 26 Movement, named after the date of the 1953 attack on the Moncada garrison. An extremely difficult task was beginning for those in charge of training these people under necessarily clandestine conditions in Mexico. They were fighting against the Mexican Government, agents of the U.S. FBI and those of Batista — against these three forces that in one way or another joined together, where money and buying people off played a large role. In addition, we had to struggle against Trujillo's spies and against the poor selection made of the human material — especially in Miami. And after overcoming all these difficulties we had to accomplish an extremely important thing: depart... and then... arrive, and all the rest, which, at the time, seemed easy to us. Today we can weigh all the costs in effort, sacrifice and lives.

Fidel Castro, helped by a small team of intimate collaborators, gave himself over entirely, with all his energies and his extraordinary spirit of work, to the task of organizing the armed fighters that would leave for Cuba. He almost never gave classes on military tactics, since for him time was in short supply. The rest of us were able to learn quite a bit from General Alberto Bayo. Listening to the first classes, my almost instantaneous impression was that victory was possible. I had thought it quite doubtful when I first enrolled with the rebel commander, to whom I was linked from the beginning by a liking for romantic adventure and the thought that it would be well worth dying on a foreign beach for such a pure ideal.

Several months passed in this way. Our marksmanship began to improve, and the best shots emerged. We found a ranch in Mexico where — under the direction of General Bayo and with myself as head of personnel — the final preparations were made, aiming to leave in March 1956. Around that time, however, two Mexican police units, both on Batista's payroll, were hunting for Fidel Castro, and one of them had the good fortune, in financial terms, of capturing him. But they made the absurd error, also in financial terms, of not killing him after taking him prisoner. Within a few days many of his followers were captured. Our ranch on the outskirts of Mexico City also fell into the hands of the police and we all went to jail.

All of this postponed the beginning of the last part of the first stage.

Some of us were imprisoned for 57 days, which we counted off one by one; with the perennial threat of extradition hanging over our heads (as Commander Calixto García and I can attest). But at no time did we lose our personal confidence in Fidel Castro. Fidel did some things that we might almost say compromised his revolutionary attitude for the sake of friendship. I remember that I explained to him my specific case: a foreigner, illegally in Mexico, with a whole series of charges against me. I told him that by no means should the revolution be held up on my account, and that he could leave me behind; that I understood the situation and would try to go fight wherever I was ordered; and that the only effort on my behalf should be to have me sent to a nearby country and not to Argentina. I also remember Fidel's sharp reply: "I will not abandon you." And that's what happened, because precious time and money had to be diverted to get us out of the Mexican jail. That personal attitude of Fidel's toward people whom he holds in esteem is the key to the fanatical loyalty he inspires. An adherence to principles and an adherence to the individual combine to make the Rebel Army an indivisible fist.

The days passed as we worked in clandestinity, hiding ourselves where we could, shunning any public presence to the extent possible, hardly going out into the street. After several months, we found out that there was a traitor in our ranks, whose name we did not know, and that he had sold an arms shipment. We also learned that he had sold the yacht and a transmitter, although he had not yet drawn up the "legal contract" of the sale. That first installment served to show the Cuban authorities that the traitor in fact knew our internal workings. But it was also what saved us, since it showed us the same thing.

From that moment on, we had to undertake feverish preparations. The *Granma* was put into shape at an extraordinary speed. We piled up as many provisions as we could get — very little, in fact — along with uniforms, rifles, equipment and two antitank guns with hardly any ammunition. At any rate, on November 25, 1956, at two o'clock in the morning, we began to make a reality of Fidel's words, scoffed at by the official press: "In 1956 we will be free or we will be martyrs."

With our lights out we left the port of Tuxpan in the midst of an infernal heap of men and equipment of every type. We had very bad weather, and although navigation was forbidden, the river's estuary remained calm. We crossed the entrance into the Gulf of Mexico and shortly thereafter turned on the lights. We began a frantic search for the antihistamines for seasickness and could not find them. We sang the Cuban national anthem and the July 26 Hymn for perhaps five minutes total, and then the whole boat took on a ridiculously tragic appearance: men with anguished faces holding their stomachs, some with their heads in buckets, and others lying immobile on the deck, in the strangest positions, with their clothing soiled by vomit. With the exception of two or three sailors, and four or five others, the rest of the 82 crew members were seasick. But after the fourth or fifth day the general panorama improved a bit. We discovered that what we thought was a leak in the boat was actually an open plumbing faucet. We had already thrown overboard everything unnecessary in order to lighten the ballast.

The route we had chosen involved making a wide turn south of Cuba, bordering Jamaica and the Grand Cayman Islands, with the landing to be someplace close to the village of Niquero in Oriente Province. The plan was being carried out quite slowly. On November 30 we heard over the radio the news of the uprising in Santiago de Cuba that our great Frank País had started, aiming to coincide with the expedition's arrival. The following day, December 1, at night, we set the bow on a straight line toward Cuba, desperately seeking the Cape Cruz lighthouse, as we ran out of water, food and fuel.

At two o'clock in the morning, on a dark and stormy night, the situation was disturbing. The lookouts walked back and forth, searching for the ray of light that would not appear on the horizon. Roque, an ex-lieutenant in the navy, once again got up on the small upper bridge, to look for the light from the cape. Losing his footing, he fell into the water. Shortly after continuing on our way, we saw the light. But the labored advance of our boat made the final hours of the trip interminable. It was already daylight when we reached Cuba at a place known as Belic on the beach at Las Coloradas.

A coast guard boat spotted us and telegraphed the discovery to Batista's army. No sooner had we disembarked and entered the swamp, in great haste and carrying only what was absolutely necessary, than we were attacked by enemy planes. Naturally, walking through the mangrove-covered swamps, we were not seen or harassed by the planes, but the dictatorship's army was already on our trail. It took us several hours to get out of the swamp, where we had ended up due to the inexperience and irresponsibility of a *compañero* who said he knew the way. We wound up on solid ground, lost, walking in circles.

We were an army of shadows, of ghosts, who walked as if following the impulse of some dark psychic mechanism. It had been seven days of continuous hunger and seasickness during the crossing, followed by three more days, terrible ones, on land. Exactly 10 days after the departure from Mexico, in the early morning hours of December 5, after a night march interrupted by fainting, exhaustion and rest for the troops, we reached a point known — paradoxically — by the name of Alegría de Pío [joy of the pious]. It was a small grove of trees, bordering a sugarcane field on one side and open to some valleys on the other, with the dense forest starting further back. The place was ill-suited for an encampment, but we stopped there to rest for a day and resume our march the following night.

Alegría de Pío

Alegría de Pío is a place in Oriente Province, Niquero municipality, near Cape Cruz, where on December 5, 1956, the dictatorship's forces surprised us.

We were exhausted from a trek not long so much as painful. We had landed on December 2, at a place known as Las Coloradas beach. We had lost almost all our equipment, and with new boots we had trudged for endless hours through salt-water marshes. Now almost the entire troop was suffering from open blisters on their feet. But boots and fungus infections were not our only enemies. We had reached Cuba following a seven-day voyage across the Gulf of Mexico and the Caribbean Sea, without food, in a boat in poor condition, with almost everyone plagued by seasickness from lack of experience in sea travel. We had left the port of Tuxpan on November 25, a day when a stiff gale was blowing and all navigation was prohibited. All this had left its mark upon our troop made up of raw recruits who had never seen combat.

All that was left of our war equipment was our rifles, cartridge belts and a few wet rounds of ammunition. Our medical supplies had disappeared, and most of our knapsacks had been left behind in the swamps. The previous night we had passed through one of the cane fields of the Niquero sugar mill, owned by Julio Lobo at the time. We had managed to satisfy our hunger and thirst by eating sugarcane, but due to our lack of experience we had left a trail of cane peelings and bagasse all over the place. Not that the guards looking for us needed any trail to follow our steps, for it had been our guide — as we found out years later — who had betrayed us and brought them there. We had let him go the night before — an error we were to repeat several times during our long struggle until we learned that civilians whose backgrounds were unknown to us were not to be trusted while in dangerous areas. We should never have permitted that false guide to leave.

By daybreak on December 5 hardly anyone could go a step further. On the verge of collapse, we would walk a short distance and then beg for a long rest. Because of this, orders were given to halt at the edge of a cane field, in a thicket close to the dense woods. Most of us slept through the morning hours.

At noon we began to notice unusual signs of activity. Piper planes as well as other types of small army planes together with small private aircraft began to circle around us. Some of our group went on peacefully cutting and eating sugarcane without realizing that they were perfectly visible to those flying the enemy planes, which were now circling at slow speed and low altitude. I was the troop physician, and it was my duty to treat the blistered feet. I recall my last patient that morning: his name was Humberto Lamothe and it was to be his last day on earth. I still remember how tired and wornout he looked as he walked from my improvised first-aid station to his post, still carrying in one hand the shoes he could not wear.

Compañero [Jesús] Montané and I were leaning against a tree talking about our respective children, eating our meager rations — half a sausage and two crackers — when we heard a shot. Within seconds, a hail of bullets — at least that's the way it seemed to us, this being our baptism of fire —

descended upon our 82-man troop. My rifle was not one of the best; I had deliberately asked for it because I was in very poor physical condition due to an attack of asthma that had bothered me throughout our ocean voyage and I did not want to be held responsible for wasting a good weapon. I can hardly remember what followed the initial burst of gunfire. [Juan] Almeida, then a captain, approached us requesting orders but there was nobody there to issue them. Later I was told that Fidel had tried vainly to get every-body together into the adjoining cane field, which could be reached by simply crossing a path. The surprise had been too great and the gunfire had been too heavy. Almeida ran back to take charge of his group. A *compañ-ero* dropped a box of ammunition at my feet. I pointed to it, and he answered me with an anguished expression, which I remember perfectly, that seemed to say "It's too late for ammunition boxes," and immediately went toward the cane field. (He was murdered by Batista's henchmen some time later.)

Perhaps this was the first time I was faced with the dilemma of choosing between my devotion to medicine and my duty as a revolutionary soldier. There, at my feet, were a knapsack full of medicine and a box of ammunition. I couldn't possibly carry both of them; they were too heavy. I picked up the box of ammunition, leaving the medicine, and started to cross the clearing, heading for the cane field. I remember Faustino Pérez, kneeling and firing his submachine gun. Near me, a *compañero* named [Emilio] Albentosa was walking toward the cane field. A burst of gunfire hit us both. I felt a sharp blow on my chest and a wound in my neck, and I thought for certain I was dead. Albentosa, vomiting blood and bleeding profusely from a deep wound made by a .45-caliber bullet, shouted, "They've killed me!" and began to fire his rifle at no-one in particular. Flat on the ground, I turned to Faustino, saying, "I've been hit!" — only I used a stronger word — and Faustino, still firing away, looked at me and told me it was nothing, but I could see by the look in his eyes that he considered me as good as dead.

Still on the ground, I fired a shot in the direction of the woods, following an impulse similar to that of the other wounded man. Immediately, I began to think about the best way to die, since all seemed lost. I recalled an old Jack London story where the hero, aware that he is bound to freeze to death in the wastes of Alaska, leans calmly against a tree and prepares to die in a dignified manner. That was the only thing that came to my mind at that moment. Someone on his knees said that we had better surrender, and I heard a voice — later I found out it was that of Camilo Cienfuegos — shout-ing: "Nobody surrenders here!" followed by a four-letter word. [José] Ponce approached me, agitated and breathing hard, and showed me a bullet wound, apparently through his lungs. He said "I'm wounded," and I replied indifferently, "Me, too." Then Ponce and other *compañeros* who were still unhurt, crawled toward the cane field. For a moment I was left alone, just lying there waiting to die. Almeida approached, urging me to go on, and despite the intense pain I dragged myself into the cane field. There I met *compañero* Raúl Suárez, whose thumb had been blown away by a bullet, being attended by Faustino Pérez, who was bandaging his hand. Then everything became a blur of airplanes flying low and strafing the field, adding to the confusion, amid Dantesque as well as grotesque scenes such as a *compañero* of considerable corpulence who was desperately trying to hide behind a single stalk of sugarcane, while in the midst of the din of gunfire another man kept on yelling "Silence!" for no apparent reason.

A group was organized, headed by Almeida, including Lt. Ramiro Valdés, now a commander, and *compañeros* [Rafael] Chao and [Reynaldo] Benítez. With Almeida leading, we crossed the last path among the rows of cane and reached the safety of the woods. The first shouts of "Fire!" were heard in the cane field and columns of flame and smoke began to rise. I cannot remember exactly what happened; I was thinking more of the bitterness of defeat and that I was sure I would die.

We walked until the darkness made it impossible to go on, and decided to lie down and go to sleep all huddled together in a heap. We were starving and thirsty, and the mosquitoes added to our misery. This was our baptism of fire on December 5, 1956, in the outskirts of Niquero. Such was the beginning of forging what would become the Rebel Army.

The battle of La Plata

Our first victory was the result of an attack on a small army garrison at the mouth of the La Plata River in the Sierra Maestra. The effect of our victory was electrifying and went far beyond that craggy region. It was like a clarion call, proving that the Rebel Army really existed and was ready to fight. For us, it was the reaffirmation of our chances for the final victory.

On January 14, 1957, a little more than a month after the surprise attack at Alegría de Pío, we came to a halt by the Magdalena River, which is separated from La Plata by a piece of land originating at the Sierra Maestra and ending at the sea. Fidel gave orders for target practice as an initial attempt at some sort of training for our troop. Some of the men were using weapons for the first time in their lives. We had not washed for many days and we seized upon the opportunity to bathe. Those who were able to do so changed into clean clothes. At that time we had 23 weapons in operating condition: nine rifles equipped with telescopic sights, five semiautomatic rifles, four bolt-action rifles, two Thompson machine guns, two submachine guns and a 16-gauge shotgun.

That afternoon we climbed the last hill before reaching the environs of La Plata. We were following a not-well-traveled trail marked specially for us with a machete by a peasant named Melquiades Elías. This man had been recommended by our guide Eutimio, who at that time was indispensable to us and seemed to be the prototype of the rebel peasant. He was later apprehended by Casillas, however, who, instead of killing him, bribed him with an offer of $10,000 and a rank in the army if he managed to kill Fidel. Eutimio came close to fulfilling his bargain but he lacked the courage to do so. He was nonetheless very useful to the enemy, since he informed them of the location of several of our camps.

At the time, Eutimio was serving us loyally. He was one of the many peasants fighting for their land in the struggle against the landowners, and anyone fighting them was also fighting against the Rural Guards, who did the landowners' bidding.

That day we captured two peasants who turned out to be our guide's relatives. One of them was released but we kept the other one as a precautionary measure. The next day, January 15, we sighted the La Plata army barracks, under construction, with its zinc roof. A group of half-naked men were moving about but we could nevertheless make out the enemy uniform. Just before sundown, about 6 p.m., a boat came in; some guards landed and others got aboard. We did not quite make out the maneuver, so we postponed the attack to the following day.

At dawn on the 16th we began watching the barracks. The boat had disappeared during the night and no soldiers could be seen anywhere. At 3 p.m. we decided to approach the road along the river leading to the barracks and take a look. By nightfall we crossed the shallow La Plata River and took up our positions on the road. Five minutes later we took two peasants into custody; one of them had a record as an informer. When we told them who we were and reassured them that no harm would befall them, they gave us some valuable information: the barracks held about 15 soldiers. They also told us that Chicho Osorio, one of the region's most notorious foremen, was to go by at any moment. These foremen worked for the Laviti family plantation. The Lavitis had established an enormous fiefdom, holding onto it by means of a regime of terror with the help of characters such as Chicho Osorio. Shortly afterward, Chicho showed up, astride a mule, with a little black boy riding "double." Chicho was drunk. Universo Sánchez gave him the order to halt in the name of the Rural Guards and immediately Chicho replied: "Mosquito." That was the password.

We must have looked like a bunch of pirates, but Chicho Osorio was so drunk we were able to fool him. Fidel stepped forward and, looking very indignant, said he was an army colonel who had come to find out why the rebels had not yet been wiped out. He bragged about going into the woods, which accounted for his beard. He added that the army was "botching things up." In a word, he cut the army's efficiency to pieces. Sheepishly, Chicho Osorio admitted that the guards spent all their time inside the barracks, eating and doing nothing but occasional useless rounds. He emphasized that the rebels must be wiped out. We began asking discreetly about friendly and unfriendly people living in the area and we noted his replies, naturally reversing the roles: when Chicho called somebody a bad man we knew he was one of our friends, and so on. We had about 20-odd names by now and he was still jabbering away. He told us how he had killed two men, adding: "But my General Batista set me free at once." He spoke of having slapped two peasants who "had gotten a little out of hand," adding that the guards would not do such a thing; on the contrary, they let the peasants talk without punishing them. Fidel asked Osorio what he would do if he ever caught Fidel Castro, and Osorio, with a very expressive gesture, replied: "We'll have to cut his — off." He said he would do the same thing to Crescencio [Pérez]. "Look," he said, showing us his shoes (they were the kind of Mexican-made shoes our men wore), "these shoes belonged to one of those sons of — we killed." Without realizing it, Chicho Osorio had signed his own death sentence. At Fidel's suggestion, he agreed to accompany us to the barracks in order to surprise the soldiers and prove to them they were badly prepared and were neglecting their duties.

As we neared the barracks, with Chicho Osorio in the lead, I still did not feel so sure he had not become wise to our trick. But he kept going on, completely unaware, for he was so drunk he could not think straight. When he crossed the river to get near the barracks Fidel told Osorio that military rules called for the prisoner to be tied up. The man did not resist and he went on, this time unwittingly as a real prisoner. He explained to us that the only guards were set up at the entrance of the barracks under construction and at the house of a foreman named Honorio. Osorio guided us to a place near the barracks, near the road to El Macío. *Compañero* Luis Crespo, now a commander, went on to scout around and returned saying that the foreman's report was correct. Crespo had seen the barracks and the pinpoints of light made by the guards' cigarettes.

We were just about ready to approach the barracks when we had to pull back into the woods to let three guards on horseback go by. The men were driving a prisoner on foot like a mule. They passed very close to me, and I remember the peasant saying: "I'm just like one of you" and the answer by one of the men whom we later identified as Corporal Basol: "Shut up and keep going or I'll use the whip on you!" At the time we thought that the peasant would be out of danger by not being in the barracks and would escape our bullets when we attacked. But the following day when the guards heard of the attack they murdered him at El Macío.

We had 22 weapons ready for the attack. It was a crucial moment because we were short of ammunition. The army barracks had to be taken at all costs, for a failure would have meant expending all our ammunition, leaving us practically defenseless. Lt. Julio Díaz — who later died heroically at the battle of El Uvero — Camilo Cienfuegos, [Reynaldo] Benítez, and Calixto Morales, armed with semiautomatic rifles, were to surround the palm-thatched house on the right side. Fidel, Universo Sánchez, Luis Crespo, Calixto García, [Manuel] Fajardo — today a commander with the same last name as our physician, Piti Fajardo, killed in the Escambray — and myself, would attack the center. Raúl [Castro] and his squad and Almeida with his, would attack the barracks from the left.

We approached to within 40 meters of the barracks. By the light of a full moon, Fidel opened the hostilities with two bursts of machinegun fire and all available rifles joined in. Immediately, we demanded the enemy's surrender, but we got no results. Murderer-informer Chicho Osorio was executed as soon as the shooting broke out.

The attack had begun at 2:40 a.m., and the guards put up a much stiffer resistance than we had expected. A sergeant, armed with an M-1, opened up with a burst every time we asked them to surrender. We were given orders to use our old Brazilian-type hand grenades. Luis Crespo and I threw ours but they did not go off; Raúl Castro threw a stick of dynamite with the same negative result. It became necessary to get close to the houses and set them on fire even at the risk of our own lives. Universo Sánchez made a futile attempt and Camilo Cienfuegos also failed. Finally, Luis Crespo and I got close to one of the buildings and set it on fire. The light from the blaze allowed us to see that it was simply a place for storing coconuts, but the soldiers had been intimidated and gave up the fight. One of them, trying to escape, ran smack into Luis Crespo's rifle; Luis shot him in the chest, took the man's rifle, and continued firing toward the house. Camilo Cienfuegos, sheltered behind a tree, fired on the fleeing sergeant and ran out of ammunition. The soldiers, almost defenseless, were being cut to pieces by our bullets. Camilo Cienfuegos was first into the house, where shouts of surrender were being heard.

Quickly, we took stock of our booty: eight Springfields, one Thompson machine gun and about 1,000 rounds; we had fired approximately 500 rounds. In addition, we now had cartridge belts, fuel, knives, clothing and some food. Casualties: they lost two dead, five wounded. Some, along with the wretched Honorio, had fled. We took three prisoners. On our side, not a scratch.

We withdrew after setting fire to the soldiers' quarters and after taking care of the wounded — three of them were seriously wounded and we were told after the final victory that they had died — leaving them in the care of the prisoners. One of the soldiers later joined the forces under Commander Raúl Castro, was promoted to lieutenant, and died in an airplane accident following the war.

Our attitude toward the wounded was in open contrast to that of Batista's army. Not only did they kill our wounded men; they abandoned their own. This difference made a great impact on the enemy over time and it was a factor in our victory. Fidel gave orders that the prisoners be given all the medicines to take care of the wounded. I was pained at this decision because, as a physician, I felt the need to save all available medicine and drugs for our own men. We freed all the civilians and at 4:30 on the morning of January 17 we started for Palma Mocha, arriving there at dawn and seeking out the most inaccessible zones of the Sierra Maestra.

A most pitiful scene awaited us: the day before, an army corporal and one of the foremen had warned all the families living in the area that the air force was going to bomb the entire zone, and the exodus toward the coast had begun. No-one knew of our presence in the area, so it was evidently a maneuver on the part of the foremen and the Rural Guards to take the land and belongings away from the peasants. But their lie had coincided with our attack and now became a reality. Terror was rampant among the peasants and it was impossible for us to stop their flight.

This was the first victorious battle of the Rebel Army. This battle and the one following it were the only times that we had more weapons than men. Peasants were not yet ready to join in the struggle, and communication with the city bases was practically nonexistent.

A betrayal in the making

It was a pleasure to look at our troop again.[3] Close to 200 men, well disciplined, with increased morale, and with some new weapons. The qualitative change I mentioned before was now quite evident in the Sierra. There was a true liberated territory, and safety measures were not as necessary. There was a little freedom to carry on relaxed conversations at night while resting in our hammocks. We were allowed to visit the villages of the people in the Sierra, developing closer ties with them. It was also a real joy to see the welcome given us by our old *compañeros*.

Felipe Pazos and Raúl Chibás were the stars of those days, although they had two totally different personalities. Raúl Chibás lived solely off the reputation of his brother [Eduardo] — who had been a real symbol of an era in Cuba — but he had none of his brother's virtues. He was neither expressive nor wise nor even intelligent. Only his absolute mediocrity allowed him to be a unique and symbolic figure in the Orthodox Party. He spoke very little and he wanted to get out of the Sierra at once.

Felipe Pazos had a personality of his own. He had the standing of a great economist and the reputation of being an honest person, won by not stealing from the public treasury while president of the National Bank under [Carlos] Prío Socarrás's regime; a regime marked by gross larceny and embezzlement. How magnificent, one might think, to remain unpolluted throughout those years. A great merit, perhaps, for a functionary who pursued his administrative career, indifferent to the country's grave problems. But how can anyone imagine a revolutionary who does not speak out daily against the inconceivable abuses rampant at the time? Felipe Pazos skillfully managed to keep his mouth shut, and following Batista's coup he left the post of president of the National Bank, adorned with a great reputation for honesty, intelligence, and talent as an economist. Petulantly, he expected to come to the Sierra and take over. This pint-sized Machiavelli thought he was destined to control the country's future. It is possible that he had already hatched the idea of betraying the movement; perhaps this came later. But his conduct was never entirely honest.

Basing himself on the joint declaration [the Sierra Manifesto] that we will analyze later on, Pazos appointed himself representative of the July 26 Movement in Miami, and he was going to be designated provisional president of the republic. In this way, Prío was assured that he had a man he could trust in the leadership of the provisional government.

We did not have much time to talk in those days, but Fidel told me about his efforts to make the document a really militant one that would lay the basis for a declaration of principles. This was a difficult task when faced by those two stone-age mentalities immune to the call of the people's struggle.

Fundamentally, the manifesto issued "the slogan of a great civic revolutionary front comprising all opposition political parties, all civic institutions and all revolutionary forces."

It made a series of proposals: the "formation of a civic revolutionary front in a common front of struggle"; the appointment of "an individual to head the provisional government." It contained an explicit declaration that the front would neither call for nor accept intervention by another nation in Cuba's internal affairs and "would not accept any sort of military junta as a provisional government of the republic." The document expressed the determination to remove the army from politics entirely and guarantee the nonpolitical nature of the armed forces. It declared that elections would be held within one year.

The program, which was to serve as a basis for a provisional government, proclaimed freedom for all political prisoners, civilian and military; absolute guarantee of freedom of the press and radio, with all individual and political rights to be guaranteed by the constitution; appointment of provisional mayors in all municipalities, after consultation with the civic institutions of the locality; suppression of all forms of government corruption, and adoption of measures designed to enhance the efficiency of all state bodies; establishment of a civil service; democratization of trade union politics, promoting free elections in all trade unions and industry-wide union federations; immediate launching of an all-out drive against illiteracy and for civic education, stressing the rights and duties of the citizen in relation to society and the homeland; "putting in place the foundations for an agrarian reform designed to distribute unused land and transform into owners all the cane growers who rent their land and all the sharecroppers, tenant farmers and squatters who work small plots of land owned either by the state or private persons, after payment of compensation to the former owners"; adoption of a healthy fiscal policy to safeguard our currency's stability and aimed at investing the nation's credit in productive works; acceleration of the industrialization process and creation of new jobs.

In addition, there were two points of special emphasis: "First: The need to appoint, at this time, the person who will preside over the provisional government of the republic, to show to the entire world that the Cuban people can unite behind a call for freedom, and support the person who, for his impartiality, integrity, capabilities and decency, can personify such a call. There are more than enough able men in Cuba who can preside over the republic." (Naturally, Felipe Pazos at least, one of the signers, knew in his heart of hearts that there were not more than enough men, there was only one and it was he.)

"Second: that this person shall be appointed by all the civic, and therefore apolitical, institutions, whose support would free the provisional president from any commitments to any party, thus ensuring absolutely clean and impartial elections."

The document also stated: "It is not necessary to come to the Sierra for discussions. We can have representatives in Havana, Mexico, or wherever necessary."

Fidel had pressed for more explicit statements regarding the agrarian reform, but it was very difficult to crash through the monolithic front of the two cavemen. "Putting in place the foundations for an agrarian reform designed to distribute unused land" — that was precisely the kind of policy that the *Diario de la Marina* might agree with. To make it worse, there was the part reading: "after payment of compensation to the former owners."

The revolution did not carry out some of the commitments as originally stated. We must emphasize that the enemy broke the tacit pact expressed in the manifesto when they refused to acknowledge the authority of the Rebel Army and made an attempt to shackle the future revolutionary government.

We were not satisfied with the agreement, but it was necessary; at the time it was progressive. It could not last beyond the moment when it would represent a brake on the revolution's development. But we were ready to comply with it. By their treachery, the enemy helped us to break uncomfortable bonds and show the people what these individuals' true intentions were.

We knew that this was a minimum program, a program that limited our efforts, but we also had to recognize that it was impossible to impose our will from the Sierra Maestra. For a long period of time, we would have to depend upon a whole series of "friends" who were trying to use our military strength and the great trust that the people already felt in Fidel Castro for their own macabre maneuvers. Above all they wanted to maintain imperialist domination of Cuba, through its comprador bourgeoisie closely linked with their masters to the north.

The manifesto had its positive sides: it mentioned the Sierra Maestra and stated explicitly: "Let no one be deceived by government propaganda about the situation in the Sierra. The Sierra Maestra is already an indestructible bulwark of freedom, which has taken root in the hearts of our countrymen, and it is here that we will know how to do justice to the faith and the confidence of our people." The words "we will know how" meant that Fidel Castro knew how. The other two proved incapable of following the development of the struggle in the Sierra Maestra, even as spectators; they came down immediately. One of them, Chibás, was surprised and roughed up by Batista's police. Both of them afterward went to the United States.

It was a well-planned coup: a group of the most distinguished representatives of the Cuban oligarchy arrived in the Sierra Maestra "in defense of freedom," signed a joint declaration with the guerrilla chief isolated in the wilds of the Sierra, and left with full freedom to play their trump card in Miami. What they failed to take into account was that political coups always depend on the opponent's strength, in this case, the weapons in the hands of the people. Quick action by our leader, who had full confidence in the guerrilla army, prevented the betrayal's success. Months later, when the results of the Miami Pact became known, Fidel's fiery reply paralyzed the enemy. We were accused of being divisive and of trying to impose our will from the Sierra; but they had to change their tactics and prepare a new trap: the Caracas Pact.[4]

The Sierra Manifesto, dated July 12, 1957, was published in the newspapers at the time. To us, this declaration was simply a brief pause on the road. Our main task — to defeat the oppressor's army on the battlefield — had to go on. A new column was being organized then, with myself in charge, and I became a captain. There were other promotions; Ramiro Valdés was promoted to captain and his platoon joined my column. Ciro Redondo, too, was promoted to captain, and was to lead a platoon. The column was made up of three platoons. The first one, the vanguard, was led by Lalo Sardiñas, who was also the detachment's second-in-command. Ramiro Valdés and Ciro Redondo led the other two platoons. This column, which was called the "Dispossessed Peasants," was made up of close to 75 men, heterogeneously dressed and armed; nonetheless, I was very proud of them. A few nights later, I was to feel even prouder, with greater affinity to the revolution, if that were possible, more anxious to prove that my officer's insignia was well deserved.

We wrote a letter of congratulations and appreciation to "Carlos," the underground name of Frank País, who was living his final days. It was signed by all the officers of the guerrilla army who knew how to write. (Many of the Sierra peasants were not very skilled in this art but were already an important component of the guerrillas.) The signatures appeared in two columns, and as we wrote down the ranks on the second one, when my turn came, Fidel simply said: "Make it commander." Thus, in a most informal manner, almost in passing, I was promoted to commander of the second column of the guerrilla army, which would later become known as Column No. 4.

The letter, written in a peasant's house, was the guerrilla fighters' warm message to their brother in the city, who was fighting so heroically in Santiago itself to obtain supplies for us and lessen the enemy's pressure on us.

There is a bit of vanity hiding somewhere within every one of us. It made me feel like the proudest man in the world that day. My insignia, a small star, was given to me by Celia [Sánchez]. The award was accompanied by a gift: one of the wristwatches ordered from Manzanillo. With my recently formed column, my first task was to set a trap for Sánchez Mosquera, but he was the wiliest of all the Batista henchmen and had already left the area.

We had to do something to justify the semi-independent life we were to lead in what was to be our new zone, the region of El Hombrito where we were headed, so we began to plan a series of great deeds.

We had to prepare to celebrate with dignity the glorious date of July 26 that was approaching, and Fidel gave me free rein to do whatever I could, as long as it was done prudently. At the final meeting we met a new doctor who had joined the guerrillas: Sergio del Valle, now head of the general staff of our revolutionary army. At that time he practiced his profession as the conditions of the Sierra allowed.

We needed to prove that we were still alive, since we had received a few setbacks on the plains. Weapons from the Miranda sugar mill that were to be used to open another front had been seized by the police, and several valuable leaders, among them Faustino Pérez, had been captured. Fidel had opposed dividing our forces but had given in at the insistence of the *Llano compañeros*. The correctness of Fidel's view was demonstrated, and from then on we devoted ourselves to strengthening the Sierra Maestra as the first step toward the expansion of the guerrilla army.[5]

The murdered puppy

For all the harshness of conditions in the Sierra Maestra, the day was superb. We were hiking through Agua Revés, one of the steepest and most intricate valleys in the Turquino basin, patiently following Sánchez Mosquera's troops. The relentless killer had left a trail of burned-out farms, sadness and despair throughout the entire region. But his trail led him, by necessity, to ascend along one of the two or three points of the Sierra where we knew Camilo would be: either the Nevada ridge, or the area we called the "Ridge of the Crippled," now known as the "Ridge of the Dead."

Camilo had left hurriedly with about a dozen men, part of his forward detachment, and this small number had to be divided up in three different places to stop a column of over a hundred soldiers. My mission was to attack Sánchez Mosquera from behind and surround him. Our fundamental aim was encirclement; we therefore followed him patiently, over a considerable distance, past the painful trail of burning peasant houses, set aflame by the enemy's rear guard. The enemy troops were far away, but we could hear their shouts. We did not know how many of them there were. Our column's march was a difficult one, along the slopes, while the enemy advanced through the center of a narrow valley.

Everything would have been perfect had it not been for our new mascot, a little hunting dog only a few weeks old. Despite repeated commands by Félix [Mendoza] for the animal to return to our center of operations — a house where the cooks were staying — the puppy continued to trail behind the column. In that part of the Sierra Maestra, crossing over the slopes is extremely difficult due to the lack of paths. We went through a difficult patch of felled trees covered over by newly grown foliage and passage became extremely arduous. We were bounding through tree trunks and bushes trying not to lose touch with our guests.

Our small column marched silently along. Not even the sound of a broken twig intruded upon the usual noises of the forest. Suddenly the silence was broken by the disconsolate, nervous barking of the little dog. It had remained behind and was barking desperately, calling on its masters to help it through the difficult patch. Someone picked up the animal, and we continued on again. However, as we rested in the middle of a creek bed with a lookout keeping watch on the enemy's movements, the little dog once again began to howl hysterically. Comforting words no longer had any effect, the animal, afraid we would leave it behind, barked desperately.

I remember my emphatic order: "Félix, that dog must stop its howling once and for all. You're in charge; strangle it. There will be no more barking." Félix looked at me with eyes that said nothing. He and the little dog were in the center of all the troops. Very slowly he took out a rope, wrapped it around the animal's neck, and began to tighten it. The cute little movements of the dog's tail suddenly became convulsive, before gradually dying out, accompanied by a steady moan that escaped from its throat, despite the firm grip. I don't know how long it took for the end to come, but to all of us it seemed like forever. With one last nervous twitch, the puppy stopped moving. There it lay, sprawled out, its little head spread over the twigs.

We continued the march without even a word about the incident. Sánchez Mosquera's troops had moved ahead of us somewhat, and within moments, shots were heard. We quickly descended the slopes, amid the difficult terrain, searching for the best path to reach the rear guard. We knew that Camilo had attacked. It took us a considerable amount of time to reach the last house before the ascent; we were taking many precautions as we walked, thinking we would confront the enemy at any moment. The exchange of fire had been intense, but it did not last long. We all waited tensely. The last house was also abandoned. The soldiers had left no traces. Two scouts climbed the "Ridge of the Crippled" and soon returned with the news: "There is a grave up above. We dug it up and found an enemy soldier buried." They also brought the identity papers of the victim, found in his shirt pocket. There had been a clash with one dead. The dead was theirs, but nothing more was known.

We returned slowly, discouraged. Two scouting parties came upon a large number of footprints along both sides of the ridge of the Maestra, but nothing else. We made the return trip slowly, this time through the valley.

We arrived during the night at a house, also vacant. It was in the settlement of Mar Verde, and there we were able to rest. Soon a pig was cooked along with some yucca, and we ate. Someone sang a tune on a guitar, since the peasant houses had been hastily abandoned with all their belongings still inside.

I don't know whether it was the sentimental tune, or the darkness of night, or just plain exhaustion. What happened, though, is that Félix, while eating seated on the floor, dropped a bone, and a house dog came out meekly and grabbed it up. Félix patted its head, and the dog looked at him. Félix returned the glance, and then he and I exchanged a guilty look. Suddenly everyone fell silent. An imperceptible stirring came over us, as the dog's meek yet roguish gaze seemed to contain a hint of reproach. There in our presence, although observing us through the eyes of another dog, was the murdered puppy.

Interlude

In the months of April and June 1958 two poles could be seen in the insurrectional wave.

Beginning in February, after the battle at Pino del Agua, the wave gradually increased until it threatened to become an uncontainable avalanche. The people were rising in insurrection against the dictatorship throughout the country, and particularly in Oriente Province. After the failure of the [April 9] general strike called by the July 26 Movement, the wave subsided until it reached its lowest point in June, when the dictatorship's troops more and more tightened their encirclement of Column No. 1.

In the first days of April, Camilo had left the protection of the Sierra area of El Cauto, where he would be appointed commander of the Antonio Maceo Column No. 2, and carried out a series of impressive feats in the plains of

Oriente. Camilo was the first army commander who went out on the plains to fight with the morale and effectiveness of the army of the Sierra, putting the dictatorship in hard straits until several days after the April 9 failure, when he returned to the Sierra.

Taking advantage of the situation, during the days of the height of the revolutionary wave, a whole series of camps was set up, composed of some people who were yearning to fight and others who were thinking only of keeping their uniforms clean so as to enter Havana in triumph. After April 9, when the dictatorship's counteroffensive began to step up, those groups disappeared or joined the Sierra forces.

Morale fell so much that the army considered it opportune to offer pardons and it prepared some leaflets, which it dropped by air in the rebel zones. The leaflets read:

> Compatriots: If by having gotten yourself involved in insurrectional plots, you are still in the countryside or in the mountains, now you have the opportunity to make amends and return to your family.
>
> The government has issued orders to offer respect for your life and your home if you lay down your weapons and abide by the law.
>
> Report to the governor of the province, the mayor of your municipality, the friendly congressman, the nearest military, navy, or police post, or to any ecclesiastic authority.
>
> If you are in a rural area, come with your weapon on one shoulder and with your hands up.
>
> If you come forward in an urban zone, leave your weapon hidden in a safe place so that it may be collected immediately after you report it.
>
> Do so without wasting time because the operations for total pacification will continue with greater intensity in the area where you are.

Then they would publish photos of people who had turned themselves in, some real, others not. What was clear was that the counterrevolutionary wave was growing. In the end, it would crash against the peaks of the Sierra, but at the end of April and the beginning of May, it was in full ascent.

Our mission, in the first phase of the period we are discussing, was to hold the front occupied by the fourth brigade, which extended to the outskirts of the town of Las Minas de Bueyecito. Sánchez Mosquera was quartered there, and our struggle consisted of fleeting clashes without either side risking a decisive battle. At night we would fire our M-26s at them, but they already knew the scant killing power of that weapon and had simply put up a large wire-mesh netting where the TNT charges exploded in their shells of condensed milk cans, causing only a lot of noise.[6]

Our camp was set up about two kilometers from Las Minas, in a place called La Otilia, in the house of a local landowner. From there we kept watch on Sánchez Mosquera's movements, and there were odd skirmishes every day. The henchmen would go out at dawn, burning the peasants' huts, looting all their belongings, and withdrawing before we intervened. At other times, they would attack some of our rifle units scattered through the area, making them flee. Any peasant suspected of an understanding with us was murdered.

I have never been able to find out why Sánchez Mosquera allowed us to be comfortably settled in a house, in a relatively flat area with no vegetation, without calling the enemy air force to attack us. Our guess was that he was not interested in fighting and that he did not want to let the air force see how close the troops were, because he would then have to explain why he did not attack. Nevertheless, there were repeated skirmishes, as I have said, between our forces.

One of those days I left with an aide to see Fidel, who was then located in El Jíbaro. It was a long walk, practically a whole day. After spending a day with Fidel, we left the following day to return to our camp in La Otilia. For some reason that I do not remember, my aide had to stay behind and I had to accept a new guide. Part of the route ran along a roadway and later through rolling pastures. In this last leg of the trip, already near the house, a strange spectacle presented itself by the light of a full moon that clearly illuminated the surroundings in one of those rolling fields, with scattered palm trees, there appeared a row of dead mules, some with their harnesses on.

When we got down from our horses to examine the first mule and saw the bullet holes, the guide's expression as he looked at me was an image out of a cowboy movie. The hero of the film arrives with his partner and sees a horse killed by an arrow. He says something like, "The Sioux," and makes a special face for the occasion. That's what the man's face was like and perhaps my own as well, but I did not bother to look at myself. A few meters further on was the second, then the third, then the fourth or fifth dead mule. It had been a convoy of supplies for us, captured by one of Sánchez Mosquera's expeditions. I think I remember that a civilian was also murdered. The guide refused to follow me. He claimed he did not know the terrain and simply got on his mount. We separated amicably.

I had a Beretta, and with it cocked, taking the horse by the reins, I went on into the first coffee field. When I reached the abandoned house, a loud noise startled me to such an extent that I almost fired, but it was only a pig, also frightened by my presence. Slowly, and very carefully, I covered the few hundred meters left to reach our position, which I found totally abandoned. After much searching, I found a *compañero* who had stayed sleeping in the house.

Universo [Sánchez], who had remained in command of the troops, had ordered the house evacuated, foreseeing some nocturnal or dawn attack. As our troops were well spread out, defending the place, I lay down to sleep with my lone companion. That whole scene has no significance for me other than the satisfaction I experienced at having overcome fear during a journey that seemed eternal until at last, alone, I reached the command post. That night I felt brave.

But the toughest confrontation with Sánchez Mosquera took place in a very small village or hamlet called Santa Rosa. As always, at dawn we were warned that Sánchez Mosquera was there and we headed quickly to the place. I had a touch of asthma and therefore was riding a bay horse with which I had made good friends. The fighting spread out over certain places in a fragmented manner. I had to abandon my mount. With the group of men that was with me, we took up positions on a small hill, scattering ourselves at two or three different heights. The enemy was firing some mortars, without very good aim.

For a moment, the shooting got more intense to my right, and I set off to check the positions, but halfway there it also began on my left. I sent my aide off to I-don't-know-where, and I remained alone, between the two extremes of fire. To my left, Sánchez Mosquera's forces, after firing some mortar shells, climbed the hill amidst tremendous shouting. Our people, with little experience, managed to fire only one or two isolated shots, and took off running down the hill. Alone, in an open field, I saw soldiers' helmets begin to appear. A henchman began to run down the hill in pursuit of our fighters, who were heading into the coffee fields. I fired my Beretta at him, missed, and immediately several rifles found me and opened fire. I began a zigzagging race, carrying 1,000 bullets in an awesome leather cartridge belt on my shoulders, greeted by the contemptuous shouts of some enemy soldiers. As I got close to the shelter of the trees, my pistol fell. My only insolent gesture of that sad morning was to stop, retrace my steps, pick up the pistol and take off running, greeted this time by the small dust clouds the rifle bullets kicked up like darts around me.

When I felt I was out of danger, without knowing about my *compañeros* or the result of the offensive, I stayed resting, barricaded behind a large rock in the middle of the woods. The asthma, mercifully, had let me run a few meters, but it was taking revenge and my heart was jumping inside my chest. I heard branches being broken by people approaching, but it was no longer possible to keep fleeing (which was what I really felt like doing). This time it was another *compañero* of ours, lost, a recruit who had recently joined our troop. His words of consolation were more or less: "Don't worry, commander, I will die with you." I had no desire to die and felt tempted to say something about his mother. I don't think I did. That day I felt cowardly.

At night we would recount all the events. A magnificent *compañero* — Mariño was his last name — had been killed in one of the skirmishes. Other than that the result was very poor for the enemy. The body of a peasant shot through the mouth, murdered who-knows-why, was all that remained in the army's abandoned positions. There, with a small box camera, the Argentine journalist Jorge Ricardo Masetti, who was visiting us in the Sierra for the first time and with whom we would later maintain a deep and lasting friendship, took a photograph of the murdered peasant.

After those battles we withdrew a bit further back from La Otilia, but I was already being replaced as commander of Column No. 4 by Ramiro Valdés, who had been promoted. I left the area, accompanied by a small group of fighters, to take charge of the school for recruits, where the men who would have to cross from Oriente to Las Villas would get their training. Moreover, we had to prepare for what was already imminent: the army's offensive. All the following days, late April and early May, were devoted to preparing the defensive points and to trying to take the largest possible quantity of food and medicine up to the hills to be able to resist what we saw coming: a large-scale offensive.

As a parallel task, we were trying to collect a tax on the sugar plantation owners and cattle ranchers. In those days, Remigio Fernández went up to see us; he was a cattle rancher who offered us the moon and the stars, but he forgot his promises when he reached the plains.

The sugar plantation owners did not give us anything either. But later, when our strength was solid, we got even, although we spent those days of the offensive without the necessary elements for our defense.

A short time later, Camilo was called to better cover our small territory, which contained countless riches: a radio station, hospitals, munitions depots and, on top of that, an airstrip located among the hills of La Plata, where a light plane could land.

Fidel maintained the principle that what mattered was not the enemy soldiers, but the number of people we needed to make a position invulnerable and that this was what we should rely on. That was our tactic, and that's why all our forces gathered around the command post to form a compact front. There were not many more than 200 usable rifles when the expected offensive began on May 25, in the middle of a meeting Fidel was having with some peasants, discussing the conditions under which the coffee harvest could be carried out, since the army did not allow day laborers to go up to pick the crop.

He had called together some 350 peasants, who were very interested in resolving their crop problems. Fidel had proposed creating a Sierra currency to pay the workers, to bring the straw and the bags for packing, to set up producer and consumer cooperatives and a supervisory commission. Moreover, he offered the Rebel Army's help for the harvest. Everything was approved, but just as Fidel himself was going to end the meeting, the machine-gunning began. The enemy army had clashed with Capt. Ángel Verdecia's men and its air force was punishing the area.

A decisive meeting

Throughout the entire day of May 3, 1958, a meeting, practically unknown until now, took place in the Sierra Maestra, in Los Altos de Mompié. This gathering, nonetheless, was of extraordinary importance in guiding our revolutionary strategy. From the early hours of the day until two o'clock the following morning the meeting analyzed the consequences of the April 9 failure and why that defeat took place. It also took the necessary measures to reorganize the July 26 Movement and to overcome the weaknesses resulting from the dictatorship's victory.

Although I was not a member of the National Directorate, I was invited to participate in the meeting at the request of *compañeros* Faustino Pérez and René Ramos Latour (Daniel), whom I had strongly criticized earlier. In addition to those named, also present were Fidel, Vilma Espín (Débora in the underground), Ñico Torres, Luis Buch, Celia Sánchez, Marcelo Fernández (Zoilo at that time), Haydée Santamaría, David Salvador and Enso Infante (Bruno), who joined us at midday. The gathering was tense, since it had to judge the actions of the *Llano compañeros*, who in practice had run the affairs of the July 26 Movement until that moment.

At that meeting decisions were taken that confirmed Fidel's moral authority, his indisputable stature, and the conviction among the majority of revolutionaries present that errors of judgment had been committed. The *Llano* leadership had underestimated the enemy's strength and subjectively overestimated their own, without taking into account the methods necessary to unleash their forces. But most importantly, the meeting discussed and

THE CUBAN REVOLUTIONARY WAR

judged two conceptions that had been at odds throughout the whole previous stage of the leadership of the war. The guerrilla conception would emerge triumphant from that meeting. Fidel's standing and authority were consolidated, and he was named commander in chief of all forces, including the militias — which until then had been under *Llano* leadership. Fidel was also named general secretary of the July 26 Movement.

There were many heated discussions when the meeting analyzed each person's participation in the events under discussion. But perhaps the most violent discussion was the one with the workers' representatives, who were opposed to any participation by the Popular Socialist Party in the organization of the struggle. The analysis of the strike demonstrated that subjectivism and putschist conceptions permeated its preparation and execution. The formidable apparatus that the July 26 Movement seemed to have in its hands, in the form of organized workers' cells, fell apart the moment the action took place. The adventurist policy of the workers' leaders had failed in the face of an inexorable reality. But they were not the only ones responsible for the defeat. Our opinion was that the largest share of the blame fell on the workers' delegate David Salvador; on Faustino Pérez, who was responsible for Havana; and on the leader of the militias for the *Llano,* René Ramos Latour.

Salvador's fault was having held and put into practice his conception of a sectarian strike, in which the other revolutionary movements would be forced to follow our lead. Faustino's was his lack of perspective in thinking that it would be possible to seize the capital with his militias, without closely examining the forces of reaction inside their principal bastion. Daniel was criticized for the same lack of vision but in reference to the *Llano* militias, which were organized as parallel troops to ours, but without the training or the combat morale, and without having gone through the rigorous process of selection in the war.

The division between the *Sierra* and the *Llano* was a real one. There were certain objective bases for it, due to the higher level of maturity achieved over the course of the guerrilla struggle by the Sierra representatives and the lower level of maturity of the fighters from the *Llano.* But there was also an extraordinarily important element, something that might be called an occupational hazard. The *compañeros* of the *Llano* had to work in their environment, and little by little they became accustomed to viewing the work methods required under those conditions as the ideal ones and as the only ones possible for the Movement. Moreover, logically enough from a human standpoint, they began to consider the *Llano* as having a greater relative importance than the *Sierra.*

After the failures in confronting the dictatorship's forces, there now arose only one authoritative leadership, the *Sierra,* and concretely one sole leader, one commander in chief, Fidel Castro. At the end of an exhaustive and often violent discussion, the meeting resolved to relieve Faustino Pérez of his duties, replacing him with [Delio Gómez] Ochoa, and to relieve David Salvador of his duties, replacing him with Ñico Torres. (This last change did not amount to a substantive step forward as far as the conception of the struggle was concerned. For when the meeting raised the need for unity of all working-class forces to prepare the next revolutionary general strike, which would be called from the Sierra, Ñico expressed his readiness to work in a disciplined manner with the "Stalinists," but said that he did not think this would lead to anything. He referred in those terms to the *compañeros* of the Popular Socialist Party.) The third change, regarding Daniel, did not lead to a replacement, since Fidel directly became commander in chief of the *Llano's* militias.

The meeting also decided to send Haydée Santamaría to Miami as a special representative of the July 26 Movement, putting her in charge of finances in the exile community. In the political sphere, the National Directorate was to be moved to the Sierra Maestra, where Fidel would occupy the post of general secretary. A secretariat of five members was constituted with one person each in charge of finances, political affairs and workers' affairs. I don't remember now who the *compañeros* assigned to these positions were. But everything related to arms shipments — or decisions about the arms — and foreign relations would from then on be the responsibility of the general secretary. The three *compañeros* relieved of their duties were to go to the Sierra, where David Salvador would hold a post as workers' delegate and Faustino and Daniel would be commanders. The latter was given command of a column that participated actively in the fighting against the army's final offensive, which was about to be unleashed. He died at the head of his troops while attacking a retreating enemy column. His revolutionary career earned him a place in the select list of our martyrs.

Faustino asked for and obtained authorization to return to Havana and take care of a number of the Movement's affairs, to hand over the leadership, and later reintegrate himself into the struggle in the Sierra. This he did, finishing the war in the José Martí Column No. 1 commanded by Fidel Castro. Although history must relate the events just as they occurred, it is necessary to make clear the high opinion we always have had of this *compañero* who at a given moment was our adversary within the Movement. Faustino was always considered an irreproachably honest *compañero,* and he was daring to the extreme. I was an eyewitness of his fearlessness, the time he burned a plane that had brought us weapons from Miami but had been discovered by enemy aircraft and was damaged. Under machine-gun fire Faustino carried out the necessary operation to prevent it from falling into the army's hands, setting it on fire with the gasoline pouring out through the bullet holes. His whole history shows his revolutionary mettle.

At that meeting other decisions of lesser importance were made, and a whole series of obscure aspects of our reciprocal relations were clarified. We heard a report, by Marcelo Fernández on the organization of the Movement in the cities, and he was assigned to prepare another report for the Movement's cells, detailing the results and decisions of the National Directorate's meeting. We also heard a report on the organization of the civic resistance, its formation, its methods of work, its components, and how to broaden and strengthen them.

Compañero Buch reported on the committee in exile, on Mario Llerena's half-hearted position and his incompatibility with Urrutia. It was decided to ratify Urrutia as our Movement's candidate for president and transfer to him a stipend that until then Llerena had been receiving as the Movement's only professional cadre in the exile community. In addition, the meeting decided that if Llerena continued his interference he would be relieved of his position as chairman of the committee in exile. There were many problems abroad; in New York, for example, the groups of [Arnaldo] Barrón, [Angel] Pérez Vidal, and Pablo Díaz worked separately, and at times clashed or interfered with each other. It was resolved that Fidel would send a letter to the emigrant and exile groups recognizing the committee in exile of the July 26 Movement as the sole official body.

The meeting analyzed all the possibilities for support by the Venezuelan Government headed at that time by Wolfgang Larrazábal. He had promised to support the Movement, which in fact he did. The only complaint we might have with Larrazábal was that along with a planeload of weapons he sent us the "worthy" Manuel Urrutia Lleó. But actually we ourselves were the ones who had made such a deplorable choice.

Other agreements were reached during the meeting. In addition to Haydée Santamaría, who would go to Miami, Luis Buch was to travel to Caracas with precise instructions regarding Urrutia. Carlos Franqui was ordered to the Sierra to take charge of the leadership of Radio Rebelde. The contacts would be made by radio via Venezuela, through codes made up by Luis Buch that worked until the end of the war.

As can be appreciated from the decisions emanating from this meeting, it was of capital importance. Various concrete problems of the Movement were finally clarified. In the first place, the war would be led militarily and politically by Fidel in his dual role as commander in chief of all forces and as general secretary of the organization. The line of the *Sierra* would be followed, that of direct armed struggle, extending it to other regions and in that way taking control of the country. We did away with various naive illusions of attempted revolutionary general strikes when the situation had not matured sufficiently to bring about an explosion of that type, and without having laid the groundwork of adequate preparations for an event of that magnitude.

In addition the leadership lay in the Sierra, which objectively eliminated some practical decision-making problems that had prevented Fidel from actually exercising the authority he had earned. In fact this did nothing more than register a reality: the political predominance of the *Sierra* people, a consequence of their correct position and interpretation of events. The meeting corroborated the correctness of our earlier doubts, when we considered the possibility of a failure of the Movement's forces in attempting a revolutionary general strike, if carried out in the manner outlined at a meeting prior to April 9.

Certain very important tasks still remained: above all resisting the approaching offensive, since the army's forces were taking up positions in a ring around the revolution's principal bastion, the command post of Column No. 1, led by Fidel. Afterward, the tasks would be the invasion of the plains, the seizure of the central provinces, and finally, the destruction of the regime's entire political-military apparatus. It would take us seven months to complete those tasks in full.

What was most urgent at the time was to strengthen the Sierra front, and to assure that a small bastion could continue speaking to Cuba and sowing the revolutionary seed among our people. It was also important to maintain communications with abroad. A few days earlier I had witnessed a radio conversation between Fidel and Justo Carrillo, who represented the Montecristi Group, that is, a group of aspiring thugs including representatives of imperialism such as Carrillo himself and [Ramón] Barquín. Justico offered the moon and the stars, but asked that Fidel make a declaration supporting the "pure" military men. Fidel answered that while this was not impossible, it would be difficult for our Movement to understand a call of this nature when our people were falling victim to soldiers of whom it was difficult to distinguish the good from the bad, since they were all lumped together. In short, the declaration was not made. Llerena was also spoken with, I seem to recall, as well as Urrutia. An attempt was made to issue a call for unity to try to prevent the breakup of the flimsy grouping of disparate personalities. From Caracas, they were trying to capitalize on the armed movement for their own gain, but they represented our aspirations for international recognition, and we therefore had to be careful.

Immediately after the meeting, the participants scattered. It was my task to inspect a whole series of zones, trying to create defensive lines with our small forces to resist the army's push. The really strong resistance would begin in the most mountainous zones, from the Sierra de Caracas, where the small and poorly armed groups of Crescencio Pérez would be located, to the zones of La Botella or La Mesa, where Ramiro Valdés's forces were distributed.

This small territory had to be defended, with not much more than 200 functioning rifles, when a few days later Batista's army began its "encirclement and annihilation" offensive.

The final offensive and the battle of Santa Clara

April 9 was a resounding defeat that never endangered the regime's stability. Not only that: after that tragic date, the government was able to transfer troops and gradually place them in Oriente Province, spreading its destruction to the Sierra Maestra. Our defense more and more had to be from within the Sierra Maestra, and the government kept increasing the number of regiments it placed in front of our positions, until there were 10,000 men. With these forces it began the offensive May 25 in the town of Las Mercedes, which was our forward position.

There, Batista's army gave proof of its poor combat effectiveness, and we showed our lack of resources; 200 usable rifles to fight against 10,000 weapons of all sorts. It was an enormous disadvantage. Our boys fought bravely for two days, with odds of one against 10 or 15; fighting moreover, against mortars, tanks, and the air force, until the small group was forced to abandon the town. It was commanded by Capt. Ángel Verdecia, who one month later would courageously die in action.

By that time, Fidel Castro had received a letter from the traitor Eulogio Cantillo, who, true to his charlatan's politicking attitude, wrote to the Rebel leader as the enemy's chief of operations, saying that the offensive would be launched in any case, but that "The Man" (Fidel) should take care to await the final result. The offensive, in fact, ran its course, and in two and a half months of hard fighting, the enemy lost over 1,000 men, counting dead, wounded, prisoners, and deserters. They also left 600 weapons in our hands, including a tank, 12 mortars, 12 tripod machine guns, over 200 submachine guns and countless automatic weapons; also, an enormous amount of ammunition and equipment of all sorts, and 450 prisoners, who were handed over to the Red Cross when the campaign ended.

Batista's army came out of that last offensive in the Sierra Maestra with its spine broken, but it had not yet been defeated. The struggle would go on. It was then that the final strategy was established, attacking through three points: Santiago de Cuba, which had been under a flexible siege; Las Villas, where I was to go; and Pinar del Río, at the other end of the island, where Camilo Cienfuegos, who was now commander of the Antonio Maceo Column No. 2, was to march in remembrance of the historic invasion by the great leader of 1895, when Maceo crossed the length of Cuban territory with epic acts, culminating in Mantua. Camilo Cienfuegos was not able to fulfill the second part of his program, as the exigencies of the war forced him to remain in Las Villas.

Once the regiments that assaulted the Sierra Maestra had been wiped out, once the front had returned to its normal level, and once our troops had increased their strength and morale, it was decided to begin the march on the central province of Las Villas. My orders were that the main strategic task was to systematically cut off communications between the two ends of the island. I was also ordered to establish relations with all the political groups that might be in the mountains of that region, and I was given broad powers to militarily govern my assigned area.

With those instructions and thinking that we would make the trip in four days, we were to begin our march, by truck, on August 30, 1958, when an unexpected accident upset our plans. A pickup truck carrying uniforms and gasoline necessary for the vehicles that were ready was arriving that night, when a cargo of arms also arrived, by air, at an airstrip near the road. The plane was sighted just as it landed, even though it was at night, and the airstrip was systematically bombed from 8:00 p.m. until 5:00 in the morning, when we burned the plane to prevent it from falling into the enemy's hands and to prevent the enemy from continuing the bombardment during the day, which would have been even worse for us. The enemy troops advanced on the airstrip. They intercepted the pickup truck carrying the gasoline, and we were left on foot.

So it was that we began the march on August 31, without trucks or horses, hoping to find them after crossing the highway from Manzanillo to Bayamo. In fact, having crossed it we found the trucks, but also — on September 1 — we encountered a fierce hurricane that made all roads impassable except for the central highway, the only paved one in this region of Cuba, forcing us to give up on using vehicles for transportation. From that moment on, we had to use horses, or walk. We were loaded down with quite a bit of ammunition, a bazooka with 40 shells and everything necessary for a long march and for rapidly establishing a camp.

One day after another went by, and they already were becoming difficult even though we were in the friendly territory of Oriente: crossing rivers that were overflowing, canals and streams that had become rivers, struggling with difficulty to prevent our ammunition, arms, and shells from getting wet; looking for horses and leaving the tired ones behind; avoiding inhabited zones as we moved away from the eastern province.

We walked through difficult flooded terrain, suffering attacks by swarms of mosquitoes that made the rest periods unbearable, eating little and poorly, drinking water from swampy rivers or simply from swamps. Each day of travel became longer and truly horrible. A week after we had left camp, by the time we crossed the Jobabo River, which marks the border between Oriente and Camagüey Provinces, our forces were greatly weakened. This river, like all the previous ones and like those we would cross later, was flooded. We were also feeling the effects of lack of footwear among our troops, many of whom were walking barefoot through the swamps of southern Camagüey.

On the night of September 9, as we were approaching a place known as La Federal, our advance guard fell into an enemy ambush, and two valuable *compañeros* were killed. But the most regrettable result was being sighted by the enemy forces, who from then on gave us no respite. After a brief clash, the small garrison there surrendered and we took four prisoners. Now we had to march very carefully, since the air force knew our approximate route. Thus, one or two days later, we reached a place known as Laguna Grande, along with Camilo's force, which was much better equipped than ours. This zone is remarkable for its extraordinary number of mosquitoes, which made it absolutely impossible for us to rest outside without a mosquito net, which some of us did not have.

These were days of tiring marches through desolate expanses where there was only water and mud. We were hungry, thirsty, and could hardly advance because our legs were as heavy as lead and the weapons were enormously heavy. We continued advancing with better horses that Camilo left for us when his column got on trucks, but we had to give them up near the Macareño sugar mill. The guides they were supposed to send us did not arrive and we set out as we were, on to the adventure.

Our vanguard clashed with an enemy outpost in a place called Cuatro Compañeros and the exhausting battle began. It was daybreak, and with great effort we managed to gather a large part of our troop in the largest woods in the area. But the army was advancing along its sides and we had to fight hard to make it possible for some of our men, who had fallen behind, to cross a railroad line, toward the woods. The air force sighted us then and the B-26s, the C-47s, the big C-3 reconnaissance planes, and the light planes began bombing an area no more than 200 meters wide. Finally, we withdrew, leaving one of our men killed by a bomb and carrying several wounded, including Captain Silva, who went through the rest of the invasion with a broken shoulder.

The following day the picture was less discouraging, since many of those who had fallen behind showed up, and we managed to gather the whole troop, except for 10 men who would go on to join Camilo's column and with him get as far as the northern front of Las Villas Province, in Yaguajay.

Despite the difficulties, we were never without the encouragement of the peasants. We always found someone who would serve as a guide, or who would give us the food without which we could not go on. Naturally, it was not the unanimous support of the whole people we had enjoyed in Oriente, but there was always someone who helped us. At times we were reported to the enemy as soon as we crossed a farm, but that was not because of a direct action by the peasants against us. Rather it was because their living conditions made these people slaves of the landowner and, fearful of losing their daily subsistence, they would report to their master that we had passed through that region. The latter in turn would take charge of graciously informing the military authorities.

One afternoon we were listening on our field radio to a report by Gen. Francisco Tabernilla Dolz. With all his thuggish bombast, he was announcing that the hordes led by Che Guevara had been destroyed and giving extensive details on the dead, the wounded, names, and all sorts of things, which were the product of the booty they took from our knapsacks after that disastrous encounter with the enemy a few days earlier. All of this was mixed in with false information cooked up by the army high command. This news of our demise produced great merriment among our troop. But pessimism was getting hold of them little by little. Hunger and thirst, weariness, the feeling of impotence against the enemy forces that were increasingly closing in on us, and above all, the terrible foot disease that the peasants call *mazamorra* — which turned each step our soldiers took into an intolerable torment — had made us an army of shadows. It was difficult to advance, very difficult. Our troop's physical condition worsened day by day, and the meals — today yes, tomorrow no, the next day maybe — in no way helped to alleviate the level of misery we were suffering.

We spent the hardest days besieged in the vicinity of the Baraguá sugar mill in stinking swamps, without a drop of water, continuously attacked by the air force, without a single horse that could carry the weakest through barren marshes, with our shoes totally demolished by the muddy sea water, full of vegetation that injured our bare feet. Our situation was really disastrous when, with difficulty, we broke out of the encirclement at Baraguá and reached the famous Júcaro-Morón trail, a historic spot, the scene of bloody fighting between patriots and the Spaniards during the war of independence.

We did not have time to recover even a little when a new downpour, bad weather, in addition to enemy attacks or reports of their presence, forced us to march on. The troop was increasingly tired and disheartened. When the situation was most tense, however, when insults, pleas and tongue lashings were the only way to get the weary men to advance, a sight far away in the distance lit up their faces and instilled new spirit in the guerrillas. That sight was a blue streak to the west, the blue streak of the Las Villas mountain range, seen for the first time by our men. From that moment on, the same hardships, or similar ones, became much more bearable, and everything seemed easier. We slipped through the last encirclement by swimming across the Júcaro River, which divides the provinces of Camagüey and Las Villas, and it seemed already that a new light was shining on us.

Two days later we were in the heart of the Trinidad-Sancti Spíritus mountain range, safe, ready to begin the next stage of the war. We rested for another two days; we had to be on our way immediately and prepare ourselves to prevent the elections scheduled for November 3. We had reached the mountain region of Las Villas on October 16. Time was short and the task was enormous. Camilo was doing his part in the north, sowing fear among the dictatorship's men.

Our task, upon arriving for the first time in the Escambray Mountains, was well defined: we had to harass the dictatorship's military apparatus, above all its communications. And, as an immediate goal, we had to prevent the elections from taking place. But the task was made difficult because time was scarce, and because of the disunity among the revolutionary forces, which resulted in internal quarrels that cost us dearly, including in human lives.

We were supposed to attack the neighboring towns to prevent the elections, and plans were worked out to do this simultaneously in the cities of Cabaiguán, Fomento, and Sancti Spíritus, in the rich plains of the center of the island. Meanwhile, the small garrison at Güinía de Miranda — in the mountains — surrendered, and later the Banao garrison was attacked with little results. The days prior to November 3, the date of the elections, were extraordinarily busy. Our columns were mobilized everywhere, almost totally preventing voters in those areas from going to the polls. Camilo Cienfuegos's troops in the northern part of the province paralyzed the electoral farce. In general, everything was halted, from the transport of Batista's soldiers to commercial traffic.

In Oriente, there was practically no voting; in Camagüey, the percentage was a bit higher; and in the western region, in spite of everything, mass abstention was clear. This abstention was achieved spontaneously in Las Villas, as there had not been time to synchronize the masses' passive resistance with the guerrillas' activity.

In Oriente successive battles were taking place on the first and second fronts, as well as on the third — with the Antonio Guiteras Column. They were insistently exerting pressure on Santiago de Cuba, the provincial capital. Except for the seats of the municipalities, the government had nothing left in Oriente.

The situation was also becoming very serious in Las Villas, with stepped-up attacks on communications routes. When we arrived, we completely changed the system of struggle in the cities, as we rapidly sent the best militiamen from the cities to the training camp to receive instruction in sabotage, which proved effective in suburban areas.

During the months of November and December 1958, we gradually closed the highways. Captain Silva totally blocked the highway from Trinidad to Sancti Spíritus, and the island's central highway was seriously damaged when the bridge across the Tuinicú River was dynamited, although it did not completely collapse. The central railroad was blocked at several points; moreover, the southern route had been cut by the second front and the northern route had been closed by Camilo Cienfuegos's troops. Therefore the island was divided into two parts. The region most in upheaval, Oriente, received aid from the government only by air and sea, and this became increasingly uncertain. The symptoms of the enemy's disintegration were increasing.

An extremely intense campaign for revolutionary unity had to be carried out in the Escambray Mountains because operating there was a group led by Commander [Eloy] Gutiérrez Menoyo (Second National Front of the Escambray), another of the Revolutionary Directorate (led by Commanders Faure Chomón and Rolando Cubela), another smaller one of the Authentic Organization, another of the Popular Socialist Party (commanded by [Félix] Torres), and us. In other words, there were five different organizations operating under different commands and in the same province. After laborious talks that I had to have with their respective leaders, we reached a series of agreements and it was possible to go on to form a more or less common front.

From December 16 onward, systematic cutting off of bridges and all kinds of communication had made it very difficult for the dictatorship to defend its forward positions and even those on the central highway. Early that day, the bridge across the Falcón River, on the central highway, was destroyed, and communications between Havana and the cities to the east of Santa Clara, the capital of Las Villas Province, were virtually cut off. Also, a number of towns — the southernmost being Fomento — were besieged and attacked by our forces. The commander of the city defended his position more or less efficiently for several days. Despite the air force's punishment of our Rebel Army, however, the dictatorship's demoralized troops would not advance overland to support their *compañeros*. Realizing that all resistance was useless, they surrendered, and more than 100 rifles joined the forces of freedom.

Without giving the enemy any respite, we decided to paralyze the central highway immediately, and on December 21 we simultaneously attacked Cabaiguán and Gudyos, both on the central highway. The latter town surrendered in a few hours, and during the following days, so did Cabaiguán with its 90 soldiers. (The surrender of the garrisons was negotiated on the political basis of letting the soldiers go free on the condition that they leave the liberated territory. Thus, they were given the opportunity to surrender their weapons and to save themselves.) Cabaiguán once again proved the dictatorship's ineffectiveness, as it never sent infantry units to reinforce those under siege.

In the northern region of Las Villas, Camilo Cienfuegos was attacking several towns, which he was subduing at the same time that he laid siege to Yaguajay, the last bastion of the dictatorship's troops. It was under the command of a captain of Chinese ancestry who resisted for 11 days, immobilizing the revolutionary troops in the region. At the same time our troops were already advancing along the central highway toward Santa Clara, the provincial capital.

After Cabaiguán had fallen, we set out — in active collaboration with the forces of the Revolutionary Directorate — to attack Placetas, which surrendered after only one day of struggle. After taking Placetas, we liberated in rapid succession Remedios and Caibarién on the northern coast, the latter an important port. The picture was turning gloomy for the dictatorship, because in addition to the continuous victories scored in Oriente, the Second Front of the Escambray was defeating small garrisons, and Camilo Cienfuegos controlled the north.

When the enemy withdrew from Camajuaní without offering resistance, we were ready to launch the definitive attack on the capital of Las Villas Province. Santa Clara is the hub of the island's central plain, with 150,000 inhabitants, center of the railway system and of all communications in the country. It is surrounded by small bare hills, which had previously been taken by the troops of the dictatorship.

At the time of the attack, our forces had considerably increased our weaponry, as we had taken several positions and some heavy weapons, for which there was no ammunition. We had a bazooka without shells, and we had to fight against about 10 tanks. But we also knew that for us to fight most effectively, we had to reach the city's populous neighborhoods, where the tanks' efficiency diminishes a lot.

While the troops of the Revolutionary Directorate were taking the Rural Guard's Garrison No. 31, we set about to besiege almost all of Santa Clara's fortified positions. Our fight focused mainly on the defenders of the armored train stationed at the entrance of the road to Camajuani. These positions were tenaciously defended by the army, which was well equipped.

On December 29 we began the struggle. At first the university served as our base of operations. Later, we established our headquarters closer to the city's downtown area. Our men were fighting against troops supported by armored units and would force them to flee, although many paid for their boldness with their lives. The dead and wounded began to fill up the improvised cemeteries and hospitals.

I remember an episode that shows the spirit of our forces in those final days. I had admonished a soldier because he was sleeping in the midst of battle, and he replied that he had been disarmed for accidentally firing his weapon. I responded with my customary dryness: "Get yourself another rifle by going disarmed to the front line… if you're up to it." In Santa Clara, while I was speaking to the wounded in the Hospital de Sangre, a dying man touched my hand and said, "Do you remember, commander? In Remedios you sent me to find a weapon… and I earned it here." He was the fighter who had accidentally fired his weapon. He died a few minutes later, and I think he was content for having proven his courage. Such was our Rebel Army.

The hills of Cápiro continued to resist, and we went on fighting there all day December 30, at the same time gradually taking different points in the city. By then, communications between downtown Santa Clara and the armored train had been cut off. Those in the train, seeing that they were surrounded on the hills of Cápiro, tried to escape by rail, with all their magnificent cargo. Arriving at the spur that we had previously destroyed, the locomotive and some cars were derailed. Then a very interesting battle began, in which the men were forced out of the armored train by our Molotov cocktails. They were very well protected, but willing to fight only at a distance, from comfortable positions, and against a virtually unarmed enemy, in the style of the colonists against the Indians of the U.S. West. Cornered by men who, from nearby points and adjoining railroad cars, were throwing bottles with burning gasoline, the train became, thanks to the armored plating, a veritable oven for the soldiers. In a few hours, the whole complement surrendered with its 22 cars, its antiaircraft guns, its machine guns of the same type and its fabulous quantity of ammunition — fabulous, of course, compared with our meager supply.

We had been able to take the power station and the city's whole northwest side. We went on the air to announce that Santa Clara was almost in the hands of the revolution. In that announcement, which I made as commander in chief of the armed forces in Las Villas, I remember I had the sorrow of informing the Cuban people of the death of Capt. Roberto Rodríguez, "El Vaquerito" [The little cowboy], small in height and young in years, leader of the Suicide Squad, who had played with death a thousand and one times fighting for freedom. The Suicide Squad was an example of revolutionary morale, and only selected volunteers joined it. But whenever a man died — and that happened in every battle — when the new candidate was named, those not chosen would be grief-stricken and even cry. How curious to see those seasoned and noble figures showing their youth in their tears of despair, because they did not have the honor of being in the front line of combat and death.

Next fell the police station, surrendering the tanks that defended it. And in rapid succession Garrison No. 31 surrendered to Commander Cubela, while the jail, the courthouse, the provincial government palace and the Grand Hotel — where snipers had kept firing from the 10th floor almost until the combat ended — surrendered to our forces.

At that moment, only the Leoncio Vidal Garrison, the largest fortress in central Cuba, had not surrendered. But by January 1, 1959, there were already signs of growing weakness among the forces defending it. That morning, we sent Captains Núñez Jiménez and Rodríguez de la Vega to negotiate the surrender of the garrison.

The reports were contradictory and extraordinary: Batista had fled that day, leaving the armed forces high command in a shambles. Our two delegates established radio contact with [Gen. Eulogio] Cantillo, telling him of the surrender offer. But he refused to go along because this constituted an ultimatum, and he had taken over command of the army in strict accordance with instructions from the leader Fidel Castro. We immediately contacted Fidel, telling him the news, but giving our opinion of Cantillo's treacherous attitude, an opinion with which he absolutely agreed. (In those decisive hours, Cantillo let all the main figures responsible for Batista's government escape. His attitude was even more wretched if one considers that he was an officer who had made contact with us and whom we had trusted as a military man of honor.)

The results that followed are known to everyone: Castro's refusal to recognize Cantillo's authority; Fidel's order to march on the city of Havana; Colonel Barquín's taking over command of the army after leaving the Isle of Pines prison; the seizure of Camp Columbia by Camilo Cienfuegos and of La Cabaña fortress by our Column No. 8; and the final installation, in a few days, of Fidel Castro as prime minister of the provisional government. All this belongs to the country's present political history.

We are now in a position in which we are much more than simple instruments of one nation. We are now the hope of the unredeemed Americas. All eyes — those of the great oppressors and those of the hopeful — are firmly on us. In great measure, the development of the popular movements in Latin America depends on the future stance that we take, on our capacity to resolve so many problems. And every step we take is being observed by the ever-watchful eyes of the big creditor and by the optimistic eyes of our brothers in Latin America.

With our feet planted firmly on the ground, we are beginning to labor and produce our first revolutionary works, confronting the first difficulties. But what is Cuba's main problem if not the same as of all Latin America, the same as even enormous Brazil with its millions of square kilometers and with its land of marvels that is a whole continent? The one-crop economy. In Cuba, we are slaves to sugarcane, the umbilical cord that binds us to the large northern market. We must diversify our agricultural production, stimulate industry. And we must ensure that our minerals and agricultural products, and — in the near future — our industrial production, go to the markets that are best suited for us and by means of our own transportation lines.

The government's first big battle will be the agrarian reform, which will be audacious, thorough, but flexible: it will destroy the latifundia in Cuba, although not Cuba's means of production. It will be a battle that will absorb a great part of the strength of the people and the government during the coming years. The land will be given free to the peasant. Landowners who prove that they came by their holdings honestly will be compensated with long-term bonds. But the peasantry will also be given technical assistance;

there will be guaranteed markets for the products of the soil. And production will be channeled with a broad national sense of development in conjunction with the great battle for agrarian reform, so that within a short time the infant Cuban industries can compete with the monstrous ones of the countries where capitalism has reached its highest level of development. Simultaneously with the creation of the new domestic market that the agrarian reform will bring about, and the distribution of new products to satisfy a growing market, there will arise the need to export some products and to have the adequate instrument to take them to this or that part of the world. That instrument will be a merchant fleet, which the already approved Maritime Development Law envisages.

With those elementary weapons, we Cubans will begin the struggle for our territory's total freedom. We all know it will not be easy, but we are all aware of the enormous historic responsibility of the July 26 Movement, of the Cuban Revolution, of the nation in general, to be an example for all peoples of Latin America, whom we must not disappoint.

Our friends of the indomitable continent can be sure that, if need be, we will struggle no matter what the economic consequence of our acts may be. And if the fight is taken further still, we shall struggle to the last drop of our rebel blood to make this land a sovereign republic, with the true attributes of a nation that is happy, democratic, and fraternal with its brothers of Latin America.

El Patojo

A few days ago a cable brought the news of the death of some Guatemalan patriots, among them Julio Roberto Cáceres Valle.

In this difficult profession of a revolutionary, in the midst of class wars that are convulsing the entire continent, death is a frequent accident. But the death of a friend, a comrade during difficult hours and a sharer in dreams of better times, is always painful for the person who receives the news, and Julio Roberto was a great friend. He was short and frail; for that reason we called him "El Patojo," Guatemalan slang meaning "Shorty" or "Kid."

El Patojo had witnessed the birth of our revolution while in Mexico and had volunteered to join us. Fidel, however, did not want to bring any more foreigners into that struggle for national liberation in which I had the honor to participate.

A few days after the revolution triumphed, El Patojo sold his few belongings and, with only a small suitcase, appeared in Cuba. He worked in various branches of public administration, and he was the first head of personnel of the Department of Industrialization of INRA (National Institute of Agrarian Reform). But he was never happy with his work. El Patojo was looking for something different; he was seeking the liberation of his own country. The revolution had changed him profoundly, as it had all of us. The bewildered boy who had left Guatemala without fully understanding the defeat had now become the fully conscious revolutionary.

The first time we met we were on a train, fleeing Guatemala, a couple of months after the [1954] fall of Arbenz. We were going to Tapachula, from where we could reach Mexico City. El Patojo was several years younger than I, but we immediately formed a lasting friendship. Together we made the trip from Chiapas to Mexico City; together we faced the same problems — we were both penniless, defeated and forced to earn a living in an indifferent if not hostile environment. El Patojo had no money and I only a few pesos; I bought a camera and, together, we undertook the illegal job of taking pictures of people in the city parks. Our partner was a Mexican who had a small darkroom where we developed the film. We got to know all of Mexico City, walking from one end to another, delivering the atrocious photographs we had taken. We battled with all kinds of clients, trying to convince them that the little boy in the photo was really very cute and it was really a great bargain to pay a Mexican peso for such a marvel. This is how we ate for several months. Little by little the contingencies of revolutionary life separated us. I have already said that Fidel did not want to bring him to Cuba, not because of any shortcomings of his, but so as to avoid turning our army into a mosaic of nationalities.

El Patojo had been a journalist, had studied physics at the University of Mexico, had left his studies and then returned to them, without ever getting very far. He earned his living in various places, at various jobs, and never asked for anything. I still do not know whether that sensitive and serious boy was overly timid, or too proud to recognize his weaknesses and his personal problems to approach a friend for help. El Patojo was an introvert, highly intelligent, broadly cultured, sensitive. He matured steadily and in his last moments was ready to put his great sensibilities at the service of his people. He belonged to the Partido Guatemalteco de Trabajo [Guatemalan Labor Party] and had disciplined himself in that life — he was developing into a fine revolutionary cadre. By then, little remained of his earlier hypersensitivity. Revolution purifies people, improves and develops them, just as the experienced farmer corrects the deficiencies of their crops and strengthens their good qualities.

After he came to Cuba we almost always lived in the same house, as was fitting for two old friends. But we no longer maintained the early intimacy in this new life, and I only suspected El Patojo's intentions when I sometimes saw him earnestly studying one of the native Indian languages of his country. One day he told me he was leaving, that the time had come for him to do his duty.

El Patojo had had no military training; he simply felt that duty called him. He was going to his country to fight, gun in hand, to somehow reproduce our guerrilla struggle. It was then that we had one of our few long talks. I limited myself to recommending strongly these three things: constant movement, constant wariness and eternal vigilance. Movement — never stay put; never spend two nights in the same place; never stop moving from one place to another. Wariness — at the beginning, be wary even of your own shadow, friendly peasants, informants, guides, contacts; mistrust everything until you hold a liberated zone. Vigilance — constant guard duty; constant reconnaissance; establishment of a camp in a safe place and, above all, never sleep beneath a roof, never sleep in a house where you can be surrounded. This was the synthesis of our guerrilla experience; it was the only thing — along with a warm handshake — which I could give to my friend. Could I advise him not to do it? With what right? We had undertaken something at a time when it was believed impossible, and now he saw that it had succeeded.

El Patojo left and in time came the news of his death. At first we hoped there had been a confusion of names, that there had been some mistake, but unfortunately his body had been identified by his own mother; there could be no doubt he was dead. And not only he, but a group of comrades with him, all of them as brave, as selfless, as intelligent perhaps as he, but not known to us personally.

Once more there is the bitter taste of defeat and the unanswered question: Why did he not learn from the experience of others? Why did those men not heed more carefully the simple advice which we had given them? There is an urgent investigation into how it came about, how El Patojo died. We still do not know exactly what happened, but we do know that the region was poorly chosen, that the men were not physically prepared, that they were not sufficiently wary and, of course, that they were not sufficiently vigilant. The repressive army took them by surprise, killed a few, dispersed the rest, then returned to pursue them, and virtually annihilated them. They took some prisoners; others, like El Patojo, died in battle. After being dispersed, the guerrillas were probably hunted down, as we had been after Alegría de Pío.

Once again youthful blood has fertilized the fields of the Americas to make freedom possible. Another battle has been lost; we must make time to weep for our fallen comrades while we sharpen our machetes. From the valuable and tragic experience of the cherished dead, we must firmly resolve not to repeat their errors, to avenge the death of each one of them with many victories, and to achieve definitive liberation.

When El Patojo left Cuba, he left nothing behind, nor did he leave any messages; he had few clothes or personal belongings to worry about. Old mutual friends in Mexico, however, brought me some poems he had written and left there in a notebook. They are the last verses of a revolutionary; they are, in addition, a love song to the revolution, to the homeland, and to a woman. To that woman whom El Patojo knew and loved in Cuba are addressed these final verses, this injunction:

> Take this, it is only my heart
> Hold it in your hand
> And when the dawn arrives,
> Open your hand
> And let the sun warm it...

El Patojo's heart has remained among us, in the hands of his beloved and in the loving hands of an entire people, waiting to be warmed beneath the sun of a new day which will surely dawn for Guatemala and for all the Americas. Today, in the Ministry of Industry where he left many friends, there is a small school of statistics named in his memory "Julio Roberto Cáceres Valle." Later, when Guatemala is free, his beloved name will surely be given to a school, a factory, a hospital, to any place where people fight and work to build a new society.

What we have learned and what we have taught

(December 1958)

This article, written in the final weeks before victory, was published on January 1, 1959, in Patria, *official organ of the Rebel Army in Las Villas Province.*

H ere in December, the month of the second anniversary of the *Granma* landing, it's worth taking a look back over the years of armed struggle and the long revolutionary battle. The initial ferment was provided by Batista's coup of March 10, 1952, and the first bell sounded on July 26, 1953, with the tragic battle of Moncada.

The road has been long and full of hardships and contradictions. In the course of every revolutionary process that is led honestly and not held back by those in positions of responsibility, there are a series of reciprocal interactions between the leaders and the revolutionary masses. The July 26 Movement has also felt the effects of this historical law. There is a gulf between the group of enthusiastic youths who attacked the Moncada garrison at dawn on July 26, 1953, and the Movement's current leaders, even though many of the individuals are the same. The five years of head-on struggle — including two of open war — have molded the revolutionary spirit of us all in the course of daily clashes with reality and with the people's instinctive wisdom.

Indeed, our contact with the peasant masses has taught us the great injustice that the current system of agrarian property relations entails. The peasants convinced us of the justice of a fundamental change in this property system. They enlightened us in daily practice about the Cuban peasant's capacity for self-sacrifice and their unbounded nobility and loyalty.

But we have also taught. We have taught how to lose all fear of the enemy's repression. We have taught that weapons in the hands of the people are superior to mercenary battalions. We have taught, in short, the popular maxim that can never be repeated enough: in unity there is strength.

And the peasant who became aware of his own strength pressed the Movement, his combative vanguard, to put forward ever more consciously bold demands that finally took shape in the recently issued Sierra Maestra Agrarian Reform Law No. 3.[7] Today this law is our pride, our battle flag, our reason for existence as a revolutionary organization.

But this was not always our approach to social questions. Besieged in our bastion in the Sierra, without vital links with the mass of the people, we could sometimes begin to feel more confident in the might of our weapons than in the correctness of our ideas. Because of this, we had our April 9, a sad date to remember, a date that represents with regard to the social struggle what Alegría de Pío — our only defeat in the field of battle — signified in the development of the armed struggle.

From Alegría de Pío we drew the revolutionary lessons necessary to not lose a single other battle. From April 9 we have also learned that the strategy of mass struggle follows established laws that cannot be bent or evaded. The lesson is clearly learned. To the work among the peasant masses — whom we have united, regardless of affiliation, in the struggle for the land — we add today the raising of workers' demands that unite the proletarian masses under a single banner of struggle, the United National Workers Front (FONU), and a single immediate tactical goal: the revolutionary general strike.

This does not represent the use of demagogic tactics in order to display political cleverness. We do not investigate the feelings of the masses out of simple scientific curiosity; we respond to their call. Because we, the combative vanguard of the workers and peasants who are shedding our blood in the mountains and plains of Cuba, are not elements isolated from the popular masses; we are very much part of the people. Our leadership role does not isolate us; rather it imposes obligations on us.

The fact that we are a Movement of all classes in Cuba, however, makes us also fight for the professional and the small businessperson who aspire to live in a framework of decent laws; for the Cuban industrialist whose efforts contribute to the nation by creating jobs; for every good man who wants to see a Cuba free from the daily sorrow of these painful times.

Now more than ever, the July 26 Movement, committed to the highest interests of the Cuban nation, wages its battle, without arrogance but without wavering, for the workers and peasants, for the professionals and small businessperson, for the national industrialists, for democracy and freedom, for the right to be the free children of a free people, for our daily bread to become the exact measure of our daily effort.

On this second anniversary, we are changing the formulation of our pledge. We will no longer "be free or be martyrs." We will be free — free by the action of the entire people of Cuba, who are breaking chain after chain with the blood and suffering of their best sons and daughters.

The essence of guerrilla struggle

(1960)

This is the first part of chapter one of Guevara's book La guerra de guerrillas *[Guerrilla warfare].*

The armed victory of the Cuban people over the Batista dictatorship has not only been the epic triumph as reported by broadcasts all over the world; it has also forced a change in the old dogmas concerning the conduct of the popular masses of Latin America. It has tangibly shown the capacity of the people to free themselves through guerrilla struggle from a government that oppresses them.

We believe that the Cuban Revolution made three fundamental contributions to the conduct of revolutionary movements in Latin America. They are:

1. Popular forces can win a war against the army.
2. It is not always necessary to wait until all the conditions for revolution exist; the insurrectional center can create them.
3. In underdeveloped Latin America the arena for armed struggle must be basically the countryside.

Of these three contributions, the first two counter the passive attitude of revolutionaries or pseudo-revolutionaries who shelter themselves and their inactivity using the pretext that nothing can be done against the professional army, and of some others who sit and wait until in some mechanical way all the necessary objective and subjective conditions come about, without working to accelerate them. Clear as these two undeniable truths appear today for the whole world, they were discussed in Cuba in the past, and are probably being discussed throughout Latin America, as well.

Naturally, when one speaks of the conditions for revolution it must not be thought that they will all be created by the impulse given by the guerrilla center. It must always be kept in mind that there are certain minimum requirements that make feasible the establishment and consolidation of the first center. That is, it is necessary to clearly demonstrate to the people that it is impossible to keep the struggle for social demands within the framework of civic dispute. The peace is broken precisely by the forces of the aggressors, who maintain their power in violation of established law.

Under these conditions popular discontent takes on ever more active shape and dimensions, and at a given moment, a stance of resistance crystallizes in the outbreak of fighting, provoked initially by the attitude of the authorities.

Where a government has come to power through some form of popular vote, fraudulent or not, and maintains at least an appearance of constitutional legality, it is impossible to produce the guerrilla outbreak, since the possibilities of civic struggle have not yet been exhausted.

The third contribution is fundamentally of a strategic nature, and is a rebuke to those who dogmatically assert that the struggle of the masses is centered in urban movements, totally forgetting the immense participation of the people from the countryside in the life of all the underdeveloped countries of Latin America. It is not a matter of slighting the struggles of the masses of organized workers. It is simply a matter of realistically analyzing the possibilities, under the difficult conditions of armed struggle, where the guarantees that usually adorn our constitutions are suspended or ignored. Under these conditions the workers' movements must go underground, without arms, illegal, and facing enormous dangers. The situation is not as difficult in the open countryside, where the inhabitants can be supported by the armed guerrillas in places beyond the reach of the repressive forces.

Although we will later make a detailed analysis, we point to these three conclusions drawn from the Cuban revolutionary experience at the start of this work because we consider them to be our fundamental contribution.

Guerrilla warfare, the basis of the struggle of a people to free itself, has diverse characteristics, different facets, even though the essential will for liberation remains the same. It is obvious — and writers on the theme have said it time and again — that war is governed by a specific set of scientific laws, and whoever goes against them will go down to defeat. Guerrilla warfare as a phase of war must be governed by all of these laws. Because of its special aspects, however, it also has an additional set of laws that must be followed in order to carry it forward. Naturally, geographical and social conditions in each country determine the mode and particular forms that guerrilla warfare will take, but its essential laws hold true for all struggles of this type.

Our task at the moment is to discover the fundamentals of this kind of struggle, the rules to be followed by peoples seeking liberation, to develop theory on the basis of the facts, to generalize and give structure to this experience for the benefit of others.

The first thing to establish is: Who are the combatants in guerrilla warfare? On one side there is the group of oppressors and their agent, the professional army (well armed and disciplined), who in many cases can count on support from abroad and from small groups of bureaucrats, servants of that group of oppressors. On the other side is the population of the nation or region involved. It is important to emphasize that the guerrilla struggle is a mass struggle, it is the struggle of a people. The guerrillas, as an armed nucleus, are the fighting vanguard of the people, and their great strength is rooted in the mass of the population. The guerrillas should not be considered numerically inferior to the army against which it fights, although its fire power may be inferior. That is precisely why guerrilla warfare is turned to when you have majority support but possess an infinitely smaller number of arms with which to defend yourselves against oppression.

The guerrilla fighter therefore relies on the complete support of the people of the area. This is absolutely indispensable. And this can be seen very clearly by taking as an example gangs of bandits that operate in a region. They have all the characteristics of a guerrilla army: homogeneity, respect for the leader, bravery, knowledge of the terrain, and often even a complete understanding of the tactics to be employed. The only thing they lack is the support of the people, and inevitably these gangs are captured or exterminated by government forces.

Having analyzed the mode of operation of the guerrillas, their form of struggle, and understanding that their base is among the masses, all that is left is the question: What is the guerrilla fighting for? We must come to the inevitable conclusion that the guerrilla is a social reformer, who takes up arms responding to the angry protest of the people against their oppressors, and who fights to change the social system that keeps all his unarmed brothers in ignominy and poverty. He rises up against the special conditions of the reigning institutional structure at a particular moment and dedicates himself with all the vigor that circumstances permit to breaking the mold of those institutions.

When we analyze more deeply the tactic of guerrilla warfare, we will see that the guerrilla fighter must have a thorough knowledge of the terrain he treads, his access and escape routes, the possibilities of rapid maneuver, the extent of popular support, naturally, and places to hide. All this indicates that the guerrilla fighter will carry out his actions in rugged, sparsely populated areas. In these places the struggle of the people for their demands is aimed primarily and almost exclusively at changing the social form of land ownership; in other words, the guerrilla fighter is above all an agrarian revolutionary. He interprets the desires of the great peasant masses to be owners of the land, of their means of production, of their livestock, of all that they have yearned for over the years, of what makes up their lives and will also be their grave.

It should be noted that in current interpretations there are two different types of guerrilla warfare, one of which — a struggle complementary to large regular armies, as in the case of the Ukrainian guerrillas in the Soviet Union — is not of interest for this analysis. We are interested in the case of an armed group that develops in the struggle against the existing power, whether colonial or not, that establishes itself as the only base, and that develops in rural areas. In all such cases, whatever the ideological aims that may inspire the struggle, the economic basis is given by the aspiration for ownership of the land.

Mao's China begins as an outbreak of workers' groups in the south, which is defeated and almost annihilated. It is able to stabilize itself and begin its forward march only when, after the long march to Yenan, it settles in rural territories and makes agrarian reform the basis of its demands. The struggle of Ho Chi Minh in Indochina is based on the rice-growing peasants, oppressed under the French colonial yoke; with this force it goes forward until it defeats the colonialists. In both cases there is an interlude of patriotic war against the Japanese invader, but the economic basis of the struggle for the land does not disappear. In the case of Algeria, the great idea of Arab nationalism has its economic counterpart in the control of nearly all of the arable land by a million French settlers. And in some countries, such as Puerto Rico, where the particular conditions of the island have not allowed a guerrilla outbreak, the nationalist spirit, deeply wounded by the acts of discrimination committed against them daily, has as its basis the aspiration of the peasants (even though often already proletarianized) for the land that the Yankee invader seized from them. This same central idea, though in different forms, inspired the small farmers, peasants and slaves of the eastern haciendas of Cuba to close ranks and together defend the right to possess land during the 30-year war of liberation [of Cuba against Spain from 1868 to 1898].

Despite the special characteristics that turn guerrilla warfare into a particular type of war, and taking into account the possibilities of its development (with the growth of the group's potential) into a war of positions, we should consider this type of struggle as an embryo of a war of positions, a plan for it. The possibilities for the growth of the guerrillas, and for changes in the type of fighting until conventional warfare is reached, are as great as the possibilities of defeating the enemy in each of the different battles, combats or skirmishes that may take place. Therefore, it is a fundamental principle that no battle, combat, or skirmish is to be fought unless it can be won. There is a malicious definition that states that "the guerrilla fighter is the Jesuit of warfare." By this is meant a quality of secretiveness, of treachery, of surprise that is obviously an essential element of guerrilla struggle. It is naturally a special kind of Jesuitism, prompted by circumstances that necessitate acting at certain moments in ways different from the romantic and sporting conceptions with which we are taught to believe war is fought.

War is always a struggle in which both contenders try to annihilate the other. Besides using force, they will have recourse to all possible tricks and stratagems in order to achieve these results. Military strategy and tactics are an expression of the guerrilla group's aspirations and of the means to carry them out; and those methods seek to take advantage of the enemy's weak points. Examined up close, the action of each platoon in a large army in a war of positions will present the same characteristics, in terms of individual combat, as those of the guerrilla unit. It uses secretiveness, treachery and surprise; and when these are not present, it is because vigilance on the other side makes surprise impossible. But since the guerrilla unit is a division in itself, and since there are large zones of territory not guarded by the enemy, it is always possible to carry out these tasks in such a way as to assure surprise; and it is the duty of the guerrilla fighter to do so.

"Hit and run," some people scornfully call this, and that's accurate. Hit and run, wait, lie in ambush, hit and run again, and do so repeatedly, without giving the enemy a moment's rest. There is in all this, it would appear, a negative attitude, an attitude of retreat, of avoiding direct confrontation. All this is consistent with the general strategy of guerrilla warfare, however, which is the same in its ultimate end as that of any warfare: to win, to annihilate the enemy.

Thus it is clear that guerrilla warfare is a phase that does not in itself afford opportunities to achieve complete victory. It is one of the primary phases of warfare and will develop and unfold until the guerrilla army, through steady growth, acquires the characteristics of a regular army. At that moment it will be ready to deal definitive blows to the enemy and register victory. Triumph will always be the product of a regular army, though its origins may be that of a guerrilla army.

Now, just as the general of a division in a modern war does not have to die at the head of his soldiers, the guerrilla fighter, who is his own general, should not die in every battle. He is ready to give his life, but the positive quality of guerrilla warfare is precisely that each one of the guerrilla fighters is ready to die, not to defend an ideal, but rather to make that ideal a reality. This is the basis, the essence of guerrilla struggle: the miracle whereby a small nucleus of men, the armed vanguard of the great popular force that supports them, able to see farther than the immediate tactical objective, advances decisively to achieve an ideal, to establish a new society, to break the mold of the old society, and to achieve, once and for all, the social justice for which they fight.

Seen in this light, all disparaging words acquire a true nobility, the nobility of what the guerrilla aims to accomplish; and mark well that we are not speaking of twisted means of reaching an end. The fighting attitude, this attitude of never losing heart, this inflexibility in confronting the great problems of the final objective, this too is the nobility of the guerrilla fighter.

Guerrilla warfare: A method

(September 1963)

G uerrilla warfare has been employed throughout history on innumerable occasions and in different circumstances to obtain different objectives. Lately it has been employed in various people's wars of liberation when the vanguard of a people have chosen the road of irregular armed struggle against enemies of superior military power. Asia, Africa and Latin America have been the scenes of such actions in attempts to obtain power in the struggle against feudal, neocolonial, or colonial exploitation. In Europe, guerrilla units have been used as supplements to native or allied regular armies.

Guerrilla warfare has been employed in the Americas on several occasions. We have had, as a case in point, the experience of César Augusto Sandino fighting against the Yankee expeditionary force on Nicaragua's Segovia [River]. Recently we had Cuba's revolutionary war. In the Americas since then the problem of guerrilla war has been raised in theoretical discussions by the progressive parties of the continent with the question of whether its utilization is possible or convenient. This has become the topic of very controversial polemics.

This article will express our views on guerrilla warfare and its correct utilization. Above all, we must emphasize at the outset that this form of struggle is a means to an end. That end, essential and inevitable for any revolutionary, is the conquest of political power. In the analysis of specific situations in different countries of America, we must therefore use the concept of guerrilla warfare in the limited sense of a method of struggle in order to gain that end.

Almost immediately the questions arise: Is guerrilla warfare the only formula for seizing power in Latin America? Or, at any rate, will it be the predominant form? Or will it simply be one formula among many used during the struggle? And ultimately we may ask: Will Cuba's example be applicable to the present situation on the continent? In the course of polemics, those who want to undertake guerrilla warfare are criticized for forgetting mass struggle, implying that guerrilla warfare and mass struggle are opposed to each other. We reject this implication, for guerrilla warfare is a people's warfare; an attempt to carry out this type of war without the population's support is a prelude to inevitable disaster. The guerrilla is the combat vanguard of the people, situated in a specified place in a certain region, armed and willing to carry out a series of warlike actions for the one possible strategic end — the seizure of power. The guerrilla is supported by the peasant and worker masses of the region and of the whole territory in which it acts. Without these prerequisites, guerrilla warfare is not possible.

> We consider that the Cuban Revolution made three fundamental contributions to the laws of the revolutionary movement in the current situation in America. First, people's forces can win a war against the army. Second, it is not always necessary to wait for all conditions favorable to revolution to be present; the insurrection itself can create them. Third, in the underdeveloped parts of America, the battleground for armed struggle should in the main be the countryside. (Ernesto Che Guevara, *Guerrilla Warfare*)

Such are the contributions to the development of the revolutionary struggle in America, and they can be applied to any of the countries on our continent where guerrilla warfare may develop.

The Second Declaration of Havana points out:

> In our countries two circumstances are linked: underdeveloped industry and an agrarian system of feudal character so no matter how hard the living conditions of the urban workers are, the rural population lives under even worse conditions of oppression and exploitation. With few exceptions, the rural population also constitutes the absolute majority, comprising more than 70 percent of the Latin American populations.
>
> Not counting the landowners who often live in the cities, this great mass earns its livelihood by working for miserable wages as peons on plantations. They till the soil under conditions of exploitation no different from those of the Middle Ages. These circumstances determine in Latin America that the poor rural population constitutes a tremendous potential revolutionary force.
>
> The armies in Latin America are set up and equipped for conventional warfare. They are the force through which the power of the exploiting classes is maintained. When they are confronted with the

irregular warfare of peasants based on their home ground, they become absolutely powerless; they lose 10 men for every revolutionary fighter who falls. Demoralization among them mounts rapidly when they are beset by an invisible and invincible army which provides them no chance to display their military academy tactics and their military fanfare, of which they boast so heavily, and which they use to repress the city workers and students.

The initial struggle of the small fighting units is constantly nurtured by new forces; the mass movement begins to grow bold, bit by bit the old order breaks into a thousand pieces, and that is when the working class and the urban masses decide the battle.

What is it that from the very beginning of the fight makes these units invincible, regardless of the numbers, strengths and resources of their enemies? It is the people's support, and they can count on an ever-increasing mass support.

The peasantry, however, is a class that because of the ignorance in which it has been kept and the isolation in which it lives, requires the revolutionary and political leadership of the working class and the revolutionary intellectuals. It cannot launch the struggle and achieve victory alone.

In the present historical conditions of Latin America, the national bourgeoisie cannot lead the antifeudal and anti-imperialist struggle. Experience demonstrates that in our nations this class — even when its interests clash with those of Yankee imperialism — has been incapable of confronting imperialism, paralyzed by fear of social revolution and frightened by the clamor of the exploited masses.

Completing the foresight of the preceding statements that constitute the essence of the revolutionary declaration of Latin America, the Second Declaration of Havana states:

The subjective conditions in each country, the factors of revolutionary consciousness, organization and leadership, can accelerate or delay revolution, depending on the state of their development. Sooner or later in each historic epoch objective conditions ripen, consciousness is acquired, organization is achieved, leadership arises, and revolution takes place.

Whether this takes place peacefully or comes into the world after painful labor does not depend on the revolutionaries; it depends on the reactionary forces of the old society, who resist the birth of the new society engendered by contradictions carried in the womb of the old. Revolution, in history, is like the doctor assisting at the birth of a new life, who will not use forceps unless necessary, but who will use them unhesitatingly every time labor requires them. It is a labor bringing the hope of a better life to the enslaved and exploited masses.

In many Latin American countries revolution is inevitable. This fact is not determined by the will of any person. It is determined by the horrifying conditions of exploitation under which the Latin American people live, the development of a revolutionary conscious- ness in the masses, the worldwide crisis of imperialism and the universal liberation movements of the subjugated nations.

We shall begin from this basis to analyze the whole matter of guerrilla warfare in Latin America.

We have already established that it is a means of struggle to attain an end. First, our concern is to analyze the end in order to determine whether the winning of power in Latin America can be achieved in ways other than armed struggle.

Peaceful struggle can be carried out through mass movements that compel — in special situations of crisis — governments to yield; thus, the popular forces would eventually take over and establish a dictatorship of the proletariat. Theoretically this is correct. When analyzing this in the Latin American context, we must reach the following conclusions: Generally on this continent objective conditions exist that propel the masses to violent action against their bourgeois and landholding governments. In many countries there are crises of power and also some subjective conditions necessary for revolution. It is clear, of course, that in those countries where all of these conditions are found, it would be criminal not to act to seize power. In other countries where these conditions do not occur, it is right that different alternatives will appear and out of theoretical discussions the tactic suitable to each country should emerge. The only thing history does not allow is that the analysts and executors of proletarian politics be mistaken.

No-one can solicit the role of vanguard party as if it were a diploma given by a university. To be the vanguard party means to be at the forefront of the working class through the struggle for achieving power. It means to know how to guide this fight through shortcuts to victory. This is the mission of our revolutionary parties and the analysis must be profound and exhaustive so that there will be no mistakes.

At the present time we can observe in America an unstable balance bet- ween oligarchical dictatorship and popular pressure. We mean by "oligar- chical" the reactionary alliance between the bourgeoisie and the landown- ing class of each country in which feudalism remains to a greater or lesser degree.

These dictatorships carry on within a certain "legal" framework adjudicated by themselves to facilitate their work throughout the unrestricted period of their class domination. Yet we are passing through a stage in which pressure from the masses is very strong and is straining bourgeois legality so that its own authors must violate it in order to halt the impetus of the masses.

Barefaced violation of all legislation or of laws specifically instituted to sanction ruling class deeds only increases the pressure from the people's forces. The oligarchical dictatorships then attempt to use the old legal order to alter constitutionality and further oppress the proletariat without a frontal clash. At this point a contradiction arises. The people no longer support the old, and much less the new, coercive measures established by the dictatorship and try to smash them. We should never forget the class character, authoritarian and restrictive, that typifies the bourgeois state. Lenin refers to it in the following manner [in *State and Revolution*]: "The state is the product and the manifestation of the irreconcilability of class antagonisms. The state arises when, where, and to the extent that class antagonisms objectively cannot be reconciled. And, conversely, the existence of the state proves that class antagonisms are irreconcilable."

In other words, we should not allow the word "democracy" to be utilized apologetically to represent the dictatorship of the exploiting classes; to lose its deeper meaning and acquire that of granting the people certain liberties, more or less adequate. To struggle only to restore a certain degree of bourgeois legality without considering the question of revolutionary power is to struggle for the return of a dictatorial order established by the dominant social classes. In other words, it is to struggle for a lighter iron ball to be fixed to the prisoner's chain.

In these conditions of conflict, the oligarchy breaks its own contracts, its own mask of "democracy," and attacks the people, though it will always try to use the superstructure it has formed for oppression. We are faced once again with a dilemma: What must be done? Our reply is: Violence is not the monopoly of the exploiters and as such the exploited can use it too and, moreover, ought to use it when the moment arrives. [José] Martí said, "He who wages war in a country when he can avoid it is a criminal, just as he who fails to promote war which cannot be avoided is a criminal."

Lenin said, "Social democracy has never taken a sentimental view of war. It unreservedly condemns war as a bestial means of settling conflicts in human society. But social democracy knows that as long as society is divided into classes, as long as there is exploitation of human by human, wars are inevitable. In order to end this exploitation we cannot walk away from war, which is always and everywhere begun by the exploiters, by the ruling and oppressing classes." He said this in 1905. Later, in *Military Program of the Proletarian Revolution*, a far-reaching analysis of the nature of class struggle, he affirmed: "Whoever recognizes the class struggle cannot fail to recognize civil wars, which in every class society are the natural, and under certain conditions, inevitable continuation, development and intensification of the class struggle. All the great revolutions prove this. To repudiate civil war, or to forget about it, would mean sinking into extreme opportunism and renouncing the socialist revolution." That is to say, we should not fear violence, the midwife of new societies, but violence should be unleashed at that precise moment in which the leaders have found the most favorable circumstances.

What will these be? Subjectively, they depend on two factors that complement each other and which deepen during the struggle: consciousness of the necessity of change and confidence in the possibility of this revolutionary change. Both of these factors — combined with the objective conditions (favorable in all of Latin America for the development of the struggle) — and the firm will to achieve revolutionary change, as well as the new correlation of forces in the world, will determine the mode of action.

Regardless of how far away the socialist countries may be, their favorable influence will be felt by the people who struggle, just as their example will give the people further strength. Fidel Castro said on July 26 [1963]:

> The duty of the revolutionaries, especially at this moment, is to know how to recognize and how to take advantage of the changes in the correlation of forces that have taken place in the world and to understand that these changes facilitate the people's struggle. The duty of revolutionaries, of Latin American revolutionaries, is not to wait for the change in the correlation of forces to produce a miracle of social revolutions in Latin America, but to take full advantage of everything that is favorable to the revolutionary movement — and to make revolution!

There are some who say, "Let us admit that in certain specific cases revolutionary war is the best means to achieve political power; but where do we find the great leaders, the Fidel Castros, who will lead us to victory?" Fidel Castro, like any other human being, is the product of history. The political and military leaders who will lead the insurrectional uprisings in the Americas, merged if possible in one person, will learn the art of war during the course of war itself. There exists neither trade nor profession that can be learned from books alone. In this case, the struggle itself is the great teacher.

Of course, the task will not be easy and it is not exempt from grave dangers.

During the development of armed struggle, there are two moments of extreme danger for the future of the revolution. The first of these arises in the preparatory stage and the way it is dealt with will give the measure of determination to struggle as well as clarity of purpose of the people's forces. When the bourgeois state advances against the people's positions, obviously there must arise a process of defense against the enemy who at this point, being superior, attacks. If the basic subjective and objective conditions are ripe, the defense must be armed so that the popular forces will not merely become recipients of the enemy's blows. Nor should the armed defense camp be allowed to be transformed into the refuge of the pursued.

The guerrilla army, the defensive movement of the people, at a given moment carries within itself the capacity to attack the enemy and must develop this constantly. This capacity is what determines, with the passing of time, the catalytic character of the people's forces. That is, guerrilla warfare is not passive self-defense; it is defense with attack. From the moment we recognize it as such, it has as its final goal the conquest of political power.

This moment is important. In social processes the difference between violence and nonviolence cannot be measured by the number of shots exchanged; rather it lies in concrete and fluctuating situations. We must be able to see the right moment in which the people's forces, conscious of their relative weakness and their strategic strength, must take the initiative against the enemy so the situation will not deteriorate. The equilibrium between oligarchic dictatorship and popular pressure must be changed. The dictatorship tries to function without resorting to force so we must try to oblige it to do so, thereby unmasking its true nature as the dictatorship of the reactionary social classes. This event will deepen the struggle to such an extent that there will be no retreat from it. The success of the people's forces depends on the task of forcing the dictatorship to a decision — to retreat, or to unleash the struggle — thus beginning the stage of long-range armed action.

Skillful avoidance of the next dangerous moment depends on the growing power of the people's forces. Marx always recommended that once the revolutionary process has begun the proletariat should strike blows again and again without rest. A revolution that does not constantly expand is a revolution that regresses. The fighters, if weary, begin to lose faith; and at this point some of the bourgeois maneuvers may bear fruit — for example, the holding of elections to turn a government over to another gentleman with a sweeter voice and a more angelic face than the outgoing tyrant, or the staging of a coup by reactionaries, generally led by the army, with the direct or indirect support of the progressive forces. There are others, but it is not our intention to analyze all such tactical stratagems.

Let us focus on the military coup mentioned previously. What can the military contribute to democracy? What kind of loyalty can be asked of them if they are merely an instrument of domination for the reactionary classes and imperialist monopolies and if, as a caste whose worth rests on the weapons in their hands, they aspire only to maintain their prerogatives?

When, in difficult situations for the oppressors, the military establishment conspires to overthrow a dictator who in reality has already been defeated, it can be said that they do so because the dictator is unable to preserve their class prerogatives without extreme violence, a method that generally does not suit the interests of the oligarchies at that point.

This statement does not mean to reject the service of military men as individual fighters who, once separated from the society they served, have in fact now rebelled against it. They should be utilized in accordance with the revolutionary line they adopt as fighters and not as representatives of a caste.

A long time ago Engels, in the preface to the third edition of *Civil War in France*, wrote:

> The workers were armed after every revolution; for this reason the disarming of the workers was the first commandment for the bourgeois at the helm of the state. Hence, after every revolution won by the workers there was a new struggle ending with the defeat of the workers. (Quoted by Lenin in *State and Revolution*)

This play of continuous struggle, in which some change is obtained and then strategically withdrawn, has been repeated for many dozens of years in the capitalist world. Moreover, the permanent deception of the proletariat along these lines has been practiced for over a century.

There is danger also that progressive party leaders, wishing to maintain conditions more favorable for revolutionary action through the use of certain aspects of bourgeois legality, will lose sight of their goal (which is common during the action), thus forgetting the primary strategic objective: *the seizure of power*.

These two difficult moments in the revolution, analyzed briefly here, become obvious when the leaders of Marxist-Leninist parties are capable of clearly perceiving the implications of the moments and of mobilizing the masses to the fullest, leading them on the correct path of resolving fundamental contradictions.

In developing the thesis, we have assumed that eventually the idea of armed struggle as well as guerrilla warfare as a method of struggle will be accepted. Why do we think that in the present situation in the Americas guerrilla warfare is the best method? There are fundamental arguments that in our opinion determine the necessity of guerrilla action as the central axis of struggle in the Americas.

First, accepting as true that the enemy will fight to maintain itself in power, one must think about destroying the oppressor army. To do this, a people's army is necessary. Such an army is not born spontaneously; rather it must be armed from the enemy's arsenal and this requires a long and difficult struggle in which the people's forces and their leaders will always be exposed to attack from superior forces and will be without adequate defense and maneuverability.

On the other hand the guerrilla nucleus, established in terrain favorable for the struggle, ensures the security and continuity of the revolutionary command. The urban forces, led by the general staff of the people's army, can perform actions of the greatest importance. The eventual destruction of these groups, however, would not kill the soul of the revolution; its leadership would continue from its rural bastion to spark the revolutionary spirit of the masses and would continue to organize new forces for other battles.

More importantly, in this region begins the construction of the future state apparatus entrusted to lead the class dictatorship efficiently during the transition period. The longer the struggle becomes, the larger and more complex the administrative problems; and in solving them, cadres will be trained for the difficult task of consolidating power and, at a later stage, economic development.

Second, there is the general situation of the Latin American peasantry and the ever more explosive character of the struggle against feudal structures within the framework of an alliance between local and foreign exploiters.

Returning to the Second Declaration of Havana:

> At the outset of the past century, the peoples of the Americas freed themselves from Spanish colonialism, but they did not free themselves from exploitation. The feudal landlords assumed the authority of the governing Spaniards, the Indians continued in their painful serfdom, the Latin American remained a slave one way or another, and the minimal hopes of the peoples died under the power of the oligarchies and the tyranny of foreign capital. This is the truth of the Americas, to one or another degree of variation. Latin America today is under a more ferocious imperialism that is more powerful and

ruthless than the Spanish colonial empire.

What is Yankee imperialism's attitude toward confronting the objective and historically inexorable reality of the Latin American revolution? To prepare to fight a colonial war against the peoples of Latin America; to create an apparatus of force establishing the political pretexts and the pseudo-legal instruments underwritten by the representatives of the reactionary oligarchies in order to curb, by blood and by iron, the struggle of the Latin American peoples.

This objective situation shows the dormant force of our peasants and the need to utilize it for Latin America's liberation.

Third, there is the continental nature of the struggle. Could we imagine this stage of Latin American emancipation as the confrontation of two local forces struggling for power in a specific territory? Hardly. The struggle between the people's forces and the forces of repression will be to the death. This also is predicted within the paragraphs cited previously.

The Yankees will intervene due to conjunction of interest and because the struggle in Latin America is decisive. As a matter of fact they are intervening already, preparing the forces of repression and the organization of a continental apparatus of repression. But from now on they will do so with all their energies; they will punish the popular forces with all the destructive weapons at their disposal. They will not allow a revolutionary power to consolidate, and, if it ever happens, they will attack again, they will not recognize such a power, and will try to divide the revolutionary forces. They will infiltrate saboteurs, create border problems, force other reactionary states to oppose it and will impose economic sanctions attempting, in one word, to annihilate the new state.

This being the panorama in Latin America, it is difficult to achieve and consolidate victory in an isolated country. The unity of the repressive forces must be confronted with the unity of the popular forces. In all countries where oppression reaches intolerable proportions, the banner of rebellion must be raised; and this banner of historical necessity will have a continental character.

As Fidel has said, the cordillera of the Andes will be the Sierra Maestra of Latin America; and the immense territories this continent encompasses will become the scene of a life or death struggle against imperialism.

We cannot predict when this struggle will reach a continental dimension or how long it will last. But we can predict its advent and triumph because it is the inevitable result of historical, economic and political conditions; and its direction cannot change.

The task of the revolutionary forces in each country is to initiate the struggle when the conditions are present there, regardless of the conditions in other countries. The development of the struggle will bring about the general strategy. The prediction of the continental character of the struggle is the outcome of the analysis of the strength of each contender but this does not exclude independent outbreaks. The beginning of the struggle in one area of a country is bound to cause its development throughout the region; the beginning of a revolutionary war contributes to the development of new conditions in the neighboring countries.

The development of revolution has usually produced high and low tides in inverse proportion. To the revolution's high tide corresponds the counterrevolutionary low tide and vice versa, as there is a counterrevolutionary ascendancy in moments of revolutionary decline. In those moments, the situation of the people's forces becomes difficult and they should resort to the best means of defense in order to suffer the least damage. The enemy is extremely powerful and has continental scope. The relative weakness of the local bourgeoisie cannot therefore be analyzed with a view to making decisions within restricted boundaries. Still less can one think of an eventual alliance by these oligarchies with a people in arms.

The Cuban Revolution sounded the bell that raised the alarm. The polarization of forces will become complete: exploiters on one side and exploited on the other. The mass of the petty bourgeoisie will lean to one side or the other according to their interests and the political skill with which they are handled. Neutrality will be an exception. This is how revolutionary war will be.

Let us think how a guerrilla foco can start. Nuclei with relatively few people choose places favorable for guerrilla warfare with the intention of either unleashing a counterattack or weathering the storm, and from there they start taking action. What follows, however, must be very clear: At the beginning the relative weakness of the guerrilla is such that they should work only toward becoming acquainted with the terrain and its surroundings while establishing connections with the population and fortifying the places that will eventually be converted into bases.

There are three conditions for survival that a guerrilla force must embrace if it is emerging subject to the premises described here: constant mobility, constant vigilance and constant distrust. Without these three elements of military tactics the guerrilla will find it hard to survive. We must remember that the heroism of the guerrilla fighter, at this moment, consists of the scope of the planned goal and the enormous number of sacrifices they must make in order to achieve it. These sacrifices are not made in daily combat or in face-to-face battle with the enemy; rather they will take subtler forms, more difficult for the guerrilla fighter to resist both physically and mentally.

Perhaps the guerrillas will be punished heavily by the enemy, divided at times into groups, while at other times those who are captured will be tortured. They will be pursued as hunted animals in the areas where they have chosen to operate; the constant anxiety of having the enemy on their track will be with them. They must distrust everyone, for the terrorized peasants will in some cases give them away to the repressive troops in order to save themselves. Their only alternatives are life or death, at times when death is a concept a thousand times present and victory only a myth for a revolutionary to dream about.

This is the guerrilla's heroism. For this it is said that walking is a form of fighting and that avoiding combat at a given moment is another. Facing the general superiority of the enemy at a given place, one must find the tactics with which to gain relative superiority at that moment, either by being capable of concentrating more troops than the enemy or by using the terrain fully and well in order to secure advantages that unbalance the correlation of forces. In these conditions tactical victory is assured; if relative superiority is not clear, it is better not to act. As long as the guerrilla army is in the position of deciding the "how" and the "when," no combat should be fought that will not end in victory.

Within the framework of the great political-military action of which they are a part, the guerrilla army will grow and reach consolidation. Bases will continue to be formed, for they are essential to the success of the guerrilla army. These bases are points the enemy can enter only at the cost of heavy losses; they are the revolution's bastions, they are both refuge and starting point for the guerrilla army's more daring and distant raids.

This point is reached if difficulties of a tactical and political nature have been overcome. The guerrillas cannot forget their function as vanguard of the people — their mandate — and as such they must create the necessary political conditions for the establishment of a revolutionary power based on the support of the masses. The peasants' aspirations or demands must be satisfied to the degree and in the form that circumstances permit so as to bring about the decisive support and solidarity of the whole population.

If the guerrillas' military situation is difficult from the very first moment, the political situation is just as delicate. If a single military error can liquidate the guerrilla, a political error can hold back its development for long periods. The struggle is political-military and it must be developed and understood as such.

In the process of the guerrilla's growth, the fighting reaches a point where its capacity for action in a given region is so great there are too many fighters in too great a concentration. Then begins the "beehive action" in which one of the commanders, a distinguished guerrilla, moves to another region and repeats the chain of development of guerrilla warfare. That commander is nevertheless subject to a central command.

It is imperative to point out that one cannot hope for victory without the formation of a popular army. The guerrilla forces can be expanded to a certain magnitude; the people's forces in the cities and in other areas can inflict losses; but the military potential of the reactionaries will still remain intact. One must always keep in mind the fact that the final objective is the enemy's annihilation. All these new zones that are being created, as well as the infiltrated zones behind enemy lines and the forces operating in the principal cities, should be unified under one command.

Guerrilla war or liberation war will generally have three stages. First is the strategic defensive stage when the small force nibbles at the enemy and runs. It is not sheltered to make a passive defense within a small circumference, but rather its defense consists of the limited attacks it can successfully strike. After this comes a state of equilibrium in which the possibilities of action on both sides — the enemy and the guerrillas — are established. Finally, the last stage consists of overrunning the repressive army leading to the capture of the big cities, large-scale decisive encounters, and ultimately the complete annihilation of the enemy.

After reaching a state of equilibrium, when both sides respect each other, the guerrilla war develops and acquires new characteristics. The concept of maneuver is introduced: large columns attacking strong points; mobile warfare with the shifting of forces and relatively potent means of attack. But due to the capacity for resistance and counterattack that the enemy still has, this war of maneuver does not replace guerrilla fighting; rather, it is only one form of action taken by the guerrillas until that time when they crystallize into a people's army with an army corps. Even at this moment the guerrilla, marching ahead of the action of the main forces, will continue the tactics of the first stage, destroying communications and sabotaging the whole defensive apparatus of the enemy.

We have predicted that the war will be continental. This means that it will be a protracted war, it will have many fronts and it will cost much blood and countless lives for a long period of time.

Another phenomenon occurring in Latin America is the polarization of forces, that is, the clear division between exploiters and exploited. When the armed vanguard of the people achieves power both the imperialists and the national exploiting class will be liquidated at one stroke. The first stage of the socialist revolution will have crystallized and the people will be ready to heal their wounds and initiate the construction of socialism.

Are there less bloody possibilities? A while ago the last dividing-up of the world took place and the United States took the lion's share of our continent. Today the imperialists of the Old World are developing again — and the strength of the European Common Market frightens the United States itself. All this might lead to the belief that the possibility exists for us merely to observe as spectators, perhaps in alliance with the stronger national bourgeoisie, the struggle among the imperialists trying to make further advances. Yet a passive policy never brings good results in class struggle and alliances with the bourgeoisie, though they might appear to be revolutionary, have only a transitory character. The time factor will induce us to choose another ally. The sharpening of the most important contradiction in Latin America appears to be so rapid that it disturbs the "normal" development of the imperialist camp's contradiction in its struggle for markets.

The majority of national bourgeoisie have united with U.S. imperialism so their fate shall be the same. Even in the cases where pacts or common contradictions are shared between the national bourgeoisie and other imperialists, this occurs within the framework of a fundamental struggle which will sooner or later embrace *all the exploited and all the exploiters.* The polarization of antagonistic forces among class adversaries is up till now more rapid than the development of the contradiction among exploiters over splitting the spoils. There are two camps. The alternative becomes clearer for each individual and for each specific stratum of the population.

The Alliance for Progress attempts to slow that which cannot be stopped. But if the advance on the U.S. market by the European Common Market, or any other imperialist group, were more rapid than the development of the fundamental contradiction, the forces of the people would only have to penetrate into the open breach, carrying on the struggle and utilizing the new intruders whilst having a clear awareness of what their true intentions are.

Not a single position, weapon or secret should be given to the class enemy, under penalty of losing all. In fact, the eruption of the Latin American struggle has begun. Will its storm center be in Venezuela, Guatemala, Colombia, Peru, Ecuador…? Are today's skirmishes only manifestations of a restlessness that has not come to fruition? The outcome of today's struggles does not matter. It does not matter in the final count that one or two movements were temporarily defeated, because what is definite is the decision to struggle which matures every day, the consciousness of the need for revolutionary change, and the certainty that it is possible.

This is a prediction. We make it with the conviction that history will prove us right. Analysis of the objective and subjective conditions of Latin America and the imperialist world indicates to us the certainty of these assertions based on the Second Declaration of Havana.

PART

THE CUBA YEARS
1959–65

"One must have a large dose of humanity, a large dose of a sense of justice and truth in order to avoid dogmatic extremes, cold scholasticism, or an isolation from the masses. We must strive every day so that this love of living humanity is transformed into actual deeds."

Social ideals of the Rebel Army

(January 29, 1959)

T onight it is necessary to invoke [José] Martí, as was suggested by the person who introduced me. When we speak of the social ideals of the Rebel Army I think we are basically referring to the dream Martí himself hoped to realize. As this is a night of remembrance, we shall briefly outline the past development of our revolution before we discuss the topic and its historical significance.

I shall not begin with the attack on the Moncada Barracks of July 26, 1953. I shall refer only to those events in which I participated and which resulted in the revolution of January 1 of this year.

Let us begin this story in Mexico, where it began for me.

It is very important for us to know the actual thinking of those who constitute our Rebel Army, the thinking of that group who embarked on the *Granma* adventure and the evolution of that thinking — born from the very heart of the July 26 Movement — and its successive changes throughout the revolutionary process that have reached the final stage in this last chapter, of which the insurrectional part has just ended.

In Mexico I met several members of the July 26 Movement. Those men had very different social ideals prior to sailing on the *Granma,* prior to the first schism of the July 26 Movement, when it comprised of the entire surviving nucleus of the attack on the Moncada Barracks. I recall an intimate discussion in a Mexico home when I spoke of the need to offer the people of Cuba a revolutionary program and a member of the July 26 Movement who had participated in the Moncada Barracks assault — he fortunately later left the Movement — answered me in a way I shall always remember: "The matter is simple. What we want to accomplish is a coup d'état. Batista staged a coup and took power in one day. We must carry out another coup to get him out... Batista has given a hundred concessions to the United States and we must give them a hundred and one." For him the main objective was achieving power. I argued that a coup must be based on principles, for it was important to know what we would do once we had taken over government.

This was the thinking of a member of the July 26 Movement in its first stage. Those who held these ideas have fortunately for us left our revolutionary movement and taken other paths.

From that time on the group constituting the *Granma* crew began to take shape, going through many difficult periods. We suffered continuous persecution from Mexican authorities that at one point almost endangered the whole expedition. In addition, certain individuals who at first wanted to participate in the adventure later left us under one pretext or another, reducing the number of expeditionaries. In the end, 82 men boarded the *Granma.* The rest is well known by the Cuban people.

What I am concerned with and what I believe to be primarily important is the social thought of those who survived Alegría de Pío, the first and only disaster the rebels suffered throughout the insurrection. Fifteen men regrouped afterward, physically and morally destroyed. We were able to move forward only because of the enormous confidence Fidel Castro gave us in those decisive moments, with his strong revolutionary caudillo's personality and his unshakeable faith in the people. We were a group with civilian origins, attached but not grafted to the Sierra Maestra. Thus we went from hut to hut; we touched nothing that did not belong to us, we did not eat unless we could pay for it and many times we went hungry because of this principle. Our group was tolerated but not joined by the peasants, and in this situation a great deal of time went by. For a few months we led a nomadic life high in the Sierra Maestra mountains. We made sporadic attacks. We went from one mountain to the next. Most of the time there was no water and living conditions were extremely difficult.

Bit by bit the peasants' attitude toward us began to change, propelled by the actions of the repressive forces of Batista who dedicated themselves to assassination and the destruction of the peasants' houses. Batista's men were hostile toward all who came in contact with the Rebel Army. This change in attitude translated into the incorporation of peasants into our guerrilla army and in this way an army of civilians began to change into an army of peasants. As the peasants were incorporated into the armed struggle for liberty and social justice, the magic words began simultaneously to spread to the oppressed masses of Cuba in their struggle for land: agrarian reform.

In this manner the first great social issue was established. Later, agrarian reform became the predominant banner of our movement even though [earlier] we went through a stage of much restlessness due to our natural preoccupation with the policy and conduct of our neighbor to the north. At the time, the presence of foreign reporters, preferably U.S. reporters, was more important to us than a military victory. More important than the incorporation in the struggle of the peasantry (who gave the revolution their ideals and faith) was to have U.S. supporters who served to export our revolutionary propaganda.

At that time a tragic event occurred in Santiago de Cuba — the assassination of *compañero* Frank País — marking a complete change in the structure of the revolutionary movement. The people of Santiago de Cuba, responding to the emotional impact of the assassination, took to the streets spontaneously, producing the first attempt at a general political strike. Even though it had no leadership it completely paralyzed Oriente Province, with repercussions in Las Villas and Camagüey provinces. The dictatorship liquidated this movement that began without preparation or revolutionary control. The phenomenon made us aware of the need to incorporate the workers into our liberation struggle. Immediately, underground work in workers' centers began to prepare a general strike which would aid the Rebel Army in gaining power.

This work led to the creation of underground organizations with an insurrectional philosophy, yet those who encouraged these movements did not really grasp the meaning or the tactics of a people's war. The masses were led down false paths because their leaders did not create revolutionary spirit and unity. They attempted to direct the strike from above without effective links to the workers at the base.

The victories of the Rebel Army and the great efforts of the underground created within the country such a state of unrest that a general strike was called on April 9, 1958. It failed — precisely because of organizational errors due primarily to the lack of contact between the leaders and the working masses and the leaders' mistaken attitude. The experience taught us a lesson. An ideological struggle developed within the July 26 Movement that brought about a radical change in the analysis of the country's realities and in its activist sectors. The July 26 Movement was strengthened by the failure of the strike and the experience taught us a precious truth — that the revolution did not belong to any one group in particular but to all the Cuban people. Consequently, the energies of the Movement's members in the mountains and cities were aimed toward that end.

Precisely at this time the Rebel Army took its first steps toward developing the theory and doctrine of the revolution; demonstrating that the insurrectional movement had grown and was achieving political maturity.

We moved from an experimental stage to a constructive one, from trials to definite deeds. Immediately we initiated "small industries" in the Sierra Maestra: like our ancestors, we moved from nomadic life into a settled life; we created centers of production in accord with our most basic needs. Weapons and shoe factories appeared and we began to build land mines from the bombs Batista dropped on us.

The men and women of the Rebel Army did not forget that their fundamental mission in the Sierra Maestra and elsewhere was the betterment of the peasantry and their incorporation into the struggle for land. We formed schools in the mountainous regions of Oriente. There we made our first experiment at distributing land through an agrarian code written by Dr. Humberto Sorí Marín, Fidel Castro and myself. The land was given to peasants in a revolutionary manner. Great farms owned by Batista's advocates were occupied, and all state land in the region was given to the peasants. We were now fully identified as a peasant movement closely bound to the land and with agrarian reform as our emblem.

Later we reaped the consequences of the ill-fated strike of April 9 [1958]. The dictatorship increased its repression toward the end of May, provoking in our cadres a loss of morale which could have had catastrophic consequences for our cause. The dictatorship began its most furious offensive. On May 25 of last year [1958], 10,000 well-equipped soldiers attacked our position, centering their offensive on Column Number One led personally by our commander in chief, Fidel Castro. At the time the Rebel Army controlled a very small area. It is incredible that we faced a force of 10,000 soldiers whilst we had 300 rifles — the only rifles in the Sierra Maestra at the time. Effective tactical leadership resulted, by July 30, in the end of the Batista offensive. From then on the rebels moved from defense into the offensive. We captured more than 600 new arms, more than twice the number of rifles we had when the action was begun. The enemy suffered more than 1,000 casualties in dead, wounded, deserters and prisoners.

The Rebel Army came out of this campaign prepared to initiate the offensive in the lowlands. This was a tactical and psychological offensive because our armaments could not compete in quality or quantity with those of the dictatorship. This was a war in which we always counted on that imponderable: the extraordinary courage of the people. Our columns were able to constantly fool the enemy and place themselves in better positions not only because of our tactical advantage and the high morale of our militia, but also because of the generous support given by the peasants. The peasant was the invisible collaborator who did everything the rebel soldier could not do: they gave us information, watched the enemy, discovered the enemy's weaknesses, rapidly brought us urgent messages and spied within the ranks of the Batista army. None of these was a miracle but a product of our energetic agrarian policy. In light of the attacks made on the Sierra Maestra and the encircling hunger established and enforced by all the landowners in the surrounding areas, 10,000 head of cattle were sent to the mountains to supply the Rebel Army and the peasants. For the first time the peasants of that region ate meat and their children drank milk. Also for the first time the peasants there received the benefits of education. Our revolution brought schools in its hand. In this way the peasants reached a positive conclusion about our regime.

At the same time the dictatorship systematically burned the peasants' houses. The peasants were removed from their land or murdered. Death came sometimes from the skies in the form of napalm given graciously to Batista by that democratic neighbor to the north for terrorizing civilian populations. They gave 500-kilo bombs that destroyed everything within a 100-meter circumference. A napalm bomb dropped over a coffee grove means the destruction of that wealth — and all those years of labor. What is destroyed in a minute will take five or six years to rebuild.

At this time we began our march to Las Villas. This is important to point out, not because I participated in it but because on our arrival in Las Villas we found a new socio-political panorama of the revolution.

When we arrived at Las Villas with the flag of the July 26 [Movement], the Revolutionary Directorate, groups of the Second Front of Escambray, groups of the Popular Socialist Party, and smaller ones of the Auténtica Organization were already there fighting against the dictatorship. It was necessary to begin to work to achieve unity — an important factor in any revolutionary struggle. The July 26 Movement, with the Rebel Army at its head, had to promote unity among the different elements that were disgruntled with one another and who had as their only unifying element the work done in the Sierra Maestra. First it was necessary to unify these groups of fighters not only in the hills but also in the plains. We therefore had to perform the very important task of classifying all the sections of workers in the province. This task was carried out amid opposition, even within our own movement, still suffering the disease of sectarianism.

We had just arrived in Las Villas and our first governmental edict — even before establishing the first school — was to pass a revolutionary law establishing an agrarian reform that ordered, among other things, that owners of small parcels of land pay no more rent until the revolution considered each case separately. Agrarian reform was the spearhead with which the Rebel Army advanced. It was not a demagogic maneuver, it was simply that after one year and eight months of revolution, the close understanding that existed between the leaders and the peasant masses was so great that many times it propelled the revolution to do things it had not even conceived of doing before. We did not invent agrarian reform, it was an idea that came from the peasants; they pushed for it. We convinced the peasants that with the weapons at hand, with organization and without fear of the enemy, victory was assured. And the peasantry, with good reasons to do so, compelled the revolution to bring about agrarian reform. They compelled the confiscation of cattle and all the other social measures adopted in the Sierra Maestra.

In the Sierra Maestra, Law Number Three was decreed on the day of the November 3 [1958] electoral farce. It established genuine agrarian reform and, though incomplete, contained very positive arrangements: state land was to be distributed as was land owned by those who served Batista, as well as land obtained by fraudulent means, like that of the land-grabbers who swallowed thousands of acres of borderlands. It gave small, rent-paying *colonos* [tenant farmers] plots not exceeding two *caballerías*. Everything was free. The principle was very revolutionary.

Agrarian reform will benefit over 200,000 families. Yet the agrarian revolution is not complete with Law Number Three. To complete it, it will be necessary to establish a law to proscribe large landholdings — as stated by the constitution. We must define exactly the concept of *latifundia* which characterizes our agrarian structure and is the source of the nation's backwardness and of the miseries of the majority of the peasantry. This has not yet been touched. The organized peasant masses now have the task of demanding a law that will prohibit *latifundia* just as they once compelled the Rebel Army to establish Law Number Three.

Another aspect must also be considered. The constitution states that land expropriation must be paid for in advance. If the agrarian reform is to follow that precept it may be a little slow and expensive. The collective action of the peasantry, who have won their right to freedom since the triumph of the revolution, is needed in order to demand the democratic derogation of that precept so they can advance toward a true and full agrarian reform.

Now we begin to consider the social ideals of the Rebel Army. Today we have an armed democracy. When we plan the agrarian reform and observe the new revolutionary laws that complement it, making it viable and immediate, our main concern is the social justice that land redistribution brings about. The creation of an extensive internal market and agricultural diversification, two of the fundamental and inseparable objectives of the revolutionary government, cannot be postponed because the interests of the people are implied in and through it.

All economic activities are related. We must increase the industrialization of the country without ignoring the many problems that this process creates. But a policy to encourage industrialization requires certain tariff measures, to protect our new industries, and an internal market capable of absorbing the new products. This market can only be increased by adding to it the peasant masses — the *guajiros* — who, though they remain needy, have until now had no buying power.

We are aware that our goals demand an enormous responsibility on our part, and these are not our only responsibilities. We must await the reaction of those who dominate more than 75 percent of our commercial trade and our market. We must prepare ourselves before this danger by applying counter-measures such as tariffs and by diversifying our markets abroad. We need to build a Cuban merchant fleet to transport sugar, tobacco and other products. Its existence will favorably influence the exchange of the type of cargoes on which the progress of underdeveloped countries like Cuba depend.

If we are to undertake an industrialization program, what are its most important features? First, the raw materials that the constitution wisely protected but that have been surrendered to foreign enterprises by the Batista dictatorship. We must rescue our subsoil, our minerals. Another element in the process of industrialization is electricity. We have to be able to rely on it. We are going to make sure that electrical power returns to Cuban hands. We must also nationalize the telephone company because of the poor service it has rendered and the high rates it maintains.

What are the tools we possess to carry out a program of this sort? We have the Rebel Army, and it must be the first instrument in our struggle, our most vigorous and positive weapon. The remains of Batista's army must be destroyed. Let it be understood that this will not be done for revenge or for a love of justice, but to assure that the people achieve their goals in the shortest possible time.

We defeated, with the support of the people, an army numerically superior to ours. We did so with appropriate tactics and a revolutionary morale. Now we must face the fact that our Rebel Army is not yet capable of performing its new responsibilities, such as the integral defense of Cuban territory. We have to rapidly restructure the Rebel Army. We initially formed an armed force of workers and peasants, many of them illiterate and without technical preparation. We must now educate this army culturally and technically for the demanding tasks they must face.

The Rebel Army is the vanguard of the Cuban people and when we refer to its technical and cultural development we should understand the contemporary meaning of these terms. We have symbolically begun this education with a reading imbued almost exclusively with the spirit and teachings of José Martí.

The process of national reconstruction must destroy many privileges and we must be on the alert to defend the nation from its real and hidden enemies. The new army must adapt to the new modes that have arisen in this war of liberation. We know that if, for example, Cuba suffers external aggression originating from a small island, it would be with the support of a nation that occupies almost an entire continent. We would have to face on our soil an immense aggressive force. That is why we must anticipate and prepare our vanguard with a guerrilla spirit and strategy — so that our defenses will not disintegrate with the first attack and will maintain their cohesive unity. All the Cuban people must become a guerrilla army — the Rebel Army is a growing institution whose capacity is limited only by our population of six million people. Each and every Cuban must learn to handle and, if necessary, to use firearms in the defense of the nation.

I have briefly outlined the social ideals of the Rebel Army after victory and its role as it moves the government toward realizing its revolutionary aspirations.

There is something most interesting thing to tell you before ending this talk.

The example our revolution has set in Latin America and the teachings implied in it have destroyed all café society theories. We have demonstrated that a small group of determined fighters with the support of the people and without fear of death can, if necessary, defeat a regular and disciplined army. This is the fundamental lesson. Another lesson that should be learned by our brothers and sisters in the Americas — because they find themselves economically in the same agrarian category as ourselves — is that agrarian revolutions must be made; we must struggle in the countryside, in the mountains, and from there take the revolution to the cities. One cannot pretend to make revolution in the cities devoid of any social substance.

Now, with all the experiences we have had, we are faced with the question of what our future will be, a future very closely related to that of all the underdeveloped countries of Latin America. This revolution is not limited to the Cuban nation — it has touched the consciousness of Latin America and has also alerted the enemies of our peoples. We have warned that any aggression will be repelled with arms in hand. The example of Cuba has provoked unrest in all of Latin America, in all oppressed countries. The revolution has placed the dictators of Latin America on death row. They, like foreign monopolies, are the enemies of popular government. We are a small country and we need the support of all democratic countries and especially of the people of Latin America.

We have to inform the entire world truthfully of the noble goals of the Cuban Revolution. We have to call on the friendship of U.S. people and Latin Americans. We have to create a spiritual unity among all of our countries, a unity that will transcend words and bureaucracy, a friendship that will transform itself into effective aid to our brothers and sisters by sharing with them our experience.

Finally, we must open new roads identifying our common interests as underdeveloped countries. We must be aware of all efforts to divide us and struggle against those who try to sow the seeds of discord among us — those who, hiding behind well-known masks, aspire to profit from our political disagreements and incite unfounded prejudices in this country.

Today the people of Cuba are conducting the struggle on their feet and must continue to do so. Their victory against dictatorship is not transitory but rather is the first step toward Latin America's victory.

Political sovereignty and economic independence

(March 20, 1960)

This speech was given as the first in a television series entitled "People's University," a program of talks by leaders of the revolution. Televised live every Sunday, the format of the program was a presentation followed by an open question-and-discussion period. This speech, the first in a series on the development of Cuba's economy, was given before a studio audience of several hundred.

aturally, when beginning an appearance of this kind we have to extend greetings to all the listeners in Cuba. We should also reiterate our *compañero's* explanation of the importance of this type of popular education directly reaching all our workers and peasants, explaining the truths of the revolution while stripping away the cover of language specifically designed to distort the truth, baring the truth of all deceptions, and showing it as it is.

I am honored to begin this series of appearances that — although initially assigned to *compañero* Raúl Castro — have fallen to me since they deal with economic issues. As soldiers of the revolution, we carry out the tasks that duty calls for, although often we don't have the ideal training, to say the least. Perhaps this is one of those tasks: to put into simple words, and into concepts that everyone can understand, the enormous importance of the issues of political sovereignty and economic independence, and to also explain the extremely close link between these two goals. One can sometimes precede the other — as happened at a certain point in Cuba — but they necessarily go together, and in a short time they must join together. In some cases this union is a positive affirmation, as in Cuba, which achieved its political independence and immediately afterward set out to win economic independence. There are also negative cases, countries that achieve or enter onto the road of political independence, but because they do not secure their economic independence, little by little the former gets weaker and finally disappears. Our revolutionary task today is to think not only of the present, with all the threats being made against us, but also to think of the future.

The watchword of this moment is planning: the conscious, intelligent restructuring of all the problems that will face the people of Cuba in future years. We cannot just think of a rejoinder, of a counterattack when faced with a more or less immediate aggression. We have to make an effort to draw up a whole plan to be able to predict the future. The men of the revolution have to advance toward their destiny consciously, but it is not enough for this to be done by the men of the revolution. It is also necessary for the entire people of Cuba to understand exactly what all the revolutionary principles are, so they can know that, after these times, in which some feel uncertain about the future, there will be — and let there be no doubt about it — a happy and glorious future. Because we have been the ones who have set the cornerstone of liberty in Latin America.

That is why a program of this kind is so important, a program in which everyone who has something to say comes and says it. Not that this is new, because every time our prime minister appears before the cameras he gives a masterful lesson, as only a teacher of his stature can give. But we have also planned our teaching; we are trying to divide it into specific topics and are not just answering interview questions. So we will go into the topic of political sovereignty and economic independence, as I said before.

But before talking about the tasks that the revolution is carrying out to make these two terms a reality — these two concepts that must always go together — it would be good to define them and make them clear to you. Definitions always have defects; they always tend to freeze terms, to make them dead. But it would be good to at least give a general idea of these twin terms.

It happens that there are some people who do not understand or do not want to understand — which is the same thing — what sovereignty is. They are frightened when our country, for example, signs an agreement — in which, by the way, I had the honor of taking part — like the trade agreement with the Soviet Union, and also receives a line of credit from that nation.

This whole struggle is something that has its antecedents in the history of Latin America. Recently — exactly two days ago — was the anniversary of the expropriation of the Mexican oil companies during the government of General Lázaro Cárdenas.[1] We young people were very young children in those days (more than 20 years have gone by), and we cannot remember exactly the commotion it brought about in Latin America. In any case, the accusations were exactly the same as the ones Cuba has to put up with today; as the ones Guatemala had to put up with in a more recent past, and that I personally lived through; and as the accusations all countries that decide to follow this road of liberty will have to put up with in the future.

We can say today, almost without making a caricature, that big business, the news media, and the opinion columnists in the United States provide us the key to a leader's importance and honesty — only in reverse. When a leader is most attacked, then undoubtedly he is better. And today we have the privilege of being the most attacked country and government, not only at this moment, but perhaps ever in the history of Latin America, much more than Guatemala, and perhaps more than Mexico in 1938, or 1936, when General Cárdenas ordered the expropriation. Oil at that time played a very important role in Mexico's life. In our case sugar has the same importance: the role of a single product that goes to a single market. "Without sugar there is no country," screamed the spokesmen of reaction. And they also believe that if the market that buys our sugar stops doing so, the country's ruin will be absolute. As if that market were buying our sugar just because they want to help us out.

For centuries political power was in the hands of slave-owners, then of feudal lords. And to facilitate their war-making against enemies and against rebellions of the oppressed, they delegated power to one man among them, the one who united them, the most determined one, the most cruel perhaps. He became king, the sovereign, the despot. Little by little, throughout various epochs of history, he imposed his will until at a certain point it became absolute.

Naturally, we are not going to recount the whole historical process of humanity. And anyway, the times of the kings are gone. There are just a few token ones left in Europe. Fulgencio Batista never thought of calling himself Fulgencio I. It was enough for him that a certain powerful neighbor recognized him as president, and that the officers of an army obeyed him. That is, he had the support and obedience of those with the physical power, with the material forces, with implements of destruction. They supported and obeyed him as the strongest among them, as the most cruel, or as the one with the best friends abroad.

Today there are kings without crowns; they are the monopolies, the true masters of entire nations and at times of entire continents. That has been the case until now on the African continent and a good part of the Asian continent and unfortunately on our Latin American continent as well. Other times they have tried to rule the world. First it was Hitler, a representative of the big German monopolies who tried to take the idea of the superiority of a race and impose it on the world in a war that cost 40 million lives.

The importance of the monopolies is immense, so great that it makes political power disappear in many of our republics. Some time ago I was reading an essay by Papini where his character, Gog, bought a republic and said that although the republic thought it had presidents, legislatures, armies and that it was sovereign, he had actually bought it. The caricature is exact. Some republics have all the formal characteristics necessary to be one, but actually depend on the all-embracing will of the United Fruit Company, for example, whose hated director was a lawyer who is now deceased. Others are dependent on Standard Oil or some other oil monopoly, while still others are under the control of the kings of tin or the coffee merchants. These are just some examples on our continent, not to mention Africa or Asia.

In other words, political sovereignty is a term not to be sought in formal definitions. Rather we have to go deeper, we have to look for its roots. All the treaties, codes of law and politicians in the world maintain that national political sovereignty is an idea inseparable from the notion of a sovereign state, of a modern state. If that were not so, some powers would not feel obliged to call their colonies associated free states, that is, to conceal colonization with a phrase.[2] Whether the internal regime of each nation allows its sovereignty to be exercised to a greater or lesser degree, or in full, or absolutely not at all — that should be a matter to be decided by that nation. However, national sovereignty means, in the first place, the right of a country to have no-one interfere in its life, the right of a people to choose whatever form of government and way of life suits it. That should depend on its will, and only that nation can decide whether a government changes or not. But all these concepts of political sovereignty, of national sovereignty, are fictitious if there is no economic independence to go along with them.

At the beginning we said that political sovereignty and economic independence go hand in hand. If a country does not have its own economy, if it is penetrated by foreign capital, then it cannot be free from the tutelage of the country it is dependent on. Much less can a country make its will prevail if it clashes with the powerful interests of the country that dominates it economically. That idea is not yet absolutely clear to the Cuban people, and it is necessary to go over it time and again. The pillars of political sovereignty, which were put in place on January 1, 1959, will be totally consolidated only when we achieve absolute economic independence. And we can say we are on the right track if every day we take measures to assure our economic independence. Anytime that governmental measures cause a halt along this road or a turning back, even if it's only one step, everything is lost and inevitably begins to return to the more or less covert systems of colonization, according to the given country's characteristics and social context.

Right now it is very important to understand these concepts. These days it is very difficult to do away with a country's national political sovereignty by the use of pure and simple violence. The most recent two examples are the merciless and treacherous attack by the English and French colonialists on Port Said in Egypt and the landing of U.S. troops in Lebanon.[3] But the marines are no longer sent in with the same impunity as before. And it is much easier to put up a veil of lies than to invade a country simply because some big monopoly's interests have been injured. It is difficult in these days of the United Nations, where all peoples want to have a voice and vote, to invade a country that is demanding its right to exercise its sovereignty.

It is not easy to calm domestic or international public opinion about this. A tremendous propaganda effort is needed to prepare the conditions to make such an intervention appear less odious. That is precisely what they are doing to us. We should never stop pointing out that they are preparing the conditions to subdue Cuba in whatever way necessary, and that it is up to us alone not to let that aggression take place. Economically they can go as far as they want, but we must secure a consciousness in our country such that if they want to launch physical aggression (directly with soldiers from the same country as the monopolies or with mercenaries from other countries), it would be so costly they cannot do it. They are trying to drown us, preparing the necessary conditions to drown this revolution in blood if need be, just because we are on the road toward economic liberation, because we are setting an example of measures aimed at totally liberating our country and at making our level of economic liberty equal the level of our political liberty and of our political maturity today.

We have taken political power. We have begun our struggle for liberation with this power firmly in the hands of the people. The people cannot even dream of sovereignty unless there is a power that defends their interests and aspirations. People's power means not only that the Council of Ministers, the police, the courts and all other government bodies are in the hands of the people. It also means that economic bodies are being transferred to the people. Revolutionary power or political sovereignty is the instrument for the conquest of the economy and for making national sovereignty a reality in its broadest sense. In Cuban terms, it means that the revolutionary government is the instrument so that in Cuba only Cubans have power, in every sense of the word: from politics, to being able to decide what to do with the riches of our land and our industry.

We cannot yet swear on our martyrs' graves that Cuba is economically independent. It cannot be so when having just one ship detained in the

United States forces a factory in Cuba to stop production, when simply at the command of any of the monopolies a workplace here is paralyzed. Cuba will be independent when it has developed all its means, all its natural resources, when it makes sure through agreements, through trade with the whole world, that no unilateral action by any foreign power can prevent it from maintaining its rhythm of production, and keeping its factories and farms producing at the best possible rate according to plans that we have drawn up.

What we can say for sure is the exact date on which Cuba won its national political sovereignty as a first step. That was the day that people's power was victorious, the day that the revolution triumphed, that is, January 1, 1959. This was a day that more and more is being established as the beginning not only of an extraordinary year in the history of Cuba, but also as the beginning of an era. And we even like to think that it is not only the beginning of an era in Cuba, but the beginning of an era in Latin America.

For Cuba, January 1 is the culmination of July 26, 1953, and August 12, 1933, and also of February 24, 1895, or October 10, 1868.[4] But for Latin America, too, it is a glorious date. It may be the continuation of that May 25, 1809, when Murillo rose up in arms in Upper Peru, or of May 25, 1810, the date of the Cabildo Abierto in Buenos Aires, or of any other date that marks the beginning of the struggle of the peoples of Latin America for their political independence at the beginning of the 19th century.[5]

This date, January 1, won at an enormously high price for the people of Cuba, sums up the struggle of generations and generations of Cubans, since the formation of the nationality, for sovereignty, for the homeland, for Cuba's liberty, and for full political and economic independence. No-one can talk now of reducing it to a bloody episode, a decisive and spectacular one perhaps, but only a moment in Cuban history. Because January 1 is the date of the death of the despotic regime of Fulgencio Batista, that small native version of Weyler.[6] But it also is the birth date of the true republic, politically free and sovereign, that takes as its supreme law the full dignity of man.

This January 1 means victory for all the martyrs who came before us, since José Martí, Antonio Maceo, Máximo Gómez, Calixto García, [Guillermo] Moncada, or Juan Gualberto Gómez, whose antecedents are to be found in Narciso López, in Ignacio Agramonte, and Carlos Manuel de Céspedes. What they started was continued by the whole constellation of martyrs from our republican history: the [Julio Antonio] Mellas, the [Antonio] Guiterases, the Frank Países, the José Antonio Echeverrías, and the Camilo Cienfuegoses.

As always, Fidel, having devoted everything to battles on behalf of his people, has been aware of the magnitude of revolutionary firmness, of the greatness of the date that made possible the collective heroism of an entire people: this marvelous Cuban people from which sprang the Rebel Army, a continuation of the *mambí* army.[7] That is why Fidel always likes to compare the tasks now to be undertaken with those that lay ahead for the handful of survivors of the legendary *Granma* landing. When they disembarked the *Granma,* all individual hopes were left behind. They were beginning the struggle in which an entire people had to either triumph or fail. Because of this, because of that great faith and that great union between Fidel and his people, they never lost heart, not even in the most difficult moments of the campaign. They knew that the struggle was not centered and isolated in the mountains of the Sierra Maestra, but that the struggle was taking place everywhere in Cuba, wherever a man or a woman raised the banner of dignity.

Fidel knew, as all of us knew later, that it was a struggle like today's, in which the entire Cuban people would triumph or be defeated. Now he insists on the same terms and says: either we are all saved or we all sink. You know the phrase. The obstacles to overcome are difficult, as they were in those days following the *Granma* landing. But now our fighters are not to be counted by the ones or by the dozens but by the millions. All of Cuba has become a Sierra Maestra to fight, wherever the enemy may be, the decisive battle for freedom, for our homeland's future and honor. And at this point, unfortunately, Cuba alone is ready to wage this struggle.

Cuba's battle is the battle of all Latin America; not the definitive one, at least not definitive in one sense. Even assuming Cuba loses the battle, it would not be lost for all Latin America. But if Cuba wins this battle, the entire continent will have won the fight. That is the importance of our island, and that is why they want to suppress this "bad example" we are setting.

Back in 1956, the strategic objective, that is, the broad objective of our war, was to overthrow the Batista dictatorship. In other words, the reestablishment of all the ideas of democracy and sovereignty and independence that were trampled underfoot by the foreign monopolies. Starting from the days of March 10, [1952] all Cuba had become a garrison — a garrison like those that we are now turning over to the people [as a school]. All of Cuba was a garrison. March 10 was not the work of one man but of a caste, a group of men united by a series of privileges. One of them, the most ambitious, the most daring, the Fulgencio I of our story, was the captain. This caste defended the interests of the reactionary class in our country, the large landowners, parasitic capitalists, and was closely linked to foreign colonialism. It was made up of a whole series of specimens who disappeared like magic — from the cheap huckster politicians to the journalists who hung around presidential halls, from the scabs to the czars of gambling and prostitution.

The fundamental strategic objective of the revolution at that time was achieved on January 1 with the destruction of the dictatorship that for almost seven years had brutalized the Cuban people. But our revolution, which is a conscious revolution, knows that political sovereignty is closely linked to economic sovereignty.

This revolution does not want to repeat the mistakes committed in the 1930s, simply getting rid of one man without realizing that this man is a representative of a class and of a status quo, and that if that whole status quo is not destroyed, then the enemies of the people create another man.[8] For that reason the revolution is compelled to destroy the roots of the evil that afflicted Cuba. We would have to imitate Martí and repeat once again that a *radical* is nothing less than that — one who goes to the roots. Those who do not see the roots of things, those who do not aid men's security and happiness, are not radicals. This revolution is determined to eliminate injustice at the roots, as Fidel has said paraphrasing Martí.

We have achieved the great strategic goal of the fall of the dictatorship and the establishment of the revolutionary power that arose from the people and is responsible to it, whose armed branch is now an army synonymous with the people. Today, the new strategic goal is the conquest of economic independence, once again the conquest of total national sovereignty.

Yesterday, the tactical objectives of the struggle were the Sierra, the plains, Santa Clara, the Presidential Palace, Camp Columbia, the production centers — which were to be conquered through direct attack, a siege or underground action. Our tactical objectives today are the triumph of the agrarian reform, which provides the basis for the country's industrialization, diversification of foreign trade, and raising the people's living standards to reach that great strategic goal of the liberation of the national economy.

The economic front has turned out to be the main battlefield, although there are others of enormous importance, such as education, for example. Recently, we talked about the importance of an education system that would make it possible to provide the necessary technicians for this battle. But that itself indicates that in this battle the economic front is the most important, and that education is aimed at providing officers for this battle in the best possible conditions.

I can call myself a military man, a military man of the people, who took up arms like so many others, simply responding to a call, who fulfilled his duty when it was necessary, and who today is assigned to the post you know. I do not pretend to be an economist. Like all revolutionary fighters, I am simply in this new trench where I have been assigned, and I have to worry, as few others do, about the fate of the national economy, since the future of the revolution depends on it.

These battles on the economic front are different from those waged in the Sierra. These are battles of positions, battles where the unexpected almost never happens, where you gather troops and prepare the attacks very carefully. Victories are the result of work, perseverance and planning. This is a war that demands collective heroism, sacrifice by all. And it does not last a day or a week or even a month. It is very long; it is longer the more isolated we are, and longer still the less we study all the characteristics of the battlefield and analyze the enemy over and over again. It has to be waged with many weapons, too, from the contribution of four percent from the workers for the country's industrialization,[9] to work in each cooperative, to the establishment of branches hitherto unknown in the national industry such as citrochemicals, heavy chemicals, or the steel industry. And the main strategic goal — and we must underline this constantly — is the conquest of national sovereignty.

In other words, in order to conquer something we have to take it away from somebody, and it is good to speak clearly and not hide behind concepts that could be misinterpreted. That something we must conquer — the country's sovereignty — has to be taken away from that somebody called monopoly. And that somebody called monopoly — although monopolies as a rule have no homeland, at least they have a common definition — all the monopolies that have been in Cuba, that have benefited from the Cuban land, have very close ties with the United States. That means that our economic war will be fought against the big power to the north, that our war is not a simple one. It means that our road to liberation will be opened up with a victory over the monopolies, and concretely over the U.S. monopolies.

Control of one country's economy by another without a doubt hurts that country's economy. Fidel asked on February 24 at the CTC: How can anyone think that a revolution would sit back and wait for a solution from private foreign investment capital? How can anyone think that a revolution that was born defending workers' rights, which had been trampled underfoot for many years, would sit back and wait for the solution to the problem from private foreign investment capital, which acts according to its interests, which is not invested in products that are the most necessary for the country, but rather the most profitable for the owners? So the revolution could not follow this road; this was a road of exploitation. In other words, another road had to be found.

We had to strike at the most troublesome of all the monopolies — the monopoly in land ownership — destroy it, turn the land over to the people, and then start the real struggle, because despite everything, this was just the first contact between two enemies. The battle was not waged at the level of the agrarian reform, that is a fact.[10] The battle will be waged now. It will be waged in the future, because although the monopolies had large land-holdings here, that is not where the most important holdings are. The most important ones are in the chemical industry, in engineering, in oil, and that is where Cuba's example worries them, the "bad example," as they call it.

We had to start with the agrarian reform, however. One and a half per-cent of the landowners — Cubans or foreigners, but owners of Cuban land — possessed 46 percent of the national territory, while 70 percent owned only 12 percent of the national territory. There were 62,000 farms that had less than three-quarters of a *caballería*. Under our agrarian reform two *caballerías* are considered to be the vital minimum, that is, the minimum required on nonirrigated land for a family of five to live satisfying their minimum needs. In Camagüey, five companies, five or six sugar companies, controlled 56,000 *caballerías* of land — 20 percent of Camagüey's total area.

Besides that, the monopolies own the nickel, the cobalt, the iron, the chromium, the manganese and all the oil concessions. In the case of oil, for example, the concessions, adding those granted and those requested, came to three times the national territory. In other words, the entire national terri-tory had been granted, as had the keys and the Cuban continental shelf. Besides that, there were zones that had been requested by two or three companies that were in litigation. We have proceeded to eliminate these holdings of U.S. companies.

Housing speculation was also hit, first by the lowering of rents and now by INAV's [National Institute of Savings and Housing] plans to prov-ide low-cost housing. Here there used to be many housing monopolies, and even though perhaps they were not U.S.-owned they were parasitic capital linked to the U.S. monopolies, at least in regard to the ideological conception of private property in the service of one person for the exploitation of a people. We put an end to speculation and the monopoly in domestic trade — or took the first step toward ending it — with the revolutionary government's intervention in the big markets and the creation of people's stores, of which there are 1,400 in the Cuban countryside.

You know how prices go up. If there are peasants listening to us, you will know of the great difference between the current prices and the prices

charged by the cutthroats throughout the Cuban countryside in those ghast-
ly days. The unbridled actions of the public utility monopolies have at
least been reined in. Telephones and electricity are two examples. Monopolies figured in all aspects of the Cuban people's life. Not only in the economy, which we are talking about today, but also in politics and culture.

Now we had to take another important step in our struggle for liberation:
dealing a blow against the monopolies' stranglehold on foreign trade. Several trade agreements have already been signed with various countries, and
new countries are constantly coming to seek the Cuban market on an absolutely equal footing. Of all the agreements signed, the most important, without
a doubt, is with the Soviet Union. It is good to emphasize this, because at
this point we have already sold something unprecedented: our entire [sugar]
quota, without having to sell anything on the world market. And we still
have requests estimated at between one million or 800,000 to a million
tons, if we do not make new contracts, new agreements, with other nations.
In addition, we have secured the sale of one million tons a year for five
years.

It is true that we are not being paid in dollars, except for 20 percent of
that sugar. But the dollar is nothing more than an instrument for buying;
the dollar has no value other than its buying power. So by getting paid
with manufactured products or raw materials, we are simply using sugar
like a dollar. Somebody told me that such a contract was ruinous, since the
distance separating the Soviet Union from Cuba would significantly increase the price of all the goods we would import. The oil agreement has
torn apart all these predictions. The Soviet Union is committed to sell Cuba
oil of different specifications at a price 33 percent lower than the U.S. monopoly companies, which are but a step away from us. That is called economic
liberation.

Naturally, there are some who claim all these sales by the Soviet Union
are political sales. Some claim that it is being done only to annoy the United
States. We can admit that this may be true. The Soviet Union, making use of
its sovereignty, can, if it feels like annoying the United States, sell us oil and
buy sugar from us to annoy the United States. But what do we care? That's
a separate question. What their intentions may or may not be is a separate
question. In our trade we are simply selling merchandise, not our national
sovereignty as we used to do. We simply intend to talk on equal terms.

Every time a representative of a new nation of the world comes here,
now, he comes to talk on equal terms. No matter what size country he
comes from, or the power of its guns. As an independent nation, Cuba has
one vote at the United Nations, just like the United States and the Soviet

Union. That has been the spirit in which all the treaties have been made, and that will be the spirit in which all new trade agreements will be made. We have to insist on what Martí understood and clearly stated many years ago: that the nation that buys is the one that commands and the nation that sells is the one that obeys.

When Fidel Castro explained that the trade agreement with the Soviet Union was very advantageous for Cuba, he was simply explaining... more than explaining, we could say he was synthesizing the sentiments of the Cuban people. Really, everyone felt a bit freer when we learned that we could sign trade agreements with whomever we pleased. Everyone should feel even freer today when we fully realize that we not only exercised the country's national sovereignty by signing a commercial agreement, but that it was also one of Cuba's most advantageous commercial agreements. When the time comes to analyze the onerous loans of the U.S. companies, and to compare them with the loan or credit granted by the Soviet Union for a 12-year term at a 2.5 percent interest rate, the lowest in the history of international trade relations, then we will see its importance.

It is true that this credit is for purchasing Soviet goods. But it is no less true that the loans, for example, from the Export Bank, which supposedly is an international agency, are made to buy goods in the United States. And furthermore, that they are granted to acquire specific goods from foreign monopolies. The Export Bank, for instance, lends (of course, this is a hypothetical example) the Burmese Electricity Company — let us assume the Burmese Electricity Company is [foreign-owned] just like the Cuban Electricity Company — so it lends that company 8, 10 or 15 million pesos. The company then sets up its equipment, begins to supply electricity at a very high price and with very bad service, charges huge prices, and then the nation pays. Those are the international credit systems.

There is a tremendous difference between that and a loan granted to really benefit a nation, so that it is worthwhile for its sons and daughters to make a sacrifice for that loan. It would be very different if the Soviet Union had loaned 100 million pesos to a subsidiary firm it owned to establish a business here and then export the dividends back to the Soviet Union. But instead we have now planned to build a big steel plant and an oil refinery, totally national and at the service of the people.

In other words, today whatever we pay represents only the payment for what we receive, and it is a correct and honest payment, as we have seen in the case of oil. I am not saying that as we sign other contracts, in the same open way that the Cuban Government explains everything, we will be able to report extraordinarily cheap prices for all goods produced by the Soviet

Union, and furthermore for all quality manufactured products. The *Diario de la Marina* — we have to quote it one more time — is opposed to the trade agreement. Unfortunately, I did not bring a very interesting article that gives five, six or seven reasons why it thinks the agreement is a bad one. Of course, they are all false. But not only is their interpretation false, which is bad enough. Even their news is false. It is false, for example, when they say that this means Cuba is committed to supporting Soviet moves in the United Nations. It is an entirely different matter that — in a declaration absolutely separate from this agreement and drafted by mutual accord — Cuba commits itself to struggle for peace within the United Nations. In other words, as Fidel has explained, Cuba is being accused of doing exactly what the United Nations was created for, according to its founding charter.

All the other economic issues raised have been refuted very well by our minister of trade, and suffer from very big flaws, including gross lies. The most important lie is related to the price. As you know the price of sugar naturally depends on the world market, on supply and demand. The *Diario de la Marina* says that if that million tons of sugar that Cuba sells is later put back on the market by the Soviet Union, then Cuba has not gained anything. That is a lie, for the simple reason that it is clearly established in the agreement that the Soviet Union can export sugar only to countries that usually buy it from them. The Soviet Union is a sugar importer, but it also exports refined sugar to some neighboring countries that have no refineries, such as Iran, Iraq, Afghanistan. And the Soviet Union will, naturally, continue to supply those countries to which it usually exports. But our sugar will be used entirely in the plans to increase that country's domestic consumption.

If up in the United States they are very worried — since they are already talking in Congress itself about the Soviet Union overtaking them — if they believe the Soviet Union, then why shouldn't we? Especially when the Soviet Union tells us — and puts it in writing besides, because it's not just verbal — that this sugar is for their domestic consumption? Why does any newspaper here have to spread doubts, doubts that are picked up internationally and that can indeed adversely affect sugar prices? It is nothing but the work of the counterrevolution, of those who do not want to resign themselves to losing their privileges.

On another point, with regard to the price of Cuban sugar, which merited an unwarranted comment by U.S. spokesman Lincoln Price, regarding a statement we made a few days ago; they insist that those extra 100 or 150 million dollars they are paying for our sugar is a gift to Cuba. That is not so. For that, Cuba signs tariff agreements that obligate us to buy $1.15 worth of U.S. goods for every dollar spent by the U.S. interests in Cuba. That means

THE CUBA YEARS ■ 109

that in 10 years $1 billion has been transferred from the hands of the Cuban people to the U.S. monopolies.

We don't have to give things away to anybody, but if they went from the hands of the Cuban people to the hands of the people of the United States we would be happier. However, they go into the monopolies' coffers, which are only used as instruments of oppression to prevent the subjugated peoples of the world from beginning their road to liberation. The loans the United States has granted Cuba have cost Cuba 61 percent interest on every dollar — and that's on a short-term agreement, not to mention what the cost would be on a long-term agreement like the one signed with the Soviet Union. That's why at every step we have followed Martí's teachings, and in foreign trade we have insisted on diversifying as much as possible, not tying ourselves to any one buyer. And we are not only diversifying our foreign trade but also our domestic production in order to be able to serve more markets.

So Cuba is moving forward. We are living a truly brilliant moment of our history, a moment in which all the countries of Latin America have their eyes on this small island, and the reactionary governments accuse Cuba of responsibility for every explosion of popular indignation anywhere in the continent.

We have stated very clearly that Cuba does not export revolutions. Revolutions cannot be exported. Revolutions take place when there are a series of insurmountable contradictions within a country. Cuba does export an example, that bad example I've mentioned. It is the example of a small people that challenges the laws of a false science called "geopolitics" and — in the very jaws of the monster, as Martí called it — ventures to hurl its cries of liberty.

That is the crime and that is the example feared by the imperialists, the U.S. colonialists. They want to crush us because we are a banner for Latin America. They want to apply the Monroe Doctrine to us, as there is a new version of the one stated by Monroe that has been presented in the U.S. Senate. Fortunately for them, I think that it was not approved or did not go beyond some committee. I had the opportunity to read the *whereases* — whereas it shows such a cave-dweller mentality, such an extraordinarily colonialist mentality that I think adopting it would have been a disgrace to the people of the United States. That motion revived the Monroe Doctrine, but it was much clearer. I remember perfectly that one of the paragraphs said: "Whereas: the Monroe Doctrine establishes very clearly that no country outside the Americas can enslave the American countries." In other words, countries inside the Americas can. And this new version of the Monroe

Doctrine went on to say that now the United States could intervene without having to notify the OAS, afterward presenting the OAS with a fait accompli. Well, these are the political dangers that stem from our campaign to win our economic liberation.

We have... first of all we have a time crunch, but anyway... we have the last problem, how to invest our foreign exchange reserves, how to invest the nation's efforts so that we can rapidly move our economic aspirations forward. Speaking to the workers on February 24, when he was presented with the symbolic total amount of that four percent, Fidel Castro said: "When the revolution came to power, the reserves could not have been more depleted, and the people were used to consuming more imports than what was exported." In that situation a country has to invest. It has to save or it has to receive capital from abroad.

Now, what was our idea? To save and save, especially our foreign exchange, to develop our own industry. It replaced the idea of importing private capital. When it is a matter of private national capital, that capital is already in the country. But when it is a matter of imports — because you need capital, and the advisable solution is the investment of private capital — we have that situation.

Private foreign capital is not motivated by generosity; it's not motivated by an act of noble charity; it's not motivated by the desire to reach the people. Foreign capital is motivated by the desire to help itself. Private foreign capital is the surplus capital of a country that is transferred to another country, where wages and living conditions are lower, where raw materials are cheaper, in order to obtain higher profits. What motivates private foreign capital is not generosity but profit. And the idea that had always been upheld here was to give guarantees to private investment capital in order to solve the problems of industrialization.

In agriculture and industry together $300 million will be invested. That is the battle to economically develop our country and solve its ills. Of course, it is not an easy road. You know we are being threatened, you know there is talk of economic retaliation, you know there is talk of maneuvers, of taking away our quota, and so on. Meanwhile we are trying to sell our products.

Does this mean we have to retreat? Does this mean that because they threaten us we have to abandon all hopes of improvement? What is the correct road for the people? Does our desire for progress harm anyone? Do we want to live off the labor of other peoples? Do we want to live off the wealth of other peoples? What do we Cubans want here?

We do not want to live off the sweat of others, but to live off our own sweat. Not to live off the wealth of others, but off our own wealth, so that all the material needs of our people are satisfied, and on that basis to solve the country's other problems. We don't talk of economics purely for the sake of economics, but of economics as a foundation for meeting all the country's other needs: education, a clean and healthy life, the need for a life not only of work but of recreation. How are we going to spend all those millions? That is something another *compañero* will explain to you in one of these talks, showing not only how but why they will be spent along the road we have chosen.

Now for the weak, for those who are afraid, for those who think that we're in a unique situation in history, that this is an insurmountable situation, and that if we don't stop or turn back we're lost, I want to read you one last quotation. It is a brief anecdote by Jesús Silva Herzog, a Mexican economist who was the author of the Oil Expropriation Law. It refers precisely to that period Mexico lived through, when international capital was also moving threateningly against the spiritual and cultural values of the peoples. The quotation is a synthesis of what is now being said about Cuba. It says:

> Of course, it was said that Mexico was a communist country. The ghost of communism appeared. Ambassador Daniels, in the book I have quoted in other lectures, tells the story of going to Washington on a visit in those difficult days, and an English gentleman speaks to him about Mexican communism. Mr. Daniels says to him: "Well, in Mexico the only communist I know is Diego Rivera; but, what is a communist?" Daniels then asks the English gentleman. The latter sits back in an easy chair, ponders, stands up, and tries to offer a definition. It does not satisfy him. He sits down again, ponders once more, perspires a little, stands up once more, and gives another definition. It is not satisfactory either. And he goes on like that until finally, desperate, he says to Daniels: "Mister, a communist is anybody who annoys us."

You can see how historical situations repeat themselves. I am sure that all of us annoy other people quite a bit. It seems I have the honor, along with Raúl [Castro], of being among the most annoying. But historical situations have their similarities. Just as Mexico nationalized its oil and was able to move forward, and Cárdenas is recognized as the greatest president that republic has had, so we will continue to forge ahead. All those who are on the other side will call us whatever names they wish. They will say whatever they wish. What is certain is that we are working for the benefit of the people, that we will not go back, and that they, the expropriated, the confiscated, will not return.

Speech to medical students and health workers

(August 20, 1960)

This speech was given at the inauguration of a series of political talks and discussions organized by the Ministry of Public Health. Opened by Commander Dr. José Machado, the minister of public health, this meeting in the assembly hall of the Confederation of Cuban Workers (CTC) was attended by several hundred medical students and health workers.

lthough this modest ceremony is only one among hundreds held as the Cuban people celebrate day by day their freedom and the advance of all their revolutionary laws, their advance along the road to total independence, I nevertheless find it interesting.

Almost everyone knows that I started my career as a doctor a number of years ago. When I started off as a doctor, when I began to study medicine, the majority of the concepts I hold today as a revolutionary were absent from the storehouse of my ideals.

I wanted to succeed, as everybody wants to succeed. I dreamed about being a famous researcher. I dreamed of working tirelessly to achieve something that could really be put at the disposal of humanity, but that, at the same time, would be a personal triumph. I was, as we all are, a child of my environment.

Through special circumstances and perhaps also because of my character, after receiving my degree I began to travel through Latin America and I got to know it intimately. Except for Haiti and the Dominican Republic, I have visited — in one way or another — all the other countries of Latin America. In the way I traveled, first as a student and afterward as a doctor, I began to come into close contact with poverty, with hunger, with disease, with the inability to cure a child because of lack of resources, with the numbness that hunger and continued punishment cause until a point is reached where a parent losing a child is an unimportant accident, as often happens among the hard-hit classes of our Latin American homeland.

And I began to see that there was something that, at that time, seemed to me almost as important as being a famous researcher or making some substantial contribution to medical science, and it was helping those people.

But I continued being, as all of us always continue being, a child of my environment, and I wanted to help those people through my personal efforts. I had already traveled a lot — I was then in Guatemala, the Guatemala of Arbenz — and I had begun to make some notes to guide the conduct of a revolutionary doctor. I began to look into what I needed to be a revolutionary doctor.

However, the aggression came, the aggression unleashed by the United Fruit Company, the State Department, Foster Dulles — in reality, they are all the same thing — and the puppet they put in named Castillo Armas; that was his name. The aggression was successful, given that the people had not yet reached the level of maturity the Cuban people have today. And one fine day, I, like so many others, took the road to exile, or at least I took the road of fleeing from Guatemala, since that was not my homeland.

Then I realized one fundamental thing: to be a revolutionary doctor or to be a revolutionary, there must first be a revolution. The isolated effort, the individual effort, the purity of ideals, the desire to sacrifice an entire lifetime to the noblest of ideals goes for naught if that effort is made alone, solitary, in some corner of Latin America, fighting against hostile governments and social conditions that do not permit progress. A revolution needs what we have in Cuba: an entire people mobilized, who have learned the use of arms and the practice of combative unity, who know what a weapon is worth and what the people's unity is worth.

Then we get to the heart of the problem that today lies ahead of us. We already have the right and even the obligation to be, before anything else, a revolutionary doctor, that is, a person who puts the technical knowledge of his profession at the service of the revolution and of the people. Then we come back to the earlier questions: How does one do a job of social welfare effectively? How does one reconcile individual effort with the needs of society?

We again have to recall what each of our lives was like, what each of us did and thought, as a doctor or in any other public health function, prior to the revolution. We have to do so with profound critical enthusiasm. We will then conclude that almost everything we thought and felt in that past epoch should be filed away, and that a new type of human being should be created. If each one of us is his own architect of that new human type, then creating that new type of human being — who will be the representative of the new Cuba — will be much easier.

It is good for you — those present, the residents of Havana — to absorb this idea: that in Cuba a new type of human being is being created, which cannot be entirely appreciated in the capital, but which can be seen in every corner of the country. Those of you who went to the Sierra Maestra on July 26 must have seen two absolutely unheard-of things: an army with picks and shovels, an army that takes the greatest pride in marching in the patriotic celebrations in Oriente Province with its picks and shovels ready, while the militia *compañeros* are marching with their rifles. But you must have also seen something much more important: You must have seen some children who by their physical stature would appear eight or nine years old, but who nevertheless are almost all 13 or 14. They are the most authentic children of the Sierra Maestra, the most authentic children of hunger and poverty in all its forms. They are the creatures of malnutrition.

In this small Cuba, with four or five television channels, with hundreds of radio stations, with all the advances of modern science, when those children arrived at school at night for the first time and saw the electric lights, they exclaimed that the stars were very low that night. Those children, whom some of you would have seen, are now learning in the collective schools, from the ABCs right up to learning a trade, right up to the very difficult science of being revolutionaries.

These are the new types of human beings born in Cuba. They are being born in isolated places, in remote parts in the Sierra Maestra and also in the cooperatives and centers of work.

All that has a lot to do with the topic of our talk today: the integration of the doctor or any other medical worker into the revolutionary movement. Because the revolution's task — the task of training and nourishing the children, the task of educating the army, the task of distributing the lands of the old absentee landlords among those who sweated every day on that same land without reaping its fruit — is the greatest work of social medicine that has been done in Cuba.

The battle against disease should be based on the principle of creating a robust body — not creating a robust body through a doctor's artistic work on a weak organism, but creating a robust body through the work of the whole collectivity, especially the whole social collectivity.

One day medicine will have to become a science that serves to prevent diseases, to orient the entire public toward their medical obligations, and that only has to intervene in cases of extreme urgency to perform some surgical operation or to deal with something uncharacteristic of that new society we are creating.

The work that is today entrusted to the Ministry of Health, to all the institutions of this type, is to organize public health in such a manner that it aids the greatest possible number of people, that it prevents everything foreseeable related to diseases, and that it orients the people. But for the organizational task, as for all revolutionary tasks, what is required, fundamentally, is the individual. The revolution is not, as some claim, a standardizer of collective will, of collective initiative. To the contrary, it is a liberator of man's individual capacity.

What the revolution does do, however, is to orient that capacity. Our task today is to orient the creative talent of all the medical professionals toward the tasks of social medicine.

We are at the end of an era, and not only here in Cuba. Despite all that is said to the contrary and despite all the hopes of some people, the forms of capitalism we have known, under which we have been raised and have suffered, are being defeated throughout the world. The monopolies are being defeated. Collective science every day registers new and important triumphs. And we have had the pride and the self-sacrificing duty of being the vanguard in Latin America of a liberation movement that began some time ago, in the other subjugated continents of Africa and Asia. That very profound social change also demands very profound changes in the mentality of the people.

Individualism as such, as the isolated action of a person alone in a social environment, must disappear in Cuba. Individualism tomorrow should be the proper utilization of the whole individual, to the absolute benefit of the community. But even when all this is understood today, even when these things I am saying are comprehended, and even when everyone is willing to think a little about the present, about the past, and about what the future should be, changing the manner of thinking requires profound internal changes and helping bring about profound external changes, primarily social. Those external changes are taking place in Cuba every day. One way of learning about this revolution, of getting to know the forces the people keep stored inside themselves, forces that have been dormant for so long, is to visit all of Cuba, visit the cooperatives and all the work centers being created. And one way of getting to the heart of the medical question is not only knowing, not only visiting these places, but also getting to know the people who make up those cooperatives and work centers. Go there and find out what diseases they have, what their ailments are, what extreme poverty they have lived in over the years, inherited from centuries of repression and total submission. The doctor, the medical worker, should then go to the heart of his new work, which is as a man among the masses, a man within the community.

Whatever happens in the world, by always being close to the patient, by knowing his psychology so deeply, by being the representative of those who come near pain and relieve it, the doctor always has a very important job, a job of great responsibility in social life.

Some time ago, a few months, it so happened here in Havana that a group of students, recently certified as doctors, did not want to go to the countryside and were demanding extra payment for going. From the viewpoint of the past it is more than logical that this would occur; at least it seems that way to me, and I understand it perfectly. I simply remember that this was the way it was, the way it was thought about some years ago. Once more it is the gladiator in rebellion, the solitary fighter who wants to ensure a better future, better conditions, and to achieve recognition of what he does.

But what would happen if it were not those boys — the majority of whose families could afford several years of study — who completed their courses and are now beginning to practice their profession? What if instead it was 200 or 300 peasants who had emerged, let's say by magic, from the university lecture halls?

What would have happened, simply, is that those peasants would have run immediately, and with great enthusiasm, to attend to their brothers and sisters. They would have requested the posts with the most responsibility and the most work, in order to show that the years of study given them were not in vain. What would have happened is what will happen within six or seven years, when the new students, children of the working class and the peasantry, receive their professional degrees of whatever type.

But we should not view the future with fatalism and divide men into children of the working class or peasantry and counterrevolutionaries. That is simplistic, it is not true, and there is nothing that educates an honorable man more than living within a revolution.

None of us, none of the first group that arrived in the *Granma*, who established ourselves in the Sierra Maestra, and who learned to respect the peasant and the worker, living together with him — none of us had a past as a worker or peasant. Naturally, there were those who had to work, who had known certain wants in their childhood. But hunger, true hunger — that none of us had known, and we began to know it, temporarily — during the two long years in the Sierra Maestra. And then many things became very clear.

We, who at the beginning severely punished anyone who touched even an egg of some rich peasant or some landowner, one day took 10,000 head of cattle to the Sierra and told the peasants simply: "Eat." And the peasants, for the first time in many years, and some for the first time in their lives, ate beef.

The respect we had for the sacrosanct property of those 10,000 head of cattle was lost in the course of the armed struggle, and we learned perfectly that the life of a single human being is worth millions of times more than all the property of the richest man on earth. We learned it there, we who were not sons of the working class or the peasantry. So why should we now shout to the four winds that we are the privileged ones and that the rest of the Cuban people cannot learn too? Yes, they can learn. In fact, the revolution today demands that they learn, demands that they understand well that the pride of serving our fellow man is much more important than a good income; that the people's gratitude is much more permanent, much more lasting than all the gold one can accumulate. Each doctor, in the sphere of his activity, can and should accumulate that prized treasure, the people's gratitude.

We must then begin to erase our old concepts and come ever closer and ever more critically to the people. Not in the way we got closer before, because all of you will say: "No, I am a friend of the people. I enjoy talking with workers and peasants, and on Sundays I go to such and such a place to see such and such a thing." Everybody has done that. But they have done it practicing charity, and what we have to practice today is solidarity. We should not draw closer to the people to say: "Here we are. We come to give you the charity of our presence, to teach you with our science, to demonstrate your errors, your lack of refinement, your lack of elementary knowledge." We should go with an investigative zeal and with a humble spirit, to learn from the great source of wisdom that is the people.

Often we realize how mistaken we were in concepts we knew so well; they had become part of us and, automatically, of our consciousness. Every so often we ought to change all our concepts, not just general, social or philosophical concepts, but also, at times, our medical concepts. We will see that diseases are not always treated as one treats an illness in a big-city hospital. We will see then that the doctor also has to be a farmer, that he has to learn to cultivate new foods and, by his example, to cultivate the desire to consume new foods, to diversify this food structure in Cuba — so small and so poor in an agricultural country that is potentially the richest on earth. We will then see that under those circumstances we will have to be a little bit pedagogic, at times very pedagogic, that we will also have to be politicians; that the first thing we will have to do is not go offering our wisdom, but showing that we are ready to learn with the people, to carry out that great and beautiful common experience — to build a new Cuba.

We have already taken many steps, and the distance between that January 1, 1959, and today cannot be measured in the conventional manner. It was some time ago that the people understood that not only had a dictator fallen here, but that a system had fallen as well. Now the people should learn that upon the ruins of a crumbled system, one must build a new one that brings about the people's absolute happiness.

I remember when *compañero* [Nicolás] Guillén arrived from Argentina early last year. He was the same great poet he is today — perhaps his books were translated into one fewer language, because every day he wins new readers in all the languages of the world — but he was the same as today. But it was difficult for Guillén to read his poems, which were the poems of the people, because that was the first period, the period of prejudices. Nobody ever stopped to think that for years and years, with incorruptible dedication, the poet Guillén had put all his extraordinary artistic gifts at the service of the people and at the service of the cause he believed in.[11] The people saw in him not the glory of Cuba, but the representative of a political party that was taboo. But all that is behind us. We have already learned that we cannot have divisions based on opinions about certain internal structures in our country, if we have a common enemy and if we are trying to reach a common goal.

We have definitively become convinced that there is a common enemy. We know that everyone looks around to see if someone will hear him, if someone is listening from some embassy who will transmit his opinion, before clearly stating an opinion against the monopolies, before saying clearly: "Our enemy, and the enemy of all Latin America, is the monopolistic government of the United States of America."

If everybody already knows that this is the enemy, and if our starting point is knowing that whoever struggles against that enemy has something in common with us, then comes the second part. What are our goals here in Cuba? What do we want? Do we want the people's happiness or not? Are we struggling for Cuba's absolute economic liberation or not? Are we or are we not struggling to be a free country among free countries, without belonging to any military bloc, without having to consult any embassy of any great power on earth about any domestic or foreign decision we make? Are we thinking of redistributing the wealth of those who have too much, to give to those who have nothing? Are we thinking here of doing creative work, a dynamic daily source of all our happiness? If so, then we already have the goals to which we referred. And everyone who shares those goals is our friend. If that person also has other ideas, if he belongs to one or another organization, those are discussions of lesser importance.

At times of great dangers, at times of great tensions and great creations, what counts are the great enemy and the great goals. If we agree, if we all already know where we are going, then whatever happens, we must begin our work.

I was telling you that to be a revolutionary requires having a revolution. We already have it. And a revolutionary must also know the people with whom he is to work. I think we still don't know one another well. I think we still have to travel a while along that road. If someone asks me how to go about getting to know the people, in addition to going into the interior, learning about cooperatives, living in cooperatives (and not everybody can do that, and there are many places where the presence of a medical workers is very important)… in those cases, I will tell you that one of the Cuban people's greatest expressions of solidarity is the revolutionary militias, militias that now give the doctor a new function and prepare him for what was at least until recently a sad and almost fatal reality in Cuba: that is, that we were going to be prey — or if not prey at least victims — of a large-scale armed attack.

As a revolutionary militia member, the doctor should be warned to always be a doctor. He should not commit the error we made in the Sierra — or perhaps it was not an error, but all the doctor *compañeros* of that period know it — that it appeared dishonorable for us to be at the side of a wounded or ill person, and we sought any means possible to grab a rifle and show on the battlefield what should be done.

Now conditions are different. The new armies being formed to defend the country should be armies that use different methods, as part of which the doctor will have an enormous importance. He should continue being a doctor, which is one of the most beautiful and most important tasks of war. And not just the doctor but also the nurses, laboratory technicians, all those who dedicate themselves to this humane profession.

But all of us — even knowing that the danger is latent and even while preparing to repel the aggression that still hangs over us — should stop thinking about that. Because if we center our efforts on war preparations, we cannot build what we want, we cannot devote ourselves to creative work.

All work, all capital that is invested in preparing for military action, is labor lost, money lost. Unfortunately, it has to be done, because there are others preparing. But the money I am most saddened to see leave the National Bank coffers — and I say this with all honesty and pride as a soldier — is the money to pay for some weapon of destruction.

The militias have a function in peacetime, however. The militias should be, in the populated areas, the arm that unifies and gets to know the people. They should practice real solidarity, as the *compañeros* have told me is being done in the medical militias. They should immediately set out to resolve the problems of the needy throughout Cuba at all times of danger. But they are also an opportunity to get to know one another, an opportunity to live alongside men of all Cuba's social classes, made equal and made brothers by a common uniform.

If we achieve this, medical workers — and allow me to use again a term I had forgotten some time ago — if we all use that new weapon of solidarity, if we know the goals, if we know the enemy, and if we know the direction in which we have to travel, then the only thing left for us is to know the daily stretch of the road and to take it. Nobody can point out that stretch; that stretch is the personal road of each individual; it is what he will do every day, what he will gain from his individual experience, and what he will give of himself in practicing his profession, dedicated to the people's well-being.

If we already possess all the elements with which to march toward the future, let us recall that phrase of Martí, which at this moment I am not putting into practice, but which we must constantly put into practice: "The best form of saying is doing." And let us then march toward the future of Cuba.

Notes for the study of the ideology of the Cuban Revolution

(October 1960)

This is a unique revolution, which for some does not fit in with one of the most orthodox premises of the revolutionary movement, expressed by Lenin: "Without revolutionary theory there can be no revolutionary movement."[12] It should be said that revolutionary theory, as the expression of a social truth, stands above any particular presentation of it. In other words, one can make a revolution if historical reality is interpreted correctly and if the forces involved are utilized correctly, even without knowing theory.

In every revolution there is always involvement by people from very different tendencies who, nevertheless, come to agreement on action and on the most immediate objectives. It is clear that if the leaders have adequate theoretical knowledge prior to taking action, many errors can be avoided, as long as the adopted theory corresponds to reality.

The principal actors of this revolution had no coherent viewpoint. But it cannot be said that they were ignorant of the various concepts of history, society, economics and revolution being discussed in the world today. A profound knowledge of reality, a close relationship with the people, the firmness of the objective being sought, and the experience of revolutionary practice gave those leaders the opportunity to form a more complete theoretical conception.

The foregoing should be considered an introduction to the explanation of this curious phenomenon that has intrigued the entire world: the Cuban Revolution. How and why did a group of men, cut to ribbons by an army enormously superior in technique and equipment, manage first to survive, then to become strong, later to become stronger than the enemy in the battle zones, move into new combat zones still later, and finally defeat that enemy in pitched battles even though their troops were still vastly outnumbered? This is a deed that deserves to be studied in the history of the contemporary world.

Naturally we, who often do not show due concern for theory, will not proceed today to expound the truth of the Cuban Revolution as if we were its owners. We are simply trying to lay the foundation for being able to interpret this truth. In fact, the Cuban Revolution must be separated into two absolutely different stages: that of the armed action up to January 1, 1959; and the political, economic and social transformations from then on.

Even these two stages deserve further subdivisions. We will not deal with them from the viewpoint of historical exposition, however, but from the viewpoint of the evolution of the revolutionary thinking of its leaders through their contact with the people.

Incidentally, here we must introduce a general attitude toward one of the most controversial terms of the modern world: Marxism. When asked whether or not we are Marxists, our position is the same as that of a physicist when asked if he is a "Newtonian" or of a biologist when asked if he is a "Pasteurian."

There are truths so evident, so much a part of the peoples' knowledge, that it is now useless to debate them. One should be a "Marxist" with the same naturalness with which one is a "Newtonian" in physics or a "Pasteurian." If new facts bring about new concepts, the latter will never take away that portion of truth possessed by those that have come before. Such is the case, for example, of "Einsteinian" relativity or of Planck's quantum theory in relation to Newton's discoveries. They take absolutely nothing away from the greatness of the learned Englishman. Thanks to Newton, physics was able to advance until it achieved new concepts of space. The learned Englishman was the necessary stepping-stone for that.

Obviously, one can point to certain mistakes of Marx, as a thinker and as an investigator of the social doctrines and of the capitalist system in which he lived. We Latin Americans, for example, cannot agree with his interpretation of Bolívar, or with his and Engels' analysis of the Mexicans, which accepted as fact certain theories of race or nationality that are unacceptable today. But the great men who discover brilliant truths live on despite their small faults and these faults serve only to show us they were human. That is to say, they were human beings who could make mistakes, even given the high level of consciousness achieved by these giants of human thought. This is why we recognize the essential truths of Marxism as part of humanity's body of cultural and scientific knowledge. We accept it with the naturalness of something that requires no further argument.

The advances in social and political science, as in other fields, belong to a long historical process whose links are constantly being connected, added up, bound together and perfected. In early human history, there existed

Chinese, Arab or Hindu mathematics; today, mathematics has no frontiers. A Greek Pythagoras, an Italian Galileo, an English Newton, a German Gauss, a Russian Lobachevsky, an Einstein, etc., all have a place in the history of the peoples. Similarly, in the field of social and political sciences, a long series of thinkers, from Democritus to Marx, have added their original investigations and accumulated a body of experience and doctrines.

The merit of Marx is that he suddenly produces a qualitative change in the history of social thought. He interprets history, understands its dynamic, foresees the future. But in addition to foreseeing it (by which he would meet his scientific obligation), he expresses a revolutionary concept: it is not enough to interpret the world, it must be transformed. Man ceases to be the slave and instrument of his environment and becomes an architect of his own destiny. At that moment Marx begins to put himself in a position where he becomes the necessary target of all those who have a special interest in maintaining the old — like what happened to Democritus, whose work was burned by Plato himself and his disciples, the ideologues of the Athenian slave-owning aristocracy. Beginning with the revolutionary Marx, a political group is established with concrete ideas, which, based on the giants, Marx and Engels, and developing through successive stages with individuals such as Lenin, Stalin, Mao Tse-tung and the new Soviet and Chinese rulers, establishes a body of doctrine and, shall we say, examples to follow.

The Cuban Revolution takes up Marx at the point where he put aside science to pick up his revolutionary rifle. And it takes him up at that point not in a spirit of revisionism, of struggling against that which came after Marx, of reviving a "pure" Marx, but simply because up to that point Marx, the scientist, standing outside of history, studied and predicted. Afterward, Marx the revolutionary took up the fight as part of history.

We, practical revolutionaries, by initiating our struggle were simply fulfilling laws foreseen by Marx the scientist. Along that road of rebellion, by struggling against the old power structure, by basing ourselves on the people to destroy that structure, and by having the well-being of the people as the foundation of our struggle, we are simply fitting into the predictions of Marx the scientist. That is to say, and it is well to emphasize this once again: The laws of Marxism are present in the events of the Cuban Revolution, independently of whether its leaders profess or fully know those laws from a theoretical point of view.

To better understand the Cuban revolutionary movement up to January 1 [1959], we should divide it into the following stages: before the *Granma* landing; from the *Granma* landing until after the victories of La Plata and

Arroyo del Infierno; from those days until El Uvero and the formation of the guerrillas' second column; from then until the formation of the third and fourth columns, the invasion of the Sierra de Cristal, and the establishment of the Second Front; the April strike and its failure; the beating back of the enemy's big offensive; the invasion of Las Villas.

Each one of those small historical moments of the guerrilla war framed different social concepts and different appraisals of Cuban reality. They shaped the thinking of the military leaders of the revolution, who in time would also reaffirm their status as political leaders.

Before the landing of the *Granma,* a mentality predominated that, to some degree, might be called subjectivist: blind confidence in a rapid popular explosion, enthusiasm and faith in being able to destroy Batista's might by a swift uprising combined with spontaneous revolutionary strikes, and the subsequent fall of the dictator. The movement was the direct heir of the Orthodox Party and its main slogan: "Honor against money." In other words, administrative honesty as the principal idea of the new Cuban Government.

Nevertheless, Fidel Castro had noted in *History Will Absolve Me* the foundations that the revolution has now almost completely fulfilled.[13] The revolution has also gone beyond these foundations, moving toward a deepening in the economic arena. This in turn has brought about a parallel deepening in the political arena, both nationally and internationally.

After the landing comes the defeat, the almost total destruction of the forces, their regroupment and formation as a guerrilla force. The small numbers of survivors, survivors with the will to struggle, were characterized by their understanding of the falsehood of the imagined schema of spontaneous outbursts throughout the island. They understood also that the fight would have to be a long one and that it would need to have a large peasant participation. At this point too, the first peasants joined the guerrillas. Also, two clashes were fought, of little importance in terms of the number of combatants, but of great psychological value, since they erased the uneasiness toward the peasants felt by the guerrillas' central group, made up of people from the cities. The peasants, in turn, distrusted the group and, above all, feared barbarous reprisals from the government. Two things were demonstrated at this stage, both very important for these interrelated factors: The peasants saw that the bestialities of the army and all the persecution would not be sufficient to put an end to the guerrillas, but would be capable of wiping out the peasants' homes, crops and families. So a good solution was to take refuge with the guerrillas, where their lives would be safe. In turn, the guerrilla fighters learned the ever-greater necessity of winning the peasant masses. This obviously meant that we had to offer them something they yearned for with all their might. And there is nothing a peasant desires more than land.

What followed then was a nomadic stage in which the Rebel Army went about conquering zones of influence. It still could not remain in them very long, but neither could the enemy army, which could hardly even enter them. Various battles established a vaguely defined front between the two sides.

May 28, 1957, marked a milestone. We attacked El Uvero, a well-armed, quite well-entrenched garrison located by the sea and equipped with an airfield, which made possible rapid reinforcement. The victory of the Rebel forces in this battle, one of the bloodiest of the war — 30 percent of the forces that went into battle were killed or wounded — totally changed the picture. There was now a territory in which the Rebel Army did as it pleased, where no news of this army filtered out to the enemy and from where it could descend in force onto the plains in rapid, sudden attacks and strike at its adversary's positions.

Shortly afterward, the first division of forces came about, and two guerrilla columns were established. The second took the name Column No. 4 in a quite infantile attempt at disguise. The two columns immediately showed signs of activity. On July 26, Estrada Palma was attacked, and five days later Bueycito, some 30 kilometers away. By then these shows of force became more important. On solid ground we would await the repressive forces, halting several of their attempts to go up into the Sierra. Battle fronts with wide no-man's lands were established, punctured by punitive incursions from both sides although the fronts remained basically unchanged.

Nevertheless, the guerrillas kept enlarging their forces with substantial additions from among the peasants in the region and some members of the July 26 Movement from the cities. The guerrillas became more combative and their fighting spirit increased. In February 1958, after suffering a number of enemy offensives that were beaten back, [Juan] Almeida's Column No. 3 left to take up positions close to Santiago, and during the first days of March Raúl [Castro]'s Column No. 6 — named after our hero Frank País, who had been killed a few months earlier — managed the feat of crossing the central highway. Going into the hills of Mayarí, it created the "Frank País" Second Front of Oriente.

News of the growing successes of our Rebel forces began to filter through the censorship, and the people were rapidly approaching the climax of revolutionary activity. At this point the proposal was raised, from Havana, of taking the struggle to the entire country through a revolutionary general strike, which was to destroy the enemy's forces by attacking them at all points simultaneously.

The Rebel Army's function in this case would be that of a catalyst or, perhaps, that of an "irritating thorn" that could unleash the movement. In those days our guerrillas stepped up their activity and Camilo Cienfuegos began creating his heroic legendary reputation, fighting for the first time in the Oriente plains, operating with a feel for organization and responding to a central leadership.

The revolutionary strike was not correctly approached, however, since the importance of working-class unity was ignored, and since no attempt was made to have the workers themselves, in exercising their own revolutionary activity, select the right moment. The strike was called over the radio in an attempt to clandestinely launch a rapid, sudden attack. Ignored was the fact that the secret of the appointed day and hour had filtered through to Batista's henchmen, but not to the people. The strike movement failed, and many valuable revolutionary patriots were mercilessly murdered.

A curious fact that should be noted at some point in the revolution's history is that Jules Dubois, the gossipmonger for the U.S. monopolies, knew ahead of time the day when the strike would break out.

At this point one of the most important qualitative changes in the war's development occurred: we acquired the certainty that the triumph could be achieved only through a gradual increase in the guerrilla forces, until the defeat of the enemy army in pitched battles.

By then broad relations had been established with the peasantry. The Rebel Army had issued its penal and civil codes, dispensed justice, distributed food supplies and collected taxes in the zones it administered. The neighboring zones also felt the influence of the Rebel Army. The enemy prepared large-scale offensives, but the balance sheet of two months of battle was 1,000 casualties for the totally demoralized invading army and an increase of our fighting capacity by 600 weapons.

We had already shown that the army could not defeat us. There was definitely no force in Cuba capable of conquering the peaks of the Sierra Maestra and the hills of the "Frank País" Second Front of Oriente. For the dictatorship's troops the roads of Oriente became impassable. With the enemy's offensive defeated, Camilo Cienfuegos and his Column No. 2, and the author of these lines, with the Ciro Redondo Column No. 8, were assigned to cross Camagüey Province, establish ourselves in Las Villas, and cut the enemy's communications. Camilo was supposed to later continue his advance in order to repeat the feat of the hero for whom his column was named, Antonio Maceo: an invasion across the entire island from east to west.

At this point the war shows a new characteristic: the relationship of forces turns in favor of the revolution. During a month and a half, two small columns, one of 80 and the other of 140 men, constantly surrounded and harassed by an army that mobilized thousands of soldiers, crossed the plains of Camagüey, arrived at Las Villas, and began the job of cutting the island in two.

At times it may seem strange, or incomprehensible, or even incredible that two columns of such small size — without communications, without transport, without the most elementary arms of modern warfare — could fight against well-trained, and above all, well-armed troops. The fundamental thing is the characteristic of each group. The fewer comforts the guerrilla fighter has, the more he is initiated into the rigors of nature, the more he feels at home, the higher his morale, the higher his sense of security. At the same time, under whatever circumstances, the guerrilla has come to put his life on the line, to trust it to the luck of a tossed coin. And in general, whether or not the individual guerrilla lives or dies weighs little in the final outcome of the battle.

The enemy soldier, in the Cuban example that we are now considering, is the junior partner of the dictator. He is the man who gets the last crumbs left by the next-to-last hanger-on in a long chain that begins on Wall Street and ends with him. He is ready to defend his privileges, but only to the degree that they are important. His salary and his benefits are worth some suffering and some dangers, but they are never worth his life. If that is the price of keeping them, better to give them up, in other words, to retreat from the guerrilla danger.

From these two concepts and these two morals springs the difference that would reach the crisis point on December 31, 1958.

The superiority of the Rebel Army was being established more and more clearly. Furthermore, the arrival of our columns in Las Villas showed the greater popularity of the July 26 Movement compared to all other groups: the Revolutionary Directorate, the Second Front of Las Villas, the Popular Socialist Party and some small guerrilla forces of the Authentic Organization. In large part this was due to the magnetic personality of its leader, Fidel Castro, but the greater correctness of its revolutionary line was also a factor.

Here ended the insurrection. But the men who arrive in Havana after two years of arduous struggle in the mountains and plains of Oriente, in the plains of Camagüey, and in the mountains, plains, and cities of Las Villas are not the same ideologically as the ones who landed on the beaches of Las Coloradas, or who joined in the first phase of the struggle. Their distrust of the peasant has turned into affection and respect for his virtues. Their total ignorance of life in the countryside has turned into a profound knowledge of the needs of our peasants. Their dabbling with statistics and with theory has been replaced by the firm cement of practice.

With agrarian reform as their banner, the implementation of which begins in the Sierra Maestra, these men come up against imperialism. They know that the agrarian reform is the basis upon which the new Cuba will be built. They know also that the agrarian reform will give land to all the dispossessed, but that it will dispossess its unjust possessors. And they know that the largest of the unjust possessors are also influential men in the State Department or in the government of the United States of America. They have learned to conquer difficulties with courage, with audacity, and above all, with the support of the people. And they have now seen the future of liberation that awaits us on the other side of our sufferings.

To reach this final understanding of our goals has been a long road, and many changes have taken place. Parallel to the successive qualitative changes that occurred on the battlefronts came the changes in the social composition of our guerrillas, and also the ideological transformations of its leaders. This came about because each one of these processes, of these changes, indeed constitutes a qualitative change in the composition, in the strength, in the revolutionary maturity of our army. The peasant contributes his vigor, his capacity to withstand suffering, his knowledge of the terrain, his love for the land, his hunger for agrarian reform. The intellectual, of whatever type, adds his small grain of sand beginning to sketch out a theory. The worker imparts his organizational sense, his innate tendency to band together and to unite.

Standing over all of this was the example of the Rebel forces themselves, who had already shown themselves to be much more than an "irritating thorn" and whose lessons aroused and awakened the masses until they lost their fear of the hangmen. Never before was the conception of this interaction as clear to us as now. We were able to feel how this interaction matured, as we taught the efficacy of armed insurrection, the strength that man has when he is called on to defend himself with a weapon in his hand and with the resolve to triumph in his eyes. And the peasant showed us the tricks of the Sierra, the strength necessary to live and triumph in it, and the dose of tenacity, of willingness to sacrifice, that it is necessary to have to be able to carry forward a people's destiny.

That's why, when the Rebel leader and his procession entered Havana, bathed in the peasants' sweat, with a horizon of mountains and clouds, beneath the burning island sun, up a new "stairway of the winter garden, climbed history with the feet of the people."

Cuba: Historical exception or vanguard in the anticolonial struggle?

(April 9, 1961)

> The working class is the creative class; the working class produces what material wealth exists in a country. And while power is not in their hands, while the working class allows power to remain in the hands of the bosses who exploit them, in the hands of landlords, the speculators, the monopolies and in the hands of foreign and national interest groups, while armaments are in the hands of those in the service of these interest groups and not in their own hands, the working class will be forced to lead a miserable existence no matter how many crumbs those interest groups should let fall from their banquet table.
>
> — Fidel Castro

Never in the Americas has an event of such extraordinary character, with such deep roots and such far-reaching consequences for the destiny of the continent's progressive movements taken place as our revolutionary war. This is true to such an extent that it has been appraised by some to be the decisive event of the Americas, on a scale of importance second only to that great trilogy — the Russian Revolution, the victory over Nazi Germany and the subsequent social transformations and the victory of the Chinese Revolution.

Our revolution, unorthodox in its forms and manifestations, has nevertheless followed the general lines of all the great historical events of this century that are characterized by anticolonial struggles and the transition toward socialism.

Nevertheless some sectors, whether out of self-interest or in good faith, claim to see in the Cuban Revolution exceptional origins and features whose importance for this great historical-social event they inflate even to the level of decisive factors. They speak of the exceptionalism of the Cuban Revolution as compared with the course of other progressive parties in Latin America. They conclude that the form and road of the Cuban Revolution are unique and that in the other countries of the Americas the historical transition will be different.

We accept that exceptions exist which give the Cuban Revolution its peculiar characteristics. It is clearly established that in every revolution there are specific factors, but it is no less established that all follow laws that society cannot violate. Let us analyze, then, the factors of this purported exceptionalism.

The first, and perhaps the most important and original, is that cosmic force called Fidel Castro Ruz, whose name in only a few years has attained historic proportions. The future will provide the definitive appraisal of our prime minister's merits, but to us they appear comparable to those of the great historic figures of Latin America. What is exceptional about Fidel Castro's personality? Various features of his life and character make him stand out far above his *compañeros* and followers. Fidel is a person of such tremendous personality that he would attain leadership in whatever movement he participated. It has been like that throughout his career, from his student days to the premiership of our country and as a spokesperson for the oppressed peoples of the Americas. He has the qualities of a great leader, added to which are his personal gifts of audacity, strength, courage, and an extraordinary determination always to discern the will of the people — and these have brought him the position of honor and sacrifice that he occupies today. But he has other important qualities — his ability to assimilate knowledge and experience in order to understand a situation in its entirety without losing sight of the details, his unbounded faith in the future, and the breadth of his vision to foresee events and anticipate them in action, always seeing farther and more accurately than his *compañeros*. With these great cardinal qualities, his capacity to unite, resisting the divisions that weaken; his ability to lead the whole people in action; his infinite love for the people; his faith in the future and with his capacity to foresee it, Fidel Castro has done more than anyone else in Cuba to create from nothing the present formidable apparatus of the Cuban Revolution.

No-one, however, could assert that specific political and social conditions existed in Cuba that were totally different from those in the other countries of the Americas, or that precisely because of those differences the revolution took place. Neither could anyone assert, conversely, that Fidel Castro made the revolution despite a lack of difference. Fidel, a great and able leader, led the revolution in Cuba, at the time and in the way he did, by interpreting the profound political disturbances that were preparing the people for their great leap onto the revolutionary road. Certain conditions were not unique to Cuba but it will be hard for other peoples to take advantage of them because imperialism — in contrast to some progressive groups — does learn from its errors.

The condition we would describe as exceptional was the fact that U.S. imperialism was disoriented and was never able to accurately assess the true scope of the Cuban Revolution. This partly explains the many apparent contradictions in U.S. policy.

The monopolies, as is habitual in such cases, began to think of a successor for Batista precisely because they knew that the people were opposed to him and were looking for a revolutionary solution. What more intelligent and expert stroke than to depose the now unserviceable little dictator and to replace him with the new "boys" who would in turn serve the interests of imperialism? The empire gambled for a time on this card from its continental deck, and lost miserably.

Prior to our military victory they were suspicious of us, but not afraid. Actually, with all their experience at this game they were so accustomed to winning, they played with two decks. On various occasions emissaries of the U.S. State Department came, disguised as reporters, to investigate our rustic revolution, yet they never found any trace of imminent danger. By the time the imperialists wanted to react — when they discovered that the group of inexperienced young men marching in triumph through the streets of Havana had a clear awareness of their political duty and an iron determination to carry out that duty — it was already too late. Thus, in January 1959, the first social revolution in the Caribbean and the most profound of the Latin American revolutions dawned.

It could not be considered exceptional that the bourgeoisie, or at least a part of it, favored the revolutionary war over the dictatorship at the same time as it supported and promoted movements seeking negotiated solutions that would permit them to substitute elements disposed to curb the revolution for the Batista regime. Considering the conditions in which the revolutionary war took place and the complexity of the political tendencies that opposed the dictatorship, it was not at all exceptional that some elements adopted a neutral, or at least a nonbelligerent, attitude toward the insurrectionary forces. It is understandable that the national bourgeoisie, choked by imperialism and the dictatorship — whose troops sacked small properties and made extortion a daily way of life — felt a certain sympathy when they saw those young rebels from the mountains punish the mercenary army, the military arm of imperialism.

Nonrevolutionary forces did indeed aid the coming of revolutionary power.

A further exceptional factor was that in most of Cuba the peasants had been progressively proletarianized due to the needs of large-scale, semi-mechanized capitalist agriculture. They had reached a new level of organization and therefore a greater class consciousness. In mentioning this we should also point out, in the interest of truth, that the first area in which the Rebel Army operated (comprising the survivors of the defeated column who had made the *Granma* voyage) was an area inhabited by peasants whose social and cultural roots were different from those of the peasants found in the areas of large-scale, semimechanized Cuban agriculture. In fact the Sierra Maestra, the site of the first revolutionary settlement, is a place where peasants who had struggled against large landholders took refuge. They went there seeking new land — somehow overlooked by the state or the voracious landholders — on which to earn a modest income. They struggled constantly against the demands of the soldiers, always allied to the landholders, and their ambitions extended no further than a property deed. The peasants who belonged to our first guerrilla armies came from that section of this social class which most strongly shows love for the land and the possession of it; that is to say, which most perfectly demonstrates the petty-bourgeois spirit. The peasants fought because they wanted land for themselves and their children, to manage and sell it and to enrich themselves through their labor.

Despite their petty-bourgeois spirit, the peasants soon learned that they could not satisfy their desire to possess land without breaking up the large landholding system. Radical agrarian reform, the only type that could give land to the peasants, clashed directly with the interests of the imperialists, the large landholders and the sugar and cattle magnates. The bourgeoisie was afraid to clash with those interests but the proletariat was not. In this way the course of the revolution itself brought the workers and peasants together. The workers supported the demands of the peasants against the large landholders. The poor peasants, rewarded with ownership of land, loyally supported the revolutionary power and defended it against its imperialist and counterrevolutionary enemies.

In our opinion no further exceptionalism can be claimed. We have been generous to extend it this far. We shall now examine the permanent roots of all social phenomena in the Americas: the contradictions that mature in the wombs of present societies and produce changes that can reach the magnitude of a revolution such as Cuba's.

First, in chronological order although not in order of importance at

present, is the large landholding system. It was the economic power base of
the ruling class throughout the entire period following the great anticolonial
revolutions of the last century. The large landholding social class, found in
all Latin American countries, generally lags behind the social developments
that move the world. In some places, however, the most alert and clear-
sighted members of this class are aware of the dangers and begin to change
the form of their capital investment, at times opting for mechanized agriculture, transferring some of their wealth to industrial investment or becoming
commercial agents of the monopolies. In any case, the first liberating revolutions never destroyed the large landholding powers that always constituted a reactionary force and upheld the principle of servitude on the land.
This phenomenon, prevalent in all the countries of the Americas, has been
the foundation of all the injustices committed since the era when the King
of Spain gave huge grants of land to his most noble *conquistadores*. In the
case of Cuba, only the unappropriated royal lands — the scraps left between
where three circular landholdings met — were left for the natives, Creoles
and mestizos.

In most countries the large landholders realized they couldn't survive
alone and promptly entered into alliances with the monopolies — the
strongest and most ruthless oppressors of the Latin American peoples.
U.S. capital arrived on the scene to exploit the virgin lands and later carried
off, unnoticed, all the funds so "generously" given, plus several times the
amount originally invested in the "beneficiary" country. The Americas
were a field of interimperialist struggle. The "wars" between Costa Rica
and Nicaragua, the separation of Panama from Colombia, the infamy committed against Ecuador in its dispute with Peru, the fight between Paraguay
and Bolivia, are nothing but expressions of this gigantic battle between the
world's great monopolistic powers, a battle decided almost completely in
favor of the U.S. monopolies following World War II. From that point on the
empire dedicated itself to strengthening its grip on its colonial possessions
and perfecting the whole structure to prevent the intrusion of old or new
competitors from other imperialist countries. This resulted in a monstrously
distorted economy which has been described by the shamefaced economists
of the imperialist regime with an innocuous vocabulary revealing the deep
compassion they feel for us inferior beings. They call our miserably exploited
Indians, persecuted and reduced to utter wretchedness, "little Indians"
and they call blacks and mulattos, disinherited and discriminated against,
"colored" — all this as a means of dividing the working masses in their
struggle for a better economic future. For all of us, the peoples of the Americas,
they have a polite and refined term: "underdeveloped."

What is underdevelopment?

A dwarf with an enormous head and a swollen chest is "underdeveloped" inasmuch as his weak legs or short arms do not match the rest of his anatomy. He is the product of an abnormal formation distorting his development. In reality that is what we are — we, politely referred to as "underdeveloped," in truth are colonial, semicolonial or dependent countries. We are countries whose economies have been distorted by imperialism, which has abnormally developed those branches of industry or agriculture needed to complement its complex economy. "Underdevelopment," or distorted development, brings a dangerous specialization in raw materials, inherent in which is the threat of hunger for all our peoples. We, the "underdeveloped," are also those with the single crop, the single product, the single market. A single product whose uncertain sale depends on a single market imposing and fixing conditions. That is the great formula for imperialist economic domination. It should be added to the old, but eternally youthful Roman formula: *Divide and Conquer!*

The system of large landholding, then, through its connections with imperialism, completely shapes so-called "underdevelopment," resulting in low wages and unemployment that in turn create a vicious cycle producing ever lower wages and greater unemployment. The great contradictions of the system sharpen, constantly at the mercy of the cyclical fluctuations of its own economy, and provide the common denominator for all the peoples of America, from the Rio Bravo to the South Pole. This common denominator, which we shall capitalize and which serves as the starting point for analysis by all who think about these social phenomena, is called the People's Hunger. The people are weary of being oppressed, persecuted, exploited to the maximum. They are weary of the wretched selling of their labor-power day after day — faced with the fear of joining the enormous mass of unemployed — so that the greatest profit can be wrung from each human body, profit later squandered in the orgies of the masters of capital.

We see that there are great and inescapable common denominators in Latin America, and we cannot say we were exempt from any of those, leading to the most terrible and permanent of all: the people's hunger.

Large landholding, whether in its primitive form of exploitation or as a form of capitalist monopoly, adjusts to the new conditions and becomes an ally of imperialism — that form of finance and monopoly capitalism which goes beyond national borders — in order to create economic colonialism, euphemistically called "underdevelopment," resulting in low wages, underemployment and unemployment: the people's hunger.

All this existed in Cuba. Here, too, there was hunger. Here, the proportion of unemployed was one of the highest in Latin America. Here, imperialism was more ruthless than in many countries of America. And here, large landholdings existed as much as they did in any other Latin American country.

What did we do to free ourselves from the vast imperialist system with its entourage of puppet rulers in each country, its mercenary armies to protect the puppets and the whole complex social system of the exploitation of human by human? We applied certain formulas, discoveries of our empirical medicine for the great ailments of our beloved Latin America, empirical medicine which rapidly became scientific truth.

Objective conditions for the struggle are provided by the people's hunger, their reaction to that hunger, the terror unleashed to crush the people's reaction and the wave of hatred that the repression creates. The rest of the Americas lacked the subjective conditions, the most important of which is consciousness of the possibility of victory against the imperialist powers and their internal allies through violent struggle. These conditions were created through armed struggle — which progressively clarified the need for change and permitted it to be foreseen — and through the defeat and subsequent annihilation of the army by the popular forces (*an absolutely necessary condition for every genuine revolution*).

Having already demonstrated that these conditions are created through armed struggle, we have to explain once more that the scene of the struggle should be the countryside. A peasant army pursuing the great objectives for which the peasantry should fight (the first of which is the just distribution of land) will capture the cities from the countryside. The peasant class of Latin America, basing itself on the ideology of the working class whose great thinkers discovered the social laws governing us, will provide the great liberating army of the future — as it has already done in Cuba. This army, created in the countryside where the subjective conditions for the taking of power mature, proceeds to take the cities, uniting with the working class and enriching itself ideologically. It can and must defeat the oppressor army, at first in skirmishes, engagements and surprises and, finally, in big battles when the army will have grown from small-scale guerrilla footing to a great popular army of liberation. A vital stage in the consolidation of the revolutionary power, as we have said, will be the liquidation of the old army.

If these conditions present in Cuba existed in the rest of the Latin American countries, what would happen in other struggles for power by the dispossessed classes? Would it be feasible to take power or not? If it was feasible, would it be easier or more difficult than in Cuba?

Let us mention the difficulties that in our view will make the new Latin American revolutionary struggles more difficult. There are general difficulties for every country and more specific difficulties for some whose level of development or national peculiarities are different. We mentioned at the beginning of this essay that we could consider the attitude of imperialism, disoriented in the face of the Cuban Revolution, as an exceptional factor. The attitude of the national bourgeoisie was, to a certain extent, also exceptional. They too were disoriented and even looked sympathetically upon the action of the rebels due to the pressure of the empire on their interests — a situation which is indeed common to all our countries.

Cuba has again drawn the line in the sand, and again we see Pizarro's dilemma: On the one hand there are those who love the people and on the other, those who hate the people. The line between them divides the two great social forces, the bourgeoisie and the working class, each of which are defining, with increasing clarity, their respective positions as the process of the Cuban Revolution advances.

Imperialism has learned the lesson of Cuba well. It will not allow itself to be caught by surprise in any of our 20 republics or in any of the colonies that still exist in the Americas. This means that vast popular struggles against powerful invading armies await those who now attempt to violate the peace of the sepulchers, pax Romana. This is important because if the Cuban liberation war was difficult, with its two years of continuous struggle, anguish and instability, the new battles awaiting the people in other parts of Latin America will be infinitely more difficult.

The United States hastens the delivery of arms to the puppet governments they see as being increasingly threatened; it makes them sign pacts of dependence to legally facilitate the shipment of instruments of repression and death and of troops to use them. Moreover, it increases the military preparation of the repressive armies with the intention of making them efficient weapons against the people.

And what about the bourgeoisie? The national bourgeoisie generally is not capable of maintaining a consistent struggle against imperialism. It shows that it fears popular revolution even more than the oppression and despotic dominion of imperialism which crushes nationality, tarnishes patriotic sentiments, and colonizes the economy.

A large part of the bourgeoisie opposes revolution openly, and since the beginning has not hesitated to ally itself with imperialism and the landowners to fight against the people and close the road to revolution.

A desperate and hysterical imperialism, ready to undertake any maneuver and to give arms and even troops to its puppets in order to annihilate any country which rises up; ruthless landowners, unscrupulous and experienced in the most brutal forms of repression; and, finally, a bourgeoisie willing to close, through any means, the roads leading to popular revolution: These are the great allied forces which directly oppose the new popular revolutions of Latin America.

Such are the difficulties that must be added to those arising from struggles of this kind under the new conditions found in Latin America following the consolidation of that irreversible phenomenon represented by the Cuban Revolution.

There are still other, more specific problems. It is more difficult to prepare guerrilla groups in those countries that have a concentrated population in large centers and a greater amount of light and medium industry, even though it may not be anything like effective industrialization. The ideological influence of the cities inhibits the guerrilla struggle by increasing the hopes for peacefully organized mass struggle. This gives rise to a certain "institutionalization," which in more or less "normal" periods makes conditions less harsh than those usually inflicted on the people. The idea is even conceived of possible quantitative increases in the congressional ranks of revolutionary forces until a point is someday reached which allows a qualitative change.

It is not probable that this hope will be realized given present conditions in any country of the Americas, although a possibility that the change can begin through the electoral process is not to be excluded. Current conditions, however, in all countries of Latin America make this possibility very remote.

Revolutionaries cannot foresee all the tactical variables that may arise in the course of the struggle for their liberating program. The real capacity of a revolutionary is measured by their ability to find adequate revolutionary tactics in every different situation and by keeping all tactics in mind so that they might be exploited to the maximum. It would be an unpardonable error to underestimate the gain a revolutionary program could make through a given electoral process, just as it would be unpardonable to look only to elections and not to other forms of struggle, including armed struggle, to achieve power — the indispensable instrument for applying and developing a revolutionary program. If power is not achieved, all other conquests, however advanced they appear, are unstable, insufficient and incapable of producing necessary solutions.

When we speak of winning power via the electoral process, our question is always the same: If a popular movement takes over the government of a country by winning a wide popular vote and resolves as a consequence to initiate the great social transformations which make up the triumphant program, would it not immediately come into conflict with the reactionary classes of that country? Has the army not always been the repressive instrument of that class? If so, it is logical to suppose that this army will side with its class and enter the conflict against the newly constituted government. By means of a more or less bloodless coup d'état, this government can be overthrown and the old game renewed again, never seeming to end. It could also happen that an oppressor army could be defeated by an armed popular reaction in defense and support of its government. What appears difficult to believe is that the armed forces would accept profound social reforms with good grace and peacefully resign themselves to their liquidation as a caste.

Where there are large urban concentrations, even when economically backward, it may be advisable — in our humble opinion — to engage in struggle outside the limits of the city in a way that can continue for a long time. The existence of a guerrilla center in the mountains of a country with populous cities maintains a perpetual focus of rebellion because it is very improbable that the repressive powers will be able, either rapidly or over a long period of time, to liquidate guerrilla groups with established social bases in territory favorable to guerrilla warfare, if the strategy and tactics of this type of warfare are consistently employed.

What would happen in the cities is quite different. Armed struggle against the repressive army can develop to an unanticipated degree, but this struggle will become a frontal one only when there is a powerful army to fight against [the enemy] army. A frontal fight against a powerful and well-equipped army cannot be undertaken by a small group.

For the frontal fight, many arms will be needed, and the question arises: Where are these arms to be found? They do not appear spontaneously; they must be seized from the enemy. But in order to seize them from the enemy, it is necessary to fight; and it is not possible to fight openly. The struggle in the big cities must therefore begin clandestinely, capturing military groups or weapons one by one in successive assaults. If this happens, a great advance can be made.

Still, we would not dare to say that victory would be denied to a popular rebellion with a guerrilla base inside the city. No one can object on theoretical grounds to this strategy; at least we have no intention of doing so.

But we should point out how easy it would be as the result of a betrayal, or simply by means of continuous raids, to eliminate the leaders of the revolution. In contrast, if while employing all conceivable maneuvers in the city (such as organized sabotage and, above all, that effective form of action, urban guerrilla warfare) and if a base is also maintained in the countryside, the revolutionary political power, relatively safe from the contingencies of the war, will remain untouched even if the oppressor government defeats and annihilates all the popular forces in the city. *The revolutionary political power should be relatively safe, but not outside the war, not giving directions from some other country or from distant places. It should be within its own country fighting.* These considerations lead us to believe that even in countries where the cities are predominant, the central political focus of the struggle can develop in the countryside.

Returning to the example of relying on help from the military class in effecting the coup and supplying the weapons, there are two problems to analyze: First, supposing it was an organized nucleus and capable of independent decisions, if the military really joins with the popular forces to strike the blow, there would in such a case be a coup by one part of the army against another, probably leaving the structure of the military caste intact. The other problem, in which armies unite rapidly and spontaneously with popular forces, can occur only after the armies have been violently beaten by a powerful and persistent enemy, that is, in conditions of catastrophe for the constituted power. With an army defeated and its morale broken, this phenomenon can occur. For that, struggle is necessary; we always return to the question of how to carry on that struggle. The answer leads us toward developing guerrilla struggle in the countryside, on favorable ground and supported by struggle in the cities, always counting on the widest possible participation of the working masses and guided by the ideology of that class.

We have sufficiently analyzed the obstacles revolutionary movements in Latin America will encounter. It can now be asked whether or not there are favorable conditions for the preliminary stage, like, for example, those encountered by Fidel Castro in the Sierra Maestra. We believe that here, too, general conditions can facilitate these centers of rebellion and specific conditions in certain countries exist which are even more favorable. Two subjective factors are the most important consequences of the Cuban Revolution: the first is the possibility of victory, knowing that the capability exists to crown an enterprise like that of the group of idealistic *Granma* expeditionaries who successfully struggled for two years in the Sierra Maestra. This immediately indicates there can be a revolutionary movement operating from the countryside, mixing with the peasant masses, that will grow from weakness to strength, that will destroy the army in a frontal fight, that will capture cities from the countryside, that will strengthen through its struggle the subjective conditions necessary for seizing power. The importance of this fact is demonstrated in the huge number of "exceptionalists" who have recently appeared. "Exceptionalists" are those special beings who say they find in the Cuban Revolution a unique event which cannot be followed — led by someone who has few or no faults, who led the revolution through a unique path. We affirm this is completely false.

Victory by the popular forces in Latin America is clearly possible in the form of guerrilla warfare undertaken by a peasant army in alliance with the workers, defeating the oppressor army in a frontal assault, taking cities by attack from the countryside, and dissolving the oppressor army — as the first stage in completely destroying the superstructure of the colonial world.

We should point out a second subjective factor: The masses not only know the possibility of triumph, they know their destiny. They know with increasing certainty that whatever the tribulations of history during short periods, the future belongs to the people; the future will bring about social justice. This knowledge will help raise revolutionary ferment to even greater heights than those prevailing in Latin America today.

Some less general factors do not appear with the same intensity from country to country. One very important one is the greater exploitation of the peasants in Latin America than there was in Cuba. Let us remind those who pretend to see the proletarianization of the peasantry in our insurrectionary stage, that we believe it was precisely this which accelerated the emergence of cooperatives as well as the achievement of power and the agrarian reform. This is in spite of the fact that the peasant of the first battles, the core of the Rebel Army, is the same one to be found today in the Sierra Maestra, proud owner of their parcel of land and intransigently individualistic.

There are, of course, characteristics specific to the Latin American countries: an Argentine peasant does not have the same outlook as a communal peasant in Peru, Bolivia or Ecuador. But hunger for land is permanently present in the peasants, and they generally hold the key to the Americas. In some countries they are even more exploited than they were in Cuba, increasing the possibility that this class will rise up in arms.

Another fact is Batista's army, which with all its enormous defects, was structured in such a way that everyone, from the lowest soldier to the highest general, was an accomplice in the exploitation of the people. They were complete mercenaries, and this gave the repressive apparatus some cohesiveness. The armies of Latin America generally include a professional officers' corps and recruits who are called up periodically. Each year, young recruits leave their homes where they have known the daily sufferings of their parents, have seen them with their own eyes, where they have felt poverty and social injustice. If one day they are sent as cannon fodder to fight against the defenders of a doctrine they feel in their own hearts is just, their capacity to fight aggressively will be seriously affected. Adequate propaganda will enable the recruits to see the justice of and the reasons for the struggle, and magnificent results will be achieved.

After this brief study of the revolutionary struggle we can say that the Cuban Revolution had exceptional factors giving it its own peculiarities as well as factors which are common to all the countries of the Americas and which express the internal need for revolution. New conditions will make the flow of these revolutionary movements easier as they give the masses consciousness of their destiny and the certainty that it is possible. On the other hand, there are now obstacles making it harder for the armed masses to achieve power rapidly, such as imperialism's close alliance with the bourgeoisie, enabling them to fight to the utmost against the popular forces. Dark days await Latin America. The latest declarations of those that rule the United States seem to indicate that dark days await the world: Lumumba, savagely assassinated, in the greatness of his martyrdom showed the tragic mistakes that cannot be committed. Once the anti-imperialist struggle begins, we must constantly strike hard, where it hurts the most, never retreating, always marching forward, counterstriking against each aggression, always responding to each aggression with even stronger action by the masses. This is the way to victory. We will analyze on another occasion whether the Cuban Revolution, having taken power, followed these new revolutionary paths with its own exceptional characteristics or if, as in this analysis, while respecting the existence of certain special characteristics, it fundamentally followed a logic derived from laws intrinsic to the social process.

A new culture of work

(August 21, 1962)

This speech was delivered to a meeting in Havana, organized by the Central Organization of Cuban Trade Unions (CTC), of workers from four factories that had surpassed their production quotas. At the meeting, CTC General Secretary Lázaro Peña also spoke.

 ompañero acting head of the mission of the sister German Democratic Republic; *compañeros* all:

As *compañero* Lázaro already pointed out, this ceremony has a dual purpose. One is to express our gratitude to the workers of the German Democratic Republic, who extended their hands in friendship across the sea, helping us in this stage of socialist construction with one of our most cherished weapons: the tools of work.

The other purpose of this gathering is for all of us here to celebrate that a group of several of our Ministry's factories, despite the difficult conditions created by the imperialist blockade, have nevertheless been able to surpass their production goals.

These factories belong to different enterprises, but all are closely linked to the people's consumption: the two flour mills that are part of the Consolidated Flour Enterprise, one of the factories of the Consolidated Tire Enterprise, and the ice factory that is part of the Consolidated Beer and Malt Enterprise.

Unfortunately, due to present conditions, the other factories that are part of the beer and malt enterprise, the breweries, have not been able to surpass many goals. We've had to significantly cut back their production, because all the raw materials must be imported.

That, in general, is the tragedy of our industry, an industry created in semicolonial conditions, dependent on getting supplies from abroad. Under these conditions we've had to develop new techniques to adapt our industry to the raw materials that come from the socialist countries. These new techniques will allow us to save more material, in some cases to find raw materials here in Cuba. We cannot stress enough the importance that saving raw materials has for our development. We have to accomplish all these things simultaneously. We must try to raise our revolutionary consciousness so that work becomes the center of our efforts in the hard struggle to build socialism.

Emulation will play a major role in this effort. And these *compañeros*, involved at times in emulation between factories, at other times between trade unions or enterprises, have topped numerous goals.

A few days ago we celebrated the production of the one hundred thousandth sack in a month by the Echeverría Flour Mill of Havana. Hours earlier its rival, the Frank País Flour Mill in Santiago, had broken its mark of 50,000 sacks. In this way, emulation — becoming a kind of collective competition in which the consciousness of the workers intervenes to make it work and to turn it into almost a sports competition — has little by little been attracting the interest of the working masses. This assembly today is a demonstration of the advances we have made.

Like any other serious gathering of revolutionaries during this period, however, this one must include a self-criticism of the systems and methods that we have used up until now to make emulation a real vehicle to mobilize the masses.

All of you worker *compañeros* know that we have been working on emulation for some time now, and that we presented some guidelines to the last congress, to the [CTC] workers' congress last November. But we could not get away from a certain formal and bureaucratic spirit. So at this point it would take a highly trained specialist to wade through all the rules and regulations for emulation and determine who is the winner or who is ahead in the competition. We have turned emulation into a formal competition. We have separated it from its logical strong point: the masses. But the workers, conscious of its importance, full of revolutionary enthusiasm, broke down the formal barriers and began on their own to organize emulation in different production units.

We have to gather the experience of our errors and talk constantly with the masses, talk things over so that emulation becomes a really collective effort. So that winners of emulation will be not only the workers who successfully reach their goals, or surpass them, as they have been surpassed in some cases. Rather, the winners will be those who surpass the goals because they have doubled or tripled them, because they have achieved fabulous results. In the future no-one should win in emulation simply by meeting the goal.

In other words, every worker at every factory must be conscious that emulation is something more than a competition during a given period. It is a vital part of our nation's work. Every worker should take an interest in emulation. Every worker should understand well the importance of the results of emulation, which is to produce more and better, increase production, increase productivity, improve the quality of products, and save raw materials. And we should strive for these basic tenets to become systematic. It is fine for us to organize on the national level so we are able to establish who the winners are after complicated tallies. But all of you should engage in emulation on all levels: shop to shop, department to department, factory to factory, enterprise to enterprise, state institution to state institution. Emulation should be part of the worker's day-to-day discussions during the hours he is not working. That would really mark the triumph of emulation.

That is very important because we are at a difficult stage of the revolution. We are at the stage of building socialism in the face of the imperialist blockade, 150 kilometers from the shores of the United States; surrounded by the enemy day and night; spied on by their planes that violate our territory and by spies sent out from the Guantánamo base; our territory trampled upon by the stain of Guantánamo; facing constant threats of an invasion that could signify the cruelest war in the history of humanity.

We feel ourselves to be, in a certain sense, the vanguard of the world proletariat, part of a broad battlefield with many vanguard positions. But we are proud of defending here what man values most: the right to develop freely, the right to build a new society under new conditions, where there are no exploiters and exploited. All this, as long as imperialist aggression does not come about, as long as it is only a threat, as long as it is not necessary to pick up the rifle, to pick up whatever weapon the revolution happens to assign us, whether by luck or by the aid of our friends, while we become increasingly stronger and better able to beat back an invasion — as long as that time doesn't come, work is our daily battlefield. It is the battlefield on which we confront imperialism every hour of our working day.

And this work should be done as well as possible, taking as much interest in it as possible. Because socialism is built on the fruits of labor, on optimum production, on the greatest productivity. It would be useless to deepen our consciousness to the maximum if we did not increase our production, if we did not have goods to share out among the people.

Socialism is a social system based on equal distribution of society's wealth. But this requires that society has wealth to distribute, that there are machines with which to work, and that these machines have raw materials to produce the necessary goods for our population's consumption. To the extent that we increase the number of products available for the whole population, we move forward in building socialism.

New factories will have to be built because socialism is based on the factory. Socialism takes root in a technologically developed society. It cannot exist under feudal conditions, under agrarian conditions. It develops on the basis of technology.

Work, therefore, contributes its fruits to production. In addition, daily work, applied with creative enthusiasm, develops socialist consciousness in all of us. Productivity, more production, consciousness — these are the foundations upon which the new society can be built.

But let's not forget that we still have not created the new society. Memories of the past, memories of struggle, and the vices of a wretched past — of a past that strangled man — have not yet been erased. Let's not forget that the working masses who today are beginning the task of building socialism are not pure. They are made up of human beings who carry along with them a whole series of bad habits inherited from the previous epoch. I say bad habits they have — we have — we all have those bad habits inherited from the previous epoch, which weighed heavily on us over many years.

We are all children of that environment. We have destroyed the fundamental thing and have changed it, but we have not been able to wipe out as rapidly those bad habits from our consciousness. Not even social labor, community labor, collective labor, is sufficient to create that new consciousness: when man begins to look upon work as a moral necessity, not just a material necessity to earn a salary for his children and relatives.

At this stage there are a whole series of measures to create closer ties between the masses and the government, to rid ourselves of the vices of the past, to build a strong and prosperous state, to have the nation's best sons and daughters contribute their work to the tasks of leading more rapidly to the period of the transition to socialism and the subsequent period of communist society. Even though it's a distant future, we should already be thinking about communism, which is the perfect society, the fundamental aspiration of the first men who could see beyond the present and foresee humanity's destiny.

Among those factors we should point to, and point to as very important, is discipline. When the structure of the old society was torn down, the worker felt freed from a series of burdens that weighed upon him. Many *compañeros* thought that reaching this new stage of society automatically meant being free from responsibilities and acquiring only rights. That is precisely the reflection of the old society in the consciousness of men who are building a new society.

Discipline, however, is fundamental to the work of construction, *compañeros*. Don't think of discipline as a negative attitude, that is, as submission to management. In this stage discipline must be absolutely dialectical. It consists of abiding by majority decisions in accordance with democratic centralism. It means following the guidelines of a government supported by the masses. It means collectively discussing, on each level, the fundamental problems of the shop, the factory or the enterprise to ensure better production. It means increasing the workers' participation through their organizations in the management of the factory, in the sense of being able to participate in discussions and decisions about production and to constantly supervise the administration in carrying out every one of the disciplinary rules that we must all impose upon ourselves.

We were undisciplined at every level, but especially in the economic sphere. Our guerrilla fighters started off with the characteristics of guerrillas, of soldiers unfamiliar with the formal discipline of the barracks, and had to begin to form new units that required a rigid discipline, because the command of soldiers in battle must be that way, rigid and automatic. But the economic apparatus marched to a different beat, and the understanding of these problems by the worker *compañeros* on all levels was not always clear.

We have had to take drastic measures to definitively reestablish discipline and establish the principle of authority, of central responsibility in state administration. One of the factory directors, the director of one of the prize-winning factories today, was penalized for not complying with a recommendation of the Central Planning Board transmitted through our Ministry.

Several enterprise directors were also penalized. We have the highest opinion of all of them as revolutionaries, as workers, and as administrators. But their enthusiasm led them to believe that their own enterprise was the most important thing, that they had to assure supplies for their own enterprise, forgetting that the enterprise is only a tiny grain within the entire administrative apparatus. So we had to take drastic measures.

It so happens that some of the penalized *compañeros* were among our best and most hardworking directors within the Ministry of Industry. In other words, their revolutionary enthusiasm in making their factory produce to the maximum made them lose perspective, and along with it, lose the necessary discipline.

But that discipline should not be applied only on the administrative level; that discipline should be adopted by the workers. And that's your job, to cooperate fully in this task through your mass organizations and also as individuals.

We lack two fundamental things, two pillars upon which this new society must be built: the establishment of work norms and salaries for all categories of the country's workers. We are way behind in these tasks; several months ago we promised to complete them right away. On the eve of May Day we announced that we would start with the mining enterprise and we did so. Today, by the middle of August, we have established work norms in one mine and we are studying them in a few others.

We cannot permit this sluggishness. Establishing norms and salaries in order to come up with new collective contracts should be the work of the masses. It must be the work of the masses not only in the sense of having lively discussion when it comes up at the workplace. Rather, the masses themselves must take initiative in the work of standardizing job categories on the national level and fixing new salaries.

This should be everyone's concern, the national trade unions, the revolutionary nuclei [of the party], the entire government, and the workers.

These norms will set the quantity and quality of what each worker must contribute to society. Every worker in every workplace must be capable of providing society with products of labor of a given quantity and quality.

We should always remember that by no means is quality at odds with this stage in the construction of socialism. We should always remember that our obligation as producers in a society that is freeing itself is to give the people the best we can, our best efforts embodied in the form of products of the highest quality.

But of course discipline is only one of the factors that will move us forward; there are many others. We can take an example from today: the aid of friendly countries, friendly countries that extend a hand in the form of technical assistance, advice, material goods and entire factories so that we can develop our society. All new value comes from human labor, and this labor will be embodied in the large factories and big machines we're going to build in our country during this four-year plan and in the planning periods that follow.

If we had to carry out the gigantic effort we are projecting alone, we would have to call upon the people to make the greatest sacrifices to get the wherewithal to build these factories. The aid of friendly countries spares us a large part of that sacrifice, and for that reason our task seems easier. Nevertheless, sacrifice is part of building a new society. We cannot hope to destroy an agency of U.S. imperialism, like our comprador bourgeoisie was, or like the big landowners who spent their summers in the United States or Europe, or the U.S. companies themselves — we cannot hope to challenge the most powerful oppressor on earth and at the same time try to do so without sacrifices. We must be ready to make the relative sacrifices we have made, as well as new ones. We must be prepared for tighter blockades, to beat back who-knows-what attempts by the invader to destroy our society. We must always hold aloft our banner as the first to begin building the socialist society in Latin America. That is an honor and an example. It is an example that will nourish the countries of Latin America.

Every time visitors come here, or every time our truths are heard over Radio Havana, a new consciousness grows throughout Latin America. Already the oppressed masses of the continent know that change is necessary, that they can no longer continue living under centuries of oppression, where injustice is the instrument for the enrichment of a few. But they know something else.

The consciousness of the masses throughout Latin America — peasants and workers mistreated, attacked, murdered — that consciousness has been transformed into something new: the certainty that change is possible. And many machetes are being sharpened throughout Latin America!

Whenever we start to lament our sacrifices we should remember that our responsibility transcends the borders of Cuba, that we are a living example, that we are showing something new in Latin America. And we must overcome whatever difficulty we may confront.

All right, *compañeros*. In order to build the society we also need a superior technique, a modern technology. An example of what can be accomplished is shown by the visit of a Soviet technician to the two flour mills that compete each month in surpassing production goals. This *compañero*, after investigating the capacity of the flour mills, discovered some bottlenecks — places where production was held up. He recommended the necessary measures to eliminate these bottlenecks.

All the measures were implemented. Today, with a very small investment and with the talent and capacity of this Soviet *compañero* — and his revolutionary enthusiasm on top of that, because he's an untiring worker — we now have almost the equivalent of an additional flour mill in Cuba. In other words, the *compañeros* of the flour mill — who have the moral incentive of being at the head of the people, being recognized as exemplary workers — must recognize that a part of this achievement belongs to that *compañero* who over several months provided all of his technical knowledge with unsurpassed enthusiasm.

To achieve this higher technology, to overcome all the stumbling blocks along our way, we need systematic training, systematic study.

One of the prize-winning enterprises today, a factory that is part of the tire enterprise — although the entire enterprise worked in the same way —

looked up one day, shortly after the factories were nationalized, and realized that the foreign technicians, and some Cubans too, had left the country. It was only through the effort of the workers of that enterprise, and of one Cuban technician who handled all the problems that arose, that the factory was kept running. They were able to overcome all the technical inconveniences, adapt technology to the new raw materials, and through continual changes they were able to increase the rate of production. Today it is one of the factories in the front ranks of production!

Enthusiasm, discipline, the spirit of self-sacrifice, working as hard as possible — none of these things will result in a great outcome if there is not also the necessary technical knowledge. Technical knowledge, then, together with constant training on all levels to obtain it, should also be a daily concern of the working class.

Let's not forget the basic technical course, the training course, nor the follow-up course! Let's not forget that each particle of knowledge we gain helps us cement the foundation of the future! Let's not think about our age or our lack of knowledge! Let's not analyze the impossibilities; let's analyze the possibilities, and sweep away the impossibilities! These should be our slogans. These should be the slogans of the working class at this time.

In other words, *compañeros*, work — the center of human activity and of the building of socialism — is what we are indirectly honoring here today. The efficiency of that work is determined by one's attitude toward it.

Once again we have to look at the past, the past that spilled over the barriers when the old society was destroyed and that continues in the workers' consciousness. In this case the past is reflected in the consciousness of many workers who see having to work every day as an oppressive necessity, a necessity one tries to avoid, thinking that the factory is still under the old boss, is still the way it was in the past.

Our attitude should be totally different. Work should be a moral necessity for us. Work should be somewhere we go every morning, every afternoon, or every night, with renewed enthusiasm and interest. We have to learn to extract from work what's interesting, what's creative, to know the tiniest secret of the machine or the work process.

If we don't like the job, let's acquire training to obtain one we do like. Work should always be part of the good life, something exciting, something associated with life's happiest moments, not its burdens.

This will be the great result when communist society is achieved in full. But in social processes, changes in men that appear abrupt actually come about little by little. At a given moment it appears that there may have been a great commotion and a single great change. But that change has been gestating among men day by day, and sometimes generation by generation.

We have to begin today adopting that new attitude toward work — new for some, because many pioneers have already begun adopting it. Each person should feel happy at work. They should feel happy with their task as creators. They should instill all those around them with their revolutionary and creative enthusiasm. They should spread their knowledge along with their enthusiasm. They should mobilize by example. They should not remain the only meritorious worker, the only exemplary worker, but should bring along all those capable of following their example. They should engage in emulation with everyone and should help them at the same time. They should make his enthusiasm take form among groups of workers. They should engage in emulation with other workers. This attitude toward work should be at the center of society, and we should always remember that the worker with the most dignity in the country is the one who can bear the title of outstanding worker in any sphere of production.

If we are going to achieve this, *compañeros* — let's not say if we'll do it today, tomorrow or yesterday, because it's a process. Alongside the most revolutionary workers there are some who don't yet feel the revolution as their own, and still others who have not resigned themselves to forgetting the past.

But if we keep on achieving as we have up to now — and at a faster pace than now — if every day each one of us who feels creative enthusiasm inside himself is able to incorporate one additional *compañero*, or can simply get him interested so that little by little he becomes incorporated into the work — if we do this, we'll advance with "seven-league boots." We'll advance rapidly toward building socialism, toward socialist society. The task has been laid out.

We should not leave this task up in the air, as something that's contained in some speech and is analyzed and discussed for one or two days after that. The task we've laid out should be taken up by the masses as the center of their activity. Let me stress and insist upon this.

Building socialism is based on the work of the masses, on the capacities of the masses to be able to organize themselves and to better guide industry, agriculture and the country's economy. It is based on the capacity of the masses to improve their knowledge every day; on their capacity to incorporate all the technicians, all the *compañeros* that have remained here to work with us in the revolution's tasks; on their capacity to create more products for all our people; on their capacity to see the approaching future — approaching in historical terms, not in the life of any one man — and to enter onto the road toward that future with enthusiasm.

Today we're honoring quite a few *compañeros*. Not merely the vanguard, they make up what we could call the spearhead of the vanguard, those who occupy the front rank, the first to confront danger.

We have issued a challenge for everyone to meet, the challenge for all of us to link arms in a single and unbroken chain, advancing as an unbroken and uncontainable wave. In this way we can arrive rapidly at the first stage of our journey and be able to say — already looking back at a past accomplishment:

We have reached socialism and we continue forward!

Venceremos! [We will win]

The cadre: Backbone of the revolution

(September 1962)

I t is not necessary to dwell on the characteristics of our revolution, on the original way, with strokes of spontaneity, that the transition took place from a revolution of national liberation to a socialist revolution. Nor on the accumulation of rapidly passing stages in the course of its development, led by the same people who participated in the initial epic of the attack on the Moncada garrison, proceeding through the *Granma* landing, and culminating in the declaration of the socialist character of the Cuban Revolution. New sympathizers, cadres and organizations joined the weak organizational structure of the early movement, until it became the flood of people that today characterizes our revolution.

When it became clear that a new social class had definitively taken command in Cuba, we also saw the great limitations that would be faced in the exercise of state power because of the conditions in which we found the state. There were no cadres to carry out the enormous number of jobs that had to be filled in the state apparatus, in the political organization, and on the entire economic front.

Immediately after the seizure of power, bureaucratic posts were filled simply by "pointing a finger." There were no major problems — there were none because the old structure had not yet been shattered. The apparatus functioned at the slow and weary pace of something old and almost lifeless. But it had an organization and within it sufficient coordination to maintain itself through inertia, disdaining the political changes that were taking place as a prelude to the change in the economic structure.

The July 26 Movement, deeply wounded by the internal struggles between its right and left wings, could not devote itself to tasks of construction; and the Popular Socialist Party, because it had endured fierce attacks and illegality for years, had not been able to develop intermediate cadres to handle the newly arising responsibilities.

When the first state interventions in the economy took place,[14] the task of finding cadres was not very complicated, and it was possible to choose from among many people who had some minimum basis for exercising positions of leadership. But with the acceleration of the process beginning with the nationalization of the U.S. enterprises and later of the large Cuban enterprises, a real hunger for administrative technicians came about. On the other hand, an urgent need was felt for production technicians because of the exodus of many who were attracted by better positions offered by the imperialist companies in other parts of Latin America or in the United States itself. While engaged in these organizational tasks, the political apparatus had to make an intense effort to provide ideological attention to the masses who had joined the revolution eager to learn.

We all performed our roles as well as we could, but not without problems and embarrassments. Many errors were committed in administrative areas on the central executive level. Enormous mistakes were made by the new administrators of enterprises, who had overwhelming responsibilities in their hands. We also committed big and costly errors in the political apparatus, which little by little degenerated into a pleasant and peaceful bureaucracy, seen almost as a springboard for promotions and for bureaucratic posts of greater or lesser importance, totally separated from the masses.

The main cause of our errors was our lack of a sense of reality at a given moment. But the tool that we lacked, which blunted our ability to see and was turning the party into a bureaucratic organization, endangering administration and production, was the lack of developed cadres at the intermediate level. It became evident that the development of cadres was synonymous with the policy of going to the masses. The watchword was to once again establish contact with the masses, a contact that had been closely maintained by the revolution in its earliest days. But this had to be established through some type of mechanism that would afford the most beneficial results, both in feeling the pulse of the masses and in the transmission of political leadership, which in many cases was only being given through the personal intervention of Prime Minister Fidel Castro or some other leaders of the revolution.

At this point, we can pose the question: What is a cadre? We should state that a cadre is an individual who has achieved sufficient political development to be able to interpret the larger directives emanating from the central authority, make them his own, and convey them as an orientation to the masses; a person who at the same time also perceives the signs manifested by the masses of their own desires and their innermost motivations.

A cadre is someone of ideological and administrative discipline, who knows and practices democratic centralism and who knows how to evaluate the contradictions in our current methods in order to make the best of them. In the field of production, he knows how to practice the principle of collective discussion and individual decision making and responsibility. He is an individual of proven loyalty, whose physical and moral courage has developed in step with his ideological development, in such a way that he is always willing to face any debate and to give even his life for the good of the revolution. He is, in addition, an individual who can think for himself, which enables him to make the necessary decisions and to exercise creative initiative in a way that does not conflict with discipline.

The cadre, therefore, is a creator, a leader of high standing, a technician with a good political level, who by reasoning dialectically can advance his sector of production, or develop the masses from his position of political leadership.

This exemplary human being, apparently cloaked in difficult-to-achieve virtues, is nonetheless present in the people of Cuba, and we encounter him daily. The essential thing is to take advantage of all the opportunities that exist to develop him to the maximum, to educate him, to draw from each individual the greatest benefit and convert it into the greatest value for the nation.

The development of a cadre is achieved through performing everyday tasks. But the tasks must be undertaken systematically, in special schools where competent teachers — examples in their own right for the students — will encourage the most rapid ideological advancement.

In a system that is beginning to build socialism, cadres must clearly be highly developed politically. But when we consider political development we must take into account not only knowledge of Marxist theory. We must also demand responsibility of the individual for his actions, a discipline that restrains any passing weaknesses and that is not at odds with a big dose of initiative. And we must demand constant preoccupation with all the revolution's problems. In order to develop a cadre, we must begin by establishing the principle of selection among the masses. It is there that we find the individuals who are developing, tested by sacrifice or just beginning to show their concerns, and assign them to special schools; or when these are not available, give them greater responsibility so that they are tested in practical work.

In this way, we have been finding a multitude of new cadres who have developed in recent years. But their development has not been an even one, since the young *compañeros* have had to face the reality of revolutionary creation without an adequate party leadership. Some have succeeded fully, but there were others who could not completely make it and were left midway, or were simply lost in the bureaucratic labyrinth, or in the temptations that power brings.

To assure the triumph and the total consolidation of the revolution, we have to develop different types of cadres. We need the political cadre who will be the foundation of our mass organizations, and who will lead the masses through the action of the United Party of the Socialist Revolution.[15] (We are already beginning to establish this foundation with the national and provincial Schools of Revolutionary Instruction and with studies and study groups at all levels.) We also need military cadres. To achieve that, we can utilize the selection the war made among our young combatants, since there are still many living who are without great theoretical knowledge but who were tested under fire. They were tested under the most difficult conditions of the struggle, with a fully proven loyalty to the revolutionary regime with whose birth and development they have been so intimately connected since the first guerrilla battles of the Sierra. We should also develop economic cadres who will dedicate themselves specifically to the difficult tasks of planning and the tasks of the organization of the socialist state in these moments of creation.

It is necessary to work with the professionals, urging the youth to follow one of the more important technical careers in an effort to give science the energy of ideological enthusiasm that will guarantee accelerated development. And it is imperative to create an administrative team that will know how to take advantage of and adapt the special technical knowledge of others and guide the enterprises and other organizations of the state to bring them into step with the powerful rhythm of the revolution.

The common denominator for all of these cadres is political clarity. This does not consist of unthinking support for the postulates of the revolution, but a reasoned support. It requires great capacity for sacrifice and a capacity for dialectical analysis, which will enable them to make continuous contributions on all levels to the rich theory and practice of the revolution. These *compañeros* should be selected from the masses solely by application of the principle that the best will come to the fore and that the best should be given the greatest opportunities for development.

In all these situations, the function of the cadre is the same, on each of the different fronts. The cadre is the key component of the ideological motor that is the United Party of the Revolution. It is something that we could call the dynamic gear of that motor. A gear inasmuch as he is a working part of the motor, making sure it works right. Dynamic inasmuch as he is not simply a transmitter of slogans or demands upward or downward, but a creator who will aid in the development of the masses and the information of the leaders, serving as a point of contact between them. The cadre has the important mission of seeing to it that the great spirit of the revolution is not dissipated, that it will not become dormant nor slacken its rhythm. It is a sensitive position. He transmits what comes from the masses and instills in the masses the party's orientation.

Therefore, the development of cadres is now a task that cannot be postponed. The development of cadres has been undertaken with great determination by the revolutionary government with its programs of scholarships based on the principles of selection; with its programs of study for workers, offering various opportunities for technological development; with the development of the special technical schools; with the development of secondary schools and universities, opening new careers. It has been done, in short, with the development of study, work and revolutionary vigilance as watchwords for our entire country, fundamentally based on the UJC, from which all types of cadres should emerge in the future, even the leading cadres of the revolution.

Intimately linked to the concept of "cadre" is the concept of capacity for sacrifice, for demonstrating through personal example the truths and watchwords of the revolution. The cadres, as political leaders, should gain the respect of the workers by their actions. It is absolutely imperative that they have the respect and affection of their *compañeros*, whom they must guide along the vanguard paths.

Because of all this, there are no better cadres than those chosen by the masses in the assemblies that select the exemplary workers, those who will join the PURS along with the old members of the ORI who pass all the required tests of selection. At the beginning they will constitute a small party, but with enormous influence among the workers. Later it will grow when the advance of socialist consciousness begins making work and total devotion to the cause of the people into a necessity. With intermediate leaders of this quality, the difficult tasks that we have before us will be accomplished with fewer mistakes. After a period of confusion and poor methods, we have arrived at a correct policy that will never be abandoned. With the ever-renewed impulse of the working class nourishing from its inexhaustible fountain the ranks of the future United Party of the Socialist Revolution, and with the leadership of our party, we fully undertake the task of forming cadres who will guarantee the vigorous development of our revolution. We must triumph in this effort.

To be a Young Communist

(October 20, 1962)

On October 21, 1960, youth from the July 26 Movement, the Revolutionary Directorate and the PSP's Socialist Youth merged into the Association of Young Rebels. On April 4, 1962, this organization adopted the name Union of Young Communists (UJC). The following speech was presented at a ceremony marking the second anniversary of the unification.

ne of the most pleasant tasks of a revolutionary is observing over the years of revolution how the institutions that were born at the very beginning are taking shape, being refined and strengthened; how they are being turned into real institutions with power, vigor and authority among the masses. Those organizations that started off on a small scale with numerous difficulties and hesitations became, through daily work and contact with the masses, powerful representatives of today's revolutionary movement.

The Union of Young Communists [UJC], with different names and organizational forms, is almost as old as the revolution. At the beginning it emerged out of the Rebel Army — perhaps that's where it also got its initial name [Association of Young Rebels]. But it was an organization linked to the army in order to introduce Cuba's youth to the massive tasks of national defense, the most urgent problem at the time and the one requiring the most rapid solution.

The Association of Young Rebels and the Revolutionary National Militia grew out of what used to be the Rebel Army's Department of Instruction. Later, each took on a life of its own. One became a powerful formation of the armed people, representing the armed people, with a standing of its own but united with our army in the tasks of defense. The other became an organization whose purpose was the political advancement of Cuban youth.

Later, as the revolution was consolidated and we could finally talk about the new tasks ahead, *compañero* Fidel proposed changing the name of the organization, a change of name that fully expresses a principle. The

UJC has its face to the future. It is organized with the bright future of socialist society in mind, after we travel the difficult road we are now on of constructing a new society, then the road of completely solidifying the class dictatorship expressed throughout the socialist stage of society, to finally arrive at a society without classes, the perfect society, the society you will be in charge of building, guiding and leading in the future. For that, the UJC raises as its symbols those of all Cubans: study, work and the rifle. On its medallions appear two of the finest examples of Cuban youth, both of whom met tragic deaths before being able to witness the final results of this battle we are all engaged in: Julio Antonio Mella and Camilo Cienfuegos.

On this second anniversary, at this time of hectic construction, of ongoing preparations for the country's defense and of the speediest possible technical and technological advance, we must always ask ourselves first and foremost: What is the Union of Young Communists and what should it be?

The Union of Young Communists should be defined by a single word: *vanguard*. You, *compañeros*, must be the vanguard of all movements, the first to be ready to make the sacrifices demanded by the revolution, whatever they might be. You must be the first in work, the first in study, the first in defense of the country. You must view this task not only as the full expression of Cuba's youth, not only as a task of the organized masses, but as the daily task of each and every member of the UJC. In order to do that, you have to set yourself real, concrete tasks, tasks in your daily work that won't allow the slightest letup.

The job of organizing must constantly be linked to all the work carried out by the UJC. Organization is the key to grasping the initiatives presented by the revolution's leaders, the many initiatives proposed by our prime minister, and the initiatives from the working class, which should also lead to precise directives and ideas for subsequent action. Without organization, ideas, after an initial momentum, start losing their effect. They become routine, degenerate into conformity, and end up simply a memory. I make this warning because too often, in this short but rich period of our revolution, many great initiatives have failed. They have been forgotten because of the lack of the organizational apparatus needed to keep them going and accomplish something.

At the same time, each and every one of you should know that being a Young Communist, belonging to the UJC, is not a favor someone has done for you, nor is it a favor that you are doing for the state or the revolution. Membership in the UJC should be the highest honor for a young person in the new society, an honor that you fight for at all times. In addition, the honor of remaining in and keeping a high individual standing in the UJC should be an ongoing effort. In that way we will advance even faster, as we become used to thinking collectively and acting on the initiatives of the working masses and of our top leaders. At the same time, in everything we do as individuals, we should always be making sure our actions will not tarnish our own name or the name of the association to which we belong.

Now, two years later, we can look back and observe the results of our work. The UJC has tremendous achievements, one of the most important and spectacular being in defense.

Those young people, or some of them, who first climbed the five peaks of Turquino,[16] others who were enrolled in a whole series of military organizations, all those who picked up their rifles at moments of danger — they were ready to defend the revolution each and every place where an invasion or enemy action was expected. The highest honor, that of being able to defend our revolution, fell to the young people at Playa Girón.[17] At Playa Girón they had the honor of defending the institutions we have created through sacrifice, defending the accomplishments won by all the people over years of struggle. Our entire revolution was defended there in 72 hours of battle. The intention of the enemy was to create a sufficiently strong beachhead there, with an airfield that would allow it to attack our entire territory, to bomb it mercilessly, reduce our factories to ashes and our means of communication to dust, ruin our agriculture — in a word, to sow chaos across the country. But our people's decisive action wiped out that imperialist attack in only 72 hours. There, young people, many of them still children, were covered in glory. Some of them are here as examples of that heroic youth. As for others, only their memory remains, spurring us on to new battles that we will surely have to fight, to new heroic responses in the face of imperialist attack.

At the moment when the country's defense was our most important task, the youth were there. Today, defense is still at the top of our concerns. But we should not forget that the watchword that guides the Young Communists — study, work and the rifle — is a unified whole. The country cannot be defended with arms alone. We must also defend the country by building it with our work and preparing the new technical cadres to speed up its development in the coming years. This is enormously important now, just as important as armed defense. When these problems were raised, the youth once again were there. Youth brigades, responding to the call of the revolution, invaded every corner of the country, and so after a few months of hard battle in which there were also martyrs of our revolution — martyrs in education — we were able to announce something new in Latin America: Cuba was a territory free of illiteracy in the Americas.[18]

Study at all levels is also a task of today's youth; study combined with work, as in the case of those students picking coffee in Oriente, using their vacations to pick that bean so important to our country, to our foreign trade and to ourselves, who consume a tremendous amount of coffee every day. That task is similar to the literacy campaign. It is a task of sacrifice that is carried out joyfully, bringing student *compañeros* together once more in the mountains of our country, taking their revolutionary message.

This task is very important because the UJC, the Young Communists, not only give in this work but also receive. In some cases they receive more than they give. They receive new experiences: new experiences in human contact, new experiences in seeing how our peasants live, in learning what life and work are like in the most out-of-the-way places, in everything that has to be done to bring those areas up to the same level as the cities and to make the countryside a better place to live. They receive experience and revolutionary maturity. *Compañeros* who go through the tasks of teaching reading and writing or picking coffee, of being in direct contact with our people, helping them while far away from home, receive — and I can vouch for this — much more than they give. And they give a lot!

This is the kind of education that best suits youth who are being educated for communism. It is a kind of education in which work stops being an obsession, as it is in the capitalist world, and becomes a pleasant social duty, done joyfully to the rhythm of revolutionary songs, amid the most fraternal camaraderie and human relationships that are mutually invigorating and uplifting.

In addition, the UJC has advanced a lot in its organization. There is a big difference between that weak embryo that was formed as a branch of the Rebel Army and this organization today. There are Young Communists all over, in every workplace, in every administrative body. Wherever they can have an effect, there they are, Young Communists working for the revolution. The organizational progress must also be considered an important achievement of the UJC.

Nevertheless, *compañeros*, there have been many problems along this difficult road, big difficulties, gross errors, and we have not always been able to overcome them all. It is obvious that the Union of Young Communists, as a youth organization, a younger brother of the Integrated Revolutionary Organizations, must drink from the fountain of experiences of *compañeros* who have worked longer in all the tasks of the revolution. It is obvious that they should always listen, and listen with respect, to the voice of that experience. But the youth also must create. Youth that does not create is really an anomaly. The UJC has been a bit lacking in that creative spirit. Through its leadership it has been too docile, too respectful and not decisive in looking at problems on its own. Now that is breaking down. *Compañero* Joel [Iglesias] was telling us about the initiatives regarding work on state farms. That is an example of how total dependency on the older organization, which became an absurdity, is beginning to break down, of how the youth are beginning to think for themselves.

Because we, and our youth along with us, are recovering from an illness that fortunately was not a very long one but that had a lot to do with the ideological development of our revolution. We are all convalescing from the illness called sectarianism. What did sectarianism lead to? It led to mechanical imitation; it led to formal analyses; it led to separation of the leadership from the masses. It led to these things even within our National Directorate, and it had a direct reflection here in the UJC.

If we, also disoriented by sectarianism, could not hear the voice of the people, which is the wisest and most instructive voice; if we could not feel the pulse of the people to be able to turn it into concrete ideas, precise guidelines, how could we communicate these guidelines to the UJC? Since the dependency was absolute and the docility very great, the UJC was like a small boat adrift, depending upon the big ship, our Integrated Revolutionary Organizations, which was also adrift. So, the UJC took a series of minor initiatives, all it was capable of then, which at times became transformed into crude slogans, manifestations of a lack of ideological depth.

Compañero Fidel made a series of criticisms of extremism and sloganeering, some well known to all of you such as "The ORI lights the way" and "We are socialists, go, go, go… " All those things you are so familiar with and that Fidel criticized were a reflection of the illness affecting our revolution. That era is over. We have completely wiped it out.

Nevertheless, organizations always lag behind a bit. It's like a disease that makes a person lose consciousness. Once the illness goes away, the brain recuperates and mental clarity returns, but the arms and legs remain slightly uncoordinated. Those first days after getting out of bed, walking is shaky, then little by little it becomes surer. That is the road we are now on. And we must objectively define and analyze all our organizations so we can continue our housecleaning. We must realize that we are still walking shakily so as not to fall, not to trip and fall to the ground. We must understand our weaknesses in order to eliminate them and gain strength.

This lack of initiative is due to a longstanding ignorance of the dialectic that moves mass organizations, forgetting that an organization like the UJC cannot be a leadership organization that simply sends directives to the ranks all the time and doesn't listen to anything they have to say. It was thought that the UJC or all Cuba's other organizations had one-way lines, one-way lines from the leadership to the ranks, without another line that came the other way and brought communication back from the ranks. It is this constant two-way exchange of experiences and ideas that should produce the most important guidelines, those that can focus the work of our youth. At the same time this can help identify the weakest areas of work, the areas where there is a slackening off.

We still see today how the youth — heroes almost like in the novels — who can give their lives a hundred times over for the revolution, who can respond as one to whatever specific task they are called upon for, nevertheless sometimes do not show up at work because they had a UJC meeting. Or because they stayed up late the night before discussing some initiative of the youth organization. Or sometimes for no reason at all, with no justifiable reason. So when a volunteer work brigade looks around to see where the Young Communists are, they are often absent; they haven't shown up. The leader had a meeting to attend, another one was sick, still another was not really told about the work.

The result is that the fundamental attitude, the attitude of being a vanguard of the people, the attitude of that moving, living example that drives everybody forward as did the youth at Playa Girón — that attitude is not duplicated at work. The seriousness that today's youth must have in meeting its great commitments — and the major commitment is the construction of socialist society — is not reflected in actual work. There are big weaknesses and we must work on them, work at organizing, work at defining the sore spot, the area with weaknesses to be corrected. Each one of you has to work on having it very clear in your consciousness that you cannot be a good communist if you think about the revolution only at the moment of decisive sacrifice, at the moment of combat, of heroic adventure, of what is out of the plain and ordinary, but in your work you are mediocre or less than mediocre. How can that be?

You already bear the name Young Communists, a name we as a leadership organization, as a leadership party, do not yet have. You have to build a future in which work will be man's greatest dignity, a social duty, a pleasure given to man, the most creative activity there is. Everyone will have to be interested in their work and the work of others, in society's daily advance. How can it be that you who bear that name today can disdain work? There is a weakness here, a weakness in organization, in clarifying what work is.

This is a natural human weakness. People — all of us, it seems to me — much prefer something that breaks the monotony of life, something every once in a while that suddenly reminds us of our own personal worth, of our worth within society. I can imagine the pride of those *compañeros* who were manning an antiaircraft battery, for example, defending their homeland from Yankee planes. Suddenly, one of them is lucky enough to see his bullets hit an enemy plane. Clearly, that is the happiest moment of a man's life, something never to be forgotten. Those *compañeros* who lived through that experience will never forget it. We have to defend our revolution, that revolution we are building, every day. And in order to defend it we have to make it, build it, fortify it, with the work that youth doesn't like today, or at least gets left as the last of its duties. That is an old-fashioned mentality that dates back to the capitalist world, where work was indeed a duty and a necessity, but a sad duty and necessity.

Why does that happen? Because we still have not been able to give work its true content. We have not been able to imbue the worker with a consciousness of the importance of that creative act that he performs every day. The worker and the machine, the worker and the object to which he applies his labor — these are still different and antagonistic things. That has to be changed, because new generations must be formed whose main interest is work and who know how to find in work a permanent and constantly changing source of fresh excitement. They need to make work something creative, something new. That is perhaps the weakest point in our UJC today, and that is why I am harping on it. That's why, amidst the happiness of celebrating your anniversary, I am adding a small drop of bitterness in order to touch that sensitive spot, and to call on the youth to respond.

Today we held a meeting at the Ministry [of Industry] where we discussed emulation. Many of you have probably already discussed emulation at your workplaces and have read that long paper about it. What is the problem with emulation, *compañeros*? The problem is that emulation cannot be led by papers containing rules, orders and models. Rules and models are necessary later on in order to compare the work of enthusiastic people who are involved in emulation. When two *compañeros* begin an emulation with each one producing something on a machine, after a while they find they have to set up some rule to know who is getting the most out of his machine, to determine product quality, the number of hours worked, what shape the machines are in when they finish, how they are taken care of, any number of things.

But if instead of giving this set of rules to these two *compañeros* who are involved in emulation, all we do is give the set of rules to two others who are thinking only about getting home, then what good are the rules? What purpose do they serve? We often set rules and models for something that does not exist. Models must have content. Rules have to limit and define an already created situation. Rules must be the result of emulation, carried out anarchistically if you will, yes, but enthusiastically, overflowing in every workplace in Cuba, and then, automatically, the need for rules will appear. But doing emulation for the sake of a set of rules, no. That's how we have dealt with a lot of problems. That's how formal we've been in dealing with a lot of things.

I asked at that meeting why the secretary of the Young Communists hadn't been there, or how many times he had been there. He had been there once or a few times, and other Young Communists had never attended. But in the course of the meeting, as we were discussing this and other problems, the Young Communists and the party nucleus and the women and the Committees for the Defense of the Revolution and the union — everyone — naturally became very enthusiastic. Or at least they were filled with internal resentment, with bitterness, with a desire to improve, with a desire to show they could do what has not been done: motivate people. And suddenly, everybody made a commitment that the whole ministry would become involved in emulation on all levels, that they would discuss rules later, after setting up the emulation, and that within two weeks the whole ministry would be actively involved in emulation. That is mobilization. That is people who have already understood and sensed — because each of those *compañeros* is a great *compañero* — that there was a weakness in their work. Their dignity was wounded, and they went about taking care of the problem.

That is what has to be done, remembering that work is the most important thing. Pardon me if I repeat it once again, but the point is that without work there is nothing. All the riches in the world, all humanity's values, are nothing but accumulated work. Without that, nothing can exist. Without the extra work that creates more surpluses for new factories and social institutions, the country will not advance. No matter how strong our armies are, we will always have a slow rhythm of growth. We have to break out of this. We have to break with all the old errors, hold them up to the light of day, analyze them everywhere, and then correct them.

Now, *compañeros*, I wanted to share my opinion as a national leader of the ORI on what a Young Communist should be, to see if we all agree. I believe that the first thing that must characterize a Young Communist is the honor he feels in being a Young Communist, an honor that moves him to let the world know he is a Young Communist. It doesn't make him go underground, nor does he reduce it to formulas. He expresses that honor at all times, so that it comes from the bottom of his soul, and he wants to show it because it is his greatest pride. In addition to that, he should have a great sense of duty, a sense of duty toward the society we are building, toward our fellow men as human beings and toward all men around the world. That is something that must characterize the Young Communist. And along with that: deep sensitivity to all problems, sensitivity to injustice; a spirit that rebels against every wrong, whoever commits it; questioning anything not understood, discussing and asking for clarification on whatever is not clear; declaring war on formalism of all types; always being open to new experiences in order to apply the many years of experience of humanity's advance along the road to socialism to our country's concrete conditions, to the realities that exist in Cuba. Each and every one of you must think about how to change reality, how to make it better.

The Young Communist must always strive to be the best at everything, struggle to be the best, feel upset when he is not and fight to improve, to be the best. Of course, we cannot all be the best. But we can be among the best, in the vanguard. We can be a living example, a model for those *compañeros* who do not belong to the Young Communists, an example for older men and women who have lost some of that youthful enthusiasm, who have lost a certain faith in life, and who always respond well to example. That is another task of Young Communists. Together with that there should be a great spirit of sacrifice, not only in heroic ventures but at all times, sacrificing to help the next *compañero* in small tasks so he can finish his work, so he can do his work at school, in his studies, so he can improve in any way.

Always paying attention to the mass of human beings he lives among — that is, every Young Communist must be essentially human and be so human that he draws closer to humanity's best qualities, that he distills the best of what man is through work, study, through ongoing solidarity with the people and all the peoples of the world. Developing to the utmost the sensitivity to feel anguished when a man is murdered in any corner of the world and to feel enthusiasm when a new banner of freedom is raised in any corner of the world.

The Young Communist cannot be limited by national borders. The Young Communist must practice proletarian internationalism and feel it as his own, reminding himself and all of us — Young Communists and those aspiring to be communists here in Cuba — that we are a real and palpable example for all our America, and for more than our America, for the other countries of the world also fighting on other continents for freedom, against colonialism, against neocolonialism, against imperialism, against all forms of oppression by unjust systems. He must always remember that we are a flaming torch, that just as we are all individually a model for the people of Cuba, we are also a model for the peoples of Latin America and the oppressed peoples of the world who are fighting for their freedom. We must be worthy of that example. At every moment and every hour we must be worthy of that example. That is what we think a Young Communist should be.

If someone says we are just romantics, inveterate idealists, thinking the impossible, that the masses of people cannot be turned into almost perfect human beings, we will have to answer a thousand and one times: Yes, it can be done; we are right. The people as a whole can advance. They can wipe out all those little human vices as we have been doing in Cuba over these four years of revolution, improving themselves as we all improve ourselves daily, intransigently casting off all those who fall back, who cannot march to the rhythm of the Cuban Revolution.

So it has to be, so it should be, and so it will be, *compañeros*. So it will be because you are Young Communists, creators of the perfect society, human beings destined to live in a new world where everything decrepit, everything old, everything that represents the society whose foundations have just been destroyed will have definitively disappeared. To reach that goal we have to work every day, work in the inner sense of improving ourselves, of gaining knowledge and understanding about the world around us, of inquiring, finding out, and knowing why things are the way they are and always considering humanity's great problems as our own.

Thus, at any given moment, on an ordinary day in the years ahead, after much sacrifice... yes, after seeing ourselves perhaps many times on the brink of destruction, perhaps after seeing our factories destroyed and having rebuilt them, after the death and massacre of many of us and the reconstruction of what is destroyed... After all this, on an ordinary day, almost without noticing it, we will have created — together with the other peoples of the world — communist society, our ideal.

Compañeros, speaking to the youth is a very pleasant task. You feel able to communicate some things and you feel that the youth understand. There are many more things I would like to say to you about all our efforts, our desires, about how, nevertheless, we have to start all over after moments of weakness, about how contact with the people — the purity and ideals of the people — fills us with new revolutionary fervor. There are many more things to talk about, but we too have duties to carry out.

By the way, I will take this opportunity to explain to you why I am saying goodbye to you, with an ulterior motive, perhaps. I am saying goodbye because I am going to fulfill my duty as a volunteer worker at a textile factory. We have been working there for some time now, involved in an emulation with the Consolidated Spinning and Textile Enterprise in another textile plant, and we are also emulating with the Central Planning Board, which works in another textile plant. I want to tell you honestly that the Ministry of Industry is in last place in the emulation. We have to make a bigger, greater effort, repeatedly, to move ahead, to meet the goals we ourselves set of being the best, of aspiring to be the best, because it hurts us to be last in socialist emulation. What happened is simply what has happened to a lot of you. The emulation is cold, a little bit artificial, and we have not known how to get in direct contact with the mass of workers in that industry. We have a meeting tomorrow to discuss these problems and try to resolve all of them, to find a common ground, a common language, an absolute identity between the workers from that industry and us workers from the Ministry. After we do that, I am sure our output will shoot up, and we will be able to at least fight a clean, honorable battle for first place. At any rate, at next year's meeting we will tell you what happens. So until then.

A party of the working class

(1963)

Guevara wrote this article as an introduction to a book entitled The Marxist-Leninist Party, *published by the National Directorate of the United Party of the Socialist Revolution.*

This small book aims to introduce party members to the extensive and very rich body of Marxist-Leninist ideas.

The choice of themes is simple and effective. It includes a chapter from the *Manual of Marxism-Leninism* by Otto V. Kuusinen and a series of speeches by Fidel Castro. The selection is good, because the chapter from the *Manual of Marxism-Leninism* synthesizes the experiences of fraternal parties and offers a general outline of what a Marxist-Leninist party should be and how it should act. The section containing speeches by *compañero* Fidel presents the course of our country's political history through the words — in some cases autobiographical — of the revolution's leader.

The two things are closely linked: the general theory as an expression of the experiences of the Communist Party of the Soviet Union and other Marxist-Leninist parties around the world, and the practical application of these general ideas to our special characteristics. From the peculiarities that form the framework of the development of social phenomena in this part of the world, one should not infer that historical exceptions exist. Rather, the specific case of Cuba fits into the general framework of the theory, which is the fruit of the experience of the international workers' movement, adding new experiences to it.

The manual shows us with dazzling clarity what a Marxist-Leninist party is: "Persons united around common ideas, who join together to give life to Marxist ideas, that is, to carry out the historic mission of the working class." It also explains that a party cannot exist isolated from the masses; that it must be in permanent contact with them; that it must practice criticism and self-criticism and be very severe with respect to its own errors; that it must base itself not only on negative concepts of struggle against something, but also on positive concepts of struggle for something. It explains that Marxist parties cannot just sit back and wait for the objective and subjective conditions — which are formed through the complex mechanism of the class struggle — to meet all the necessary requirements for power to fall into the hands of the people like ripe fruit. The manual teaches about the leading and catalyzing role of the party: the vanguard of the working class, the leader of its class, which knows how to show it the road to victory and speed the way to new social conditions. It insists that even in moments of social ebb, it is necessary to know how to retreat and keep cadres firm in order to gain strength from the next wave and thereby advance closer toward the party's fundamental goal in the first revolutionary period: conquering power.

Naturally, the party must be a class party. A Marxist-Leninist party could hardly be anything else. Its mission is to find the shortest route to achieving the dictatorship of the proletariat. Its best members, its leading cadres, and its tactics all come from the working class.

One cannot conceive of beginning the building of socialism with a party of the bourgeois class, with a party having a lot of exploiters in its ranks, and with these exploiters entrusted with setting its political line. Clearly, a group of this sort can lead the struggle only in a national liberation stage, up to a certain level and under specific circumstances. In the following stage, the revolutionary class would become reactionary, and new conditions would be established that would require the appearance of a Marxist-Leninist party as the leader of the revolutionary struggle. Already, in Latin America at least, it is practically impossible to speak of liberation movements led by the bourgeoisie. The Cuban Revolution has polarized the forces. Faced with the dilemma of choosing between the people or imperialism, the weak national bourgeoisies choose imperialism and definitively betray their country. In this part of the world the possibility is almost totally gone for there to be a peaceful transition to socialism.

If the Marxist-Leninist party is able to foresee the coming historical stages, and is capable of becoming the banner and vanguard of the people even before having completed the national liberation stage — speaking of the colonial countries — then this party will have accomplished a dual historical mission, and it will be able to face the tasks of building socialism with greater strength, with greater authority among the masses.

Then there is the Cuban experience — a rich experience because of all that is new, because of all its vigor in this period of the development of the Latin American revolution, and also because of the rich lessons to be drawn from its mistakes, which are analyzed and corrected publicly, in contact with the masses and facing the judgment of public opinion.

Particularly important are the speeches of *compañero* Fidel referring to the United Party of the Socialist Revolution and to the methods of work employed in the ORI, which mark two fundamental stages of our development. In the first speech [of December 2, 1961], Fidel talks about the previous confusion of a thoroughgoing revolutionary who, having now arrived at the pinnacle of the ascending road in the evolution of his thinking, proclaims, without any doubts and to the whole world, his Marxist-Leninist convictions. He does this not by making a simple verbal affirmation, but by pointing out the features, the most outstanding events in his evolution as a leader, in the evolution of the movement and the party toward a fusion aimed at forming the United Party of the Socialist Revolution.

Analyzing himself, *compañero* Fidel recognizes that he had absorbed a large number of backward ideas from society. He recounts how instinctively he struggled against these and how he was forged through the struggle. He recounts his doubts and explains the reasons for them and how they were resolved.

During this stage, the July 26 Movement was something new, something very difficult to define: Fidel Castro, the hero of Moncada, a prisoner on the Isle of Pines, trains a group of expeditionaries who have as their mission to reach the shores of Oriente Province, to start the revolutionary fire in that province and separate it from the rest of the island at first, or to advance inexorably, in accordance with objective conditions, to Havana itself, in a succession of more or less bloody victories.

Reality struck us hard. The subjective conditions needed to bring about that end had not yet been established. We had not followed all the rules of revolutionary warfare, which we would later learn with our blood and the blood of our brothers during two years of hard struggle. We were defeated, and it was then that the most important history of our movement began. Then it showed its true strength, its true historical merit. We realized we had committed tactical errors and that some important subjective factors were missing. The people were conscious of the need for change but were not certain it was possible. The task was to create that certainty, and it was in the Sierra Maestra that the long process began that served as the catalyst for the entire movement on the island, eventually provoking uninterrupted hurricanes, uninterrupted revolutionary fires throughout the territory.

It began to be demonstrated with deeds that the revolutionary army — providing a correct orientation to the faith and enthusiasm of the people, and given favorable conditions for the struggle — could gradually increase its strength through the proper use of weapons and one day destroy the enemy army. That is a great lesson in our history. Before achieving victory, the relationship of forces kept changing until it became overwhelmingly favorable to the revolutionary movement. The necessary subjective conditions to carry out the change were created, and we brought about the crisis of power essential for a change to take place. Latin America was given a new revolutionary experience. It was demonstrated that the great truths of Marxism-Leninism are always fulfilled. In this case, it was shown that the mission of the leaders and of the parties is to create all the necessary conditions for taking power and not to become new spectators of the revolutionary wave being born from within the people.

At the same time, by demonstrating the need for the armed nuclei that can defend the people's sovereignty against surprises, attacks and destruction, the Cuban experience shows how important it is for the armed struggle to be fought on the terrain most favorable for guerrilla warfare, that is, the most rugged rural areas. This is another of the revolution's contributions to our struggle for the emancipation of Latin America. We went from the countryside to the city, from lesser to greater, creating the revolutionary movement that culminated in Havana.

Elsewhere, Fidel clearly states that the essential quality of a revolutionary is to know how to interpret reality. Referring to the April 1958 strike, he explains that we were unable to interpret the situation at that time and thus we suffered a catastrophe. Why was the April strike declared? Because within the movement there were a series of contradictions between what we called the *Sierra* and the *Llano*. These surfaced over the analysis of what elements should be considered fundamental to a victory in the armed struggle, and each wing had a diametrically different view of what these elements were.

The *Sierra* was ready to defeat the army as many times as necessary, to win battle after battle, to seize its weapons and to arrive some day at the total seizure of power on the basis of its Rebel Army. The *Llano* was for generalized armed struggle throughout the country culminating in a revolutionary general strike that would expel the Batista dictatorship and establish the rule of "civilian" authority, making the new army "apolitical."

The clash between these views was constant and not the most appropriate for the unity of command necessary at moments like that. The April strike was prepared and decreed by the *Llano* with the consent of the *Sierra* leadership, which despite serious doubts about the outcome did not feel capable of preventing it, and with the explicit reservations of the PSP, which warned of the danger in time. The revolutionary commanders went down into the plains to help with the strike and that was how Camilo Cienfuegos, our unforgettable army chief, began his first incursions into the Bayamo region.

The roots of those contradictions went deeper than mere tactical disagreements. The Rebel Army was already proletarian in its ideology, and it thought in terms of the dispossessed class. The *Llano* continued to be petty bourgeois, with future traitors among its leadership and heavily influenced by the milieu in which it worked.

It was a secondary struggle for internal control within the framework of the great revolutionary struggle for power. The recent events in Algeria can be explained clearly through analogy with the Cuban Revolution. The revolutionary wing did not allow itself to be displaced from power and fought until power was completely in its hands. The liberation army was the genuine representative of the revolution that triumphed.

The clashes broke out periodically, and a unified command was achieved (although it was still not heeded by everyone) only when Fidel was appointed prime minister, some months after the triumph of the revolution. Until that point, what had we accomplished? As Fidel put it, we had acquired the right to begin. We had only reached the end of one stage, based on a fight to the death against the existing system in Cuba, represented by the dictator Batista. But the fact that we had consistently followed a revolutionary line aimed at improving the condition of our society and liberating it as much as possible from all economic shackles forced us into a head-on struggle with imperialism.

Imperialism has been a very important factor in the development and deepening of our ideology. Each blow dealt by imperialism called for a response. Each time the Yankees reacted with their habitual arrogance, by taking some action against Cuba, we had to adopt the necessary countermeasures, and thereby the revolution deepened.

The Popular Socialist Party entered this front, and the *compañeros* who had long been members of the revolutionary movement and the *compañeros* who had come to power through the struggle in the Sierra began the task of fusion. Already at that time Fidel had warned against some dangers of sectarianism, and he criticized those who rubbed other people's noses in their own 15 or 20 years of party membership, as well as the sectarianism of the "bearded ones" from the Sierra or the "shoot'em-ups" from the cities.

During the period of the armed struggle, there was a group of *compañeros* who tried to protect the movement from *compañero* Fidel's apparent caudillismo and they made the mistake — which would be repeated later on during the period of sectarianism — of confusing the great merits of the revolution's leader and his undeniable talent of commanding, with an individual whose only concern was assuring the unconditional support of his followers and establishing a caudillo system. It was a fight waged by a group of *compañeros* on the basis of false principles; a fight that did not end on January 1 nor even when Fidel became Prime Minister, but only much later, when the right wing of the July 26 Movement was destroyed. That is how, for opposing the people's will, traitors such as [Manuel] Urrutia, [José] Miró Cardona, [Manuel] Ray, Huber Matos, David Salvador, and many others fell.

After the total victory over the right wing, there arose the need to structure a party: the United Party of the Revolution, the champion of Marxism-Leninism in the new conditions of Cuba. It had to be an organization linked to the masses through rigorously selected cadres of a centralized, yet flexible, organization. For all of this, we blindly put our confidence in the authority gained by the Popular Socialist Party over many years of struggle, giving up almost all of our organizational criteria. In this way, a series of conditions were created that allowed the fruit of sectarianism to ripen.

In this process of structuring, *compañero* Aníbal Escalante was put in charge of organization and a dark — although happily, very short — stage in our development began. Mistakes were made in methods of leadership. The party was losing its essential links with the masses, losing democratic centralism and its spirit of self-sacrifice. At times, through real juggling acts, persons without experience and without merit were put in leadership positions simply because they had accommodated themselves to the status quo.

The ORI lost its function as an ideological motor force — and its corresponding control over the entire productive apparatus — and became an administrative apparatus. Under these circumstances, warnings that should have come from the provinces explaining the series of problems that existed there got lost, since those who were supposed to analyze the work of the administrative officials were precisely the ORI leaders who were carrying out a dual function: party and public administration.

Fortunately, the stage of mistaken concepts, great big mistakes, and mechanical transplants has come to an end. The old foundations of this sectarian concoction have been broken.

In the face of these problems, the decision of the National Directorate, headed by Fidel, was to turn to the masses, to appeal to the masses. A system of consultation with all work centers was established in order for the masses to elect exemplary workers, with the possibility that these would be selected to join the nuclei of the party, of a party intimately linked to the masses.

As part of these changes in the party, its education system was reformed. In the past period the "enlightened" and the "professors of Marxism" had been given priority. Now, first place would go to the best workers, to men who — through their attitude toward the revolution, their daily work, their enthusiasm, and their spirit of self-sacrifice — had demonstrated the superior qualities required of members of the leading party.

In keeping with this we changed all the criteria and began a new period of strengthening the party and its methods. Opening up before us is a wide and bright road of socialist construction, in which the party's task is to lead. This leadership will not be a leadership of mechanical and bureaucratic orders; of narrow and sectarian control; of issuing commands; of advice that has to be followed just because some leaders say so, or because of their past ideas or long record, rather than on the basis of the living example that they are setting.

The party of the future will be intimately linked to the masses and will absorb from them those great ideas that will then take shape as concrete guidelines. It will be a party that will strictly apply its discipline in keeping with democratic centralism and, at the same time, where there will permanently be discussion and open criticism and self-criticism, in order to continuously improve our work. At this stage it will be a party of cadres, of the best. These cadres will have to carry out their dynamic task of being in contact with the people, of transmitting their experiences to higher bodies, of transmitting concrete guidelines to the masses, and of marching in the front ranks. The cadres of our party must be first in study, first in work, first in revolutionary enthusiasm, first in sacrifice. At all times they must be better, purer, and more humane than all the others.

One must always remember that a Marxist is not an automatic, fanatical machine aimed at a certain target like a guided missile.

Fidel deals explicitly with this problem in one of his speeches [on April 11, 1962]:

> Who says that Marxism is the renunciation of human feelings, comradeliness, love for a *compañero*, respect for a *compañero*, consideration for a *compañero*? Who says that Marxism means not having a soul, not having feelings? Indeed it was precisely love of man that gave birth to Marxism. It was love of man, of humanity, the desire to combat the distress of the proletariat, the desire to fight poverty, injustice, suffering and all the exploitation of the proletariat, that gave rise to Marxism from Karl Marx's mind precisely when it had become possible for Marxism to emerge. It arose precisely when a real possibility emerged — and more than a real possibility, the historical

necessity — of the social revolution, of which Karl Marx was the interpreter. But what made him become that interpreter if not the abundance of human feelings of men like him, like Engels, like Lenin?

Fidel's assessment is fundamental for the member of the new party. Always keep it in mind, *compañeros*, engrave it in your memories as the most effective weapon against all deviations. A Marxist must be the best, the fullest, the most complete of human beings — but, above all, a human being. He must be a party member who lives and vibrates in contact with the masses; a leader who shapes into concrete guidelines the masses' sometimes unformulated wishes; a tireless worker who gives all to his people — a self-sacrificing worker who gives up his hours of rest, his personal tranquility, his family or his life for the revolution, but who is never a stranger to the warmth of human contact.

On the international arena our party will have extremely important duties. We are the first socialist country in Latin America, an example for other countries to follow, a living experience for other fraternal parties to grasp; a living, recurring, and changing experience that brings all its successes and errors out into the light of public knowledge. In this way its example is more educational, and its aspiration is not to be held up solely to those already professing their conviction in Marxism-Leninism, but before the popular masses of Latin America.

The Second Declaration of Havana [of February 4, 1962] is a guide for the proletariat, the peasantry, and the revolutionary intellectuals of Latin America. Our own attitude will be a permanent guide. We must be worthy of the position we hold. We must work every day thinking of our America and must increasingly strengthen the foundations of our state, its economic organization, and its political development. We must do this so that, at the same time that we improve ourselves internally, we can also convince the peoples of Latin America more and more of the practical possibility of starting on the road to socialist development, at the current stage in the world relationship of forces.

All this without forgetting that the breadth of our emotions in the face of the aggressors' outrages and the peoples' sufferings cannot be limited to the framework of Latin America, nor even to the framework of Latin America and the socialist countries together. We must practice true proletarian internationalism and feel as an affront to ourselves every aggression, every insult, every act against human dignity and against man's happiness anywhere in the world.

We, the members of a new party in a newly liberated region of the world and in new situations, must always hold high the banner of human dignity raised by our [José] Martí, who was a guide for so many generations and is present today, as fresh as ever, in Cuba's reality: "Every true man must feel on his own cheek every blow dealt against the cheek of another."

Against bureaucratism

(February 1963)

Our revolution was essentially the product of a guerrilla movement that initiated the armed struggle against the dictatorship and brought it to fruition in the seizure of power. The first steps of the revolutionary state, like the whole of the primitive epoch of our management of the government, were strongly tinged by fundamental elements of guerrilla tactics as a form of state administration. "Guerrillaism" translated the experience of the armed struggle in the Cuban mountains and countryside into the work of the different administrative and mass organizations, and this meant that only the main revolutionary slogans were followed — and often interpreted in different ways — by bodies in the administration and in society in general. The method of solving concrete problems was chosen at will by each leader.

Because they occupied the whole complex apparatus of society, the fields of action of these "administrative guerrillas" clashed among themselves, producing constant friction, orders and counter-orders, and different interpretations of the laws. This reached the point, in some cases, of state institutions countering laws by issuing their own dictates in the form of decrees, ignoring the central administrative apparatus. After a year of painful experiences we reached the conclusion that we had to totally revamp our style of work and reorganize the state apparatus in a rational manner, utilizing planning techniques known in the fraternal socialist countries.

As a countermeasure, the strong bureaucratic apparatus that characterized this first period in the building of our socialist state began to be organized. But the swing went too far, and a whole number of institutions, including the Ministry of Industry, initiated a policy of centralization that put too many restrictions on the initiative of administrators. This idea of centralization can be explained by the shortage of middle-level cadres and the previous anarchic spirit, which required enormous zeal in ensuring that instructions were being carried out. At the same time, the lack of adequate control mechanisms made it difficult to correctly spot administrative errors in time, which were often hidden by the general chaos. In this way, cadres — the most conscious ones as well as the most timid ones — curbed their initiatives in order to adjust them to the sluggish motion of the administrative machinery. Others continued doing as they pleased, without feeling obliged to respect any authority, and this called for new control measures to put a stop to their activity. This is how our revolution began to suffer from the evil called bureaucratism.

Bureaucratism, obviously, is not the offspring of socialist society, nor is it a necessary component of it. The state bureaucracy existed in the period of bourgeois governments with its retinue of hangers-on and lackeys, as a great number of opportunists — who made up the "court" of the politicians in power — flourished in the shade of the government budget. In a capitalist society, where the entire state apparatus is at the service of the bourgeoisie, the state bureaucracy's importance as a leading body is very small. The main thing is that it be permeable enough to allow opportunists to pass through, yet impenetrable enough to keep the people trapped in its nets. Given the weight of the "original sins" in the old administrative apparatus and the situations created after the triumph of the revolution, the evil of bureaucratism began to develop strongly. If we were to search for its roots today, we would have to add new motives to the old causes, coming up with three fundamental reasons.

One is the lack of inner motivation. By this we mean the individual's lack of interest in rendering a service to the state and in overcoming a given situation. It is based on a lack of revolutionary consciousness or, at any rate, on acquiescence in things that are wrong.

We can establish a direct and obvious relationship between the lack of inner motivation and the lack of interest in resolving problems. In this case, whether the weakness in ideological motivation is due to an absolute lack of conviction or to a certain dose of desperation in the face of repeated insoluble problems, the individual or group of individuals take refuge in bureaucratism, filling out papers, shirking their responsibility, and establishing a written defense in order to continue vegetating or to protect themselves from the irresponsibility of others.

Another cause is the lack of organization. Attempting to destroy "guerrillaism" without sufficient administrative experience has produced dislocations and bottlenecks that unnecessarily curb the flow of information from below, as well as the instructions or orders emanating from the central apparatus. Sometimes, the former or the latter take the wrong course; other times, they are translated into poorly formulated, absurd instructions that contribute even more to the distortion.

The lack of organization is fundamentally characterized by the weakness of the methods used to deal with a given situation. We can see examples in the ministries, when attempts are made to solve problems at an inappropriate level or when problems are dealt with through the wrong channels and get lost in the labyrinth of paperwork. Bureaucratism is like a ball and chain weighing down the type of official who is trying as best he can to solve his problem but keeps crashing time and again into the established way of doing things, without finding a solution. It's common to observe how the only way out for many officials is to ask for more personnel to do a task, when an easy solution requires only a little logic. This in turn creates new reasons for unnecessary paperwork.

As a healthy self-criticism, we must never forget that the revolution's economic management is responsible for the majority of bureaucratic ills. The state apparatus was not developed by means of a single plan and with well-worked out relationships; this left a wide margin for conjecture about administrative methods. The central economic apparatus, the Central Planning Board, did not fulfill its task of leadership and could not do so because it lacked sufficient authority over the other bodies. It was unable to issue precise orders based on a single system and with adequate supervision, and it lacked the requisite assistance of an overall plan. In the absence of good organization, excessive centralization curbed spontaneous action without replacing it in time with correct methods. An accumulation of minor decisions obstructed our view of the big problems, and finding solutions for all of them came to a standstill without rhyme or reason. Last-minute decisions, made hastily and without analysis, became characteristic of our work.

The third cause, a very important one, is the lack of sufficiently developed technical knowledge to be able to make correct decisions on short notice. Not being able to do this meant we had to gather many experiences of little value and try to draw some conclusion from them. Discussions became endless and no-one had sufficient authority to settle things. After one, two, or more meetings, the problem remained until it resolved itself or until a decision had to be made willy-nilly, no matter how bad it might be.

The almost total lack of knowledge, which as I mentioned earlier was made up for by a long series of meetings, led to "meetingitis" — basically a lack of perspective for solving problems. In these cases bureaucratism — the brake that endless paper shuffling and indecision place on society's development — becomes the fate of the bodies affected.

These three fundamental causes, one by one or acting together in various combinations, affect the country's entire institutional life to a greater or lesser degree. The time has come to break away from these malignant influences. Concrete measures must be taken to streamline the state apparatus, in such a way as to establish the strict central control that enables the leadership to have in its hands the keys to the economy while also releasing initiative as much as possible, thus developing on a logical basis the relationships among the productive forces.

If we know the causes and effects of bureaucratism, we can analyze accurately the possibilities of correcting the malady. Of all the fundamental causes, we can consider the need for organization to be our central problem, and we can tackle it with all the necessary rigor. To do so we must modify our style of work. We must prioritize problems, assigning each body and each decision-making level its particular task. We must establish the concrete relationships between each one of them and all the others, from the center of economic decision making to the last administrative unit, as well as the relationships among their different components — horizontally — until we establish all the interrelationships within the economy. This is the task most within our reach at the present time, and it will afford us an additional advantage: redirecting to other areas of work a large number of employees who are not needed, who are not working, who carry out minimal duties, or who duplicate the work of others with no results whatsoever.

Simultaneously, we must develop our political work with dogged determination to rid ourselves of the lack of internal motivation, that is, the lack of political clarity, which translates into things not getting done. This can be done, first, through continuous education, through concrete explanations of the tasks, through instilling in administrative employees an interest in their work, and through the example set by the vanguard workers. And, second, by taking drastic measures to eliminate the parasites, whether it be those who conceal in their stance a deep enmity to socialist society, or those who are irremediably opposed to work.

Finally, we must correct the inferiority that comes from our lack of knowledge. We have begun the gigantic task of transforming society from top to bottom in the midst of imperialist aggression, of an increasingly tighter blockade, of a complete change in our technology, of drastic shortages of raw materials and foodstuffs, and of a massive exodus of the few qualified technicians we have. In these conditions, we must set ourselves the task of working seriously and persistently with the masses to fill the vacancies left by the traitors and to meet our need for a skilled work force resulting from the rapid rate of our development. That is why training is a top priority of all the revolutionary government's plans.

The training of active workers begins in the workplace at the most basic educational level: the elimination of any remaining illiteracy in the most remote areas; continuing education courses and, later, workers' improvement courses for those who have reached the third grade; courses in basic technical skills for the better educated workers; extension courses to turn skilled workers into assistant engineers; university courses for all types of professionals and also for administrators.

The revolutionary government intends to turn our country into one big school where study and success in one's studies become a basic factor for bettering the individual, both economically and in his moral standing in society, to the extent of his abilities.

If we manage to unravel the massive amount of red tape, the intricate relationships among institutions and among departments, the duplication of functions and frequent "potholes" into which our institutions fall, we will find the roots of the problem. We will develop organizational norms, elementary at first and later more complex. We will wage a head-on battle against those who are confused, indifferent, or lazy. We will educate and reeducate that mass of people, incorporate them into the revolution and eliminate what should be thrown out. At the same time we will tirelessly continue the great task of education at all levels, whatever obstacles we may face. If we do all this, we will be in a position to do away in a short time with bureaucratism.

The experience of the last mobilization [during the October 1962 Missile Crisis] motivated us in the Ministry of Industry to discuss and analyze what happened: in the middle of the mobilization, when the entire country steeled itself to resist the enemy attack, industrial production did not drop, absenteeism disappeared and problems were solved with surprising speed. Upon analyzing this, we concluded that a number of factors came together that destroyed the basic causes of bureaucratism. There was a great patriotic and national impulse to resist imperialism, and this sentiment was shared by the immense majority of the Cuban people. Each worker, at his own level, became a soldier of the economy, ready to solve any problem.

In this way the stimulus of foreign aggression became an ideological driving force. Organizational norms were boiled down strictly to pointing out what could not be done and the fundamental problem that needed to be solved: to maintain production at all costs, to maintain certain production with even greater emphasis, and to free the enterprises, factories and institutions from all functions that, although necessary in normal social periods, are not essential.

Each individual had a special responsibility, which forced him to make rapid decisions. We were faced with a situation of national emergency, and decisions had to be made whether they were correct or not; we had to make them, and quickly. This was done in many cases.

We have yet to draw a balance sheet of the mobilization and, obviously, it will not be a positive balance sheet in financial terms. But it was positive in terms of ideological mobilization, in the deepening of the masses' consciousness. What lesson do we draw? That we must make our workers, toilers, peasants and office workers realize that the danger of imperialist aggression still hangs over our heads, that there is no peace, and that our duty is to continue to strengthen the revolution day by day, which is also the best guarantee an invasion will not occur. The costlier it is for the imperialists to take this island, the stronger our defenses and the higher our people's awareness, the more they will think twice. But at the same time, the economic development of the country eases our situation and brings greater material well-being. The ideological task is to make permanent the great example of the mobilization in response to imperialist aggression.

We must analyze each official's responsibilities and define them as strictly as possible within limits that must not be overstepped on penalty of severe sanctions. On that basis we can grant officials the broadest possible authority. At the same time we must examine what is fundamental and what is incidental in the work of the different units of the state institutions and limit all that is incidental in order to emphasize the fundamental, thereby permitting quicker action. We must demand action from our officials, establishing deadlines for carrying out instructions from the central bodies, correctly supervising them and making them reach decisions in a reasonable amount of time.

If we succeed in all this work, bureaucratism will disappear. This is not a task for a single economic body or even all the economic bodies in the country. It is the task of the entire nation, which is to say, of the leading bodies, fundamentally the United Party of the Revolution and the mass organizations. We must all work to implement the following pressing slogans of the day:

War on bureaucratism. Streamline the state apparatus. Production without restraints, and responsibility for production.

On the budgetary finance system

(February 1964)

In 1963-64 a discussion began among Cuban leaders about the relative merits of two systems of economic management, both of which were in use during the opening years of the revolution. One was called the budgetary finance system (sometimes referred to as the consolidated enterprise system). The other was known as the economic accounting system (sometimes referred to as the financial self-management system). The discussion touched on a broad range of fundamental questions concerning the period of transition from capitalism to socialism. Guevara wrote a number of articles as contributions to this discussion. The one below was published in the Cuban magazine, Nuestra Industria, Revista Económica *[Our Industry, A Journal of Economics], February 1964.*

General background

his subject has already been discussed to some extent, but not sufficiently, and I consider it imperative to begin analyzing it more thoroughly in order to be able to present a clear idea of its scope and methodology.

It was officially sanctioned in the Law Regulating the Budgetary System of Financing State Enterprises and had its baptism in the process of the internal work of the Ministry of Industry.

Its history is brief, barely going back to 1960, when it began to take shape. Our purpose, however, is to analyze not its development but rather the system as it exists today, with the understanding that its evolution has by no means come to an end.

We are interested in making a comparison with what is called the "economic accounting system." With regard to this system we will emphasize the financial self-management aspect, since it is a fundamental distinguishing characteristic, as well as attitudes toward material incentives, which are the basis of financial self-management.

It is difficult to explain these differences, because they are often subtle and obscure. Moreover, the budgetary finance system has not been studied thoroughly enough for its description to compete in clarity with the economic accounting system.

We will begin with some quotations. The first is from Marx's economic manuscripts, which date back to the time of his work described as that of the "young Marx," when the weight of the philosophical ideas that contributed to his education is very noticeable even in the language he used, and his thoughts on economics were more imprecise. Nevertheless, Marx was in the prime of his life, and he had already embraced the cause of the poor and explained it philosophically, although without the scientific rigor of *Capital*. He thought more like a philosopher, and therefore he referred more specifically to man as a human individual and to the problems of his liberation as a social being. He had not as yet gone into the analysis of the inevitability of the break-up of the social structures of this epoch, which would open the way to the transition period, the dictatorship of the proletariat. In *Capital*, Marx appears as the scientific economist who meticulously analyzes the transitory nature of social epochs and their identification with particular relations of production. He does not engage in philosophical discussion.

The weight of this monument of human intelligence is such that we frequently forget the humanistic character (in the best sense of the word) of his concerns. The mechanisms of the relations of production and their result, the class struggle, obscure to a certain degree the objective fact that it is men who are the actors in history. At the moment, our interest is man. We therefore quote the following, which, although belonging to his youth, is no less valuable as an expression of the philosopher's thought:

> *Communism* as the *positive* transcendence of *private property as human self-estrangement,* and therefore as the real *appropriation* of the *human* essence by and for man; communism therefore as the complete return of man to himself as a *social* (i.e., human) being — a return accomplished consciously and embracing the entire wealth of previous development. This communism, as fully developed naturalism, equals humanism, and as fully developed humanism equals naturalism; it is the *genuine* resolution of the conflict between man and nature and between man and man — the true resolution of the strife between existence and essence, between objectification and self-confirmation, between freedom and necessity, between the individual and the species. Communism is the riddle of history solved, and it is *conscious* that it is this solution.[19]

The word *conscious* is emphasized because it is considered basic to the statement of the problem. Marx analyzed the problem of man's liberation and saw communism as the solution to the contradictions that brought about his alienation — but as a conscious act. In other words, communism cannot be seen merely as the product of class contradictions in a highly developed society, contradictions that would be resolved during a transition stage in order to reach the summit. Man is the conscious actor in history. Without this *consciousness,* which encompasses his consciousness as a social being, there can be no communism.

Marx did not abandon his militant attitude while preparing Capital. When the Gotha congress met in 1875 to unite the workers' organizations that existed in Germany (the Social Democratic Workers Party and the General Association of German Workers), and its program was drafted, Marx's response was the *Critique of the Gotha Program.*

This document, written in the midst of his fundamental work and having a clear polemical character, is important because in it he touches on, although in passing, the subject of the transition period. In the analysis of point three of the Gotha Program, he deals to some extent with several of the most important issues of the transition period, which he considered to be the result of a decisive break from the developed capitalist system. He did not foresee the use of money in this period, but he did see individual payment for labor, because:

> What we have to deal with here is a communist society, not as it has *developed* on its own foundations, but, on the contrary, just as it *emerges* from capitalist society; which is thus in every respect, economically, morally and intellectually, still stamped with the birth marks of the old society from whose womb it emerges. Accordingly, the individual producer receives back from society — after the deductions have been made — exactly what he gives to it. What he has given to it is his individual quantum of labor.[20]

Marx could only intuitively anticipate the development of the world imperialist system; Lenin examined it and diagnosed it:

> Uneven economic and political development is an absolute law of capitalism. Hence, the victory of socialism is possible first in several or even in one capitalist country alone. After expropriating the capitalists and organizing their own socialist production, the victorious proletariat of that country will arise *against* the rest of the world — the capitalist world — attracting to its cause the oppressed classes of other countries, stirring uprisings in those countries against the capitalists, and in case of need using even armed force against the exploiting classes and their states. The political form of a society

wherein the proletariat is victorious in overthrowing the bourgeoisie will be a democratic republic, which will more and more concentrate the forces of the proletariat of a given nation or nations, in the struggle against states that have not yet gone over to socialism. The abolition of classes is impossible without a dictatorship of the oppressed class, of the proletariat. A free union of nations in socialism is impossible without a more or less prolonged and stubborn struggle of the socialist republics against the backward states.[21]

A few years later Stalin systematized the idea to the point of believing the socialist revolution to be possible in the colonies:

The *third contradiction* is the contradiction between the handful of ruling, "civilized" nations and the hundreds of millions of the colonial and dependent peoples of the world. Imperialism is the most barefaced exploitation and the most inhuman oppression of hundreds of millions of people inhabiting vast colonies and dependent countries. The purpose of this exploitation and of this oppression is to squeeze out super-profits. But in exploiting these countries imperialism is compelled to build there railways, factories and mills, industrial and commercial centers. The appearance of a class of proletarians, the emergence of a native intelligentsia, the awakening of national consciousness, the growth of the liberation movement — such are the inevitable results of this "policy." The growth of the revolutionary movement in all colonies and dependent countries without exception clearly testifies to this fact. This circumstance is of importance for the proletariat inasmuch as it saps radically the position of capitalism by converting the colonies and dependent countries from reserves of imperialism into reserves of the proletarian revolution.[22]

Lenin's theory was proven in practice by the victory in Russia that gave birth to the Soviet Union.

We are faced by a new phenomenon: the advent of the socialist revolution in a single country, economically backward, with 22 million square kilometers, a low population density, further impoverished as a result of the war, and, as if all this were not enough, under attack by the imperialist powers.

After a period of war communism, Lenin laid the bases of the NEP [New Economic Policy] and, with it, the basis for the development of Soviet society up to today.

It is important to describe here the conjuncture the Soviet Union was living through, and no-one can do this better than Lenin:

Thus, in 1918, I was of the opinion that with regard to the economic situation then prevailing in the Soviet Republic, state capitalism would be a step forward. This sounds very strange, and perhaps even absurd, for already at that time our Republic was a socialist republic and we were every day hastily — perhaps too hastily — adopting various new economic measures which could not be described as anything but socialist measures. Nevertheless, I then held the view that in relation to the economic situation then existing in the Soviet Republic state capitalism would be a step forward, and I explained my idea simply by enumerating the elements of the economic system of Russia. In my opinion these elements were the following: "(1) patriarchal, i.e., the most primitive form of agriculture; (2) small commodity production (this includes the majority of the peasants who trade in grain); (3) private capitalism; (4) state capitalism, and (5) socialism." All these economic elements were present in Russia at that time. I set myself the task of explaining the relationship of these elements to each other, and whether one of the nonsocialist elements, namely, state capitalism, should not be rated higher than socialism. I repeat: it seems very strange to everyone that a nonsocialist element should be rated higher than, regarded as superior to, socialism in a republic which declares itself a socialist republic. But the fact will become intelligible if you recall that we definitely did not regard the economic system of Russia as something homogeneous and highly developed; we were fully aware that in Russia we had patriarchal agriculture, i.e., the most primitive form of agriculture, alongside the socialist form. What role could state capitalism play in these circumstances?...

Now that I have emphasized the fact that as early as 1918 we regarded state capitalism as a possible line of retreat, I shall deal with the results of our New Economic Policy. I repeat: at that time it was still a very vague idea, but in 1921, after we had passed through the most important stage of the Civil War — and passed through it victoriously — we felt the impact of a grave — I think it was the gravest — internal political crisis in Soviet Russia. This internal crisis brought to light discontent not only among a considerable section of the peasantry but also among the workers. This was the first and, I hope, the last time in the history of Soviet Russia that feeling ran against us among large masses of peasants, not consciously but instinctively. What gave rise to this peculiar, and for us, of course, very unpleasant, situation? The reason for it was that in our economic offensive we had run too far ahead, that we had not provided ourselves with adequate resources, that the masses sensed what we ourselves were not then able to formulate consciously but what we admitted soon after, a few weeks later, namely, that the direct transition to purely socialist forms, to purely socialist distribution, was beyond our available strength, and that if we were unable to effect a retreat so as to confine ourselves to easier tasks, we would face disaster.[23]

As can be seen, the economic and political situation in the Soviet Union made necessary the retreat Lenin spoke of. The entire policy, therefore, can be characterized as a tactic closely linked to the country's historical situation. Therefore, not all of Lenin's statements should be accorded universal validity. It seems to us that two extremely important factors should be considered regarding their introduction into other countries.

1. The characteristics of czarist Russia at the time of the revolution, including the development of technique on every level; the special character of its people; and the country's general condition — adding to this the destruction caused by a world war, the devastation wrought by the White hordes and the imperialist invaders.

2. The general characteristics of the period with respect to techniques of economic administration and control.

Oskar Lange, in his article, "Current Problems of Economic Science in Poland," says the following:

Bourgeois economic science performs yet another function. The bourgeoisie and the monopolies do not allocate substantial resources to creating schools of higher education and institutes of scientific study in the field of economic sciences merely for the purpose of having them help with an apology for the capitalist system. They expect something more from economists, that is, help in finding solutions to the numerous problems related to political economy. During the period of competitive capitalism the tasks to be done in this area were quite limited, having to do with financial administration, monetary and credit policy, customs policy, transportation, etc. But under the conditions of monopoly capitalism, and especially under the conditions of the growing penetration of state capitalism into economic life, problems of this nature increase. We can list a few of these: market analysis to facilitate the formulation of pricing policy by the big monopolies; methods of centralized administration in a complex of industrial enterprises; reciprocal accounting systems among these enterprises; the planned interlocking of their activity and development; their proper location; their amortization or investment policy. All this gives rise to questions concerning the activity of the capitalist state during the present period; the criteria for the activity of nationalized industries; investment and location policy (as, for example, in the energy field); forms of political-economic intervention in the national economy as a whole; etc.

To all these problems have been added a number of technical-economic acquisitions in certain fields, such as for example, market analysis or programming the activity of enterprises that form part of a group; internal accounting regulations within each factory or group of factories; in the criteria for amortization, and others. We can partially utilize these methods in the process of building socialism (as they will doubtless be used in the future by workers in countries that are today capitalist when they effect the transition to socialism.)[24]

It should be noted that Cuba had not made its transition nor even begun its revolution at the time this was written. Many of the advanced techniques described by Lange existed in Cuba; that is, the conditions of Cuban society in those days permitted centralized control over some enterprises, with headquarters in Havana or New York.

The Consolidated Petroleum Enterprise, which was created by the merger of the three existing imperialist refineries (Esso, Texaco, and Shell), maintained and, in some cases, perfected its control systems and is considered a model in this Ministry [of Industry]. In enterprises where neither the tradition of centralization existed nor the practical conditions for it, these systems were created on the basis of national experience. An example of this is the Consolidated Flour Enterprise, which merited first place among the enterprises in the vice-ministry of light industry.

Although the experience of the early days of industrial management fully convinces us of the impossibility of rationally following another course, it would be useless now to discuss whether the organizational measures taken at that time would have yielded similar or better results had financial self-management been introduced at the factory level. The important thing is that centralization could be done under very difficult conditions and that it made possible the elimination of — in the case of the footwear industry, for example — a great many inefficient small shops, and permitted the reallocation of 6,000 workers to other branches of production.

With this series of quotations, we have tried to lay out the themes that we consider basic to explaining the budgetary finance system.

1. Communism is a goal of humanity that is achieved consciously. Therefore, education, the elimination of the vestiges of the old society in people's consciousness, is an extremely important factor. It should be kept in mind, however, that without parallel advances in production, such a society will never be achieved.

2. The forms of economic administration, from the technological stand-point, must be borrowed from wherever they are most developed and can be adapted to the new society. The socialist camp can use the petrochemical technology of the imperialist camp without fear of being "infected" by bourgeois ideology. This also applies to the economic field, in all that refers to technical norms of administration and control of production.

At the risk of being considered pretentious, we could paraphrase Marx's reference to the use of Hegel's dialectics and say that such techniques have been turned right side up.

An analysis of the accounting techniques commonly used today in the socialist countries shows us that there is a conceptual difference between theirs and ours, perhaps comparable to the one that exists in the capitalist camp between competition and monopoly. Finally, the past techniques were the basis for the development of both systems; from the moment they are "turned right side up," the roads diverge, since socialism has its own relations of production and therefore its own requirements.

We could say, then, that as a technique the predecessor of the budgetary finance system was the imperialist monopoly implanted in Cuba. It had already gone through the variations inherent in the long process of the development of the techniques of administration and control — a process extending from the beginning of the monopoly system until today, when it reaches its higher levels. When the monopolists left, they took with them their top management and some middle management. At the same time, our immature conception of the revolution led us to destroy a number of established procedures merely because they were capitalist. Because of this our system has still not reached the level of efficiency in relation to management and control over production that the local branches of the monopolies had. We are on that road, however, clearing it of whatever rubbish is left over from the past.

General differences between the economic accounting system and the budgetary finance system

There are differences of varying degrees between the economic accounting system and the budgetary finance system. We will attempt to divide them into two general categories and explain them briefly. There are methodological differences — practical, we might say — and differences of a more serious character, but whose nature can make the analysis appear Byzantine if one does not proceed very cautiously.

It is useful to clarify at this point that what we are looking for is a more efficient way of reaching communism. There is no disagreement in principle. Economic accounting has demonstrated its practical effectiveness, and, having the same bases, both systems seek the same ends. We believe that our system's plan of action, if properly developed, can increase the effectiveness of economic management in the socialist state, deepen the consciousness of the masses, and through joint action, further strengthen the bonds of the world socialist system.

The most immediate difference arises with regard to the enterprise. For us, an enterprise is a collection of factories or production units that have a similar technological base, possess a common destination for their output, or in some cases are located in the same geographical area. For the economic accounting system, an enterprise is a production unit with its own juridical identity. One sugar mill is an enterprise under the economic accounting system, while for us all sugar mills, together with other production units connected with the sugar industry, constitute the Consolidated Sugar Enterprise. There have been recent experiments of this type in the Soviet Union adapted to the specific conditions of that fraternal country. (See I. Ivonin, "Los combinados de empresas soviéticas: la nueva forma de administración de las industries" [The combined Soviet enterprises: the new form of industrial administration], *Nuestra Industria, Revista Económica*, no. 4.)

Another difference is the way money is used. Under our system, it functions only as money of account, as a reflection, in prices, of an enterprise's performance that can be analyzed by the central bodies in order to control its functioning. Under the system of economic accounting, money serves not only this purpose but is also a means of payment that acts as an indirect instrument of control, since it is these funds that permit the production unit to operate. The production unit's relations with the bank are similar to those a private producer maintains with capitalist banks, to whom it must thoroughly explain plans and prove its solvency. Naturally, in such cases decisions are not arbitrary but are subject to a plan, and these relations take place between state bodies.

Consistent with the way in which money is used under the budgetary finance system, our enterprises have no funds of their own. At the bank there are separate accounts for withdrawals and for deposits. The enterprise may withdraw funds in accordance with the plan from the general expense account and the special wage account. But its deposits automatically pass into the hands of the state.

In the majority of the fraternal countries, enterprises have their own funds in the banks, which they can add to with bank loans for which they pay interest. But it must not be forgotten that the enterprise's "own" funds, as well as the loans, belong to society, and their movement reflects the enterprise's financial situation.

As to work norms, enterprises operating under economic accounting use work measured by the hour as well as work measured by output per hour (piecework). We are trying to institute work measured by the hour in all our factories, including bonuses for over-fulfillment of quotas, capped at the highest wage scale. We will deal with this subject at greater length below.

Under a fully developed system of economic accounting, contracts are rigorously enforced, with monetary penalties for failure to comply, based on a legal framework established after years of experience. In our country such a structure does not yet exist, even for bodies such as INRA that operate on the basis of financial self-management. It is particularly difficult to establish because of the coexistence of two such dissimilar systems. For the time being, there is the Arbitration Commission, which lacks executive powers but which is gradually growing in importance and may in the future provide a basis for our legal structure. Internally, among bodies under the budgetary finance system, the contractual decisions are easy, since only administrative procedures are involved if the accounts are well kept and up-to-date (which is already the case in most of the Ministry of Industry's enterprises).

Starting from the fact that under both systems the state's general plan is the highest authority, which must be adhered to, the practical similarities and differences can be summed up as follows:

Financial self-management is based on overall centralized control and greater decentralization. Control is exercised indirectly by means of the "ruble," through the bank, and the monetary results of the enterprise's operation provide a measure for any bonuses. Material interest is the great lever that moves workers both individually and collectively.

The budgetary finance system is based on centralized control of the activity of the enterprise. The enterprise's plan and its economic management are directly controlled by central administrative bodies. It has no funds of its own nor does it receive bank credits. It uses material incentives on an individual basis, that is, individual monetary bonuses and penalties and, at the proper time, will also use collective incentives. But direct material incentives are limited by the method of wage payment.

More subtle contradictions:
Material incentives versus consciousness

Here we come up against more subtle contradictions, which must be better explained. The subject of material incentives versus moral incentives has given rise to many discussions among those interested in such matters. We must make one thing clear: *we do not deny the objective need for material incentives,* although we are reluctant to use them as the main lever. We believe that in economics this kind of lever quickly takes on an existence of its own and then imposes its strength on the relations among men. It should not be forgotten that it comes from capitalism and is destined to die under socialism.

How will we make it die?

"Little by little, through the gradual increase of consumer goods for the people, making these incentives unnecessary," we are told. This concept seems too mechanical, too rigid. "Consumer goods" — that is the slogan and definitely the great molder of consciousness for the defenders of the other system. In our view, direct material incentives and consciousness are contradictory terms.

This is one of the points where our differences get concrete. We are no longer dealing with nuances. For the advocates of financial self-manage-ment, direct material incentives extending into the future and accompanying society in all of the various stages of building communism are not counter-posed to the "development" of consciousness. For us they are. It is for this reason that we struggle against the predominance of material incentives, for it would signify delaying the development of socialist morality.

If material incentives are counterposed to the development of conscious-ness, but are a great lever for increasing production, does this mean that giving priority to the development of consciousness retards production? In comparative terms, in a given period, that may be, although no-one has made the relevant calculations. We maintain that in a relatively short time, however, the development of consciousness does more for the development of production than material incentives do. We state this based on the overall development of society toward communism, which presupposes that work will cease to be a tedious necessity and become a pleasant duty. Being very much a matter of subjective judgment, such a statement requires proof by experience, which is what we are in the middle of doing. If in the course of this experience it were to be demonstrated that our method is a dangerous brake on the development of the productive forces, then we would have to decide to cut our losses and return to well-trodden paths. Up until now, this has not happened, and our method, with improvements through practice, is more and more taking shape and demonstrating its internal coherence.

What then is the correct way to handle material interest? We believe that its existence can never be overlooked, whether it be as a collective expression of the masses' desires or as an individual factor, a reflection in the worker's consciousness of the habits of the old society. We do not yet have a well-defined approach to collective material interest. This is because of insufficiencies in the planning apparatus that prevent us from basing ourselves on it with absolute confidence. And we have been unable so far to devise a method that would allow us to get around the difficulties. The biggest danger we see is in the antagonism that is created between the state administration and the production bodies. The Soviet economist Liberman has analyzed this antagonism and has concluded that the methods of collective incentives must be changed. He proposes that the old formula of bonuses based on fulfillment of the plan should be abandoned in favor of more advanced methods.

Although we do not agree with his emphasis on material interest (as a lever), we think he is correct in his concern about the aberrations that the concept of "fulfillment of the plan" has been subject to over the years. Relations between enterprises and central bodies become too much ones of conflict. And the methods used by the enterprises to make a profit sometimes take on characteristics that diverge considerably from the image of socialist morality.

We believe that, in a way, there is a squandering of the possibilities for development offered by the new relations of production that could accelerate man's progress toward the "kingdom of freedom." To be precise, in presenting the basic arguments for our system, we describe in detail the interrelationship that exists between education and the development of production. We can undertake the task of creating the new consciousness because we have new forms of relations of production. Although in a general historical sense consciousness is a product of the relations of production, we must still take into account the characteristics of the current epoch, whose principal contradiction (on a world scale) is the contradiction between imperialism and socialism. Socialist ideas have touched the consciousness of all the world's peoples. That is why the development of consciousness can advance ahead of the particular state of the productive forces in any given country.

During the early years of the Soviet Union, its character was that of a socialist state, despite relations of a much more backward kind that existed within it. Under capitalism remnants of the feudal stage survive; yet it is capitalism that characterizes a country after it conquers the basic sectors of the economy. In Cuba, the development of the contradictions between the two world systems permitted the establishment of the socialist character of the revolution, which was the result of a conscious act, thanks to the knowledge acquired by its leaders, the deepening of the masses' consciousness and the relationship of world forces.

If all this is possible, why not consider the role of education as a persistent helper of the socialist state in the task of eliminating the vestiges of a society that has died and is carrying the old relations of production to its grave? Let us see what Lenin has to say:

> Infinitely stereotyped, for instance, is the argument they learned by rote during the development of West European Social-Democracy, namely, that we are not yet ripe for socialism, that, as certain "learned" gentlemen among them put it, the objective economic premises for socialism do not exist in our country. It does not occur to any of them to ask: but what about a people that found itself in a revolutionary situation such as that created during the first imperialist war? Might it not, influenced by the hopelessness of its situation, fling itself into a struggle that would offer it at least some chance of securing conditions for the further development of civilization that were somewhat unusual?
>
> "The development of the productive forces of Russia has not attained the level that makes socialism possible." All the heroes of the Second International, including, of course, Sukhanov, beat the drums about this proposition. They keep harping on this incontrovertible proposition in a thousand different keys, and think that it is the decisive criterion of our revolution.
>
> But what if the situation — which drew Russia into the imperialist world war that involved every more or less influential West European country and made her a witness of the eve of the revolutions maturing or partly already begun in the East — gave rise to circumstances that put Russia and her development in a position which enabled us to achieve precisely that combination of a "peasant war" with the working-class movement suggested in 1856 by no less a Marxist than Marx himself as a possible prospect for Prussia?
>
> What if the complete hopelessness of the situation, by stimulating the efforts of the workers and peasants tenfold, offered us the opportunity to create the fundamental requisites of civilization in a different way from that of the West European countries? Has that altered the general line of development of world history? Has that altered the basic relations between the basic classes of all the countries that

are being, or have been, drawn into the general course of world history?

If a definite level of culture is required for the building of socialism (although nobody can say just what that definite "level of culture" is, for it differs in every West European country), why cannot we begin by first achieving the prerequisites for that definite level of culture in a revolutionary way, and *then*, with the aid of the workers' and peasants' government and the Soviet system, proceed to overtake the other nations?[25]

As for the presence of material interest in an individualized form, we recognize it (although fighting it and attempting to speed up its elimination through education) and apply it in our norms of hourly work including bonuses and wage penalties for nonfulfillment of these norms.

On this subject, the subtle difference between the proponents of financial self-management and ourselves resides in the arguments regarding payment of a wage based on work quotas using bonuses and penalties. The production norm is the average amount of labor that creates a product in a certain time, given average skill and under the specific conditions of equipment utilization. It is the contribution of a set amount of labor to society by one of its members. It is the fulfillment of his social duty. If the quotas are over-fulfilled, there is a greater benefit for society, and it may be assumed that the worker who does it fulfills his duties better and therefore deserves a material reward. We accept this as a necessary evil during a transitional period. But we do not agree that the maxim "from each according to his ability, to each according to his work" should be literally interpreted as meaning full payment, in additional wages, for the percentage that a given quota is over-fulfilled. (There are cases in which payment exceeds the percentage of fulfillment as a special incentive to individual productivity.) Marx explains very clearly in the *Critique of the Gotha Program* that a considerable part of the worker's wages goes to purposes far removed from any direct connection to him:

> Let us take first of all the words "proceeds of labor" in the sense of the product of labor, then the co-operative proceeds of labor are the *total social product*.
> From this must now be deducted:
> *First,* cover for replacement of the means of production used up.
> *Secondly,* additional portion for expansion of production.
> *Thirdly,* reserve or insurance funds to provide against accidents, dislocations caused by natural calamities, etc.
> These deductions from the "undiminished proceeds of labor"

are an economic necessity and their magnitude is to be determined according to available means and forces, and partly by computation of probabilities, but they are in no way calculable by equity.

There remains the other part of the total product, intended to serve as means of consumption.

Before this is divided among the individuals, there has to be deducted, again, from it:

First, the general costs of administration not belonging to production.

This part will, from the outset, be very considerably restricted in comparison with present-day society and it diminishes in proportion as the new society develops.

Secondly, that which is intended for the common satisfaction of needs, such as schools, health services, etc.

From the outset this part grows considerably in comparison with present day society and it grows in proportion as the new society develops.

Thirdly, funds for those unable to work, etc., in short, for what is included under so-called official poor relief today.

Only now do we come to the "distribution" which the program, under Lassallean influence, alone has in view in its narrow fashion, namely, to that part of the means of consumption which is divided among the individual producers of the cooperative society.

The "undiminished proceeds of labor" have already unnoticeably become converted into the "diminished" proceeds, although what the producer is deprived of in his capacity as a private individual benefits him directly or indirectly in his capacity as a member of society.

Just as the phrase "undiminished proceeds of labor" has disappeared, so now does the phrase of the "proceeds of labor" disappear altogether.[26]

All this shows that the size of the reserve fund depends on a series of political-economic or political-administrative decisions. As all the goods existing in the reserve always derive from unpaid labor, we must deduce which decisions regarding the size of the funds that Marx has analyzed imply changes in payments, that is, variations in the amount of labor not directly paid. To all this it is necessary to add that no mathematical norm is known to exist by which to determine the "fairness" of the bonus for over-fulfillment (or even the base wage). The size of this payment to the individual, therefore, must be based primarily on the new social relations, on the legal structure that sanctions the form of distribution by society of a part of the individual worker's labor.

Our system of norms has the merit of establishing compulsory professional training as a condition for promotion to higher job categories. Over time, this will bring about a significant increase in the level of technical skills.

Nonfulfillment of a norm means nonfulfillment of a social duty. Society punishes the offender by deducting a part of his income. The norm is more than a mere measuring stick marking a realizable or customary amount of labor; it is the expression of the workers' moral obligation, *it is his social duty.* Here is where the action of administrative control and ideological control must come together. The party's great role in the production unit is to be its internal driving force and to use the myriad examples set by its members to assure that productive labor, training, and participation in economic matters of the unit become integral parts of the workers' lives, gradually becoming an irreplaceable habit.

On the law of value

There is a profound difference (at least in the rigor of the terms employed) between our position and that of the proponents of economic accounting regarding the concept of the law of value and the possibility of using it consciously.

The *Manual of Political Economy* says:

> Unlike capitalism, where the law of value operates as a blind, spontaneous force imposed on man, the socialist economy is conscious of it. The state takes it into account and *uses* it in the planned administration of the economy.
>
> A knowledge of the operation of the law of value and its *intelligent use* must necessarily help the economy's directors to channel production rationally, to systematically improve work methods, and to make use of untapped reserves in order to increase and improve production.[27]

The words we have italicized indicate the spirit of the paragraphs.

The law of value would act as a blind force, but once it is understood it can be handled, or used, by man.

But this law has certain characteristics: First, it assumes the existence of a commodity society. Second, its results cannot be measured a priori; they have to reveal themselves in the market, where exchange takes place between producers and consumers. Third, it is a coherent whole, including the world market; changes and distortions in certain branches of production are reflected in the total result. Fourth, given its nature as an economic law, it operates fundamentally as a tendency, and, in the transition periods, its tendency must logically be to disappear.

Some paragraphs further on, the *Manual* states:

> The socialist state uses the law of value, exercising — through the financial and credit system — control over production and distribution of the social product.
>
> Control over the law of value, and its use in conformity with a plan, represent an enormous advantage of socialism over capitalism. Thanks to control over the law of value, its operation in the socialist economy does not imply the waste of social labor, characteristic of capitalism's anarchy of production. The law of value and its related categories — money, prices, commerce, credit, finance — are used successfully in the Soviet Union and the people's democracies in the interests of building socialism and communism, in the planned administration of the national economy.

This may be considered accurate only as regards the total amount of value produced for direct use by the population and the respective funds available to purchase them — which any capitalist treasury minister could do with relatively balanced finances. Within this framework all of the law's partial distortions apply.

Further on, the *Manual* states:

> Commodity production, the law of value, and money will disappear only when the higher stage of communism is reached. But in order to make the disappearance of commodity production and circulation possible in the higher stage of communism, it is necessary to *develop* and use the law of value as well as monetary and commodity relations during the period when the communist society is being built.

Why *develop*? We understand that the capitalist categories are retained for a time and that the length of this time cannot be determined beforehand. But the characteristics of the transition period are those of a society throwing off its old bonds in order to arrive quickly at the new stage.

The tendency must be, in our opinion, to eliminate as vigorously as possible the old categories, including the market, money, and, therefore, the lever of material interest — or, to put it better, to eliminate the conditions for their existence. Otherwise, one would have to assume that the task of building socialism in a backward society is something in the nature of a historical accident and that its leaders, in order to make up for the "mistake," should set about consolidating all the categories inherent in the intermediate society. All that would remain as foundations of the new society would be the distribution of income according to work and the tendency toward elimination of man's exploitation of man. These things by themselves seem inadequate to bring about the gigantic change in consciousness necessary to tackle the transition. That change must take place through the multifaceted action of all the new relations, through education and socialist morality — with the individualistic way of thinking that direct material incentives instill in consciousness acting as a brake on the development of man as a social being.

To summarize our differences: We consider the law of value to be partially operative because remnants of the commodity society still exist. This is also reflected in the type of exchange that takes place between the state as supplier and the consumer. We believe that particularly in a society such as ours, with a highly developed foreign trade, the law of value on an international scale must be recognized as a fact governing commercial transactions, even within the socialist camp. We recognize the need for this trade to assume a higher form in countries of the new society, to prevent a widening of the differences between the developed and the more backward countries as a result of the exchange. In other words, it is necessary to develop terms of trade that permit the financing of industrial investments in the developing countries even if it contravenes the price systems prevailing in the capitalist world market. This would allow the entire socialist camp to progress more evenly, which would naturally have the effect of smoothing off the rough edges and of unifying the spirit of proletarian internationalism. (The recent agreement between Cuba and the Soviet Union is an example of the steps that can be taken in this direction.)

We reject the possibility of consciously using the law of value in the absence of a free market that automatically expresses the contradiction between producers and consumers. We reject the existence of the *commodity* category in relations among state enterprises. We consider all such establishments to be part of the single large enterprise that is the state (although in practice this has not yet happened in our country). The law of value and the plan are two terms linked by a contradiction and its resolution. We can therefore state that centralized planning is the mode of existence of socialist society, its defining characteristic, and the point at which man's consciousness finally succeeds in synthesizing and directing the economy toward its goal: the full liberation of the human being within the framework of communist society.

On setting prices

We also have profound disagreements regarding the theory of setting prices. Under financial self-management, prices are set "in relation to the law of value," but what is not explained, to our knowledge, is which expression of the law is used. The starting point is to calculate the socially necessary labor required to produce a given article, but what has been overlooked is the fact that socially necessary labor is an economic and historical concept. Therefore, it changes not only on the local (or national) level but in world terms as well. Continued technological advances, a result of competition in the capitalist world, reduces the expenditure of necessary labor and therefore lowers the value of the product. A closed society can ignore such changes for a certain time, but it would always have to come back to these international relations in order to compare product values. If a given society ignores such changes for a long time without developing new and accurate formulas to replace the old ones, it will create internal interrelationships that will shape its own value structure in a way that may be internally consistent but would be in contradiction with the tendencies of more highly developed technology (for example, in steel and plastics). This could result in relative reverses of some importance and, in any case, would produce distortions in the law of value on an international scale, making it impossible to compare economies.

The "circulation tax" is an accounting fiction through which an enterprise is assured of maintaining certain levels of profitability. The price of the product to the consumer is raised in such a way as to level off the supply of goods with effective demand. We believe that such a tax, although imposed by the system, is not an absolute necessity, and we are working on other formulas that take all these aspects into account.

We feel that an overall equilibrium between the supply of commodities and effective demand is essential. The Ministry of Domestic Trade would be in charge of bringing about a balance between the population's buying power and commodity prices, always bearing in mind that a whole series of necessities of life must be supplied at low prices, while we can go overboard in the other direction with less-important goods, openly ignoring the law of value in each concrete case.

Here, a big problem arises. What basis for setting real prices should the economy adopt in analyzing the relations of production? It could be an analysis of necessary labor in Cuban terms. This would bring with it immediate distortions, and cause us to lose sight of world problems, because of the automatic interrelationships that would necessarily be created. On the other hand, the world-market price could be used. This would cause us to lose sight of national problems, since in no branch of industry is our productivity up to world standards.

We propose, as a first approximation to solving the problem, that consideration be given to the creation of price indexes based on the following:

All imported raw materials would have a fixed, stable price based on an average international market price, plus a few points to cover the costs of transportation and the Ministry of Foreign Trade's administration costs. All Cuban raw materials would have a price based on real production costs in monetary terms. In both cases we would add planned labor costs plus depreciation of the means of production used to produce the raw materials. This would be the price of products supplied by domestic enterprises to each other and to the Ministry of Domestic Trade. However, these prices would be constantly affected by indexes reflecting the prices of those commodities on the world market plus the costs of transportation and of the Ministry of Foreign Trade. Enterprises operating under the budgetary finance system would work on the basis of their planned costs and would make no profits. Instead, all profits would accrue to the Ministry of Domestic Trade. (Naturally, this refers to that part of the social product sold as commodities, the fundamental part of the consumption fund.) The indexes would continuously tell us (the central administration and the enterprise) how efficient we really are and would prevent our making wrong decisions. The population would not suffer at all as a result of all these changes, since the prices of the commodities they buy are established independently, in relation to the demand and essential need of each product.

For example, in order to calculate the amount of an investment, we would calculate the cost of raw materials and directly imported equipment; expenditure on construction and installation equipment; and planned wage costs — making allowances for contingencies and leaving a certain margin for administration costs. This would yield, upon completing the investment, three figures: (1) the real cost of the project in money terms; (2) what the project should have cost according to our plans; and (3) what it should cost in terms of world productivity. The difference between the first and the second would be chalked up to administrative inefficiency during construction; the difference between the second and the third would be the index of our backwardness in that particular sector.

This would allow us to make fundamental decisions regarding the alternative use of materials such as concrete, iron, or plastics; cement, aluminum, or zinc roofs; iron, lead, or copper piping; wood, iron, or aluminum windows, etc.

All decisions could diverge from the mathematical optimum for political reasons, for foreign trade reasons, etc. But we would always have the real world as a mirror by which to compare our work. Prices would never be detached from their corresponding world market levels, which will fluctuate in given years according to advances in technology, and in which the socialist market and the international division of labor will increasingly gain preeminence, once a world socialist pricing system is achieved that is more logical than the one now used.

We could continue at length on this very interesting subject, but it is preferable to outline a few basic ideas here and point out that all this needs to be developed later.

Collective bonuses

With regard to collective bonuses for an enterprise's performance, we would first like to refer to the experiments described by Fikriat Tabayev, in "Investigación económica y dirección de la economia" [Economic research and management of the economy] in *Revista Internacional, no.* 11, 1963, where he says:

> What, then, should be the fundamental and decisive index for evaluating the enterprise's work? Economic research has yielded several proposals in this regard.
>
> Some economists suggest that the principal index should be average accumulation, while others believe it should be labor costs, and so on. The pages of the Soviet press have reflected the broad discussion provoked by an article by Professor Liberman, who proposes that the fundamental indicators of enterprise performance should be the degree of profitability, average accumulation, and profit. We believe that in judging the operation of an enterprise, the most important thing to take into account is the contribution made by its personnel to the given type of production. This, which in the final analysis is not in contradiction with the struggle for high enough profitability, allows an enterprise's personnel to concentrate their efforts on perfecting the production process. The social organizations of [the Autonomous Soviet Socialist Republic of] Tataria have proposed as the main index one based on the average value of production of each piece. In order to verify the feasibility of putting this proposal into practice, they have conducted an economic experiment.
>
> In 1962, average values of production were calculated and approved for all branches of industry in Tataria. That year was a

transitional period, during which the new index was used in planning alongside the gross production index. The index based on the average value of production expresses technologically justified costs, including wages and benefits paid to workers, plus workshop and general plant costs for the production of each article.

It should be noted that the application of this index has nothing to do with the "infernal" labor accounting systems used in capitalist countries. We consistently seek to organize work processes along rational lines, not to intensify work beyond reasonable bounds. All the effort devoted to establishing work norms is made with the direct participation of the personnel of the enterprises and social organizations, particularly the trade unions.

Unlike the gross production index, the average value of manufacture does not include the great majority of materials costs — the congealed labor of other enterprises — or profit. In other words, it does not include those components of the value of gross production and of commodities that lessen the true volume of the enterprise's productive activity. By more accurately reflecting the labor expended on the production of each article, the index expressing the average value of production allows us to determine on a more realistic basis what tasks we face having to do with raising output, lowering costs, and the profitability of the given type of production. This index is also the most convenient from the standpoint of planning within a factory and for the organization of economic accounting in the enterprise. In addition, it allows one to compare labor productivity in similar enterprises.

This Soviet investigation very much deserves study and coincides, in some respects, with our thesis.

Summary of ideas regarding the budgetary finance system

In order to summarize our ideas on the budgetary finance system, we should begin by making clear that it is a comprehensive concept. That is, its objective operation would take effect when applied to all areas of the economy, in a single whole that — having political decisions as a starting point and going through JUCEPLAN — would reach the enterprises and production units through the channels of the ministries. There it would merge with the people to work its way back up to the policy-making body, thereby forming a giant, well-balanced wheel, within which given production rates could be changed more or less automatically, because the control over production would allow it. The ministries would have the specific responsibility of drawing up and supervising the plans. Enterprises and production units would do this according to more-or-less-flexible levels of decision making, depending on how thoroughly the enterprise has been organized, the type of production, or the situation at any given time. JUCEPLAN would be in charge of the economy's overall central control, assisted by the Ministry of Finance in all matters of financial control and by the Ministry of Labor in matters connected with the planning of the labor force.

Since all this does not really take place in this way, we will describe our present situation with all its limitations, its small achievements, its deficiencies, and its failures — some of them justified or justifiable, others the product of our inexperience or gross shortcomings.

JUCEPLAN furnishes only the general outlines of the plan, together with target figures for those products that are considered essential and that are more or less tightly regulated. The central administrative bodies, in which we include the Ministry of Industry, regulate what are called centralized products, and other products are dealt with by contracts between enterprises. Once the plan is established and made consistent, the contracts are signed — sometimes this has been done beforehand — and work begins.

The ministry's central administration is in charge of assuring the fulfillment of production quotas at the enterprise level, and the enterprise should be in charge of fulfilling them at the factory level. The fundamental thing is that the accounting is consolidated at these two points: the enterprise and the ministry. The basic means of production and inventories must be controlled at the central level so that resources that are idle in given factories for one reason or another can be easily transferred anywhere throughout the whole body of production units. The ministry also has authority to transfer basic means of production from one enterprise to another. These resources do not have the character of commodities; all that happens is that the corresponding entry is made on the books, debiting them on one side and crediting them on the other. A part of production is supplied directly to the population through the Ministry of Domestic Trade, while another part is supplied to different production units for which our products are intermediate goods.

Our fundamental concept is that in this whole process value is successively added to the product by the labor expended on it, but that there is no need for commodity relations between enterprises. Contracts for supplies and corresponding purchase orders, or whatever document might be required at the given moment, simply register that an enterprise has fulfilled its obligation to produce and deliver a given product. Acceptance of an article by an enterprise would mean (in somewhat ideal terms at present, it must be admitted) acceptance of product quality. The product becomes a commodity once it undergoes a legal change of ownership by entering the sphere of individual consumption. The means of production intended for other enterprises are not commodities. But a value has to be placed on them in accordance with the indexes proposed above — using the average neces-sary labor allocated to the production of consumer goods as a standard of comparison — in order to arrive at a price for the equipment or raw material under consideration.

Quarterly plans must be met with regard to product quality, quantity, and assortment. The production unit, in accordance with its labor norms, would pay wages to its workers directly. We will leave blank one point that has not yet been taken care of: the method of rewarding a production unit collectively for particularly outstanding performance or above-average per-formance in the context of the economy as a whole. We also have not con-sidered the question of whether or not to penalize those other factories that have not been able to adequately fulfill their role.

Current state of the budgetary finance system

What is happening right now? One of the first things that happens is that the factory can never count on receiving supplies in the manner and at the time they are needed, so it does not fulfill its production plans. What's worse, however, is that in many cases it receives raw materials that require a different technology. This results in changes in the production process that make technological changes necessary. Direct production costs are affected, as are labor requirements, and, at times, investment needs. The entire plan is often disrupted, forcing frequent adjustments.

Until now, at the ministerial level we have had to simply accept all these anomalies, simply record them. But we are now entering a phase in which we will be able to act, at least with respect to certain categories of the plan, to demand that any distortions be foreseen by accounting methods or mathematical methods, so they can be controlled. We do not yet have the automatic devices needed to ensure that controls are put into effect rapidly and that indexes are accurately analyzed. We do not have sufficient capa-city to analyze the indexes and figures nor the capacity needed to supply correct data for interpretation.

The enterprises are in direct contact with their factories, sometimes by telephone or telegraph or through some provincial representative. In other cases, they communicate through the ministerial representatives who serve as inspectors. And in the municipalities, or political-economic localities of that type, there are the so-called CILOS. These are simply committees of administrators from neighboring factories, responsible for analyzing their problems and making decisions regarding small matters of mutual assistance, which would otherwise require long bureaucratic procedures through all the proper channels. In some cases, they may also lend each other machinery and equipment, but always bearing in mind that permanent transfers require consultation with the corresponding enterprise.

At the beginning of each month, production statistics are sent to the ministry. There they are analyzed up to the highest levels, and basic measures are taken to correct defects. More detailed statistics come in during the following days, on the basis of which more specific measures are also taken at various levels to solve problems.

What are the system's basic weaknesses? We believe that first of all there is its lack of maturity. Second, at all levels there is a scarcity of really qualified cadres. Third, there is a lack of widely disseminated information on the system and its operation so that the people understand it better. We could also cite the lack of a central planning apparatus that would operate in a uniform way and with an absolute hierarchical order, which would make the job easier. We can list shortcomings in the supply of materials, in the transportation system, that sometimes force us to stockpile products and at other times impede production. There are shortcomings in our entire quality control apparatus and in relations (which should be very close, very harmonious, and very well defined) with distribution agencies, particularly the Ministry of Domestic Trade, and with some supply organizations, especially the Ministry of Foreign Trade and INRA. It is still difficult to specify exactly which shortcomings result from inherent weaknesses in the system and which are due largely to our present level of organization.

Neither the factory nor the enterprise use collective material incentives at the moment. This is not due to any overriding idea, but because we are not yet well enough organized to be able to do so on a basis other than the simple fulfillment or over-fulfillment of the enterprise's main plans. The reasons for this have already been noted above.

The system is said to have a tendency toward bureaucratism. One point that must therefore be constantly stressed is the rational organization of the entire administrative apparatus so that there is as little bureaucratism as possible. Now, from the standpoint of objective analysis, it is evident that the more we centralize all the recording and controlling operations of the enterprise or unit, the less bureaucracy there will be. If all the enterprises could centralize all their administrative activities, their apparatus would be reduced to a small nucleus of unit directors plus whatever might be necessary to collect information to pass on to the central administration.

That, for the moment, is impossible. We must, however, proceed with setting up production units of optimum size. This is something that is very much facilitated by the budgetary finance system. The establishment of work norms with a single wage scale breaks down narrow ideas about the enterprise as the center of an individual's activity, and he will more and more turn to society as a whole.

General advantages of the system

To our way of thinking, the budgetary system has the following advantages:

1. By tending toward centralization, it tends toward more rational utilization of national funds.

2. It tends toward greater rationalization of the entire state administrative apparatus.

3. This same tendency toward centralization compels the creation of larger units, within proper limits, which economizes on labor power and increases labor productivity.

4. Once integrated into a single regulatory system, it converts the entire ministry, and all ministries together if possible, into a single large state enterprise. Within this enterprise, a worker could transfer from one place to another, or advance in different branches or locations, with no wage problems. He would simply work under a national wage scale.

5. With regard to bodies responsible for budgeted construction projects, investment control can be much simplified. The task of overseeing the project itself would be carried out by the body contracting for the investment, while the financial supervision would be done by the Ministry of Finance.

It is important to point out that the general idea of mutual cooperation is being instilled in the worker, the idea of belonging to a great whole made up of the country's people. There is an impulse to the development of his consciousness of social duty.

The following quotation from Marx is interesting because, taking out the words that assume the existence of the capitalist regime, it describes the process by which work traditions are formed and might thereby serve as an antecedent for the construction of socialism:

It is not enough that the conditions of labor are concentrated at one pole of society in the shape of capital, while at the other pole are grouped masses of men who have nothing to sell but their labor-power. Nor is it enough that they are compelled to sell themselves voluntarily. The advance of capitalist production develops a working class which by education, tradition and habit looks upon the requirements of that mode of production as self-evident natural laws. The organization of the capitalist process of production, once it is fully developed, breaks down all resistance. The constant generation of a relative surplus population keeps the law of the supply and demand of labor, and therefore wages, within narrow limits which correspond to capital's valorization requirements. The silent compulsion of economic relations sets the seal on the domination of the capitalist over the worker. Direct extra-economic force is still of course used, but only in exceptional cases. In the ordinary run of things, the worker can be left to the "natural laws of production," i.e. it is possible to rely on his dependence on capital, which springs from the conditions of production themselves, and is guaranteed in perpetuity by them.[28]

The productive forces are being developed. The relations of production are changing. Everything awaits the direct action of the workers' state on consciousness.

With respect to material interest, what we want to achieve with the budgetary system is for the lever not to become something that compels the individual — either individually or collectively — to struggle desperately with others in order to assure certain conditions of production or distribution that would put him in a privileged situation. We must make social duty the fundamental point of all the worker's efforts. At the same time we must supervise work conscious of his weaknesses, rewarding or penalizing, using material incentives or disincentives, either individual or collective, when the worker or the unit of production is or is not able to fulfill his social duty. In addition, compulsory training as a requirement for promotion, when it can be implemented on a national scale — and not restricted by any particular local conditions, because the framework is the country as a whole — stimulates a general tendency to study on the part of all the country's working masses. Consequently, it results in a tendency toward very substantial improvements in technical skills.

It should also be considered that, through a policy of subsidies, worker-students can easily be taken out and given the skills to move on to other jobs. In this way we can gradually do away with areas where there is a surplus of living labor, in order to set up more productive factories, that is, more in accordance with the central idea of moving toward communism, toward a society of large-scale production and the satisfaction of man's basic needs.

What remains for us is to emphasize the educational role that the party should play in transforming the work center into the collective expression of the workers' aspirations and concerns and a place where their desire to serve society will take shape.

One could think of the work center as the basis of the future society's political nucleus. Its suggestions, passed on to more complex political organizations, would lead to fundamental decisions by the party and government with regard to the economy or the cultural life of the individual.

Socialism and man in Cuba

(1965)

This article was written in the form of a letter to Carlos Quijano, editor of Marcha, *a weekly published in Montevideo, Uruguay. Guevara wrote it while on a three-month overseas trip, during which he addressed the United Nations General Assembly and then visited a number of countries in Africa. Subheads have been added.*

Dear *compañero,*[29]

Though belatedly, I am completing these notes in the course of my trip through Africa,[30] hoping in this way to keep my promise. I would like to do so by dealing with the theme set forth in the title above. I think it may be of interest to Uruguayan readers.

A common argument from the mouths of capitalist spokespeople, in the ideological struggle against socialism, is that socialism, or the period of building socialism into which we have entered, is characterized by the abolition of the individual for the sake of the state. I will not try to refute this argument solely on theoretical grounds but rather to establish the facts as they exist in Cuba and then add comments of a general nature. Let me begin by broadly sketching the history of our revolutionary struggle before and after the taking of power.

As is well known, the exact date of the beginning of the revolutionary struggle — which would culminate in January 1959 — was July 26, 1953. A group led by Fidel Castro attacked the Moncada barracks in Oriente Province on the morning of that day. The attack was a failure; the failure became a disaster; and the survivors ended up in prison, beginning the revolutionary struggle again after they were freed by an amnesty.

In this process, in which there was only the germ of socialism, the individual was a fundamental factor. We put our trust in him — individual, specific, with a first and last name — and the triumph or failure of the mission entrusted to him depended on that individual's capacity for action.

Then came the stage of guerrilla struggle. It developed in two distinct environments: the people, the still sleeping mass that had to be mobilized; and its vanguard, the guerrillas, the motor force of the mobilization, the generator of revolutionary consciousness and militant enthusiasm. This vanguard was the catalyzing agent that created the subjective conditions necessary for victory.

Here again, in the framework of the proletarianization of our thinking, of this revolution that took place in our habits and our minds, the individual was the basic factor. Every one of the combatants of the Sierra Maestra who reached an upper rank in the revolutionary forces has a record of outstanding deeds to his or her credit. They attained their rank on this basis.

First heroic stage

This was the first heroic period, and in which combatants competed for the heaviest responsibilities, for the greatest dangers, with no other satisfaction than fulfilling a duty. In our work of revolutionary education we frequently return to this instructive theme. In the attitude of our fighters could be glimpsed the man and woman of the future.[31]

On other occasions in our history the act of total dedication to the revolutionary cause was repeated. During the October [1962 missile] crisis and in the days of Hurricane Flora [in October 1963] we saw exceptional deeds of valor and sacrifice performed by an entire people.[32] Finding the method to perpetuate this heroic attitude in daily life is, from the ideological standpoint, one of our fundamental tasks.

In January 1959, the revolutionary government was established with the participation of various members of the treacherous bourgeoisie. The presence of the Rebel Army was the basic element constituting the guarantee of power.

Serious contradictions developed right away. In the first instance, in February 1959, these were resolved when Fidel Castro assumed leadership of the government, taking the post of prime minister. This process culminated in July of the same year with the resignation under mass pressure of President Urrutia.[33]

In the history of the Cuban Revolution there now appeared a character, well defined in its features, which would systematically reappear: the mass.

This multifaceted being is not, as is claimed, the sum of elements of the same type (reduced, moreover, to that same type by the ruling system), which acts like a flock of sheep. It is true that it follows its leaders, basically

Fidel Castro, without hesitation. But the degree to which he won this trust results precisely from having interpreted the full meaning of the people's desires and aspirations, and from the sincere struggle to fulfill the promises he made.

Participation of the masses

The mass participated in the agrarian reform and in the difficult task of administering state enterprises;[34] it went through the heroic experience of the Bay of Pigs;[35] it was hardened in the battles against various groups of bandits armed by the CIA; it lived through one of the most important decisions of modern times during the October [missile] crisis; and today it continues to work for the building of socialism.

Viewed superficially, it might appear that those who speak of the subordination of the individual to the state are right. The mass carries out with matchless enthusiasm and discipline the tasks set by the government, whether in the field of the economy, culture, defense, sports, etc.

The initiative generally comes from Fidel, or from the revolutionary leadership, and is explained to the people, who make it their own. In some cases the party and government take a local experience and generalize it, following the same procedure.

Nevertheless, the state sometimes makes mistakes. When one of these mistakes occurs, one notes a decline in collective enthusiasm due to the effect of a quantitative diminution in each of the elements that make up the mass. Work is paralyzed until it is reduced to an insignificant level. It is time to make a correction. That is what happened in March 1962, as a result of the sectarian policy imposed on the party by Aníbal Escalante.[36]

Clearly this mechanism is not enough to ensure a succession of sensible measures. A more structured connection with the mass is needed, and we must improve it in the course of the coming years. But as far as initiatives originating in the upper strata of the government are concerned, we are currently utilizing the almost intuitive method of sounding out general reactions to the great problems we confront.

In this Fidel is a master. His own special way of fusing himself with the people can be appreciated only by seeing him in action. At the great public mass meetings one can observe something like the dialogue of two tuning forks whose vibrations interact, producing new sounds. Fidel and the mass begin to vibrate together in a dialogue of growing intensity until they reach the climax in an abrupt conclusion crowned by our cry of struggle and victory. The difficult thing to understand for someone not living through the experience of the revolution is this close dialectical unity between the individual and the mass, in which both are interrelated and, at the same time, in which the mass, as an aggregate of individuals, interacts with its leaders.

Some phenomena of this kind can be seen under capitalism, when politicians appear capable of mobilizing popular opinion. But when these are not genuine social movements — if they were, it would not be entirely correct to call them capitalist — they live only so long as the individual who inspires them, or until the harshness of capitalist society puts an end to the people's illusions.

Invisible laws of capitalism

In capitalist society individuals are controlled by a pitiless law usually beyond their comprehension. The alienated human specimen is tied to society as a whole by an invisible umbilical cord: the law of value.[37] This law acts upon all aspects of one's life, shaping its course and destiny.

The laws of capitalism, which are blind and are invisible to ordinary people, act upon the individual without he or she being aware of it. One sees only the vastness of a seemingly infinite horizon ahead. That is how it is painted by capitalist propagandists who purport to draw a lesson from the example of Rockefeller[38] — whether or not it is true — about the possibilities of individual success. The amount of poverty and suffering required for a Rockefeller to emerge, and the amount of depravity entailed in the accumulation of a fortune of such magnitude, are left out of the picture, and it is not always possible for the popular forces to expose this clearly.

(A discussion of how the workers in the imperialist countries gradually lose the spirit of working-class internationalism due to a certain degree of complicity in the exploitation of the dependent countries, and how this at the same time weakens the combativity of the masses in the imperialist countries, would be appropriate here, but that is a theme that goes beyond the scope of these notes.)

In any case, the road to success is portrayed as beset with perils — perils that, it would seem, an individual with the proper qualities can overcome to attain the goal. The reward is seen in the distance; the way is lonely. Furthermore, it is a contest among wolves. One can win only at the cost of the failure of others.

The individual and socialism

I would now like to try to define the individual, the actor in this strange and moving drama of the building of socialism, in a dual existence as a unique being and as a member of society.

I think the place to start is to recognize the individual's quality of incompleteness, of being an unfinished product. The vestiges of the past are brought into the present in one's consciousness, and a continual labor is necessary to eradicate them.[39] The process is two-sided. On the one hand, society acts through direct and indirect education; on the other, the individual submits to a conscious process of self-education.

The new society in formation has to compete fiercely with the past. This past makes itself felt not only in one's consciousness — in which the residue of an education systematically oriented toward isolating the individual still weighs heavily — but also through the very character of this transition period in which commodity relations still persist. The commodity is the economic cell of capitalist society. So long as it exists its effects will make themselves felt in the organization of production and, consequently, in consciousness.

Marx outlined the transition period as resulting from the explosive transformation of the capitalist system destroyed by its own contradictions. In historical reality, however, we have seen that some countries that were weak limbs on the tree of imperialism were torn off first — a phenomenon foreseen by Lenin.

In these countries, capitalism had developed sufficiently to make its effects felt by the people in one way or another. But it was not capitalism's internal contradictions that, having exhausted all possibilities, caused the system to explode. The struggle for liberation from a foreign oppressor; the misery caused by external events such as war, whose consequences privileged classes place on the backs of the exploited; liberation movements aimed at overthrowing neo-colonial regimes — these are the usual factors in unleashing this kind of explosion. Conscious action does the rest.

A complete education for social labor has not yet taken place in these countries, and wealth is far from being within the reach of the masses through the simple process of appropriation. Underdevelopment, on the one hand, and the usual flight of capital, on the other, make a rapid transition without sacrifices impossible.[40] There remains a long way to go in constructing the economic base, and the temptation is very great to follow the beaten track of material interest as the lever with which to accelerate development.

There is the danger that the forest will not be seen for the trees. The pipe dream that socialism can be achieved with the help of the dull instruments left to us by capitalism (the commodity as the economic cell, profitability, individual material interest as a lever, etc.) can lead into a blind alley. When you wind up there after having traveled a long distance with many crossroads, it is hard to figure out just where you took the wrong turn. Meanwhile, the economic foundation that has been laid has done its work of undermining the development of consciousness. To build communism it is necessary, simultaneous with the new material foundations, to build the new man and woman.

New consciousness

That is why it is very important to choose the right instrument for mobilizing the masses. Basically, this instrument must be moral in character, without neglecting, however, a correct use of the material incentive — especially of a social character.[41]

As I have already said, in moments of great peril it is easy to muster a powerful response with moral incentives. Retaining their effectiveness, however, requires the development of a consciousness in which there is a new scale of values. Society as a whole must be converted into a gigantic school.

In rough outline this phenomenon is similar to the process by which capitalist consciousness was formed in its initial period. Capitalism uses force, but it also educates people in the system. Direct propaganda is carried out by those entrusted with explaining the inevitability of class society, either through some theory of divine origin or a mechanical theory of natural law. This lulls the masses, since they see themselves as being oppressed by an evil against which it is impossible to struggle.

Next comes hope of improvement — and in this, capitalism differed from the earlier caste systems, which offered no way out. For some people, the principle of the caste system will remain in effect: The reward for the obedient is to be transported after death to some fabulous other world where, according to the old beliefs, good people are rewarded. For other people there is this innovation: class divisions are determined by fate, but individuals can rise out of their class through work, initiative, etc. This process, and the myth of the self-made man, has to be profoundly hypocritical: it is the self-serving demonstration that a lie is the truth.

In our case, direct education acquires a much greater importance.[42] The explanation is convincing because it is true; no subterfuge is needed. It is carried on by the state's educational apparatus as a function of general, technical and ideological education through such agencies as the Ministry of Education and the party's informational apparatus. Education takes hold among the masses and the foreseen new attitude tends to become a habit. The masses continue to make it their own and to influence those who have not yet educated themselves. This is the indirect form of educating the masses, as powerful as the other, structured, one.

Conscious process of self-education

But the process is a conscious one. Individuals continually feel the impact of the new social power and perceive that they do not entirely measure up to its standards. Under the pressure of indirect education, they try to adjust themselves to a situation that they feel is right and that their own lack of development had prevented them from reaching previously. They educate themselves.

In this period of the building of socialism we can see the new man and woman being born. The image is not yet completely finished — it never will be, since the process goes forward hand in hand with the development of new economic forms.

Aside from those whose lack of education makes them take the solitary road toward satisfying their own personal ambitions, there are those — even within this new panorama of a unified march forward — who have a tendency to walk separately from the masses accompanying them. What is important, however, is that each day individuals are acquiring ever more consciousness of the need for their incorporation into society and, at the same time, of their importance as the motor of that society.

They no longer travel completely alone over lost roads toward distant aspirations. They follow their vanguard, consisting of the party, the advanced workers, the advanced individuals who walk in unity with the masses and in close communion with them.[43] The vanguard has its eyes fixed on the future and its reward, but this is not a vision of reward for the individual. The prize is the new society in which individuals will have different characteristics: the society of communist human beings.

The road is long and full of difficulties. At times we lose our way and must turn back. At other times we go too fast and separate ourselves from the masses. Sometimes we go too slow and feel the hot breath of those treading at our heels. In our zeal as revolutionaries we try to move ahead as fast as possible, clearing the way. But we know we must draw our nourishment from the mass and that it can advance more rapidly only if we inspire it by our example.

Despite the importance given to moral incentives, the fact that there remains a division into two main groups (excluding, of course, the minority that for one reason or another does not participate in the building of socialism) indicates the relative lack of development of social consciousness. The vanguard group is ideologically more advanced than the mass; the latter understands the new values, but not sufficiently. While among the former there has been a qualitative change that enables them to make sacrifices in their capacity as an advance guard, the latter see only part of the picture and must be subject to incentives and pressures of a certain intensity. This is the dictatorship of the proletariat operating not only on the defeated class but also on individuals of the victorious class.

All of this means that for total success a series of mechanisms, of revolutionary institutions, is needed.[44] Along with the image of the multitudes marching toward the future comes the concept of institutionalization as a harmonious set of channels, steps, restraints and well-oiled mechanisms which facilitate the advance, which facilitate the natural selection of those destined to march in the vanguard, and which bestow rewards on those who fulfill their duties and punishments on those who commit a crime against the society that is being built.

Institutionalization of the revolution

This institutionalization of the revolution has not yet been achieved. We are looking for something new that will permit a complete identification between the government and the community in its entirety, something appropriate to the special conditions of the building of socialism, while avoiding at all costs transplanting the commonplaces of bourgeois democracy — such as legislative chambers, for example — into the society in formation.

Some experiments aimed at the gradual institutionalization of the revolution have been made, but without undue haste. The greatest brake has been our fear lest any appearance of formality might separate us from the masses and from the individual, which might make us lose sight of the ultimate and most important revolutionary aspiration: to see human beings liberated from their alienation.

Despite the lack of institutions, which must be overcome gradually, the masses are now making history as a conscious collective of individuals fighting for the same cause. The individual under socialism, despite apparent standardization, is more complete. Despite the lack of a perfect mechanism for it, the opportunities for self expression and making oneself felt in the social organism are infinitely greater.

It is still necessary to deepen conscious participation, individual and collective, in all the structures of management and production, and to link this to the idea of the need for technical and ideological education, so that the individual will realize that these processes are closely interdependent and their advancement is parallel. In this way the individual will reach total consciousness as a social being, which is equivalent to the full realization as a human creature, once the chains of alienation are broken.

This will be translated concretely into the reconquering of one's true nature through liberated labor, and the expression of one's own human condition through culture and art.

New status of work

In order to develop a new culture, work must acquire a new status.[45] Human beings-as-commodities cease to exist, and a system is installed that establishes a quota for the fulfillment of one's social duty. The means of production belong to society, and the machine is merely the trench where duty is performed.

A person begins to become free from thinking of the annoying fact that one needs to work to satisfy one's animal needs. Individuals start to see themselves reflected in their work and to understand their full stature as human beings through the object created, through the work accomplished. Work no longer entails surrendering a part of one's being in the form of labor power sold, which no longer belongs to the individual, but becomes an expression of oneself, a contribution to the common life in which one is reflected, the fulfillment of one's social duty.

We are doing everything possible to give work this new status as a social duty and to link it on the one hand with the development of technology, which will create the conditions for greater freedom, and on the other hand with voluntary work based on the Marxist appreciation that one truly reaches a full human condition when no longer compelled to produce by the physical necessity to sell oneself as a commodity.

Of course, there are still coercive aspects to work, even when it is voluntary. We have not transformed all the coercion that surrounds us into

conditioned reflexes of a social character and, in many cases, is still produced under the pressures of one's environment. (Fidel calls this moral
compulsion.) There is still a need to undergo a complete spiritual rebirth in
one's attitude toward one's own work, freed from the direct pressure of the
social environment, though linked to it by new habits. That will be communism.

The change in consciousness does not take place automatically, just as
change in the economy does not take place automatically. The alterations
are slow and not rhythmic; there are periods of acceleration, periods that
are slower, and even retrogressions.

Furthermore, we must take into account, as I pointed out before, that we
are not dealing with a period of pure transition, as Marx envisaged in his
Critique of the Gotha Program, but rather with a new phase unforeseen by
him: an initial period of the transition to communism, or of the construction
of socialism. This transition is taking place in the midst of violent class
struggles, and with elements of capitalism within it that obscure a complete
understanding of its essence.[46]

If we add to this the scholasticism that has held back the development
of Marxist philosophy and impeded a systematic treatment of the transition
period, whose political economy has not yet been developed, we must agree
that we are still in diapers and that it is necessary to devote ourselves to investigating all the principal characteristics of this period before elaborating
an economic and political theory of greater scope.

The resulting theory will, no doubt, put great stress on the two pillars of
the construction of socialism: the education of the new man and woman
and the development of technology. Much remains to be done in regard to
both, but delay is least excusable in regard to the concept of technology as
a basic foundation, since this is not a question of going forward blindly but
of following a long stretch of road already opened up by the world's more
advanced countries. This is why Fidel pounds away with such insistence
on the need for the technological and scientific training of our people and
especially of its vanguard.

Individualism

In the field of ideas that do not lead to activities involving production, it is
easier to see the division between material and spiritual necessity. For a
long time individuals have been trying to free themselves from alienation
through culture and art. While a person dies every day during the eight or

more hours in which he or she functions as a commodity, individuals come to life afterward in their spiritual creations. But this remedy bears the germs of the same sickness: that of a solitary being seeking harmony with the world. One defends one's individuality, which is oppressed by the environment, and reacts to aesthetic ideas as a unique being whose aspiration is to remain immaculate. It is nothing more than an attempt to escape. The law of value is no longer simply a reflection of the relations of production; the monopoly capitalists — even while employing purely empirical methods — surround that law with a complicated scaffolding that turns it into a docile servant. The superstructure imposes a kind of art in which the artist must be educated. Rebels are subdued by the machine, and only exceptional talents may create their own work. The rest become shamefaced hirelings or are crushed.

A school of artistic experimentation is invented, which is said to be the definition of freedom; but this "experimentation" has its limits, imperceptible until there is a clash, that is, until the real problems of individual alienation arise. Meaningless anguish or vulgar amusement thus become convenient safety valves for human anxiety. The idea of using art as a weapon of protest is combated.

Those who play by the rules of the game are showered with honors — such honors as a monkey might get for performing pirouettes. The condition is that one does not try to escape from the invisible cage.

New impulse for artistic experimentation

When the revolution took power there was an exodus of those who had been completely housebroken. The rest — whether they were revolutionaries or not — saw a new road. Artistic inquiry experienced a new impulse. The paths, however, had already been more or less laid out, and the escapist concept hid itself behind the word "freedom." This attitude was often found even among the revolutionaries themselves, a reflection in their consciousness of bourgeois idealism.

In countries that have gone through a similar process, attempts have been made to combat such tendencies with an exaggerated dogmatism. General culture became virtually taboo, and the acme of cultural aspiration was declared to be the formally exact representation of nature. This was later transformed into a mechanical representation of the social reality they wanted to show: the ideal society, almost without conflicts or contradictions, that they sought to create.

Socialism is young and has its mistakes. We revolutionaries often lack the knowledge and intellectual audacity needed to meet the task of developing the new man and woman with methods different from the conventional ones; conventional methods suffer from the influences of the society that created them. (Once again the theme of the relationship between form and content is posed.) Disorientation is widespread, and the problems of material construction absorb us. There are no artists of great authority who also have great revolutionary authority. The members of the party must take this task in hand and seek the achievement of the main goal: to educate the people.

What is sought then is simplification, something everyone can understand, something functionaries understand. True artistic experimentation ends, and the problem of general culture is reduced to assimilating the socialist present and the dead (therefore, not dangerous) past. Thus socialist realism arises upon the foundations of the art of the last century.[47]

The realistic art of the 19th century, however, also has a class character, more purely capitalist perhaps than the decadent art of the 20th century that reveals the anguish of the alienated individual. In the field of culture, capitalism has given all that it had to give, and nothing remains but the stench of a corpse, today's decadence in art.

But why try to find the only valid prescription in the frozen forms of socialist realism? We cannot counterpose "freedom" to socialist realism, because the former does not yet exist and will not exist until the complete development of the new society. We must not, from the pontifical throne of realism-at-all-costs, condemn all art forms since the first half of the 19th century, for we would then fall into the Proudhonian mistake of going back to the past, of putting a strait-jacket on the artistic expression of the people who are being born and are in the process of making themselves.

What is needed is the development of an ideological-cultural mechanism that permits both free inquiry and the uprooting of the weeds that multiply so easily in the fertilized soil of state subsidies.

In our country the error of mechanical realism has not appeared, but rather its opposite. This is because the need for the creation of a new individual has not been understood, a new human being who would represent neither the ideas of the 19th century nor those of our own decadent and morbid century.

What we must create is the human being of the 21st century, although this is still a subjective aspiration, not yet systematized. This is precisely one of the fundamental objectives of our study and our work. To the extent that we achieve concrete success on a theoretical plane — or, vice versa, to the extent that we draw theoretical conclusions of a broad character on the basis of our concrete research — we will have made a valuable contribution to Marxism-Leninism, to the cause of humanity.

By reacting against the human being of the 19th century we have relapsed into the decadence of the 20th century. It is not a very grave error, but we must overcome it lest we leave open the door for revisionism.

The great multitudes continue to develop. The new ideas are gaining a good momentum within society. The material possibilities for the integrated development of absolutely all members of society make the task much more fruitful. The present is a time of struggle; the future is ours.

New revolutionary generation

To sum up, the fault of many of our artists and intellectuals lies in their original sin: they are not true revolutionaries. We can try to graft the elm tree so that it will bear pears, but at the same time we must plant pear trees. New generations will come that will be free of original sin. The probability that great artists will appear will be greater to the degree that the field of culture and the possibilities for expression are broadened.

Our task is to prevent the current generation, torn asunder by its conflicts, from becoming perverted and from perverting new generations. We must not create either docile servants of official thought, or "scholarship students" who live at the expense of the state — practicing freedom in quotation marks. Revolutionaries will come who will sing the song of the new man and woman in the true voice of the people. This is a process that takes time.

In our society the youth and the party play a big part.[48] The former is especially important because it is the malleable clay from which the new person can be built with none of the old defects. The youth are treated in accordance with our aspirations. Their education is every day more complete, and we do not neglect their incorporation into work from the outset. Our scholarship students do physical work during their vacations or along with their studies. Work is a reward in some cases, a means of education in others, but it is never a punishment. A new generation is being born.

The party is a vanguard organization. It is made up of the best workers, who are proposed for membership by their fellow workers. It is a minority, but it has great authority because of the quality of its cadres. Our aspiration is for the party to become a mass party, but only when the masses have reached the level of the vanguard, that is, when they are educated for communism.

Our work constantly strives toward this education. The party is the living example; its cadres must teach hard work and sacrifice. By their action, they must lead the masses to the completion of the revolutionary task, which involves years of hard struggle against the difficulties of construction, class enemies, the maladies of the past, imperialism.

Role of the individual

Now, I would like to explain the role played by the personality, by men and women as individuals leading the masses that make history. This is our experience; it is not a prescription.

Fidel gave the revolution its impulse in the first years, and also its leadership.[49] He always set its tone; but there is a good group of revolutionaries who are developing along the same road as the central leader. And there is a great mass that follows its leaders because it has faith in them. It has faith in those leaders because they have known how to interpret its aspirations.

It is not a matter of how many kilograms of meat one has to eat, or of how many times a year someone can go to the beach, or how many pretty things from abroad you might be able to buy with present-day wages. It is a matter of making the individual feel more complete, with much more inner wealth and much more responsibility.

People in our country know that the glorious period in which they happen to live is one of sacrifice; they are familiar with sacrifice. The first ones came to know it in the Sierra Maestra and wherever they fought; later, everyone in Cuba came to know it. Cuba is the vanguard of America and must make sacrifices because it occupies the post of advance guard, because it shows the masses of Latin America the road to full freedom.

Within the country the leadership has to carry out its vanguard role. It must be said with all sincerity that in a real revolution, to which one gives his or her all and from which one expects no material reward, the task of the vanguard revolutionary is both magnificent and agonizing.

Love of living humanity

At the risk of seeming ridiculous, let me say that the true revolutionary is guided by great feelings of love. It is impossible to think of a genuine revolutionary lacking this quality. Perhaps it is one of the great dramas of the leader that he or she must combine a passionate spirit with a cold intelligence and make painful decisions without flinching. Our vanguard revolutionaries must idealize this love of the people, of the most sacred causes, and make it one and indivisible. They cannot descend, with small doses of daily affection, to the level where ordinary people put their love into practice.

The leaders of the revolution have children just beginning to talk, who are not learning to say "daddy"; their wives, too, must be part of the general sacrifice of their lives in order to take the revolution to its destiny. The circle of their friends is limited strictly to the circle of comrades in the revolution. There is no life outside of it.

In these circumstances one must have a large dose of humanity, a large dose of a sense of justice and truth in order to avoid dogmatic extremes, cold scholasticism, or an isolation from the masses. We must strive every day so that this love of living humanity is transformed into actual deeds, into acts that serve as examples, as a moving force.

The revolutionary, the ideological motor force of the revolution within the party, is consumed by this uninterrupted activity that comes to an end only with death, unless the construction of socialism is accomplished on a world scale. If one's revolutionary zeal is blunted when the most urgent tasks have been accomplished on a local scale and one forgets about proletarian internationalism, the revolution one leads will cease to be a driving force and sink into a comfortable drowsiness that imperialism, our irreconcilable enemy, will utilize to gain ground. Proletarian internationalism is a duty, but it is also a revolutionary necessity. This is the way we educate our people.

Danger of dogmatism

Of course there are dangers in the present situation, and not only that of dogmatism, not only that of freezing the ties with the masses midway in the great task. There is also the danger of the weaknesses we can fall into. The way is open to infection by the germs of future corruption if a person thinks that dedicating his or her entire life to the revolution means that, in return, one should not be distracted by such worries as that one's child lacks certain things, that one's children's shoes are worn out, that one's family lacks some necessity.

In our case we have maintained that our children must have, or lack, those things that the children of the ordinary citizen have or lack; our families should understand this and struggle for it to be that way. The revolution is made through human beings, but individuals must forge their revolutionary spirit day by day.

Thus we march on. At the head of the immense column — we are neither ashamed nor afraid to say it — is Fidel. After him come the best cadres of the party, and immediately behind them, so close that we feel its tremendous force, comes the people in its entirety, a solid structure of individual beings moving toward a common goal, men and women who have attained consciousness of what must be done, people who fight to escape from the realm of necessity and to enter that of freedom.

This great throng organizes itself; its organization results from its consciousness of the necessity of this organization. It is no longer a dispersed force, divisible into thousands of fragments thrown into the air like splinters from a hand grenade, trying by any means to achieve some protection from an uncertain future, in desperate struggle with their fellows.

We know that sacrifices lie ahead and that we must pay a price for the heroic fact that we are, as a nation, a vanguard. We, as leaders, know that we must pay a price for the right to say that we are at the head of a people that is at the head of America.[50] Each and every one of us readily pays his or her quota of sacrifice, conscious of being rewarded with the satisfaction of fulfilling a duty, conscious of advancing with everyone toward the new man and woman glimpsed on the horizon.

Allow me to draw some conclusions:[51]

We socialists are freer because we are more fulfilled; we are more fulfilled because we are freer.

The skeleton of our complete freedom is already formed. The flesh and the clothing are lacking; we will create them.

Our freedom and its daily sustenance are paid for in blood and sacrifice.

Our sacrifice is a conscious one: an installment paid on the freedom that we are building.

The road is long and, in part, unknown. We recognize our limitations. We will make the human being of the 21st century — we, ourselves.

We will forge ourselves in daily action, creating a new man and woman with a new technology.

Individuals play a role in mobilizing and leading the masses insofar as they embody the highest virtues and aspirations of the people and do not wander from the path.

Clearing the way is the vanguard group, the best among the good, the party.

The basic clay of our work is the youth; we place our hope in it and prepare it to take the banner from our hands.

If this inarticulate letter clarifies anything, it has accomplished the objective that motivated it. Accept our ritual greeting — which is like a handshake or an "Ave Maria Puríssima":

Patria o muerte! [Homeland or death!]

PART

INTERNATIONAL
SOLIDARITY

"From all the sister countries of the Americas, and from our own land, if it should remain standing as an example, from such a moment and forever, the voice of the peoples will answer: 'Thus it shall be: Let freedom triumph in every corner of the Americas'."

Speech to the First Latin American Youth Congress

(July 28, 1960)

Compañeros of the Americas and the entire world:

It would take a long time to extend individual greetings on behalf of our country to each of you, and to each of the countries represented here. We nevertheless want to draw attention to some of those who represent countries afflicted by natural catastrophes or catastrophes caused by imperialism.

We would like to extend special greetings to the representative of the Chilean people, Clotario Blest, whose youthful voice you heard a moment ago. His maturity can serve as an example and a guide to our fellow working people from that unfortunate land, which has been devastated by one of the most terrible earthquakes in history.

We would also like to extend special greetings to Jacobo Arbenz, [former] president of the first Latin American nation [Guatemala] to raise its voice fearlessly against colonialism, and to express the cherished desires of its peasant masses, through a deep and courageous agrarian reform. We would like to express our gratitude to him and to the democracy that fell in that country for the example it gave us, and for enabling us to make a correct appreciation of all the weaknesses his government was unable to overcome. In this way, it has been possible for us [here in Cuba] to get at the roots of the matter, and to decapitate with one strike those who held power, as well as the henchmen serving them.

We would also like to greet two of the delegations representing countries that perhaps have suffered the most in the Americas. First of all, Puerto Rico, which today, 150 years after freedom was first proclaimed in the Americas, continues to fight to take the first, and perhaps most difficult step of achieving, at least in formal terms, a free government. I ask Puerto Rico's delegates to convey my greetings, and those of all Cuba, to Pedro Albizu Campos. We would like to convey to him our heart-felt respect, our recognition of the example he has shown with his valor, and our fraternal feelings as free men toward a man who, despite being in the dungeons of so-called U.S. democracy, is still free.

Although it may seem paradoxical, I would also like to greet today the delegation representing the purest of the U.S. people. I would like to salute them because the U.S. people are not to blame for the barbarity and injustice of their rulers, and because they are innocent victims of the rage of all the peoples of the world, who sometimes confuse a social system with a people.

All of Cuba, myself included, open our arms to the individuals and the delegations, to show you what is good here and what is bad, what has been achieved and what has yet to be achieved, the road traveled and the road ahead. Because even though all of you come to deliberate at this Latin American Youth Congress on behalf of your respective countries, I am sure each of you also comes here full of curiosity to find out exactly what is this phenomenon of the Cuban Revolution, born on a Caribbean island.

Many of you, from diverse political tendencies, will ask yourselves, as you did yesterday and as perhaps you will do tomorrow: What is the Cuban Revolution? What is its ideology? Immediately the question will arise, as it always does, among both adherents and adversaries: Is the Cuban Revolution communist? Some say yes, hoping the answer is yes, or that the revolution is heading in that direction. Others, disappointed perhaps, will also think the answer is yes. There will be disappointed people who believe the answer is no, as well as those who hope the answer is no.

I might be asked whether this revolution before you is a communist revolution. After the usual explanations about communism (leaving aside the hackneyed accusations by imperialism and the colonial powers, who confuse everything), I would answer that if this revolution is Marxist — and listen well that I say Marxist — it is because the revolution discovered, by its own methods, the road pointed out by Marx.

In saluting the Cuban Revolution recently, Vice Premier [Anastas] Mikoyan, one of the leading figures of the Soviet Union and a lifelong Marxist, said that the revolution was a phenomenon Marx had not foreseen. He noted that life teaches more than the wisest books and the most profound thinkers.

The Cuban Revolution was moving forward, without worrying about labels, without checking what others were saying about it, but constantly scrutinizing what the Cuban people wanted of it. The revolution quickly found that it had achieved, or was on the way to achieving, the happiness of its people; and that it had also become the object of inquisitive looks from friend and foe alike — hopeful looks from an entire continent, and furious looks from the king of monopolies.

This did not come about overnight. Permit me to relate some of my own experience — an experience that could help many people in similar circumstances gain an understanding of how our current revolutionary thinking came about. Even though there is certainly continuity, the Cuban Revolution you see today is not the Cuban Revolution of yesterday, even after the victory. Much less is it the Cuban insurrection prior to our victory, when those 82 youths made the difficult crossing of the Gulf of Mexico [in November–December 1956] in a leaky boat to reach the shores of the Sierra Maestra. Between those young people and the representatives of Cuba today there is a distance that cannot be accurately measured in years, with 24-hour days and 60-minute hours. All the members of the Cuban Government — young in age, young in character, and young in the illusions they held — have nevertheless matured in an extraordinary school of experience; in living contact with the people and with their needs and aspirations.

Our collective hope had been to arrive one day somewhere in Cuba, and after a few shouts, a few heroic actions, a few deaths and a few radio broadcasts, to take power and drive out the dictator Batista. History showed us it was far more difficult to overthrow a government backed and partnered by an army of murderers, and backed by the greatest colonial power on earth.

Little by little, each of our ideas changed. We, the children of the cities, learned to respect the peasants. We learned to respect their sense of independence, their loyalty; we learned to recognize their age-old yearning for the land that had been snatched from them; and to recognize their experience in the thousand paths across the hills. From us, the peasants learned how valuable someone is when they have a rifle in their hand, and when they are prepared to fire that rifle at another person, regardless of how many rifles that other person has. The peasants taught us their know-how and we taught the peasants our sense of rebellion. From that moment until now, and forever, the peasants of Cuba and the rebel forces of Cuba — today the Cuban revolutionary government — have united as one.

The revolution continued to progress, and we drove the troops of the dictatorship from the steep slopes of the Sierra Maestra. We came face-to-face with another reality of Cuba: the workers — both in agricultural and industrial centers. We learned from them too, while we taught them that at the right moment, a well-aimed shot fired at the right person is much more powerful and effective than the most powerful and effective peaceful demonstration. We learned the value of organization, while again we taught the value of rebellion. Out of this, organized rebellion arose throughout the entire territory of Cuba.

By then much time had passed. Many deaths marked the road of our victory — many in combat, others innocent victims. The imperialist forces began to see there was something more than a group of bandits in the heights of the Sierra Maestra, something more than a group of ambitious assailants arrayed against the ruling power. The imperialists generously offered their bombs, bullets, planes and tanks to the dictatorship. With those tanks in the lead, the government's forces again attempted, for the last time, to ascend the Sierra Maestra.

By then, columns of our forces had already left the Sierra to invade other regions of Cuba and had formed the "Frank País" Second Eastern Front under Commander Raúl Castro. Our strength within public opinion was growing — we were now headline material in the international pages of newspapers from every corner of the world. Yet despite all this, the Cuban Revolution at that time possessed only 200 rifles — not 200 men, but 200 rifles — to stop the regime's last offensive, in which the dictatorship amassed 10,000 soldiers and every type of instrument of death. Each one those 200 rifles carries a history of sacrifice and blood. They were rifles of imperialism that the blood and determination of our martyrs dignified and transformed into rifles of the people.

In this way, the last stage of the army's great offensive unfolded, under the name of "encirclement and annihilation."

What I am saying to you, young people from throughout the Americas who are diligent and eager to learn, is that if today we are putting into practice what is known as Marxism, it is because we discovered it here. In those days, after defeating the dictatorship's troops and inflicting 1,000 casualties on their ranks — five times as many casualties as the sum total of our combat forces, and after seizing more than 600 weapons — a small pamphlet written by Mao Tse-tung fell into our hands. The pamphlet dealt with strategic problems of the revolutionary war in China and described the campaigns that the dictator Chiang Kai-shek carried out against the popular forces, which just like here were called "campaigns of encirclement and annihilation."

Not only had the same words been used on opposite sides of the globe to describe their campaigns, but both dictators had resorted to the same types of campaigns to try to destroy the popular forces. The popular forces here, without knowing of the manuals already written about the strategy and tactics of guerrilla warfare, used the same methods as those used on the opposite side of the world to combat the dictatorship's forces. Naturally, when somebody lives through an experience, that experience can be utilized by somebody else. But it is also possible to go through the same experience without knowing of the earlier one.

We were unaware of the experiences the Chinese troops accumulated during 20 years of struggle in their territory. But we knew our own territory, we knew our enemy, and we used something every person has on their shoulders — which is worth a lot if they know how to use it — we used our heads to guide our fight against the enemy. As a result, we defeated it.

The westward invasions came later, and the breaking of Batista's communication lines, and the crushing fall of the dictatorship when no-one expected it. Then came January 1 [1959] and the revolution, without thinking about what it had read, but hearing what it needed to from the lips of the people, decided first and foremost to punish the guilty, and it did so.

Immediately the colonial powers splashed the story all over the front pages, calling it murder, immediately trying to do what imperialists always try to do: sow division. "Communist murderers are killing people," they said. "There is, however, a naive patriot Fidel Castro, who had nothing to do with it and can be saved." In this way they tried to sow divisions among those who had fought for the same cause. They maintained this hope for some time.

One day they happened upon the Agrarian Reform Law, and saw that it was much more violent and profound than the law their very intellectual, self-appointed advisers had counselled. All of those advisers, by the way, are today in Miami or some other U.S. city, like Pepin Rivero of *Diario de la Marina*, or Medrano of *Prensa Libre*. Others, including a prime minister in our government, also counseled great moderation, being that "one must handle such things with moderation."

"Moderation" is one of those words colonial agents like to use. Those who are afraid, or who think of betraying in one way or another, are moderates. In no sense, however, are the people moderates.

The advice given was to divide up marabú land — marabú is a wild shrub that plagues our fields — and have the peasants cut marabú with machetes, or settle in swamps, or grab pieces of public land that might somehow have escaped the voraciousness of the large landowners. To touch the holdings of the large landowners was a sin greater than anything they imagined to be possible. But it *was* possible.

I recall a conversation I had in those days with a gentleman who said he had no problems at all with the revolutionary government because he owned only 900 *caballerías*. Nine hundred *caballerías* comes to more than 10,000 hectares [25,000 acres]. This gentleman, of course, did eventually have problems with the revolutionary government; his lands were seized, divided up, and turned over to individual peasants. In addition, cooperatives were created on lands where agricultural workers were already beginning to work collectively for a wage.

This is one of the peculiar features of the Cuban Revolution that must be studied. For the first time in Latin America, a revolution carried out an agrarian reform that attacked property relations other than feudal ones. There were feudal remnants in the tobacco and coffee industries, and in these areas land was turned over to individuals who had been working small plots and wanted their land. But given how sugarcane, rice and cattle were cultivated and worked in Cuba, that land was seized as a unit and worked by workers who were granted joint ownership. Those workers are not owners of single parcels of land, but of the whole great joint enterprise called a cooperative. This has enabled our far-reaching agrarian reform to move rapidly. Each of you should let it sink in, as an incontrovertible truth, that no government here in Latin America can call itself revolutionary unless its first measure is agrarian reform.

A government that says it will implement timid agrarian reform cannot call itself revolutionary. A revolutionary government carries out agrarian reform that transforms the system of property relations — that doesn't just give peasants unused land, but primarily gives peasants land that *was* in use, land that belonged to large landowners, the best land with the greatest yield, land that moreover had been stolen from the peasants in past epochs.

That is agrarian reform, and that is how all revolutionary governments must begin. On the basis of agrarian reform the great battle for the industrialization of a country can be waged, a battle that is very complicated, in which one must fight against very big things.

We could very easily fail, as in the past, if it weren't for the existence of very great forces in the world today that are friends of small nations like ours. I must note here for everyone's benefit — for those who like it and those who hate it — that at the present time countries like Cuba, revolutionary, non-moderate countries, cannot respond half-heartedly as to whether the Soviet Union or People's China are our friends. They must answer with all their might that the Soviet Union, China and all the socialist countries are our friends, as are many colonial or semicolonial countries that have freed themselves.

These friendships with governments throughout the world is why it is possible to carry out a revolution in Latin America. When the imperialists carried out aggression against us using sugar and petroleum, the Soviet Union was there to give us petroleum and to buy sugar from us. Without that, we would have needed all our strength, all our faith, and the devotion of the people, which is enormous, to withstand the blow this would have signified. These measures taken by "U.S. democracy" against this "threat to the free world" would have had huge effects on the living standards of the Cuban people, and the forces of disunity would have done their work, viciously playing on the effects.

There are government leaders in Latin America who still advise us to lick the hand that wants to hit us; to spit on the one who wants to help us. We answer these government leaders who, in the middle of the 20th century, recommend bowing our heads: We say, first of all, that Cuba does not bow down before anyone. Secondly, we say that Cuba, from its own experience, knows the weaknesses and defects of the governments advising this approach — and the rulers of these countries know them too; they know them very well. Nevertheless, Cuba has not deigned or allowed itself, or thought it permissible, to advise the rulers of these countries to shoot every traitorous official or nationalize all the monopoly holdings in their countries.

The people of Cuba shot their murderers and dissolved the army of the dictatorship. Yet they have not been telling governments in Latin America to put the murderers of the people before the firing squads or to stop propping up dictatorships. Cuba knows there are murderers in each one of these nations. We can attest to that fact because a Cuban belonging to our own movement [Andrés Coba] was killed, in a friendly country [Venezuela], by henchmen left over from the previous dictatorship.

We do not ask that they put the person who assassinated one of our members before a firing squad, although we would have done so in this country. What we ask, simply, is that if it is not possible to act with solidarity in the Americas, at least don't be a traitor to the Americas. Let no-one in the Americas parrot the notion that we are bound to a continental alliance that includes our great enslaver. That is the most cowardly and denigrating lie a ruler in Latin America can utter.

We, the entire people of Cuba who belong to the Cuban Revolution, call our friends friends, and our enemies enemies. We do not allow for halfway terms: one is either a friend or an enemy. We, the people of Cuba, don't tell any nation on earth what they should do with, for example, the International Monetary Fund. But we will not tolerate them coming to tell us what to do. We know what has to be done. If they want to do what we would do, good; if not, that's up to them. We will not tolerate anyone telling us what to do. We were here on our own until the last moment, awaiting the direct aggression of the mightiest power in the capitalist world, and we did not ask for help from anyone. We were prepared, together with our people, to resist through to the final consequences of our rebel spirit.

We can speak with our heads held high, and with very clear voices, in all the congresses and councils where our brothers of the world meet. When the Cuban Revolution speaks, it may make mistakes, but it will never tell a lie. In every place where it speaks, the Cuban Revolution expresses the truths that its sons and daughters have learned, and it does so openly to its friends and its enemies alike. It never throws stones from behind corners; it never gives advice containing daggers cloaked in velvet.

We are subject to attacks. We are attacked a great deal because of what we are. But we are attacked much, much more because we show to each nation of the Americas what is possible. What is important for imperialism — more than Cuba's nickel mines or sugar mills, Venezuela's oil, Mexico's cotton, Chile's copper, Argentina's cattle, Paraguay's grasslands or Brazil's coffee — is the totality of these raw materials upon which the monopolies feed.

They place obstacles in our path every chance they get, and when they themselves are unable to erect obstacles, others in Latin America are unfortunately willing to do so. Names are not important, because no single individual is to blame. We cannot say that [Venezuelan] President Betancourt is to blame for the death of our compatriot and co-thinker [Andrés Coba]. President Betancourt is not to blame; he is simply a prisoner of a regime that calls itself democratic. That democratic regime could have set another example in Latin America, but it nevertheless committed the great mistake of not using the firing squad in a timely way. Today the democratic government of Venezuela is again a prisoner of the henchmen Venezuela was familiar with a short while ago — and with whom Cuba was familiar, and with whom the majority of Latin America remains familiar.

We cannot blame President Betancourt for this death. We can only say the following, supported by our record as revolutionaries and by our conviction as revolutionaries: the day President Betancourt, elected by his people, feels himself a prisoner to such a degree that he cannot go forward and decides to ask the help of a fraternal people, Cuba is here to show Venezuela some of our experiences in the field of revolution.

President Betancourt should know that it was not — and could not have been — our diplomatic representative who started the affair that ended in a death. It was the North Americans, or in the final analysis the U.S. Government. A bit closer to the events, it was Batista's men, and closer still, it was those dressed up in anti-Batista clothing, the U.S. Government's reserve forces in this country, who wanted to defeat Batista yet maintain the system: people like [José] Miró Cardona, [Miguel Angel] Quevedo, [Pedro Luis] Díaz Lanz and Huber Matos. In direct line of sight it was the reactionary forces operating in Venezuela. It is very sad to say, but the leader of

Venezuela is at the mercy of his own troops, who may at any moment try to assassinate him, as happened a while ago in the case of the car packed with dynamite. The Venezuelan President, at this moment, is a prisoner of his repressive forces.

This hurts, because the Cuban people received from Venezuela the greatest amount of solidarity and support when we were in the Sierra Maestra. It hurts, because much earlier than us Venezuela was able to rid itself of the hateful and oppressive system represented by [Marcos] Pérez Jiménez. It hurts, because when our delegations went to Venezuela — first Fidel Castro, and later our president Dorticós — they received great demonstrations of support and affection.

A people who have achieved the high degree of political consciousness, who have the high fighting spirit of the Venezuelan people, will not remain prisoners of a few bayonets or bullets for long. Bullets and bayonets can change hands, and the murderers themselves can wind up dead.

But it is not my mission to list here all the stabs in the back we have received from Latin American governments in recent days and to add fuel to the fire of rebellion. That is not my task because, in the first place, Cuba is still not free of danger. Today Cuba is still the focus of the imperialists' attention in this part of the world. Cuba needs your solidarity, the solidarity of those from the Democratic Action Party in Venezuela, the URD [Democratic Republican Union], or the Communists, or COPEI [Independent Political Electoral Committee], or any other party. It needs the solidarity of the Mexican people, the Colombian people, the Brazilian people and the people of every nation in Latin America.

The colonialists are scared. They, like everyone else, are afraid of missiles, they too are afraid of bombs. Today they see, for the first time in their history, that bombs of destruction can also fall on their families, on everything they have built with so much love — as far as anyone can love wealth and riches. They began to make estimates; they put their electronic calculators to work, and they saw this set-up would be self-defeating.

This in no way means that they have renounced the suppression of Cuban democracy. Once again they are making laborious estimates on their calculating machines as to which of the available methods is best for attacking the Cuban Revolution. They have the methods of Ydígoras, Nicaragua, Haiti. For the moment, they do not have the Dominican method. They also have the mercenaries in Florida, the OAS [Organization of American States] and many other methods. And they have power to continue improving these methods.

[Former] President Arbenz and his people know they had many methods and a great deal of might. Unfortunately for Guatemala, President Arbenz had an army of the old style, and was not fully aware of the solidarity of the peoples and their capacity to repel any type of aggression.

One of our greatest strengths is being exerted throughout the world — regardless of partisan differences in any country — the strength to defend the Cuban Revolution at any given moment. Permit me to say this is a duty of Latin America's youth. What we have here in Cuba is something new and it's worth studying. You will have to assess what is good here for yourselves.

There are many bad things, I know. There is a lot disorganization, I know. If you have been to the Sierra Maestra, then you already know this. We still use guerrilla methods, I know. We lack technicians in necessary quantities commensurate to our aspirations, I know. Our army has still not reached the necessary degree of maturity and the militia members have not achieved sufficient coordination to constitute themselves as an army, I know.

But what I also know, and I want all of you to know, is that this revolution has always acted with the will of the entire people of Cuba. Every peasant and worker who handles a rifle poorly is working every day to handle it better, to defend *their* revolution. And if at this moment they can't understand the complicated workings of a machine whose technician fled to the United States, then they are studying every day to learn it, so *their* factory runs better. The peasants are studying *their* tractor, to fix its mechanical problems, so the fields of *their* cooperative yield more.

All Cubans, from both the city and country, share the same sentiments and are marching toward the future, totally united in their thinking, with a leader they have absolute confidence in because he has shown in a thousand battles and on a thousand different occasions his capacity for sacrifice and the power and foresight of his thought.

The nation before you today might disappear from the face of the earth because an atomic conflict may be unleashed on its account, and it might be the first target. Even if this entire island were to disappear along with its inhabitants, Cuba's people would consider themselves satisfied and fulfilled if each of you, upon returning to your countries, would say:

> Here we are. Our words come from the humid air of the Cuban forests. We have climbed the Sierra Maestra and seen the dawn, and our minds and our hands are filled with the seeds of that dawn. We are prepared to plant them in this land, and defend them so they can grow.

From all the sister countries of the Americas, and from our own land, if it should still remain standing as an example, from such a moment on and forever, the voice of the peoples will answer: "Thus it shall be: Let freedom triumph in every corner of the Americas!"

The OAS conference at Punta del Este

(August 8, 1961)

Che Guevara headed Cuba's delegation to the 1961 ministerial meeting of the Inter-American Economic and Social Council sponsored by the Organization of American States (OAS). The conference was held at Punta del Este, Uruguay. Upon his arrival in Uruguay, Guevara was met by a crowd of thousands of supporters. At the meeting, the U.S. delegation, headed by C. Douglas Dillon, presented Washington's recently proclaimed Alliance for Progress for official ratification by the OAS. The conference was presided over by Uruguayan President Eduardo Haedo.

Mr. President;
Distinguished delegates:

Like all the delegations, we must begin by expressing our appreciation to the government and people of Uruguay for the cordial reception they have given us during this visit.

I would also like to personally thank the distinguished president of this gathering for the gift he made to us of the complete works of Rodó, and would like to explain to him the two reasons why we are not beginning this presentation with a quotation from that great Latin American. The first is that I went back to *Ariel* after many years, looking for a passage that would express, at the present time, the ideas of someone who is, more than an Uruguayan, a man of our America, an American from the Río Bravo [Rio Grande] to the south. But Rodó expresses throughout his *Ariel* the violent struggle and the contradictions of the Latin American peoples against the nation that 50 years ago was already interfering in our economy and in our political freedom. And it was not proper to quote this in someone else's house.[1]

And the second reason, Mr. President, is that the head of one of the delegations here offered us a quotation from Martí to begin his presentation.[2] Well, we will answer Martí with Martí. But with the antiimperialist and antifeudal Martí who died facing Spanish bullets fighting for the liberty of his homeland and — as he put it in one of his last letters — trying, with Cuba's liberty, to prevent the United States from falling upon Latin America.

At that international monetary conference to which the distinguished president of the Inter-American Bank referred in his inaugural address when he spoke of the 70 years of waiting,[3] Martí said:

> Whoever speaks of economic union speaks of political union. The nation that buys, commands; the nation that sells, serves. Commerce must be balanced to assure freedom. A nation that wants to die sells to one nation only, and a nation that would be saved sells to more than one. The excessive influence of one country over another's commerce becomes political influence. Politics is the work of men, who surrender their feelings to an interest. When a strong nation supplies another with food, she requires that the recipient serve her. When a strong nation wants to engage another in battle, she forces those who have need of her to become her allies and to serve her. A nation that wants to be free must be free in matters of trade. It must distribute its trade among nations that are equally strong. If one is to be preferred, give preference to the one who needs it the least. Let there be no unions of the Americas against Europe, nor with Europe against a nation of the Americas. Only the mind of some university student can deduce an obligation to political union from the geographic coincidence of our living together in the Americas. Commerce follows the land and sea routes of the earth, going to whatever country has anything to exchange, be it a monarchy or a republic. Let us be in union with the whole world and not with just a part of it; not with one part against another. If the republics of the Americas have any function at all, it is certainly not to be herded by one of them against the future republics.

That was Martí 70 years ago, Mr. President.

Well, having complied with the elementary duty of honoring the dead and of repaying the kindness that the distinguished delegate showed us before, we pass on to the fundamental part of our presentation: the analysis of why we are here, to characterize the conference. And I must say, Mr. President, that I disagree, in the name of Cuba, with almost all the statements that have been made, although I don't know if I disagree with all the private thoughts of everyone.

I must say that Cuba's interpretation is that this is a political conference. Cuba does not agree that economics can be separated from politics, and understands that they always go together. That is why you cannot have experts who speak of models when the destinies of a people are at stake. And I am also going to explain why this conference is political. It is political because all economic conferences are political. But it is also political because it was conceived against Cuba, and because it has been conceived to counter the example that Cuba represents throughout Latin America.

And if there is any doubt about that, on the 10th, in Fort Amador in the [Panama] Canal Zone, General Decker, while instructing a group of Latin American military men in the art of repressing the people, spoke of the technical conference in Montevideo and said that it had to be backed.

But that's nothing. In the inaugural message on August 5, 1961, President Kennedy asserted: "Those of you at this conference are present at an historic moment in the life of this Hemisphere. For this is far more than an economic discussion, or a technical conference on development. In a very real sense it is a demonstration of the capacity of free nations to meet the human and material problems of the modern world."

I could continue quoting the prime minister of Peru, where he also refers to political themes. But in order not to tire the distinguished delegates, for I can foresee that my presentation will be a bit long, I will refer to some statements made by the "experts" — a term we place within quotation marks — on point 5 of the draft text.

At the end of page 11, it is stated as a definitive conclusion: "To establish, on a hemispheric and national level, regular consultative procedures with the trade union advisory committees, so that they may play an influential role in the political formulation of programs that might be approved in the special session."

And to drive home my point, so that there may not remain any doubt as to my right to speak of political matters — which is what I plan to do in the name of the Cuban Government — here is a quotation from page seven of that same report on point 5 in question: "Delay in accepting the responsibility of the democratic information media to defend the essential values of our civilization, without any weakening or commitments of a material sort, would signify irreparable damage to democratic society and the imminent danger of the disappearance of the freedoms enjoyed today, as has occurred in Cuba…" — Cuba is spelled out — "…where today all newspapers, radio, television and movies are controlled by the absolute power of the government."

In other words, distinguished delegates, in the report we are to discuss, Cuba is put on trial from a political point of view. Very well then, Cuba will state its truths from a political point of view, and from an economic point of view, as well.

We agree with only one thing in the report on point 5 by the distinguished experts, with only one phrase, which defines the present situation:

"A new stage is beginning in relations between the peoples of the Americas," it says, and that's true. Except that the new stage begins under the star of Cuba, free territory of the Americas. And this conference, and the special treatment that the delegations have received, and the credits that may be granted, all bear the name of Cuba, whether the beneficiaries like it or not, because a qualitative change has taken place in the Americas. A country can take up arms, destroy an oppressing army, form a new popular army, stand up to the invincible monster, wait for the monster's attack, and also defeat it. And that is something new in Latin America, gentlemen. That is what makes this new language possible and what makes relations easier between everyone — except, of course, between the two great rivals of this conference.

Cuba at this time cannot even speak of Latin America alone. Cuba is part of a world that is in anguished tension, because we don't know if one of the parts — the weakest, but the most aggressive — will commit the stupid mistake of unleashing a conflict that would necessarily be a nuclear one. Cuba is on the alert, distinguished delegates, because she knows that imperialism would perish enveloped in flames, but that Cuba would also suffer in its own flesh the price of imperialism's defeat, and she hopes that it can be accomplished by other means. Cuba hopes that her children will see a better future, and that victory will not have to be won at the cost of millions of human lives destroyed by the atomic bomb.

The situation of the world is tense. We are not gathered here just for Cuba, not in the least. Imperialism has to protect its rearguard because the battle is being fought on all sides, in a moment of great tension.

The Soviet Union has reaffirmed its decision to sign the Berlin peace treaty, and President Kennedy has announced that he can even go to war over Berlin. But there's not only Berlin; there's not only Cuba; there's Laos; elsewhere there's the Congo, where Lumumba was assassinated by imperialism; there's divided Vietnam, divided Korea, Formosa in the hands of Chiang Kai-shek's gang; Algeria is bleeding to death, and now they also want to divide it; and there is Tunisia, whose population was machine-gunned the other day for committing the "crime" of wanting to regain their territory.

That is the world today, distinguished delegates. That is how we have to see it in order to understand this conference and draw the conclusions that will permit our peoples either to head toward a happy future of harmonious development, or else become appendages of imperialism in the preparation of a new and terrible war. Or they may shed blood in internal strife when — as almost all of you have foreseen — the people, tired of waiting, tired of being fooled once again, begin the road that Cuba once began: that of taking weapons away from the enemy army, which represents reaction, and destroying to its very foundations a whole social order designed to exploit the people.

The history of the Cuban Revolution is short in years, Mr. President. But it is rich in accomplishments, rich in positive accomplishments, and rich also in the bitterness of the aggressions it has suffered.

We will point out a few of them so that it may be well understood that there is a long chain of events that leads us here.

In October 1959 the only fundamental economic measure that the revolutionary government had carried out was the agrarian reform. Pirate airplanes coming from the United States flew over Havana's airspace and as a result of the bombs that they dropped and the fire of our antiaircraft batteries, two people were killed and 50 were wounded. Then, there was the burning of the sugarcane fields, which constitutes economic aggression, an aggression against our wealth. The United States denied all responsibility until an airplane blew up — pilot and all — and the origin of those pirate craft was indisputably demonstrated. This time the U.S. Government was kind enough to offer apologies. The España sugar mill was also bombed in February 1960 by these planes.

In March of that year the steamship *La Coubre*, which was bringing arms and munitions from Belgium, exploded at the Havana docks in an accident that the experts said was intentional and that killed 100 people.

In May 1960 the conflict with imperialism became direct and sharp. The oil companies operating in Cuba, invoking the right of force and scorning the laws of the republic, which clearly specified their obligations, refused to refine the crude oil that we had bought from the Soviet Union, in the exercise of our free right to trade with the whole world and not with just a part of it, as Martí said.

Everyone knows how the Soviet Union responded by sending us, in a real effort, hundreds of ships to transport 3.6 million tons of oil annually — the total of our crude oil imports — to keep our whole industrial apparatus moving, which today runs on the basis of oil.

In July 1960 there was the economic aggression against Cuban sugar, although some governments have not yet realized it has taken place. The contradictions became sharper and the meeting of the OAS took place in August 1960, in Costa Rica. There — in August 1960, I repeat — it was stated: "The intervention or threat of intervention by an extra-continental power in the affairs of the American republics, even when it is invited, is energetically condemned, and it is declared that the acceptance of a threat of extra-continental intervention by an American state endangers American solidarity and security, which obligates the Organization of American States to condemn and reject it with equal energy."

In other words, the sister nations of the Americas, gathered in Costa Rica, denied us the right to be defended. It is one of the strangest denials that the history of international law has seen. Of course our people are a bit disobedient to the dictates of technical assemblies and they met in the Assembly of Havana and approved unanimously — more than a million hands raised to the sky, one-sixth of the total population of the whole country — the declaration that was called the Declaration of Havana, one of whose points states:

> The National General Assembly of the People of Cuba — confident that it is expressing the general opinion of the peoples of Latin America — reaffirms that democracy is not compatible with financial oligarchy; with discrimination against blacks and outrages by the Ku Klux Klan; nor with the persecution that drove scientists like Oppenheimer from their posts, deprived the world for years of the marvelous voice of Paul Robeson, held prisoner in his own country, and sent the Rosenbergs to their death against the protests of a shocked world, including the appeals of many governments and of Pope Pius XII.
>
> The National General Assembly of the People of Cuba expresses the Cuban conviction that democracy cannot consist solely of elections that are nearly always fictitious and managed by rich land-owners and professional politicians, but rather it lies in the right of the citizens to determine their own destiny, as this Assembly of the People is now doing. Furthermore, democracy will come to exist in Latin America only when people are really free to make choices, when the poor are not reduced — by hunger, social discrimination, illiteracy and the legal system — to the most wretched impotence....
>
> The National General Assembly of the People of Cuba condemns, in sum: the exploitation of human by human and the exploitation of the underdeveloped countries by imperialist finance capital.

That was a declaration of our people made before the whole world, to show our resolve to defend with arms, with our blood, and with our lives, our freedom and our right to determine the destiny of our country in the way our people think best.

There followed many skirmishes and battles, verbal at times, with deeds at others, until in December 1960 the Cuban sugar quota in the American market was cut once and for all. The Soviet Union responded in the manner that you know. Other socialist countries did likewise and contracts were signed to sell to the whole socialist area four million tons of sugar, at a preferential price of four cents. That naturally saved the situation for Cuba, which unfortunately is still today as much of a one-crop country as are the majority of the countries of Latin America, and it was as dependent upon a single market, on a single product — at that time — as the rest of her sister countries are today.

It seemed that President Kennedy was initiating the new era that has been so talked about. And in spite of the fact that the verbal battle had been intense between President Kennedy and the prime minister of our government, we hoped things would improve. President Kennedy made a speech clearly warning of a series of positions to be taken in Latin America, but he appeared to announce to the world that the case of Cuba must be considered now as a fait accompli.

We were mobilized at that time. The day after Kennedy's speech demobilization was ordered. Unfortunately, on March 13, 1961 — the day President Kennedy was talking about the Alliance for Progress — the pirate attack on our refinery at Santiago de Cuba took place, endangering the installations and taking the life of one of the defenders. We were thus again faced with an accomplished fact.

In that speech, which I have no doubt will be memorable, Kennedy also said that he hoped the peoples of Cuba and the Dominican Republic, for whom he felt great sympathy, could join the community of free nations. Within a month there was Playa Girón, and a few days later President Trujillo was mysteriously assassinated. We were always enemies of President Trujillo; we merely take note of the bare fact, which has not been clarified in any way up to the present time.

Afterward, a true masterpiece of belligerence and political naiveté was created, which was called the White Paper. According to the magazines that talk so much in the United States, even provoking the ire of President Kennedy, its author is one of the distinguished advisers of the U.S. delegation that is with us today.[4] It is an accusation filled with distortions about Cuban reality, and was conceived as a preparation for what was already coming.

"The revolutionary regime betrayed their own revolution," said the White Paper, as if it were the judge of revolutions and of how to make revolutions, the great appraiser of revolutions in the Americas.

"The Castro regime offers a clear and present danger to the authentic revolutions of the Americas." The word *revolution* also needs the barnacles scraped off it now and then, as one of the members presiding here said.

"The Castro regime refuses to negotiate amicably." This in spite of our having said many times that we will sit down on an equal basis to discuss our problems with the United States. I take advantage of the opportunity now, on behalf of my government, Mr. President, to state once more that Cuba is ready to sit down to discuss as equals everything that the U.S. delegation wishes to discuss, but on the strict basis that there be no prior conditions. In other words, our position is very clear on the matter.

In the White Paper the Cuban people were called to subversion and to revolution "against the Castro regime." Yet, in spite of this, on April 13, President Kennedy once more spoke and affirmed categorically that he would not invade Cuba and that the armed forces of the United States would never intervene in Cuba's internal affairs. Two days later, unmarked airplanes bombed our airports and reduced to ashes the greater part of our ancient air force, the remnants of what Batista's men had left behind when they fled.

In the United Nations Security Council Mr. Adlai Stevenson gave emphatic assurances that they were Cuban pilots, from our air force, "unhappy with the Castro regime," who had carried out such a deed. And he stated that he had spoken with them.

On April 17, the unsuccessful invasion took place. Our entire people, united and on a war footing, once more demonstrated that there are forces stronger than widespread propaganda, that there are forces stronger than the brutal force of arms, that there are higher values than the value of money. They threw themselves in a mad rush onto the narrow paths that led to the battlefield, many of them massacred on the way by the enemy's air superiority. Nine Cuban pilots were the heroes of that struggle, with the old planes. Two of them gave their lives; seven of them are exceptional witnesses to the triumph of freedom's weapons.

Playa Girón was over, and — to be brief, for there's no need to offer proof when the guilty party confesses, distinguished delegates — President Kennedy assumed full responsibility for the aggression. Perhaps at that time he did not remember the words he had spoken a few days before.

You might think that the history of aggressions was over. Nevertheless, I'll give you a scoop, as the newspaper people say. On July 26 of this year, counterrevolutionary groups armed at the Guantánamo naval base were waiting for Commander Raúl Castro at two strategic places in order to assassinate him. The plan was intelligent and macabre. They would fire upon Commander Raúl Castro while he was on the road from his house to the mass meeting at which we celebrate the date of our revolution. If they failed, they would dynamite the base, or rather, they would detonate the already dynamited bases of the stand from which our *compañero* Raúl Castro would preside over that patriotic meeting. And a few hours later, distinguished delegates, U.S. mortars would begin firing from Cuban territory against the Guantánamo naval base. So the whole world would clearly understand the matter: the Cubans, exasperated because in the middle of their personal quarrels one of those "Communists over there" was assassinated, were attacking the Guantánamo naval base, and the poor United States would have no recourse but to defend itself.

That was the plan that our security forces, which are much more efficient than you might imagine, discovered a few days ago.

All that I have just told you is why I believe that the Cuban Revolution cannot come to this conference of illustrious experts to speak about technical matters. I know that you think, "It's because they don't know about these things." And perhaps you're right. But the fundamental thing is that politics and facts, so obstinate, which are constantly present in our situation, prevent us from coming here to speak about numbers or to analyze the perfections of the IESC [Inter-American Economic and Social Council] specialists.

There are a series of political problems that are making the rounds. One of them is a political-economic question: the tractors.[5] Five hundred tractors is not an exchange value. Five hundred tractors is what our government estimates would allow it to repair the material damages caused by the 1,200 mercenaries. They do not pay for a single life, because we are not accustomed to placing a dollar value on the lives of our citizens, or a value in equipment of any kind. And much less on the lives of the children who died there, of the women who died there at Playa Girón.

But we want to make it clear that if the exchange of human beings — ones we call *gusanos* [worms] — for tractors seems to be an odious transaction, something from the days of piracy, we could make an exchange of human beings for human beings. We direct our remarks to the gentlemen from the United States. We reminded them of the great patriot Pedro Albizu Campos, on the verge of death after being in a dungeon of the empire for years and years, and we offered them whatever they wanted for the freedom of Albizu Campos. We reminded the nations of the Americas who might have political prisoners in their jails that we could make an exchange. No-one responded.

Naturally, we cannot force that trade. It is simply up to those who think that the freedom of those "valiant" Cuban counterrevolutionaries — the only army in the world that surrendered in its entirety, with almost no losses — whoever thinks that these individuals should be set free, let them set free their political prisoners. Then all the jails of the Americas will be resplendent, or at least their political prisons will be empty.

There is another problem, also of a political-economic nature. That is,

Mr. President, that our air transport fleet is being brought, plane by plane, to the United States. The procedure is simple: a few ladies enter a plane with guns hidden in their clothing, they hand them over to their accomplices, the accomplices murder the guard, they put a gun to the pilot's head, the pilot heads for Miami, and a company, legally of course — because in the United States everything is done legally — files a suit for debts against the Cuban Government, and then the plane is confiscated.

But it so happens that there was one of those many Cuban patriots — and in addition there was a U.S. patriot, but he is not ours — there was a Cuban patriot around there. And he, all by himself, without anyone telling him anything, decided to better the record of the hijackers of the two-engine planes, and he brought to Cuban shores a beautiful four-engine plane. Naturally, we are not going to use this four-engine plane, which is not ours. We respect private property, but we demand the right to be respected in kind, gentlemen. We demand that there be an end to shams; the right for there to be organizations in the Americas that can say to the United States: "Gentlemen, you are committing a vulgar outrage. You cannot take the planes of another country even though it may be opposed to you. Those planes are not yours. Return those planes, or sanctions will be imposed against you."

Naturally we understand that, unfortunately, there is no inter-American body strong enough to do that. Nevertheless, in this august conclave, we appeal to the sense of fairness and justice of the U.S. delegation, in order to normalize the situation in regard to the hijacking of our respective planes.

It is necessary to explain what the Cuban Revolution is, what this special event is that has made the blood of the world's empires boil, and that has also made the blood of the dispossessed of the world, or of this part of the world at least, boil with hope. It is an agrarian, antifeudal, and antiimperialist revolution that under the imperatives of its internal evolution and of external aggressions became transformed into a socialist revolution, and that declares itself as such before all the Americas: a socialist revolution.

A socialist revolution that took the land from those who had much and gave it to those who used to be hired to work that land, or distributed it in cooperatives among other groups of people who had no land on which to work, even as hired hands.

It is a revolution that came to power with its own army and on the ruins of the oppressor's army; a revolution that looked around when it came to power and dedicated itself to the systematic destruction of all the old forms of the structure that upheld the dictatorship of an exploiter class over the exploited class. It destroyed the army completely, as a caste, as an institution

— not as men, except for the war criminals who were shot before a firing squad; this too was done openly before the public opinion of the continent and with a clear conscience.

It is a revolution that has reaffirmed national sovereignty and that, for the first time, has called in its own name and in the name of all the peoples of the Americas and of the world for the return of all territories unjustly occupied by foreign powers.

It is a revolution that has an independent foreign policy, that comes here to this meeting of American states as one more Latin American country, that goes to the meeting of the Nonaligned countries as one of its important members, and that participates in the deliberations of the socialist countries and is considered by them to be a fraternal nation.

It is, then, a revolution with humanist characteristics. It is in solidarity with all the oppressed peoples of the world. It is in solidarity, Mr. President, because as Martí also said: "Every true human must feel on their own cheek every blow dealt against the cheek of another." And every time that an imperialist power subjugates a territory, it is a blow against every inhabitant of that territory.

That is why we struggle for the independence of other countries, for the independence of the occupied territories, indiscriminately, without asking about the political regime or about the aspirations of those who fight for their independence. We support Panama, which has a piece of its territory occupied by the United States. We call the islands near the south of Argentina the Malvinas and not the Falkland Islands. And we call the island that the United States snatched from Honduras and from which it is insulting us over radio and telegraph, Isla del Cisne.[6]

Here in the Americas we are constantly fighting for the independence of the Guianas and of the British Antilles. We accept the fact of an independent Belize, because Guatemala has already renounced its sovereignty over that piece of its territory. And we also fight in Africa, in Asia, in any part of the world where the strong oppress the weak, so that the weak may achieve independence, self-determination, and the right to self-rule as a sovereign state.

Permit us to say that when the earthquake struck Chile, our people came to her aid to the extent of our resources, with our only product, sugar. It was a small amount of aid, but nevertheless it was a type of aid for which nothing was demanded in return. It was simply handing over to a sister nation some food to tide her over those anxious hours. Nor does that country have to thank us, and much less does she owe us anything. It was our duty to give what we gave.

Our revolution nationalized the domestic economy; it nationalized basic industry, including mining. It nationalized all foreign trade, which is now in the hands of the state, and which we proceeded to diversify by trading with the whole world. It nationalized the banking system in order to have in its hands the efficient instrument with which to exercise the function of credit in accordance with the country's needs.

It provides for the participation of the workers in the management of the planned national economy. It carried out the urban reform just a few months ago, through which every inhabitant of the country was made the owner of the home he or she occupied on the sole condition that he or she continue to pay the same rent that they were already paying, in accordance with a table, for a set number of years.

It instituted many measures to affirm the dignity of the human being. Among the first was the abolition of racial discrimination, which existed in our country, distinguished delegates, in a somewhat subtle form, but it existed. The beaches of our island were not for the black nor for the poor to swim at, because they belonged to some private club to which the tourists came from other beaches because they did not like to swim with blacks.

Our hotels — Havana's great hotels, which were built by foreign companies — did not allow blacks to sleep there, because the tourists from other countries did not like blacks.

That is the way our country was. A woman did not have anything approaching equal rights. She was paid less for the same work. She was discriminated against, as she is in the majority of our countries.

The city and the countryside were in perpetual conflict, and from that conflict imperialism drew a work force, which it paid poorly and denied steady work.

In all these areas we carried out a revolution, and we also carried out a true revolution in education, culture and health care. This year illiteracy will be eliminated in Cuba. Some 104,000 literacy volunteers of all ages are all over the Cuban countryside teaching reading and writing to 1.25 million illiterates, because in Cuba there were many illiterates. There were 1.25 million illiterates, many more than the official statistics used to report.

This year primary education has been made compulsory through the ninth grade, and secondary education has been made free and compulsory for the whole school-age population. We have converted the fortresses into schools. We have carried out university reform and have given the whole people free access to higher culture, to science and modern technology. We have greatly promoted national values to overcome the cultural deformation produced by imperialism, and the expressions of our art receive the applause of the peoples of the world — not of all the peoples, since in some places they are not allowed to enter. We have promoted the cultural heritage of all Latin America through the awarding of annual prizes to writers from all latitudes of the Americas — and whose poetry prize, Mr. President, was won by the [Uruguayan] poet laureate, Roberto Ibañez, in the last contest. We have extended the social function of medicine to benefit the peasants and the poor urban workers. Sports for all the people, to the extent that on July 25, 75,000 people marched in a sports celebration given in honor of the world's first cosmonaut, Commander Yuri Gagarin. Popular beaches have been opened to all, of course, without distinction of color or ideology, and free besides. And the exclusive social clubs of our country, of which there were many, were transformed into workers' social clubs.

All right, gentlemen experts, fellow delegates, the time has come to address the economic section of the text. Point 1 is very broad. Prepared by very brainy experts, it aims at planning the social and economic development of Latin America.

I'm going to refer to some of the statements of the gentlemen experts in order to refute them from the technical point of view, and then present the Cuban delegation's viewpoint on what development planning is.

The first incongruity that we observe in this work is expressed in this passage:

> Sometimes the idea is expressed that an increase in the level and in the diversity of economic activity necessarily results in the improvement of sanitary conditions. Nevertheless, the group is of the opinion that the improvement of sanitary conditions is not only desirable per se, but that it constitutes an indispensable prerequisite to economic growth, and that it should therefore form an essential part of the programs for the development of the region.
>
> On the other hand, this is also reflected in the structure of the loans granted by the Inter-American Development Bank, for in the analysis that we made of the $120 million loaned in the first period, $40 million, in other words one-third, corresponds directly to loans of this type; for housing, for aqueducts, for sewers.

It's a bit like... I don't know, but I would almost classify it as a colonial condition. I get the impression that they are thinking of making the latrine the fundamental thing. That would improve the social conditions of the poor Indian, of the poor black, of the poor person who lives under subhuman conditions. "Let's make latrines for them and after we've made latrines for them, and after their education has taught them how to keep themselves clean, then they can enjoy the benefits of production." Because it should be noted, distinguished delegates, that the topic of industrialization does not figure in the analysis of the distinguished experts. Planning for the gentlemen experts is the planning of latrines. As for the rest, who knows how it will be done!

If the president will allow me, I will express my deepest regrets in the name of the Cuban delegation for the loss of the services of such an efficient technician as the one who directed this first group, Dr. Felipe Pazos. With his intelligence and capacity for work, and with our revolutionary activity, within two years Cuba could have become the paradise of the latrine, even if we did not have a single one of the 250 factories that we are beginning to build, even if we had not carried out the agrarian reform.

I ask myself, distinguished delegates, if they aren't trying to make fun of us — not of Cuba, because Cuba is not included, since the Alliance for Progress is not for Cuba but against her, and since it is not established to give one cent to Cuba — but if they aren't trying to make fun of all the rest of the delegates.

Don't you get the impression, just a little bit, that your leg is being pulled? You are given dollars to build highways, you are given dollars to build roads, you are given dollars to dig sewers. Gentlemen, what do you build roads with, what do you dig the sewers with, what do you build houses with? You don't have to be a genius for that. Why don't they give dollars for equipment, dollars for machinery, dollars so that our underdeveloped countries, all of them, can become industrial-agricultural countries, at one and the same time? Really, it's sad.

On page 10, in the part about the planning of development under point 6, it is made evident who the real author of this plan is. Point 6 says: "To establish more solid bases for the granting and utilization of external financial aid, especially to provide effective criteria to evaluate individual projects."

We are not going to establish the most solid foundations for granting and utilization, because we are not the ones granting; you are the ones who are receiving, not granting. We, Cuba, are watching, and it is the United States that is making the grants. This point 6, then, is drafted directly by the United States. It is the recommendation of the United States, and this is the spirit of the whole abortive scheme called point 1.

But I want to impress upon you one thing. We have spoken a good deal about politics. We have denounced what is a political plot here. We have emphasized in conversations with the distinguished delegates Cuba's right to express these opinions, because Cuba is directly attacked in point 5. Nevertheless, Cuba does not come here to sabotage the meeting, as some of the newspapers or many of the mouthpieces of the foreign information agencies are claiming.

Cuba comes to condemn what is worthy of condemnation from the point of view of principles. But Cuba also comes to work harmoniously, if possible, in order to straighten out this thing that has been born so twisted, and Cuba is ready to collaborate with all the distinguished delegates to set it right and make it into a beautiful project.

The honorable Mr. Douglas Dillon in his speech cited financing; that is important. We must speak of financing if we are all to get together and speak of development, and we have all assembled here to talk with the one country that has the capital for financing.

Mr. Dillon says: "Looking at the years to come and at the sources of external financing — international entities such as Europe and Japan as much as the United States; new private investments and investments of public funds — if Latin America takes as a precondition the necessary internal measures, it can logically expect that its efforts..." — he doesn't even say, "if it takes these measures this will happen," but only "it can logically expect"! — "...will be matched by an influx of capital on the order of at least $20 billion in the next 10 years, with the majority of these funds coming from official sources."

Is this how much there is? No, only $500 million are approved; this is what is being talked about. This must be emphasized, because it is the nub of the question. What does it mean? And I assure you that I'm not asking this for us, but for the good of all. What does it mean "if Latin America takes the necessary internal measures"? And what does "it can logically expect" mean?

I think that later in the work of the committees or at a time that the representative of the United States deems opportune, this detail should be cleared up a little, because $20 billion is an interesting sum. It is no less than two-thirds of the figure that our prime minister announced as necessary for the development of the Americas; push it a little more and we arrive at $30 billion. But that $30 billion has to arrive in jingling cash, dollar by dollar, into the national coffers of each one of the countries of the Americas, with the exception of this poor Cinderella who probably will receive nothing.

That's where we can help, not in a plan of blackmail, such as is foreseen, because it is said: "Cuba is the goose that lays the golden egg. Cuba exists, and while there is a Cuba, the United States will continue to give." No, we don't come here for that reason. We come to work, to try and struggle on the level of principles and ideas, for the development of our peoples. Because all or nearly all of the distinguished representatives have said it: if the

Alliance for Progress fails, nothing can hold back the wave of popular movements — I say this in my own words, but that's what was meant. Nothing can hold back the wave of popular movements if the Alliance for Progress fails. And we are interested in it not failing, if and insofar as it means a real improvement for Latin America in the standard of living of all its 200 million inhabitants. I can make this statement honestly and with all sincerity.

We have diagnosed and foreseen the social revolution in the Americas, the real one, because events are unfolding in a different way, because there is an attempt to hold the people back with bayonets, and when the people realize that they can take the bayonets and turn them against the ones who brandish them, then those who brandish them are lost. But if the road that the people want to take is one of logical and harmonious development, through long-term loans with low interest, as Mr. Dillon said, with 50 years to pay, we also are in agreement.

The only thing is, distinguished delegates, that we all have to work together here to make that figure concrete, and to make sure that the Congress of the United States approves it. Because don't forget that we are faced with a presidential and parliamentary regime, not a "dictatorship" like Cuba, where a representative of Cuba stands up, speaks in the name of his government, and takes responsibility for his actions. What is said here also has to be ratified over there, and the experience of all the distinguished delegates is that many times the promises made here were not approved there.

Well, what I have to say on each of these points is very long, and I'll shorten it so that we can discuss them in the commissions in a fraternal spirit. These are simply some general facts, some general considerations.

The rate of growth that is presented as a most beautiful thing for all Latin America is a 2.5 percent net growth. Bolivia announced 5 percent for 10 years. We congratulate the representative of Bolivia and say to him that with just a little effort and the mobilization of the popular forces he could say 10 percent. We speak of 10 percent growth with no fear whatsoever; 10 percent growth is the rate that Cuba foresees for the coming years.

What does this indicate, distinguished delegates? That if each country maintains its current course Latin America as a whole — which today has a per capita income of approximately $330 and a 2.5 percent annual growth rate — by around the year 1980 will have a per capita income of $500. Certainly for many countries that is really a phenomenon.

What does Cuba intend to have by the year 1980? A net income per capita of around $3,000; more than the United States currently has. And if you don't believe us, fine, here we are ready for a competition, ladies and gentlemen. Let us be left in peace. Let us be allowed to develop, so that we can come together again in 20 years to see if the siren's song is revolutionary Cuba's or someone else's. But we are announcing, quite responsibly, that rate of annual growth.

The experts suggest the substitution of well-equipped farms for ineffic-ient latifundia and very small farms. We say: Do they want to make an ag-rarian reform? Take the land from those who have a lot and give it to those who don't have any. That's the way to make an agrarian reform. The rest is a siren's song. The way to do it? Whether a piece of land is given out in par-cels, in accord with all the rules of private property; whether it is transformed into collective property; whether these are combined, as we have done — all that depends on the peculiarities of each nation. But the agrarian reform is carried out by eliminating the latifundia, not by sending people to colonize far-off places.

In the same way I could talk about the redistribution of income, which is a reality in Cuba. Because those who have more have it taken away and those who have nothing or very little are allowed to have more. Because we've made the agrarian reform. Because we've made the urban reform. Because we've reduced electric and telephone rates — which, by the way, was the first skirmish with the foreign monopolies. Because we've made social centers for workers and child-care centers, where the children of the workers go to receive food and stay there while their parents work. Because we've created public beaches. And because we've nationalized education, which is absolutely free. In addition, we are working on an extensive health plan.

I shall speak of industrialization separately, because it is the basic foundation for development and we interpret it as such.

But there is one point that is very interesting — it is the filter, the purifier: the experts, I think there were seven — the danger of the "latrinocracy" stuck in the middle of the agreements with which the peoples want to improve their living standards. Once again, politicians in the guise of spec-ialists, saying here yes and here no. Because you have done such and such a thing, yes, but in reality because you are a willing tool of the one who is handing out the favors. And nothing for you because you have done this wrong, but in reality because you are not a tool of the one handing out the favors — because you say, for example, that you can't accept as the price of any loan that Cuba be attacked.

That is the danger, without mentioning that the small countries, as in everything, are the ones who receive little or nothing. Distinguished dele-gates, there is only one place where the small countries have the right to "kick up a fuss," and that is here, where each vote is one vote, and where this question has to be put to a vote. And the small countries, if they have a mind to, can count on the militant vote of Cuba against the measures of the "seven," measures that are "sterilized," "purified," and aimed at channeling credits, with technical disguises, in another direction.

What is the stand that really leads to authentic planning, planning that must be coordinated with everyone, but that cannot be subject to any supranational body?

We understand — and we did it this way in our country, distinguished delegates — that the precondition for real economic planning is for political power to be in the hands of the working class.

That is the sine qua non of genuine planning for us. Moreover, the total elimination of imperialist monopolies and state control of the fundamental productive activities are necessary. Having those three points well nailed down, you then proceed with the planning of economic development. Otherwise, everything will be lost in words, speeches and meetings.

Besides this, there are two requirements that will decide whether or not this development makes use of the potential lying dormant in the heart of the peoples, now waiting to be awakened. They are, on the one hand, the rational, centralized direction of the economy by a single authority, which has the ability to make decisions (I'm not speaking of dictatorial powers, but the power to decide) and, on the other, the active participation of all the people in the tasks of planning.

Naturally, for the entire people to participate in the tasks of planning, they will have to own the means of production. Otherwise, it will be difficult for them to participate. The people will not want to, and it seems to me that the owners of the enterprises where they work will not want them to either.

Now, we can speak for a few minutes about what Cuba has achieved by trading with the whole world, "following the flow of commerce," as Martí said.

To date, we have signed agreements for $357 million in credits with the socialist countries, and we are in negotiations, real negotiations, for a little over $140 million more, which makes a total in loans of $500 million for the next five years.

That loan, which gives us the ownership and control of our economic development, comes to, as we said, $500 million — the sum that the United States is giving to all of Latin America — just for our little republic. This, divided by the population of the Republic of Cuba and translated to Latin America, would mean that the United States, in order to provide an equivalent amount, would have to give 15 billion pesos in five years, or $30 billion in 10 years — I speak of pesos or dollars, because in our country their value is the same. That is the sum that our prime minister asked for. With that amount, if there were a proper leadership of the economic process, Latin America in only five years would be quite a different place.

We now pass on to point 2 of the text. And naturally, before analyzing it, we will ask a political question. Some friends of ours at these meetings — of whom there are many, although it might not appear that way — were asking us if we were ready to come back into the fold of Latin American nations. We have never abandoned the Latin American nations, and we are struggling not to be expelled, not to be forced to leave the fold of Latin American republics. What we do not want is to be a herd of cattle, as Martí said. Simply that.

We denounced the dangers of the economic integration of Latin America because we are familiar with the example of Europe. In addition, Latin America knows from bitter experience what European economic integration has cost. We denounced the danger of the international monopolies completely manipulating trade relations inside the free trade associations. But we also announce here, within this conference, and we hope we are accepted, that we are willing to join the Latin American Free Trade Association, like any other member, also criticizing when necessary, but complying with all the rules, as long as Cuba's particular economic and social organization is respected and as long as its socialist government is accepted as an accomplished and irreversible fact.

In addition, equal treatment and equitable enjoyment of the advantages of the international division of labor must also be extended to Cuba. Cuba must participate actively and can contribute a great deal to alleviate many of the serious bottlenecks that exist in the economies of our countries, with the aid of the centrally managed, planned economy, and with a clear and defined goal.

Nevertheless, Cuba also proposes the following measures:

We propose the initiation of immediate bilateral negotiations for the evacuation of bases or territories in member countries occupied by other member countries, so that there are no more cases like the one reported by the delegation of Panama, where Panama's wage policy cannot be implemented in a piece of her own territory. The same is happening to us, and, speaking from the economic point of view, we would like to see that anomaly disappear.

We propose the study of rational plans of development and the coordination of technical and financial assistance from all the industrialized countries, without ideological or geographic distinctions of any kind. We also propose that guarantees be obtained to safeguard the interests of the weaker member countries; the banning of acts of economic aggression by some members against others; the guarantee of protection of Latin American entrepreneurs against the competition of foreign monopolies; the reduction of U.S. tariffs on industrial products of the integrated Latin American countries.

And we state that, as we see it, foreign financing should take place only through indirect investments that fulfill the following conditions: that they not be subject to political demands or discriminate against state enterprises; that they be allotted in accord with the interests of the receiving country; that they carry interest rates no higher than three percent, with repayment in no less than 10 years, and renewable in case of difficulties with the balance of payments; that the attachment or confiscation of ships and aircraft by one member country against another be banned; that tax reforms be initiated that don't fall upon the working masses and that are protection against the action of foreign monopolies.

Point 3 of the text has been treated with the same delicacy as the others by the distinguished experts: they have taken up the matter with two gentle little tweezers, raised the veil a little bit, and let it fall immediately, because it's a tough one.

"It would have been desirable," they say, "and even tempting for the group to have formulated ambitious and spectacular recommendations. However, this was not done owing to the numerous complex technical problems that would have had to be resolved. That is why the recommendations that are formulated necessarily had to be limited to what was considered technically feasible."

I don't know if I'm being too shrewd, but reading between the lines, there do not seem to be any pronouncements. The Cuban delegation therefore proposes concretely that from this meeting we should obtain the following: a guarantee of stable prices, without any "coulds" or "might haves," without "we would examine" or "we shall examine," but, simply, guarantees of stable prices; expanding, or at least stable, markets; guarantees against economic aggression; guarantees against the unilateral suspension of purchases in traditional markets; guarantees against the dumping of subsidized agricultural surpluses; guarantees against protectionism aimed at the production of primary materials; and the creation of conditions in the industrialized countries for the purchase of primary materials with a greater degree of processing.

Cuba declares that it would be desirable for the U.S. delegation to answer, in the commissions, whether it will continue to subsidize its production of copper, lead, zinc, sugar, cotton, wheat and wool. Cuba asks whether the United States will continue to apply pressure against member countries to prevent them from selling their surplus primary products to the socialist countries and thus broadening their market.

And now comes point 5 of the text, since point 4 is nothing but a report. This point 5 is the other side of the coin.

Fidel Castro said at the time of the Costa Rica conference that the United States had gone there "with a sack of gold in one hand and a club in the other." Here today, the United States comes with the sack of gold — fortunately even bigger — in one hand, and the barrier to isolate Cuba in the other. It is, anyway, a triumph of historical circumstances.

But point 5 of the text establishes a program of measures for Latin America aimed at the regimentation of thought, the subordination of the trade union movement, and, if possible, the preparation of military aggression against Cuba.

Three steps are contemplated throughout the whole document: the mobilization, beginning immediately, of the Latin American mass media against the Cuban Revolution and against the struggles of our peoples for their freedom; the formation at a later meeting of an inter-American federation of press, radio, television and movies, which would allow the United States to direct the policy of all the organs of opinion in Latin America, of all of them — and there are not many now that are outside their sphere of influence, but they want all of them — to exercise monopoly control over new information agencies and to absorb as many of the old ones as possible.

All this, in order to do something unprecedented, which has been announced here with such tranquility and which in my country provoked deep discussion when something similar was done in only one case. They are attempting, distinguished delegates, to establish a cultural common market, organized, managed, paid for and domesticated. All the culture of Latin America at the service of imperialism's propaganda plans, to demonstrate that the hunger of our peoples isn't hunger at all, but laziness. Magnificent!

Confronted with this, we reply: a call must be made to the organs of opinion in Latin America, that they take up and share in the ideals of national liberation of each Latin American people. There must be a call for the exchange of information, cultural media, organs of the press, and the attainment of direct visits without discrimination between our peoples, ladies and gentlemen, because today a U.S. citizen who goes to Cuba faces five years in prison when they return to their country. A call must be made to the Latin American governments for them to guarantee the freedoms that allow the working-class movement to organize independent trade unions, to defend the interests of the workers, and to struggle for the true independence of its peoples. And we call for a total, absolute condemnation of point 5 as an attempt by imperialism to domesticate the one thing that our peoples had been saving from disaster: the national culture.

Distinguished delegates, permit me to give an outline of the objectives of Cuba's first plan of economic development for the next four-year period. The overall rate of growth will be 12 percent, that is to say, more than 9.5 percent net per capita growth, transforming Cuba into the most industrial country in Latin America in relation to its population, as the following data indicate:

First place in Latin America in per capita production of steel, cement, electrical energy and, except for Venezuela, oil refining. First place in Latin America in tractors, rayon, footwear, textiles, etc. Second place in the world in the production of metallic nickel (up until now Cuba had only produced concentrates); the production of nickel in 1965 will be 70,000 metric tons, which constitutes approximately 30 percent of the world's production. In addition, Cuba will produce 2,600 metric tons of metallic cobalt. The production of 8.5 to 9 million tons of sugar. The beginning of the transformation of the sugar industry into a sucro-chemical industry.

In order to accomplish these measures — which are easy to list but demand enormous work and the effort of an entire people in order to succeed, plus a great deal of external financing for the purpose of aid and not exploitation — the following measures have been taken: more than a billion pesos (the Cuban peso is equivalent to the dollar) are going to be invested in industry in the installation of 800 megawatts of electrical generating capacity. In 1960, the installed capacity — not counting the sugar industry, which works seasonally — was 621 megawatts. Building or expanding 205 factories, among which the following 22 are the most important: a new plant to refine metallic nickel, which will raise the total to 70,000 tons; a petroleum refinery with a capacity of two million tons of crude oil; the first steel plant, for 700,000 tons, which in this four-year period will produce 500,000 tons of steel; the expansion of our seamed steel-pipe plants to produce 25,000 metric tons; tractors, 5,000 units annually; motorcycles, 10,000 units annually; three cement plants and the expansion of the existing ones for a total of 1.5 million metric tons, which will raise our production to 2.5 million tons annually; metal containers: 291 million units; expansion of our glass factories to 23,700 metric tons annually; a million square meters of window glass; a new factory for making 10,000 cubic meters of plywood from bagasse; a plant for making 60,000 metric tons of bagasse cellulose, in addition to one for wood cellulose of 40,000 metric tons annually; a 60,000-ton ammonium nitrate plant; 60,000 tons of simple superphosphate; 81,000 metric tons of triple superphosphate; 132,000 metric tons of nitric acid; 85,000 metric tons of ammonia; new textile plants and the expansion of the existing ones with 451,000 spindles; a kenaf-sack factory producing 16 million sacks. And there are other factories of less importance, for a total of 205 to date.

These credits have been contracted for, up until now, in the following way: $200 million with the Soviet Union; $60 million with the People's Republic of China; $40 million with the Socialist Republic of Czechoslovakia; $15 million with the Romanian People's Republic; $15 million with the Hungarian People's Republic; $12 million with the Polish People's Republic; $10 million with the German Democratic Republic and $5 million with the Bulgarian Democratic Republic. The total contracted for to date is $357 million. The new negotiations that we expect will culminate soon are mostly with the Soviet Union, which, as the most industrialized country in the socialist area, is the one that has offered the most extensive support.

In terms of agriculture, Cuba has set itself the goal of reaching self-sufficiency in the production of food, including fats and rice, not wheat; self-sufficiency in cotton and coarse fibers; the creation of exportable surpluses of tropical fruits and other agricultural products, whose contribution to exports will triple the present levels.

As regards foreign trade: the value of exports will increase by 75 percent over 1960; diversification of the economy — sugar and its derivatives will make up about 60 percent of the value of the exports, and not 80 percent as now.

As regards construction: the elimination of 40 percent of the present housing shortage, including the *bohíos,* which are Cuban huts; the rational combination of construction materials to increase the use of local materials without sacrificing quality.

There is one point I would like to spend a minute on: that is education. We have laughed at the group of experts who would put education and sanitation as the condition sine qua non to begin the path of development. That seems to us to be an aberration, but that does not make it less true that once the path of development is taken, education must proceed parallel with it. Without an adequate technological education, development is retarded. Therefore, Cuba has carried out a complete reform of education. It has expanded and improved educational services and has developed an overall educational plan.

At present Cuba occupies first place in Latin America in the allocation of resources to education: 5.3 percent of the national income. The developed nations devote 3 to 4 percent and Latin America from 1 to 2 percent of their national income to education. In Cuba, 28.3 percent of the current expenses of the state are for the Ministry of Education. Including other organizations that spend for education, that percentage rises to 30 percent. Among the Latin American countries, the next highest employs 21 percent of its budget.

An increase in the budget for education, from $75 million in 1958 to $128 million in 1961, an increase of 71 percent. The total expenses for education, including the literacy campaign and building schools, come to $170 million, 25 pesos per capita. In Denmark, for example, $25 per capita a year are spent on education; in France, $15; in Latin America, $5.

The creation, in two years, of 10,000 schoolrooms and the appointment of 10,000 new teachers. Cuba is the first country in Latin America that fully satisfies the needs of primary instruction for the entire student population, an aspiration of the principal project of UNESCO in Latin America for 1968, already achieved today in Cuba.

These really marvelous measures and figures, absolutely true, that we present here, distinguished delegates, have been made possible by the following measures: the nationalization of instruction, making it secular and free and allowing complete utilization of its services; the creation of a system of scholarships, which guarantees meeting all the students' needs, in accordance with the following plan: 20,000 scholarships for basic secondary schools from seventh to ninth grade; 3,000 for the pre-university institutes; 3,000 for art instructors; 6,000 for universities; 1,500 for courses in artificial insemination; 1,200 for courses in agricultural machinery; 14,000 for courses in tailoring and sewing and home economics for peasant women; 1,200 for the preparation of rural school teachers; 750 for introductory courses in elementary education; 10,000 scholarships and study stipends for students of technological education; and, in addition, hundreds of scholarships to study technology in the socialist countries; the creation of 100 centers of secondary education, with each municipality having at least one.

This year in Cuba, as I announced, illiteracy is being wiped out. It is a marvelous sight. Up to the present moment, 104,500 *brigadistas*, almost all of them students between 10 and 18 years old, have flooded the country from one end to the other, going directly to the peasant's *bohío*, to the worker's house, to convince the old man who doesn't want to study anymore, and to thus wipe out illiteracy in Cuba.

Each time a factory wipes out illiteracy among its workers, it raises a flag announcing that fact to the people of Cuba. Each time a cooperative wipes out illiteracy among its peasants, it hoists the same standard. And the 104,500 young students have as their symbol a book and a lantern, to bring the light of learning to the backward regions. They belong to the Conrado Benítez brigades, which is to honor the name of the first martyr for education in the Cuban Revolution, who was lynched by a group of counterrevolutionaries for the grave crime of being in the mountains of our country, teaching the peasants to read.

That is the difference, distinguished delegates, between our country and those who combat us. A total of 156,000 literacy volunteers, who are not full-time since they are workers or professionals, are working in education; 32,000 teachers are leading this army. And only with the active cooperation of all the Cuban people are they able to achieve such significant statistics.

All this has been done in one year, or rather, in two years: seven regimental barracks have been converted into school-cities; 27 barracks into schools; and all this while facing the danger of imperialist aggressions. The Camilo Cienfuegos School-City today has 5,000 pupils from the Sierra Maestra, and units are under construction for 20,000 pupils. The construction of a similar school-city in each province is projected. Each school-city will be self-sufficient in foodstuffs, introducing peasant children to agricultural techniques.

Moreover, new methods of teaching have been established. From 1958 to 1959, primary school enrollment went from 602,000 to 1,231,700 pupils; basic secondary school, from 21,900 to 83,800; commercial, from 8,900 to 21,300; technical schools, from 5,600 to 11,500.

A total of $48 million has been invested in school construction in only two years. The National Printing Plant guarantees textbooks and other printed matter for all students, free of charge. There are two television networks that cover the entire national territory, and we can use that powerful media for the massive dissemination of learning. Likewise, the entire national radio is at the disposal of the Ministry of Education. The Cuban Institute of Cinematographic Art and Industry, the National Library, and the National Theater, with departments throughout the country, round out the great apparatus for the dissemination of culture.

The National Institute of Sports, Physical Education, and Recreation, whose initials are INDER, promotes physical development on a mass scale.

That, distinguished delegates, is the cultural panorama of Cuba at this time.

Now comes the final part of our presentation, the part of definitions, because we want to make our position completely clear.

We have denounced the Alliance for Progress as a vehicle designed to separate the people of Cuba from the other peoples of Latin America, to sterilize the example of the Cuban Revolution, and then to subdue the other peoples according to imperialism's instructions. I would like to be allowed to fully demonstrate this.

There are many interesting documents in the world. We shall distribute among the delegates some documents that came into our hands and that demonstrate, for example, the opinion that imperialism has of the Venezuelan Government, whose foreign minister harshly attacked us a few days ago, perhaps because he thought we were violating rules of friendship with his people or his government.

Nevertheless, it is interesting to point out that friendly hands brought us an interesting document. It is a report of a secret document addressed to Ambassador Moscoso in Venezuela by his advisers John M. Cates, Jr., Irving Tragen and Robert Cox.

In one of its paragraphs, speaking of the measures that must be taken in Venezuela to make a real Alliance for Progress directed by the United States, this document states:

Reform of the bureaucracy: All the plans that are formulated...

They are speaking of Venezuela.

...all the programs that are initiated for the economic development of Venezuela, whether they be by the Venezuelan Government or by U.S. experts, will have to be put into practice through the Venezuelan bureaucracy. But as long as the public administration of this country is characterized by incompetency, indifference, inefficiency, formalism, factional favoritism in the granting of jobs, theft, duplication of functions, and the creation of private empires, it will be practically impossible to put into effect dynamic and efficient projects through the governmental machinery. For that reason the reform of the administrative apparatus is possibly now the most fundamental necessity, which is not only directed to correcting basic economic and social injustice, but which also could imply reconditioning the very instrument by which all the other basic reforms and development projects will be molded.

There are many interesting things in this document that we will put at the disposal of the distinguished delegates, in which they speak, also, of the natives. After teaching the natives, they let the natives work. We are natives, nothing more. But there is something very interesting, distinguished delegates, and that is the recommendation that Mr. Cates makes to Mr. Moscoso about what must be done in Venezuela and why it must be done. He says as follows:

The United States will be faced with the necessity, probably sooner than it is thought, of pointing out to the conservatives, the oligarchy, the newly rich, the national and foreign moneyed sectors in general, the military, and the clergy, that they will in the last analysis have to choose between two things: to contribute to the establishment in Venezuela of a society based on the masses, in which they retain part of their status quo and wealth, or to be faced with the loss of both (and very possibly their own death at the hands of a firing squad)...

This is a report of the U.S. advisers to their ambassador.

...if the forces of moderation and progress are routed in Venezuela.

After this, we are given the complete picture of the whole deception to be practiced in this conference, with other reports of the secret instructions given in Latin America by the U.S. State Department in reference to the "Cuba case."

This is very important, because it is what uncovers the wolf in sheep's clothing. This is what it says. I am going to read an extract in deference to the brevity that I have already violated, but afterward we will circulate all of it:

From the beginning, it was widely taken for granted in Latin America that the invasion was backed by the United States and that, for that reason, it would be successful. The majority of the governments and responsible sections of the population were prepared to accept a fait accompli, although there were misgivings about the violation of the principle of nonintervention.

The communists and other vehemently pro-Castro elements immediately took the offensive with demonstrations and acts of violence directed against U.S. agencies in various countries, especially in Argentina, Bolivia and Mexico. Nevertheless, such anti-U.S. and pro-Castro activities received a limited backing and had less effect than might have been expected.

The failure of the invasion discouraged the anti-Castro sectors, who thought that the United States should have done something dramatic that would restore its damaged prestige, but it was received with joy by the communists and other pro-Castro elements.

It continues:

In most cases, the reactions of the Latin American governments were not surprising. With the exception of Haiti and the Dominican Republic, the republics that had already broken or suspended their relations with Cuba expressed their understanding of the U.S. position. Honduras joined the anti-Castro camp, suspending its relations in April and proposing the formation of an alliance of Central American and Caribbean nations to deal with Cuba through force. The proposal, which was also suggested independently by Nicaragua, was quietly abandoned when Venezuela refused to back it.

Venezuela, Colombia and Panama expressed a serious concern about Soviet and international communist penetration in Cuba, but they remained in favor of carrying out some type of collective action by the OAS to deal with the Cuban problem.

"Collective action by the OAS" — here we enter familiar territory.

A similar opinion was adopted by Argentina, Uruguay and Costa Rica. Chile, Ecuador, Bolivia, Brazil and Mexico refused to back any position that might imply an intervention in the internal affairs of Cuba. This attitude was probably very strong in Chile, where the government met strong opposition in all spheres to an open military intervention by any state against the Castro regime. In Brazil and Ecuador the question provoked serious divisions in the cabinet, in the congress and in the political parties.

In the case of Ecuador, the intransigently pro-Cuba position of President Velasco was shaken but not altered by the discovery that Ecuadoran Communists were being trained inside the country in guerrilla tactics by pro-Castro revolutionaries.

Parenthetically, I will state that this is a lie.

Likewise, there is little doubt that some of the formerly uncommitted elements in Latin America have been favorably impressed by Castro's ability to survive a military attack supported by the United States against his regime. Many who had hesitated to commit themselves before, because they believed that the United States would eliminate the Castro regime in the course of time, may have changed their opinion now. The victory of Castro has demonstrated to them the permanent and viable character of the Cuban Revolution.

This is the report by the United States.

Moreover, his victory has undoubtedly aroused the latent anti-U.S. attitude that prevails in a great part of Latin America.

In all respects, the member states of the OAS are now less hostile to U.S. intervention in Cuba than before the invasion, but a majority — including Brazil and Mexico, who together account for more than half the population of Latin America — are not ready to actively intervene or even to join in a quarantine against Cuba. Nor could it be expected that the OAS would give beforehand its approval of direct intervention by the United States, except in the event that Castro might be involved, beyond any doubt, in an attack on a Latin American government.

Even when the United States might be successful ...

Which looks improbable.

... in persuading the majority of Latin American states to join in a quarantine of Cuba, it would not be totally successful. Certainly Mexico and Brazil would refuse to cooperate and would serve as a channel for travel and other communication between Latin America and Cuba.

Mexico's long-standing opposition to intervention of any kind would not represent an insuperable obstacle to collective action by the OAS against Cuba. The attitude of Brazil, however, which exercises a strong influence over its South American neighbors, is decisive for hemispheric cooperation. As long as Brazil refuses to act against Castro, it is probable that a number of other nations, including Argentina and Chile, would not want to risk adverse internal repercussions to accommodate the United States.

The magnitude of the threat that Castro and the communists constitute in other parts of Latin America will probably continue to depend, fundamentally, on the following factors: (a) the ability of the regime to maintain its position; (b) its efficacy in demonstrating the success of its mode of coping with the problems of reform and development; and (c) the ability of the non-communist elements in other Latin American countries to provide feasible and popularly acceptable alternatives.

If, by means of propaganda, etc., Castro can convince the disaffected elements of Latin America that basic social reforms are really being made...

That is to say, if the distinguished delegates are convinced that what we are saying is true.

...that benefit the poorest classes, the attraction of the Cuban example will increase and will continue to inspire imitators on the left in the whole region. The danger is not so much that a subversive apparatus, with its center in Havana, could export revolution, as that growing extreme poverty and discontent among the masses of the Latin American people may provide the pro-Castro elements opportunities to act.

After considering whether or not we are intervening, they argue:

> It is probable that the Cubans will act cautiously in this respect for some time. Probably they do not wish to risk the interception or discovery of any military adventure or military supply operation originating in Cuba. Such an eventuality would lead to a hardening of official Latin American opinion against Cuba, possibly to the point of providing tacit support to U.S. intervention, or at least giving possible motives for sanctions on the part of the OAS. For these reasons and owing to Castro's concern with the defense of his own territory at this time, the use of Cuban military forces to support insurrection in other places is extremely improbable.

So, distinguished delegates who might have doubts, the government of the United States is announcing that it is very difficult for our troops to interfere in the internal affairs of other countries.

> As time goes on, and with the absence of direct Cuban intervention in the internal affairs of neighboring states, the present fears of Castroism, of Soviet intervention in the regime, of its "socialist" nature...

They put it in quotation marks.

> ...and of repugnancy for the repression of Castro's police state, will tend to decrease and the traditional policy of nonintervention will reassert itself.

It says further on:

> Apart from its direct effect on the prestige of the United States in that area...

Which undoubtedly has decreased as a result of the failure of the invasion.

> ...the survival of the Castro regime could have a profound effect on Latin American political life in coming years. Likewise, it prepares the scene for a political struggle in the terms promoted by communist propaganda for a long time in this hemisphere, with the anti-United States, "popular"...

In quotation marks.

> ...forces on one side, and the ruling groups allied to the United States on the other. The governments that promise an evolutionary reform over a period of years, even at an accelerated pace, will be confronted by political leaders who promise an immediate remedy for the social

ills by means of the confiscation of property and the overturning of the society. The most immediate danger of Castro's army for Latin America could very well be the danger to the stability of those governments that are presently attempting evolutionary social and economic changes, rather than to those that have tried to prevent such changes, in part due to the tensions and heightened expectations that accompany social changes and economic development. The urban unemployed and the landless peasants of Venezuela and Peru, for example, who have hoped that Acción Democrática and the APRA would implement reforms, constitute a quick source of political strength for the politician who convinces them that change can be implemented much more rapidly than the social democratic movements have promised. The popular support that the groups seeking evolutionary changes presently enjoy or the potential backing that they normally could obtain as the Latin American masses become more active politically, would be lost to the degree that the extremist political leaders, utilizing the example of Castro, can rally support for revolutionary change.

And in the last paragraph, gentlemen, appears our friend who is present here:

The Alliance for Progress could very well provide the stimulus to carry out more intensive reform programs. But unless these are initiated rapidly and begin soon to show positive results, it is probable that they will not be sufficient to counterbalance the growing pressure of the extreme left. The years ahead will witness, almost surely, a race between those who are attempting to initiate evolutionary reform programs and those who are trying to generate mass support for fundamental economic and social revolution. If the moderates are left behind in this race they could, in time, see themselves deprived of their mass support and caught in an untenable position between the extremes of right and left.

These are, distinguished delegates, the documents that the Cuban delegation wanted to place before you, in order to analyze frankly the Alliance for Progress. Now we all know the private judgment of the U.S. State Department: the economies of the Latin American countries have to grow, because if they do not, a phenomenon called Castroism will come, which will be dreadful for the United States.

Well then, gentlemen, let us make the Alliance for Progress on those terms: let the economies of all the member countries of the Organization of Latin American States really grow. Let them grow so that they consume their own products and not so that they are turned into a source of income for the U.S. monopolies. Let them grow to assure social peace, not to create new reserves for an eventual war of conquest. Let them grow for us, not for those abroad.

And to all of you, distinguished delegates, the Cuban delegation says with all frankness: we wish, on our conditions, to be within the Latin American family. We want to live with Latin America. We want to see you grow, if possible, at the same rate that we are growing, but we don't oppose your growing at another rate. What we do demand is the guarantee of nonaggression for our borders.

We cannot stop exporting our example, as the United States wants, because an example is something intangible that crosses borders. What we do guarantee is that we will not export revolution. We guarantee that not one rifle will be moved from Cuba, that not one weapon will be moved from Cuba for fighting in any other country in Latin America.

What we cannot guarantee is that the idea of Cuba will not take root in some other country of Latin America, and what we do guarantee this conference is that if urgent measures of social prevention are not taken, the example of Cuba will take root in the people. And then that statement that once gave people a lot to think about, which Fidel made one July 26 and which was interpreted as an aggression, will again be true. Fidel said that if the social conditions continued as they have been until now, "the Andes would become the Sierra Maestra of Latin America."

Distinguished delegates, we call for an Alliance for Progress, an alliance for our progress, a peaceful alliance for the progress of all. We are not opposed to being left out in the distribution of loans, but we are opposed to being left out in participating in the cultural and spiritual life of our Latin American people, to whom we belong.

What we will never allow is a restriction on our freedom to trade and have relations with all the peoples of the world. And we will defend ourselves with all our strength against any attempt at foreign aggression, be it from an imperial power or be it from some Latin American body that concurs in the desire of some to see us wiped out.

To conclude, Mr. President, distinguished delegates, I want to tell you that some time ago we had a meeting of the general staff of the Revolutionary Armed Forces in my country, a general staff to which I belong. An aggression against Cuba was being discussed, which we knew would come, but we did not know when or where. We thought it would be very big; in fact, it was going to be very big. This happened prior to the famous warning of the prime minister of the Soviet Union, Nikita Khrushchev, that their rockets could fly beyond the Soviet borders. We had not asked for that aid and we did not know about their readiness to aid us. Therefore, we met knowing that the invasion was coming, in order to face our final destiny as revolutionaries.

We knew that if the United States invaded Cuba, there would be a massive slaughter, but that in the end we would be defeated and expelled from every inhabited place in the country. We then proposed, the members of the general staff, that Fidel Castro retire to a secure place in the mountains and that one of us take charge of the defense of Havana. Our prime minister and leader answered at that time with words that exalt him, as do all his acts — that if the United States invaded Cuba and Havana was defended as it should be defended, hundreds of thousands of men, women and children would die before the drive of the Yankees' weapons, and that the leader of a people in revolution could not be asked to take shelter in the mountains; that his place was there, where the cherished dead were to be found, and that there, with them, he would fulfill his historic mission.

That invasion did not take place, but we maintain that spirit, distinguished delegates. For that reason I can predict that the Cuban Revolution is invincible, because it has a people and because it has a leader like the one leading Cuba.

That is all, distinguished delegates.

The Cuban Revolution's influence in Latin America

(May 18, 1962)

This speech was given as an address to the members of the Cuban Department of State Security [DSE]. It was not published until after Che Guevara's death.

First of all, I would like to apologize, because I had intended to prepare some data and figures that would clearly express some analyses on Latin America in general, its relations with imperialism and the relations Latin America will have with the Cuban revolutionary government. However, as always in these cases, my good intentions have remained nothing more than intentions, and I will have to speak from memory, so I will talk in terms of general concepts and not quote any figures.

I won't recount at length the history of imperialism's penetration in Latin America, but it is useful to know that the part of the Americas which is called Latin America has nearly always lived under the yoke of the big imperialist monopolies. Spain dominated a large part the Americas and other European countries penetrated this area later on, just after the birth of capitalism, in the stage of capitalist expansion. England and France were among the countries that acquired some colonies here.

After the wars of independence, several countries fought over Latin America, and, with the birth of economic imperialism at the end of the 19th and beginning of the 20th century, the United States quickly came to dominate all of North, South and Central America. Other imperialismt powers persisted in the southern part of the Americas; England had a strong position in the extreme south, in Argentina and Uruguay, until the end of the last war.

At times, our countries have been the scenes of wars caused by monopolies of different nationalities fighting over spheres of influence. The War of the Chaco is one of the examples of the struggle for oil waged between Shell (owned by English and German groups) and Standard Oil. It was a very bloody war lasting four years; in it, Bolivia and Paraguay lost the best of their young men in the Chaco jungle.

There are other examples of this kind: the action in which Peru, representing Standard Oil, grabbed a part of Ecuador's territory, where Shell was influential. Wars have also been waged for other kinds of products. The United Fruit Company has caused wars in Central America in order to control banana-raising territories. Wars have also been waged in the south, between Chile, Bolivia and Peru, over possession of nitrate deposits — which were very important before a method of creating synthetic nitrate was discovered. At most, we have been unwitting actors in a struggle between empires.

After the war, however, the last redoubts of British imperialism — German imperialism had already been ousted — ceded to U.S. imperialism.

The fact that the economic domination of the Americas has since been completely unified has brought about a trend toward unity among the forces that are struggling against imperialism. We must be ever more closely united in the struggle, because it is a struggle all of us share. It is expressed now, for example, in all of the peoples' solidarity with Cuba. Everyone is quickly learning that there is only one enemy, which is imperialism, and that here in Latin America it bears the name of U.S. imperialism.

Imperialism's penetration has varied greatly depending on historical, political and economic circumstances — and also, perhaps, reflecting how far our countries are from the imperialist capital. Some countries, such as Panama, are completely colonized and this determines their system of life. Other countries retain more of their national characteristics and are still in a stage of cultural struggle against imperialism. All, however, have the common denominator of imperialism's control over their great reserves of materials for use in its industries. Such reserves are strategic not only for war but for its many other industries, its control of banking and its near monopoly on foreign trade.

We are very interested in Latin America for several reasons: because we are a part of it culturally and historically; because we belong to a group that is fighting for its freedom; and because Latin America's attitude is closely related to our future and to our revolution's future and its desire to spread its ideology. Revolutions have this characteristic, they expand ideologically. They do not remain limited to a single country but expand to other areas — or, to use an economic term, even though this isn't the case — to other spheres of influence.

The Cuban Revolution has had an enormous influence in Latin America, although to varying degrees in every country. We should analyze the reasons for the influence of the Cuban Revolution and why this has been greater in some countries than in others. We should also analyze in detail the political life in each of the countries and the attitudes of the progressive parties in each of them — with all due respect and without interfering in the internal affairs of any party — because those attitudes are very important for analyzing the current situation.

In some countries the peoples' struggles have developed acutely; in other countries, the peoples' struggles have been slowed down. In some countries, Cuba is a sacred symbol for all the people; in others, Cuba symbolizes a liberation movement that is viewed from afar. The origins are complex, but always related to each country's approach regarding how to seize power, and they are greatly influenced by solutions that have been found for this problem. In some cases, they are also related to the greater or lesser predominance of the working class and its influence; in others, they are related to their proximity to our revolution.

We can analyze these countries in groups.

Two countries in South America are very important in terms of their ideological influence. One of them is Argentina, which is one of the relatively strong powers in Latin America. In the extreme south, Uruguay presents very similar characteristics. Both are cattle-raising countries and have very powerful oligarchies which control foreign trade on the basis of their ownership of large landholdings and cattle — although they have now to share these with the United States.

They are countries with a very concentrated urban population. In Uruguay's case, we cannot say that the working class is prevalent, because Uruguay is a country with very little development. In Argentina, the working class prevails, but it is in a very difficult situation, because it is employed only in processing industries and is dependent on raw materials from abroad. The country doesn't yet have a solid industrial base. It has one enormous city, Buenos Aires, where close to 30 percent of the total population lives, and has close to three million square kilometers of habitable land, not counting the territory in Antarctica that is under dispute and is of no demographic value.

This immense country has a population of over six million people in its capital, an area a little larger than Havana. It has enormous expanses of uncultivated land where the farming class has a relatively large amount of land and a small group of agricultural workers wander from one place to another, following the crops, much as the cane-cutters used to do here, who could pick coffee or harvest tobacco and alternate this with other seasonal crops.

In Argentina and Uruguay, which have these characteristics, and in Chile, where the working class is in the majority, the philosophy of civil wars against despotic powers has been rejected and the taking of power in the future by means of elections or in some other peaceful way has been proposed more or less directly and explicitly.

Just about everyone knows of the latest events in Argentina, where some relatively leftist groups arose to more or less real power. These groups represent the progressive sector of the Argentine working class but are distorting many of the people's aspirations through a clique of the Peronist party that is completely out of touch with the people. And when elections were proposed, the *gorillas* — as the ultra-reactionary groups in the Argentine Army are called — intervened and put an end to that situation.

Something similar happened in Uruguay, though the army there has no real clout. Nardone (the ultra-reactionary now in power) carried out a kind of coup. The situation created by repeated rightist coups, combined with the leftist philosophy of taking power by means of elections and peoples' fronts, creates a certain apathy with regard to the Cuban Revolution.

The Cuban Revolution embodies an experience that Cuba does not want to be unique in Latin America. It reflects a way to take power. Naturally, it isn't a form that appeals to the masses of people who are under great pressure, oppressed by domestic oppressive groups and by imperialism. Some explanations of a theoretical nature concerning the Cuban Revolution are in order, and these will condition stances toward the revolution.

In countries where groups have openly proclaimed their determination to seize power by armed struggle there is more understanding. This position is of course very difficult and very controversial to adopt, and we don't have to participate directly in it. Every country and every party in its own country should seek the formulas of struggle recommended by its own historical experience. Yet the Cuban Revolution is a fact, and one of continental scope. Cuban reality has at least some ongoing influence in the lives of the Latin American countries.

Those known as ultra-leftists — or sometimes, provocateurs — try to implant the Cuban experience without thinking particularly about whether or not this would be the right place to do so. Such people, who exist everywhere, simply take an experience that has occurred in Latin America and attempt to transfer it to each of the other countries. This causes more friction among the leftist groups. The history of the defense of Cuba in those countries by each of the political organizations is also a history of division. It is good to say this here so you will understand something of those problems, including their histories of pettiness and their struggles to achieve small advances in controlling organizations.

Without intending to, Cuba has therefore been viewed as being mixed up in the polemics. I say "without intending to": this experience has been enough for us; we will never aspire to lead the politics or the method of carrying out a revolution, achieving power, in any other country. We are again, however, at the heart of the polemics.

In Chile where the parties of the left have greater ascendancy, a vigorous trajectory and an ideological firmness which may well be greater than that of other parties in Latin America, the situation has been similar. The difference being that the Chilean Communist Party and the other leftist parties have themselves already posed the dilemma: to take power either through peaceful means or by the way of violence. They are all preparing for a future struggle which I think will come about, because there isn't any other historical experience, nor is one possible here in Latin America in the present conditions of the conflict developing between the superpowers. The exacerbation of the struggle between imperialism and the peace camp proves that imperialism will never simply hand over control. From a strategic point of view, such a thing would be ridiculous, if the imperialists still have the weapons. To gain control, the left must be very powerful and must force the reactionaries to capitulate. Those conditions don't as yet exist in Chile. This is the part of South America where for the people of the region the Cuban Revolution presents different characteristics.

Moving north we come to the countries where the Cuban Revolution is really a beacon for the peoples. We can leave Bolivia aside, because some years ago it had a very timid bourgeois revolution that was severely weakened by concessions it had to make to its economy, which is single-crop and completely tied to the imperialist economy. Its bourgeoisie has had to be maintained in part by imperialism. Imperialism of course takes its wealth with one hand and using a quarter of the wealth it takes out it then props up the government with the other. This has created a situation of dependence and in spite of the Bolivian Government's efforts to throw off the imperialist yoke — many of these efforts have obviously been sincere — it has not managed to do so. Bolivia does maintain a correct attitude on some Cuban stances and they remain as friendly as possible in international conferences. It has carried out agrarian reform, though in a very truncated form: the church's possessions have not been seized; cooperatives have no real development; and, importantly, they are cooperatives of a traditional kind, based on earlier regional experiences of primitive communism. Such cooperatives, worked by Indians, have been maintained through tradition and operate now as they have always done. The struggle isn't manifested very strongly in Bolivia. The terms are changing a little; it isn't a case of direct struggle by the oppressed masses of farmers and workers against imperialism, but one of struggle against a national bourgeoisie which has made a series of concessions, like overthrowing the feudal overlords and the domestic large landowners, so the class struggle isn't so acute.

Paraguay, Bolivia's former rival in the War of the Chaco is, however, nearby. There are now guerrillas in Paraguay. It is a very poor country. It has around one and a half million inhabitants in a territory that is much larger than Cuba's, with extensive jungles. It has very few cattle and some agricultural products. It has terrible endemic diseases such as leprosy, which has reached enormous proportions, and there is practically no health care.

Almost all of the people live in three or four relatively large cities. There have been several guerrilla forays in the forests. The most important and most serious of these from an ideological point of view have been directed by a people's revolutionary front with the participation of the Paraguayan Communist Party. Its guerrillas have been systematically defeated. I think that tactical mistakes have been made in the conduct of the revol-utionary struggle — which has a series of laws that must not be broken — but, even so, uprisings continue. Some rebel groups are living in the forests and they know that if they turn themselves in they will be killed. They are far from the borders.

Paraguay is an ideal country for guerrilla warfare. It is agriculturally very rich and has wonderful natural conditions. There are no high mountains but there are forests, very large rivers and zones of operation that would be very difficult for regular armies and very easy to wage a struggle with the help of the farming population.

It has a dictatorship of the extreme right which used to be very influenced by the Argentine oligarchy. Paraguay was a semicolony of Argentina but with the latest penetrations of U.S. capital has now become directly dependent on the United States. It maintains a bestial dictatorship and has all of the seeds of an intensive short-term people's struggle.

A little farther to the north is Peru. Peru should be watched attentively in the future. It has very special characteristics: 80 percent of its population is indigenous or mestizo and there are very clear racial separations. Whites own the land and the capital; the mestizos generally work as overseers for the whites, and Indians as serfs.

In Peru, farms are still sold complete with their Indian workers. Farms are advertised in the newspapers along with the number of workers or the number of Indians who are forced to work for the feudal lord. You cannot even imagine how terrible the situation is unless you have been there.

Peru is the only country in Latin America with vast agricultural regions where the leftist parties have decisive influence and control. Peru and the indigenous region of Cuzco, where the Peruvian Communist Party has a strong influence, are the only areas in the Americas where any Marxist party has a strong influence. Some years ago the Peruvian Communist Party seized the city of Cuzco by force of arms, but revolutionary conditions didn't exist and there was a kind of tacit truce: the rebels returned the city and the oppressors, the government troops, took no reprisals. A tense situation ensued, and it remains one of the areas where a revolution is threatening — or, rather, where there are hopes of a revolution in Latin America.

All of Peru is in a similar situation, with extreme poverty and extreme oppression, the essential characteristics of the heavily populated Andes and factors for carrying out a revolution. The people don't speak Spanish; the most commonly spoken languages are Quechua and Aimará, closely related to each other. Anybody wanting to communicate with the Indians has to speak those languages; if they don't, communication will be impossible.

Nationalities aren't defined by the borders of those countries. Aimarás in Bolivia relate better with Aimarás in Peru than with whites in either Bolivia or Peru. First the colonizers and then the imperialists have taken pains to maintain that situation. There is therefore a natural affinity between those two countries, and in Peru and Ecuador and even as far as Colombia, between the areas where the Andeans and Quechuas live. In all of those countries the prevailing languages are dialects.

These countries have great geographical differences. Peru has three mountain chains crossed by valleys, and the eastern half of the country leads into the great Amazon River Basin, which is where *la montaña* begins — an area of medium to high mountain ranges with a subtropical climate, similar to the climate in our mountains, but with more difficult natural conditions.

The little-developed bourgeoisie in Peru lives on the coast, a narrow, desert-like strip which runs parallel to very high mountains. The highest peak in Peru's western mountain range is just 100 kilometers from the coast and 5,000 meters above sea level. It sits there like a shell washed ashore. A month or two ago there were uprisings you probably heard about, in the mining area in the middle of the country. Mining is very developed in Peru and you know that mine workers in general are very combative. They don't necessarily have great political awareness, because of the conditions in the country, but they are very combative. The Peruvian Army consists of a caste of officers at the top, all from the same class, and masses of Indians at the bottom; if a serious uprising were to occur, there would be no way to crush it.

Ecuador has the same conditions with just one difference: the Ecuadoran bourgeoisie — or a part of it — and, in general, all the supporters of the left have much more influence in the cities and are much clearer about the need for an uprising. Several leaders of these Ecuadoran leftist groups have been in Cuba and have been considerably influenced by the effects and results of the Cuban Revolution. They openly uphold the banner of an immediate agrarian revolution. There is also a strong repressive army and the United States has stationed some of its troops in Ecuador. I think that Ecuador, too, is a country where intensive revolutionary struggle will soon appear.

Continuing up the Andes, the backbone of the continent, we come to Colombia where, with periods of greater or lesser activity, a war has been going on for the past 12 years. The Colombian guerrillas have made mistakes that have kept them from achieving a people's victory like ours. There has been a lack of ideological leadership. The guerrillas are dispersed and lack a central command (which we had in Cuba), they have been under the personal leadership of caudillos from rural areas, and they began to rob and kill just like their rivals in order to survive. Naturally, they gradually fell into banditry. Other guerrilla groups adopted a position of self-defense and did nothing other than defend themselves when attacked by the government. The situation of struggle and of war to the death led these guerrillas to be weakened. Some of them were completely wiped out.

Right now, influenced by the Cuban Revolution, the guerrilla movement in Colombia has grown stronger.

One group of young people, the MOE, did something similar to what the July 26 Movement did here in the beginning. They espouse a series of rightist tendencies toward anarchy — that are sometimes mixed with anti-communist ideas — but they reflect the seeds of a determination to fight. Some of their leaders have been in Cuba. The most determined and enthusiastic of them was Comrade Larrota, who was with us during the April [1961 Bay of Pigs] invasion and some time before that. He was murdered when he returned to Colombia. MOE is probably not important as a political movement and in some cases could be dangerous, but the group is an example of what is happening there.

Clearly the Colombian parties of the left are trying to hold back the insurrectional movement and move toward electoral struggle, in an absurd situation where there are only two legal parties, each taking turns at power.

In such absurd conditions, the more impetuous Colombian revolutionaries consider that resorting to elections simply wastes time, and in spite of all obstacles they are doing everything they can to further a struggle that is no longer latent but has developed into open fighting in several parts of the country.

It's difficult to say whether the struggle in Colombia may or may not be important. It isn't directed by a well-structured leftist movement; it consists of efforts by a series of social groups and elements from different classes all trying to do something, but there is no ideological leadership and that is very dangerous. There is no way to know where it's going, but the conditions are being created for the future development of a well-structured revolutionary struggle in Colombia.

The situation in Venezuela is much more active. The Communist Party and the Movement of the Revolutionary Left (MIR) are heading an armed movement of liberation, and civil war has practically broken out in Venezuela. We should be very interested in this Venezuelan movement; we should be watching it carefully and with great affinity.

Some tactical disagreements have arisen over how to wage that struggle. As a result of our own experience, in which our nation was born from a unilateral experience, we favor guerrilla warfare based on farmers' groups and seizing the cities from the countryside. This is based on our masses' great hunger for land and on the mercenary armies' extreme weakness when moving through large territories in Latin America. Imperialism's attacks can't be effective in areas that are favorable for the guerrillas and the people's forces. The government is unable to move beyond areas where the population is concentrated.

Some Venezuelan comrades have said several times that something violent may happen in Venezuela, that special conditions exist, with some military groups ready to support an insurrection. Partial results were seen in the last insurrectional attempt made at Carúpano, showing once again that in a revolution Latin America's professional military men serve only as a source of weapons for the people. The only mission an army group can have is to let itself be disarmed. From then on, it should be left alone; at most, isolated individuals should be taken from it.

I don't know that specific area very well, but I am familiar with neighboring areas and in that region impenetrable forests and mountains are nearby. There, a guerrilla unit can create an extremely difficult situation. The area is near oil-exporting ports, such as Caripito, and a guerrilla unit can threaten one of the key areas of the imperialist economy in Venezuela. The marines, however, didn't set foot outside their garrison. The marines who rebelled couldn't go anywhere in the interior of the country. They surrendered as soon as they saw that the loyal troops outnumbered them.

A revolution cannot be carried out in those conditions. As you know, guerrilla struggle is long and drawn-out; battles follow one another very slowly and the greatest difficulties aren't direct action by the enemy but rather struggle against the rigors of the climate; lack of provisions and medicine; the struggle to ideologically awaken the rural masses; the political struggle to incorporate those masses in the people's movement; the slowness of the revolution's advance; and surely, in the case of Venezuela, U.S. intervention to defend its oil possessions. All these things influence the guerrilla struggle.

This time — though this time only, it can't be said differently — the path adopted in Venezuela was to try to deliver a violent blow via some of the units of the army. Even if they had triumphed, it would only have been a victory of one part of the army over the other. What would the army then have done? It's very simple: they would have pardoned the losing faction, maintained their caste status and allowed them to retain all of their caste privileges and their class control in the country. The exploiting class has the weapons that maintain that army of exploitation.

When one part of the army has triumphed over the other — say, the constitutional section over the anti-constitutional section — it is nothing more than a tiny distortion or a small clash within the group of exploiters. This is a contradiction that in present-day Latin America will never be decisive, with imperialism maintaining its tools of exploitation.

One of the premises of the Cuban Revolution is that it is absolutely necessary to immediately destroy the army in order to take power seriously.

Brazil is another big country in South America that is in a strange situation of unstable equilibrium. As you know, Brazil is the largest country in Latin America, the third largest in the world and the country with the largest reserves of raw materials owned by U.S. interests. It has 60 million inhabitants and is a real power. All of its raw materials are being developed by U.S. capital, and all of the contradictions of Latin America have appeared.

Two trends can be noted in the forces of the left: some of them want a revolution, while others want to take power by more peaceful or institutional means. The forces of the left that are represented, above all, by the peasant masses of the northeast are clearly willing to seize power despite the opposition of the bourgeoisie (the bourgeoisie puts up little opposition; imperialism is the real enemy).

Brazil is really several different countries. The northeast region is one of them. It is a very poor, densely populated area where there are terrible droughts and the very large peasantry is particularly combative. In the center of the country there is a largely unpopulated jungle area with small agricultural plots. To the south is the industrial area with São Paulo and Río de Janeiro, the most important cities in Brazil.

The northern area is ideal for insurrection. Exploitation has reached such an extreme that farmers cannot stand it any more. Every day there are reports that Brazilian comrades have been killed in their struggle against the large landowners. After Quadros resigned and the military tried to stage a coup, the country reached a compromise: the present government is in power thanks to a compromise between the exploiting groups, the Brazilian national bourgeoisie and imperialism. This compromise will of course be violated and the two will start fighting among themselves. If they haven't yet done so openly, it is because they face one great enemy, the Brazilian people.

When Quadros resigned, Fidel explained more or less what the Brazilian people should do. His words were broadcast to the Brazilian people and caused a lot of disquiet. Some thought it to be an act of interference by our government and prime minister in Brazil's internal affairs. I believe that revolutionaries should give such advice in times of great danger and great need for decisiveness. If a decisive battle had been won in Brazil, the panorama of Latin America would have changed rapidly. Brazil shares borders with all of the other South American countries except Chile and Ecuador. It has enormous influence. It is really a place for waging a battle.

In our relations with the other Latin American countries, we should always consider that we are part of a single family — a family with more or less special characteristics — and we must not forget our duty of solidarity or our duty to express our opinion at specific moments. It is not a matter of always interfering or of tediously pointing to our own example — an example not all the other countries can follow. But at moments like that, when Brazilians were debating the future of a large part of Latin America, we should speak out.

Part of the Brazilian battle was lost — and could be lost — without too many consequences, but it was nevertheless a moment of tremendous tension. If the battle had been won, we would have won a great deal. What happened in Brazil was not a triumph of the people's forces; it was simply a compromise, in which the group that has power, weapons, decisiveness to use them and great clarity about what has to be done gave up some of the privileges it had won. It will try to regain them later on, and then there will be a clash, too.

This year has already been one of violent clashes between the peoples' forces and those of oppression. The coming years will be similar. It cannot be said exactly when a collision will occur between such forces in each Latin American country, but it is clear that the contradictions are more and more exacerbated, and this is creating subjective conditions that are so important for developing a revolution. Two such conditions are particularly important: awareness of the need to effect urgent social change in order to do away with the situation of injustice and the certainty that it is possible to bring about that change.

All Latin Americans are training to bring change about. Training takes the form of uprisings and daily struggle, at times through legal means and at other times through illegal ones; at times in overt struggle and at other times underground. In all cases, the people are training constantly in all possible ways and that training is maturing in terms of quality and intensity, which presages very great future battles in Latin America.

Central America is like one country sharing the same characteristics and huge imperialist domination. It is one of the places where the peoples' struggle has already reached a climax but where the exact results are hard to see. In the short term I do not think they are very encouraging, because of the extensive domination of the United States. In Guatemala there has been a relative failure by the progressive forces, and Mexico is fast becoming a U.S. colony. There is a kind of bourgeoisie in Mexico, but it has made a pact with imperialism. It is a difficult country that has been greatly harmed by the so-called Mexican Revolution, and no important actions against its government can be foreseen there.

I have concentrated my attention on the countries that have entered into the sharpest contradictions with us and in which special conditions have been created for struggle. We have responded to the aggression through our mass media and explained as much as possible to the masses, telling them what can be done, and we are waiting. We aren't waiting as if in an orchestra pit preparing to watch the fight; we aren't spectators but rather are a part — an important part — of the struggle. The future of the peoples' revolutions in Latin America is very closely linked to the development of our revolution.

We have friends that are more powerful than all of the forces in Latin America. The United States knows this; if it attacks us directly it will seriously endanger its own territory. Even so it has chosen and meticulously followed a policy of isolating us in the Americas. First, it has ensured that our economic ties with the other Latin American countries are weak, excepting Chile. Second, it has seen to it that our relations with most of the other Latin American countries have been broken, and it is still working on this.

It appears that the United States will engage in more acts of aggression, such as the seemingly imminent one in Jamaica, to keep us from competing — that is, to do away with the influence of the Cuban Revolution, to break our contact. This is what Jesuits do; they put on long cassocks, hiding their desires. The United States is trying to do this with us, cloaking us so nobody will see us and we won't have any pernicious influence.

It is very important to struggle against this, because our contact with the rest of Latin America also depends on the way in which the Latin American peoples react to imperialism's attacks, and our safety depends to a great extent on how they react.

We shouldn't forget that imperialism makes mistakes. Imperialism may or may not know what the Soviet Union is willing to do to defend us, though I think it does know — if it didn't, we would have been attacked already. But it may be mistaken, and this time we must not let imperialism be mistaken. If it is, imperialism will be totally destroyed, but very little will be left of us. We must be fighters for peace and convinced champions of peace, because we ourselves will be hurt if the peace is broken. At the same time, we must talk freely of peoples' revolutions.

Though it seems paradoxical, advocating revolutions and peoples' struggle is the way to defend peace. Imperialism cannot fight against people when they are armed; it has to come to some kind of a compromise. Moreover, it isn't profitable for it to test its implements of war against something that doesn't exist, so it tries to foment wars between other nations. Imperialism wins in the local wars, the wars between nations. In them, its war matériel wins; the countries go into debt, and imperialism sells to one or to both of the countries. In short, everything depends on the circumstances, but it will gain from testing its war machinery, its tactics and its new inventions.

Now, a people's war has armies that appear and disappear in the early stages and fronts of struggle that don't exist — a war such as that in the southern part of Indochina, where a death zone has been declared 40 kilometers from Saigon; that is, the guerrillas hold territory just 40 kilometers from the capital. The imperialists can't maintain this kind of war, and moreover it teaches them nothing. They want to fight with their weapons to defend their privileges; they can't learn from fighting against small units in places where there is no visible enemy. They would have to make war against the Soviet Union, fighting with atomic missiles and using another, totally different kind of strategy.

Even though it isn't really drained — its losses are small — imperialism is losing points of support. We should remember one important thing: the U.S. imperialists are quite foresighted; they aren't as stupid as they seem.

They make mistakes, true, but they aren't as stupid as they seem. Some years ago they realized their own reserves were decreasing. The United States is a very wealthy country, but its reserves were on the decline, and so it began to seek reserves elsewhere, all over the world.

There are tin deposits close to Indochina and in Malaya. Bolivia also has tin. Peru has deposits of several precious metals, including iron and copper, and there are also large deposits of copper in Chile. Among other things, Argentina has uranium, and I believe the imperialists are taking that, too. Mexico has sulfur. Venezuela has oil, which the imperialist machine needs in order to survive. The United States needs Latin America, in addition to the parts of Asia and Africa it controls, to keep itself going.

Why did it fight in the Congo? The Congo has uranium, copper, diamonds — a whole realm of natural riches. The United States fought hard in the Congo; it ousted Belgian imperialism and took over. The United States is applying this policy all over the world, preparing for the future. If we take away its access to resources, take away imperialism's economic base, we will wound it mortally. You have to remember that imperialism functions outside its own territory. The United States isn't a power operating only within its own territory. It has invested capital all over the world and it plays with it, investing it and retracting its investments. Weakening imperialism's economic base will help to break its strength and will contribute to peace — world, global peace — which is what interests us.

We have to try to ensure that imperialism is not mistaken. We have so far warned it of the steps we would take to counter its blows — and we have taken them, which has hurt it. We have warned the imperialists several times. The radio station here in Havana hurts them. The truth hurts them, and that radio broadcasts to all of Latin America. Peasants throughout Latin America listen to the radio; cinema is the only media more influential than radio there. We have taught imperialism about our modest strength, and we must encourage their belief in our strength.

The imperialists are trying to isolate us, but also to attack us, through acts of sabotage like those in recent days and by trying to influence the people so as to create a certain climate. What happened in Hungary [in 1956] is an interesting example of mistakes made by a people's government, and there a counterrevolution paid for and prepared by the U.S. Government was unleashed.

Here in Latin America there was a very similar example, though the relevant government had different characteristics from the Hungarian people's government. It happened in Bolivia. In Bolivia there was a bourgeois government, headed by Major Villarroel, opposing the United

States. It advocated nationalizing the mines and other measures that the Bolivian people wanted. That people's government ended in a terrible way: Major Villarroel was hanged from a street-lamp in the public square. Why did that happen? Because the U.S. specialists manipulated the weaknesses arising in his government — and all governments have weaknesses, no matter how progressive they are.

We've had our weaknesses for some time, and all of you are in part responsible for them — in a very small way, of course; the leaders of the government, who are obliged to be far-sighted, are much more to blame. We took the road of sectarianism — which, more than simply being sectarian, is just plain stupid. We took the road of separation from the masses, of being too rigid, of strictly implementing correct measures and absurd ones. We took the road of suppressing criticism, and not only the people's criticism, who have a legitimate right to criticize, but also suppressing vigilant criticism by part of the party apparatus, which turned into an executive officer and, as such, lost its characteristics of vigilance and inspection. That led us to making serious economic mistakes. Remember that economics lies at the base of all political movements, and we made economic mistakes. That is, we took the road imperialism wanted us to take; they want to destroy our economic base by means of the blockade, and we have been assisting them with our own actions.

Why do I say that you're partly responsible? The Committees for the Defense of the Revolution (CDRs), institutions created for the people's vigilance and to represent the people's wish to defend their revolution, were instead imposed on the people as all-purpose dens of opportunism that were antipathetic to the people. I do think I'm entitled to describe the CDRs as being antipathetic to the people. Some of them took arbitrary measures, though this didn't happen so much here in Havana.

The fact is, we have totally ignored and abandoned the countryside, which is our base, the origin and, for two years, the source of replenishment for our guerrilla army, which triumphed over the cities — and we have left it in the hands of the CDRs.

The CDRs are filled with extremists, opportunists of all kinds who never stopped to think about the damage they were causing to the revolution. Imperialism began to work on these weaknesses — always present in the struggle — and as they worked they became quite successful. In some regions, it created real antagonism between the revolution and sectors of the petty bourgeoisie, who were overwhelmed by revolutionary activities. This is a lesson from which we should learn, and it also constitutes a great truth: that no matter what form they take, security bodies must be controlled by the people.

Sometimes it may seem, and at times it is, absolutely necessary to take prompt (and seemingly arbitrary) measures to counter the danger we are in. Half measures cannot be taken in moments of excessive tension; many people have been arrested without absolute proof that they were guilty. In the Sierra Maestra we shot some people without knowing if they bore full guilt, but it was a time when the revolution could not stop to fully investigate; it had the sacred obligation to win.

As soon as it is possible to restore natural relations among people, we should reestablish those relations, and not continue with the relations of the strong and the weak, based on the precept of "Do what I say." It is not fair not to do otherwise, and most importantly, we must do it because failure to do so would be politically unwise. Just as the CDRs have become antipathetic organizations, or at least have lost a large part of the prestige and affection they used to command, the security bodies may follow suit; in fact, they have already made similar mistakes.

Our great virtue is that we have never engaged in torture or other similarly terrible behavior, that some peoples have fallen into in many other countries in the course of defending correct principles. We established a principle energetically defended by Fidel: that no prisoner, even if they are to face execution, must be touched in any way. There may have been exceptions and I personally know of one, but we continue to uphold and defend that attitude. This is extremely important: anything and everything that happens makes the news, including things we don't publish in the [Cuban] newspapers and things we ourselves don't even want to know about. We hear about them later on. When I get home my partner says, "So-and-so took asylum in an embassy," or "A soldier shot up a bus." Everything becomes known. Everybody would find out about abuses and other bad things if there were any, no matter how secretly and far from the public eye they were carried out. The people know and evaluate all such things.

You have a very important role in the defense of the country, but it is less important than the development of the economy. Remember this: your role is less important. For us, it is much more important to have *malanga* than to have you. Even so you have an important role and must carry it out well.

Very hard battles lasting for who knows how long still lie ahead of us, and we must be ready to give our lives for the revolution in one field or another, with greater or lesser urgency, in a more or less immediate future. The battles will continue. I'm no prophet and I can't tell you what level of tension they will reach or to what degree they will consist of open combat; I hope and wish they will not reach an extreme degree. If they do, neither yours or my actions will be very important for the final outcome. But if they don't, and none of us wants them to reach an extreme degree and will struggle to hold imperialism in its place because, as Nikita said, the elephant is strong, though the tiger is still a tiger. Your task of finding out what the enemy is planning to do, and also of passing on what the people think, takes on full importance. You can be great conduits, passing on the people's feelings to the government.

The leaders of the revolution in Matanzas went through the streets with some rope, saying that INRA (National Institute of the Agrarian Reform) would provide the rope but it was up to the people to decide who should be hanged. There weren't any reports, at least I haven't read any, that any such thing happened. Those leaders didn't do their duty correctly. That's like the example of the so-called red terror that people tried to impose against the white terror, not realizing that the white terror existed only in the minds of some extremists. We ourselves unleashed a white terror with our absurd measures, and then we introduced a red terror.

The absurd measures that an uncontrolled revolutionary group took in Matanzas were both saddening and strange. They may be repeated and we must all be vigilant to prevent that from happening. Everything that goes against revolutionary morality is counterrevolutionary; don't forget that. Anyone who fights against the revolution is a counterrevolutionary, but so is a man who uses his influence to buy a house, an extra car, food beyond his ration book quota and other things the people don't have, whether or not he flaunts them. He is a counterrevolutionary and should be denounced immediately. Anyone who uses his influence for his personal benefit or for that of his friends is a counterrevolutionary, and he should be relentlessly pursued and removed. Opportunism is an enemy of the revolution and flourishes wherever the people don't have control. For this reason it is so important to control the security bodies.

In bodies where control is exercised from far above — where, because of the body's work, the steps that each of its members takes cannot be controlled — we must be inflexible. Only this is justice and we have made a revolution against injustice; moreover it is politically correct to do so, because those who violate revolutionary morality while speaking of revolution are not only potential traitors to the revolution but are also the worst detractors of the revolution. The people see them and know what they are doing, even when we ourselves don't know about such things, or don't want to know. Our revolution, having taken that mistaken path for some months, was destroying the most sacred thing it owns, the people's faith in it, and we must now work together with more enthusiasm and self-sacrifice than ever, to restore what we destroyed.

It will be a hard task; there isn't the same enthusiasm this year as last; something has been lost and must be recovered. It will take a lot of effort, but it will be done, because the will to create beats in the hearts of the people and in the revolution is great. It was easier in the past. After faith has been betrayed or weakened, it won't be so easy to restore and you must work hard to do this while at the same time, be inflexible with the counter-revolution. You must be inscrutable about state matters and remain constantly vigilant.

When making analyses you should always consider that Cuba is part of Latin America, that it is directly linked to the rest of Latin America. What we have wrought here is of great historical importance and, even if we didn't wish it, it will extend to the rest of Latin America. Like it has already extended to some peoples, it will extend to others as well. The Second Declaration of Havana will be very important in the development of the revolutionary movements in Latin America. As a document it calls on the masses to struggle, and we should retain our respect for great documents. This Second Declaration of Havana is like a Latin American Communist Manifesto of the period, and is based on our reality and on a Marxist analysis of Latin American reality.

I thought it would be correct for me to touch on Latin America with you this evening. Please forgive me because lack of data kept me from being more convincing and from going into the economic aspect of the struggle, which is so important. It would have been very interesting — for me, at least; I don't know about you — to examine data demonstrating the extent of imperialist penetration, that brings out the relations between political movements and the economic situations of our countries and clearly shows how reaction corresponds to penetration and how penetration takes place because of a specific historical or economic background.

The continent shares many features: imperialism's efforts to penetrate the bourgeoisie in some places in Latin America, the development of the struggles between different empires, and now the absolute U.S. monopoly over the economies of Latin American countries and over Latin America as a whole. The brand name Colgate, for example, is a word repeated in nearly all of the Latin American nations, just like Mejoral, Palmolive and the names of thousands of other articles consumed here every day. Imperialism uses Latin America as a source of raw materials and as an area of expansion for its monopolies. But this has also unified us, creating a unity that must be held sacred and must be defended and strengthened.

As a moral footnote to this conversation, you should study Latin America more. I have noted that generally in Cuba we know more about practically every other part of the world than we do about Latin America, and this is wrong. By studying Latin America, we will also learn a little about ourselves, draw closer together and understand more about our relations and our history. Studying Latin America means studying imperialist penetration — that is, studying its economy. There, you will discover the seeds of everything that is growing and happening now.

Tactics and strategy of the Latin American Revolution

(October–November 1962)

This essay was first published in Verde Olivo, *October 9, 1968. Written whilst in Cuba, it was not published until after Che Guevara's death.*

> Tactics show us how to use armed forces in combat and strategy teaches us how to use combat encounters in order to obtain the war's objective.
> — Karl von Clausewitz

 began this work with a quotation from Clausewitz, the military author who fought against Napoleon and who theorized so brilliantly about war; Lenin loved to quote him because of the clarity of his thinking, in spite of the fact that he was, of course, a bourgeois analyst.

Tactics and strategy are the two main elements in the art of war, but war and politics are intimately related by a common denominator: the effort to reach a specific goal, whether it be annihilation of the adversary in armed conflict or the taking of political power.

But analysis of the essential tactics and strategies that rule political or military struggles cannot be reduced to a schematic formula.

The richness of each one of these concepts can be measured only by combining practice with the analysis of the complex activities that they imply.

There are no unalterable tactical and strategic objectives. Sometimes tactical objectives attain strategic importance, and other times strategic objectives become merely tactical elements. The thorough study of the relative importance of each element permits the full utilization, by the revolutionary forces, of all of the facts and circumstances leading up to the great and final strategic objective: *the taking of power.*

Power is the *sine qua non* strategic objective of the revolutionary forces, and everything must be subordinated to this basic endeavor.

But the taking of power, in this world polarized by two forces of extreme disparity and absolute incompatibility of interests, cannot be limited to the boundaries of a single geographic or social unit. The seizure of power is a worldwide objective of the revolutionary forces. To conquer the future is the strategic element of revolution; freezing the present is the counterstrategy motivating the forces of world reaction today, for they are on the defensive.

In this worldwide struggle, position is very important. At times it is decisive. Cuba, for example, is a vanguard outpost overlooking the extremely broad stretches of the economically distorted world of Latin America. Cuba's example is a beacon, a guiding light for all the peoples of the Americas. The Cuban outpost is of great strategic value to the major contenders who at this moment dispute their hegemony of the world: imperialism and socialism.

Its value would be different if it had been located in another geographic or social setting. Its value was different prior to the revolution when it merely constituted a tactical element for the imperialist world. Its value has increased, not only because it is an open door to the Americas but because, added to the strength of its strategic, military and tactical position, is the power of its moral influence. "Moral missiles" are such a devastatingly effective weapon that they have become the most important element in determining Cuba's value. That is why, to analyze each element in the political struggle, one cannot extract it from its particular set of circumstances. All the antecedents serve to reaffirm a line or position consistent with its great strategic objectives.

Relating this discussion to the Americas, one must ask the necessary question: What are the tactical elements that must be used to achieve the major objective of taking power in this part of the world? Is it possible or not, given the present conditions in our continent, to achieve it (socialist power, that is) by peaceful means? We emphatically answer that, in the great majority of cases, it is not possible. The most that could be achieved would be the formal takeover of the bourgeois superstructure of power, and the transition to socialism by that government; having achieved formal power under the established bourgeois legal system there would still be a very violent struggle against all who attempt in one way or another to check its progress toward new social structures.

This is one of the most debated and most important topics, and possibly, it is a topic on which our revolution most disagrees with other revolutionary movements of Latin America. We must clearly state our position and try to analyze its rationale.

Today, Latin America is a volcano. Although not in a state of eruption it is shocked by subterranean vibrations announcing the volcano's coming. There are visible and audible signs everywhere. The Second Declaration of

Havana is the concrete expression of those subterranean movements. It strives to achieve an awareness of its objective, that is, an awareness of the necessity and even the certainty of revolutionary change. This volcano in the Americas is not divorced from the revolutionary movements appearing in the contemporary world in this crucial moment of confrontation between two opposing forces and conceptualizations of history.

We could refer to our homeland with the following words from the Declaration of Havana:

> What is the history of Cuba if it is not the history of Latin America? And what is the history of Latin America if it is not the history of Asia, Africa and Oceania? And what is the history of all of these peoples if it is not the history of the most merciless and cruel exploitation by imperialism in the modern world?

The Americas, like Africa, Asia and Oceania, are part of a single whole where economic forces have been distorted by imperialism. But not all the continents present similar characteristics; the forms of economic exploitation — imperialist, colonialist, or neocolonialist — employed by the European bourgeois forces have had to cope not only with the liberation struggles of the oppressed peoples of Asia, Africa and Oceania, but also with the penetration of U.S. imperialist capital. This has created different correlations of forces in different areas, and has permitted peaceful transition toward national independent or neocolonialist bourgeois systems.

But in the Americas such systems have not developed. Latin America is the parade ground of U.S. imperialism, and there are no economic forces in the world capable of supporting the struggle that national bourgeoisies have waged against imperialism elsewhere; and these forces, relatively much weaker than in other regions, back down and compromise with imperialism.

The frightened bourgeoisie is faced with a terrible choice: submission to foreign capital or destruction by domestic popular forces. The Cuban Revolution has accentuated this dilemma; the polarization created by its example means the only alternative that remains is to sell out. When this takes place, when the pact is sanctified, domestic reactionary forces ally themselves with the most powerful international reactionary forces, and the peaceful development of social revolutions is prevented.

Pointing out the present situation, the Second Declaration of Havana states:

> In many Latin American countries revolution is inevitable. This fact is not determined by the will of any one person. It is determined by

the horrible conditions of exploitation under which the Latin American people live, the development of a revolutionary consciousness in the masses, the worldwide crisis of imperialism and the universal liberation movements of the subjugated nations.

Today's restlessness is an unmistakable symptom of rebellion. The insides of the continent are stirring after having witnessed four centuries of slavery, semislavery, and feudal exploitation of human by human; from the indigenous peoples and slaves brought from Africa to the national groups that arose later — whites, blacks, mulattoes, mestizos and Indians — who today share pain, humiliation and the Yankee yoke, and share hope for a better tomorrow.

We can conclude, then, that when faced with the decision to bring about more socially just systems in the Americas, we must think fundamentally in terms of armed struggle. There exists, nevertheless, some possibility of peaceful transition; this is pointed out in the studies of classical Marxist authors and it is sanctioned in the declaration of the parties. Yet under the current conditions in Latin America, every minute that goes by makes a peaceful commitment more difficult. The latest events in Cuba are an example of the cohesion that exists between the bourgeois governments and the imperialist aggressor on the fundamental aspects of the conflict.

Remember this point we have continually emphasized: Peaceful transition is not the achievement of formal power by elections or through public opinion without direct combat, but rather it is the establishment of socialist power, with all of its attributes, without the use of armed struggle. It is reasonable, then, that all the progressive forces do not have to initiate the road of armed revolution but must use — until the very last moment — every possibility of legal struggle within the bourgeois conditions.

With regard to the form the revolutionary movements must adopt after seizing power, a number of very interesting questions of interpretation arise characterizing the times. The Declaration of the 81 Communist Parties states:

> Our epoch, whose main feature is the transition from capitalism to socialism, as initiated by the great October Socialist Revolution, is the epoch of the struggle between two diametrically opposed social systems; it is the epoch of socialist revolutions and of national liberation revolutions; it is the epoch of the collapse of imperialism and of the liquidation of the colonial system; it is the epoch of the constant advance of more and more peoples on the socialist road; it is the epoch of the triumph of socialism and of universal communism.

The main feature of our epoch is the fact that the international socialist system is becoming the decisive factor in the development of human society.

It is stated, therefore, that although the people's struggle for liberation is very important, that which characterizes the present time is the transition from capitalism to socialism.

There are countries from all the exploited continents whose social systems have reached different levels of development, but almost all of them have strong social divisions with feudal characteristics and a heavy dependence on foreign capital. It would be logical to think that in the struggle for liberation, following the natural process of development, countries could obtain national democratic governments in which the bourgeoisie more or less predominates. This has occurred in many cases. Nevertheless, those peoples who have had to use force to achieve independence have made greater advances in the path of social reforms and many of them are building socialism. Cuba and Algeria are the most recent examples of the effects of armed struggle on the development of social transformation. If we conclude that the possibility of the peaceful road is almost nonexistent in the Americas, we can point out that it is very probable that the outcome of victorious revolutions in this area of the world will produce regimes of a socialist structure.

Rivers of blood will flow before this is achieved. Algeria's wounds have not yet healed; Vietnam continues to bleed; Angola struggles bravely and alone for its independence; Venezuela, whose patriots identify with the Cuban cause, has recently demonstrated its lofty and expressive solidarity with our revolution; Guatemala is waging a difficult, almost underground struggle. All of these are good examples.

The blood of the people is our most sacred treasure, but it must be used in order to save more blood in the future.

Other continents have achieved liberation from colonialism and have established more or less strong bourgeois regimes. This has been accomplished without, or almost without, violence but we must realize that following the logic of events up to this moment, this constantly developing national bourgeoisie will at a given moment find itself in contradiction with other strata of the population. When the yoke of the oppressor country is removed, this national bourgeoisie is no longer a revolutionary force and transforms itself into an exploiting class, renewing the cycle of social struggle. It may or may not advance on a peaceful road, but irrevocably two great forces will confront each other: the exploiters and the exploited.

The dilemma of our time, regarding how power should be seized, has not escaped the attention of Yankee imperialists. They also want a "peaceful transition." They favor the liquidation of the old feudal structures still existing in Latin America and want to ally with the most advanced sectors of the national bourgeoisies, carrying out some monetary reforms, some kinds of reform in the land structure, and a moderate industrialization, preferably in consumer goods, with technology and raw materials imported from the United States.

The perfected formula consists of allying the national bourgeoisie with foreign interests; together they create new industries in the country, setting up tariff advantages in these industries of such magnitude that they permit the total exclusion of competition from other imperialist countries. Profits obtained in this manner can be taken out of the country with protection afforded by the many loopholes in exchange regulations.

Through this new and more intelligent system of exploitation, the "nationalist" country assumes the role of protecting U.S. interests — setting up tariffs that allow extra profit, which the North Americans re-export to their country. Naturally, the sale price of articles, without competition, is fixed by the monopolies.

All of this is reflected in the projects of the Alliance for Progress which are nothing more than imperialist attempts to block the development of the revolutionary conditions of the people by sharing a small quantity of the profits with the native exploiting classes, thus making them into firm allies against the highly exploited classes. In other words, they suppress the internal contradictions of the capitalist system as much as possible.

As we mentioned previously, there are no forces in America capable of intervening in this economic struggle and therefore the game of imperialism is very simple. The only possibility left is the impetuous development of the European Common Market, under German leadership, which could reach an economic strength sufficient to compete with Yankee capitalists in this region. But the development of contradictions and their violent resolution is so rapid and so eruptive today that it appears that Latin America will much earlier become the battlefield of exploiters and exploited than the scene of an economic struggle between two imperialisms.

It should be said that the intentions of the Alliance for Progress will not materialize because objective conditions and the consciousness of the masses have matured too far for them to fall into such a naive trap.

The decisive factor today is whether the imperialist-Creole-bourgeois front is consistent. During the recent OAS [Organization of American States] voting there were no discordant voices on fundamental problems and only a few governments tried to cover up their shame with legalistic formulas, without denouncing the aggressive tendency of these resolutions, which are contrary to law.

The fact that Cuba had atomic missiles served as a pretext for all to side with the United States; Playa Girón [Bay of Pigs] did not produce any different responses. They know very well that these are defensive weapons, they also know who the aggressor is.

Even though they do not say so, the fact is that they all recognize the true danger posed by the Cuban Revolution. The most submissive countries and consequently, the most cynical, talk about the threat of Cuban subversion, and they are right. The greatest threat of the Cuban Revolution is its own example, its revolutionary ideas, the fact that the government has been able to increase the combativity of the people, led by a leader of world stature, to heights seldom equalled in history.

Here is the electrifying example of a people prepared to suffer atomic immolation so that its ashes may serve as a foundation for new societies. When an agreement was reached by which the atomic missiles were removed, without asking our people, we were not relieved or thankful for the truce; instead we denounced the move with our own voice. We have demonstrated our firm stand, our own position, our decision to fight, even if alone, against all dangers and against the atomic menace of Yankee imperialism.

This causes other peoples to stir. They hear the call of the new voice emanating from Cuba, stronger than all fears, lies or prejudices, stronger than hunger and all the techniques used to try and destroy our people. It is stronger than the fear of any reprisal, the most barbarous punishment, the cruellest death, or the most bestial oppression of the exploiters. A new voice, clear and precise, has sounded in every corner of Our America.

That has been our mission and we have fulfilled it, and we shall continue to fulfil it with all the decisiveness of our revolutionary convictions.

We could ask: Is this the only road? Why not utilize the imperialist contradictions? Why not seek the backing of the bourgeois sectors that have been struck and humiliated by imperialism? Could we not find a less severe, less self-destructive formula than this Cuban position? Is it not possible to ensure Cuba's survival through a combination of force and diplomatic maneuvers? We answer: When faced with brute force, use force and determination; when faced by those who want to destroy you, you can only reply with the will to fight to the very last person in order to defend yourselves.

This formula is valid for all of Latin America in the face of those who want to remain in power, against the will of the people, at any cost. Fire and blood must be used until the last exploiter has been annihilated.

How can the revolution be carried out in Latin America? Let us listen again to the Second Declaration of Havana:

> In our countries two circumstances are linked: underdeveloped industry and a feudal agrarian system. No matter how hard the living conditions of the urban workers are, the rural population lives under even worse conditions of oppression and exploitation. With few exceptions, the rural population also constitutes the absolute majority, sometimes more than 70 percent of the population in the Latin American countries.
>
> Not counting the landowners who often live in the cities, this great mass earns its livelihood by working for miserable wages as peons on plantations. They till the soil under conditions of exploitation no different from those of the Middle Ages. These circumstances determine in Latin America that the poor rural population constitutes a tremendous potential revolutionary force.
>
> The armies in Latin America are set up and equipped for conventional warfare. They are the force through which the power of the exploiting classes is maintained. When they are confronted with the irregular warfare of peasants based on their home ground, they become absolutely powerless; they lose 10 men for every revolutionary fighter who falls. Demoralization among them mounts rapidly when they are beset by an invisible and invincible army which provides them with no opportunity to display their military academy tactics and their military fanfare, of which they boast so heavily, and which they use to repress the city workers and students.
>
> The initial struggle of the small fighting units is constantly nurtured by new forces; the mass movement begins to grow bold, bit by bit the old order breaks into a thousand pieces, and that is when the working class and the urban masses decide the battle.
>
> What is it that from the very beginning of the fight makes these units invincible, regardless of the numbers, strengths and resources of their enemies? It is the people's support, and they can count on ever-increasing mass support.
>
> The peasantry, however, is a class that because of the ignorance in which it has been kept and the isolation in which it lives, requires the revolutionary and political leadership of the working class and the revolutionary intellectuals. It cannot launch the struggle and achieve victory alone.
>
> In the present historical conditions of Latin America, the national bourgeoisie cannot lead the antifeudal and anti-imperialist struggle. Experience demonstrates that in our nations this class — even when its interests clash with those of Yankee imperialism — has been incapable of confronting imperialism, paralyzed by fear of social revolution and frightened by the clamor of the exploited masses.

That is what the Second Declaration of Havana says and it can be seen as an outline of revolution in Latin America. We cannot think of alliances that are not entirely led by the working class, we cannot think of collaboration with a frightened and treacherous bourgeoisie that destroys the forces on which it based itself to attain power. The weapons must be in the hands of the people and all of Latin America must become a battlefield. The peasants have to fight for their land, the oppressor must be killed mercilessly in ambushes, and the revolutionary must fight and die with honor. This is what counts.

This is the panorama of Latin America, a continent preparing to fight, and the sooner the people take up arms and bring their machetes down on the landowners, industrialists, bankers, and all exploiters, as well as their main instrument, the oppressor army, the better.

Whether guerrilla action should always be the tactic or whether it is feasible to institute other actions as the central axis of the struggle can be argued at length. Our opposition to using any other tactic in Latin America is based on two arguments:

First: Accepting as truth the statement that the enemy will fight to stay in power, one must think in terms of the destruction of the oppressor army. In order to destroy it, a people's army must be raised to oppose it directly. This army will not spring up spontaneously; it will have to arm itself with the weapons taken from the enemy's arsenal and this implies a very long and hard struggle in which the popular forces and their leaders will always be exposed to attack from superior forces, without adequate conditions for defense and maneuverability. On the other hand, a guerrilla nucleus established in favorable terrain guarantees the security and permanence of the revolutionary command and the urban contingents can be directed from this central command of the people's army. They can carry out actions of incalculable importance.

The eventual destruction of urban groups will not destroy the soul of the revolution; its leadership, from its rural bastion, will continue catalyzing the revolutionary spirit of the masses and organizing new forces for other battles.

Second: The continental character of the struggle. Can we conceive of this new epoch in the emancipation of Latin America as the contest between two local forces struggling for power over a given territory? Obviously not. It will be a fight to the death between all the popular forces and all the repressive forces.

The Yankees will intervene because of shared interests and because the struggle in Latin America is decisive. They will intervene with all of their resources and will also turn all available destructive weapons upon the popular forces. They will not allow revolutionary power to consolidate itself, and if it succeeds in doing so, they will attack it again and again. They will not recognize defeat and will try to divide the revolutionary forces, introducing saboteurs of every kind. They will try to destroy the new state economically; in a word, they will try to annihilate it.

Given this overall panorama of Latin America, we find it difficult to believe that victory can be achieved in one isolated country. The union of repressive forces must be countered with the unity of the popular forces. In every country where oppression reaches the limits of tolerance, the banner of rebellion must be raised, and this banner will, of historical necessity, be continental in character. The Andean cordillera is destined to be the Sierra Maestra of the Americas, as Fidel has said, and all the immense territories of this continent are destined to be the scene of a struggle to death against imperialist power.

We cannot say when the struggle will take on these continental characteristics or how long it will last, but we can predict its coming, for it is the product of historical, political and economic circumstances. Its advance cannot be stopped.

Faced with this continental tactic and strategy, some people offer limited formulas: minor election campaigns; an election victory here or there; two deputies, a senator, four mayors; a large popular demonstration broken up by gunfire; an election lost by fewer votes than the preceding one; one labor strike won, 10 strikes lost; one step forward, 10 steps back. And then, at any precise moment, the rules of the game are changed and one has to start all over again.

Why such formulas? Why such weakening of the people's energies? There is only one reason: Among the progressive forces of some Latin American nations there exists a terrible confusion between tactical and strategic objectives. Small tactical positions have been interpreted as great strategic objectives. One must credit the reactionary forces with the success of having forced their class enemy to make minimal offensive positions their fundamental objective.

When and where these grave errors occur, the people organize their legions year after year to achieve gains which cost them immense sacrifices and do not have the least value.

There is the hill of parliament, of legal economic strikes, of salary increases, of bourgeois constitutions, of the liberation of a popular figure... and worst of all, in order to gain these positions one must enter into the political games of the bourgeois state. In order to get permission to play this dangerous game one must show that one is a good child, that one is not dangerous, that one would never think of assaulting army garrisons or trains, destroying bridges, or bringing revolutionary justice to hired thugs or to torturers, or going to the mountains. One cannot state resolutely the only and violent affirmation of Latin America: the final struggle for her redemption.

Latin America offers a contradictory picture. There are progressive forces which are not up to the level of those they lead — people who can rise to unknown heights, people who boil with a desire to act and leaders who frustrate those desires. The catastrophe is almost here and the people have no fear; they try to move toward the moment of sacrifice, which will mean the definitive achievement of redemption. The educated and prudent ones, on the other hand, put all available brakes on the movement of the masses, attempting to divert the irrepressible yearnings of the masses for the great strategic objectives: the taking of political power, the annihilation of the army and the destruction of the system of exploitation of man by man. The picture is contradictory but full of hope because the masses know that "the role of Job is not for the revolutionary," so they prepare for battle.

Will imperialism continue to lose one position after another or will it, in its bestiality and as it threatened not long ago, launch a nuclear attack and burn the entire world in an atomic holocaust? We cannot say. We do assert, however, that we must follow the road of liberation even though it may cost millions of atomic war victims. In the struggle to death between two systems we cannot think of anything but the final victory of socialism or its relapse as a consequence of the nuclear victory of imperialist aggression.

Cuba is at the brink of an invasion, threatened by the most powerful imperialist forces of the world, and as such, threatened with atomic death. From its trench, refusing to retreat, Cuba issues a call to arms to all of Latin America. This is a struggle that will not be decided in a few minutes or an hour of terrible battle. The end of the struggle will take years of bitter encounters causing atrocious suffering. The attack of the allied imperialist and bourgeois forces will time and again force the popular movements to the brink of destruction, but those movements will always come back strengthened by the support of the people until total liberation is achieved.

From here, from its lonely vanguard trench, our people make their voices heard. This is not the song of a revolution heading for defeat; it is a revolutionary anthem destined to be sung eternally from the lips of Latin American fighters. It will be echoed by history.

The philosophy of plunder must cease

(March 25, 1964)

Guevara headed Cuba's delegation to the United Nations Conference on Trade and Development in Geneva, Switzerland, where he presented this speech.

Mr. President;
Distinguished delegates:

T his is the delegation of Cuba speaking, an island country situated at the mouth of the Gulf of Mexico in the Caribbean Sea. It is addressing you under the protection of its right to come to this forum and proclaim the truth. It addresses you, first of all, as a country that is going through the gigantic experience of building socialism. It does so also as a country belonging to the group of Latin American nations, even though illegal decisions have temporarily severed it from the regional organization, owing to the pressure exerted and the action taken by the United States of America.[7] Its geography indicates it is an underdeveloped country that addresses you, one that bears the scars of colonialist and imperial exploitation and that knows from bitter experience the subjection of its markets and its entire economy or — what amounts to the same thing — the subjection of its entire governmental machinery to a foreign power. Cuba also addresses you as a country under attack.

All these features have given our country a prominent place in the news throughout the world, despite our small size, our lack of economic importance and our limited population.

At this conference, Cuba will express its views from the various standpoints that correspond to its particular situation in the world. But we will base our analysis on our most important and positive attribute: that of a country building socialism. As a Latin American and underdeveloped country, we will support the main demands of our sister countries, and as a country under attack we will denounce from the very outset all the schemes being cooked up by the coercive machinery of that imperialist power, the United States of America.

We preface our statement with these words of explanation because our country considers it imperative to define exactly the scope of the conference, its meaning, and its possible importance.

We come to this meeting 17 years after the Havana conference, whose aim was to create a world order suited to the competitive interests of the imperialist powers.[8] Although Cuba was the site of that conference, our revolutionary government does not consider itself bound in the slightest by the role then played by a government subordinated to imperialist interests. Nor do we feel bound by the content or scope of the so-called Havana Charter.

At that conference, and at the previous meeting at Bretton Woods, a number of international bodies were set up whose activities have been harmful to the interests of the dependent countries of the contemporary world. And even though the United States of America did not ratify the Havana Charter because it considered it too "daring," the various international credit and financial bodies and the General Agreement on Tariffs and Trade (GATT) — the tangible outcome of those two meetings — have proved to be effective weapons for defending U.S. interests. What is more, they have been weapons for attacking our countries. These are subjects we will deal with at length later on.

Today, the conference agenda is broader and more realistic because it includes, among others, three of the crucial problems facing the modern world: the relations between the camp of the socialist countries and that of the developed capitalist countries, the relations between the underdeveloped countries and the developed capitalist powers, and the great problem of development for the dependent world.

The participants at this new meeting far outnumber those who met at Havana in 1947. Nevertheless, we cannot say with complete accuracy that this is a forum of the world's peoples. As a result of the strange legal interpretations that certain powers still use with impunity, countries of great importance in the world are missing from this meeting: for example the People's Republic of China, the sole lawful representative of the most populous nation on earth, whose seats are occupied by a delegation that falsely claims to represent that nation and that, to add to the anomaly, even enjoys the right of veto in the United Nations.[9]

It should also be noted that delegations representing the Democratic Republic of Korea and the Democratic Republic of Vietnam, the genuine governments of those nations, are absent, while representatives of the governments of the southern parts of both those divided states are present. To add to the absurdity of the situation, while the German Democratic Republic is unjustly excluded, the Federal Republic of Germany is attending this conference and is given a vice-presidency. And while the socialist republics I mentioned are not represented here, the government of the Union of South Africa, which violates the United Nations Charter with the inhuman and fascist policy of apartheid embodied in its laws, and which defies the United Nations by refusing to transmit information on the territories that it holds in trust, makes bold to occupy a seat in this hall.[10]

Because of all these anomalies, this conference cannot be defined as the forum of the world's peoples. It is our duty to point this out and draw it to the attention of those present. Because so long as this situation persists and justice remains the tool of a few powerful interests, legal interpretations will continue to be tailored to the convenience of the oppressor powers and it will be difficult to ease the prevailing tension: a situation that entails real dangers for humanity. We also stress these facts in order to call attention to the responsibilities incumbent upon us and to the consequences that may flow from the decisions taken here. A single moment of weakness, wavering, or compromise may discredit us in the eyes of history, just as we member states of the United Nations are in a sense accomplices and, in a manner of speaking, bear on our hands the blood of Patrice Lumumba, Congolese Prime Minister, who was shamefully murdered at a time when United Nations troops supposedly guaranteed the stability of his government.[11] What is worse, those troops had been expressly called in by the martyr, Patrice Lumumba. Events of such gravity or of a similar nature, or that have negative implications for international relations and jeopardize our standing as sovereign nations, must not be allowed to happen at this conference.

We live in a world that is deeply and antagonistically divided into groupings of nations very dissimilar in economic, social and political outlook. In this world of contradictions, the one existing between the socialist countries and the developed capitalist countries is spoken of as the fundamental contradiction of our time. The fact that the Cold War, conceived by the West, has shown itself lacking in real effectiveness and in political realism is one of the factors that have led to the convening of this conference. While that is the most important contradiction, however, it is nevertheless not the only one. There is also the contradiction between the developed capitalist countries and the world's underdeveloped nations. And at this conference on trade and development, the contradictions existing between these groups of nations are also of fundamental importance. In addition there is the inherent contradiction between the various developed capitalist countries, which struggle unceasingly among themselves to divide up the world and to gain stable possession of its markets so that they may enjoy substantial development based, unfortunately, on the hunger and exploitation of the dependent world.

These contradictions are important. They reflect the realities of the planet today, and they give rise to the danger of new conflagrations that, in the nuclear age, may spread throughout the world.

If, at this egalitarian conference — where all nations can express, through their votes, the hopes of their peoples — a solution satisfactory to the majority can be reached, a unique step will have been taken in the history of the world. There are many forces at work to prevent this from happening, however. The responsibility for the decisions to be taken falls on the representatives of the underdeveloped peoples. If all the peoples who live under precarious economic conditions and who depend on foreign powers for some vital aspects of their economy and for their economic and social structure are capable of resisting — coolly, although in the heat of the moment — the temptations offered them and imposing a new type of relationship here, then humanity will have taken a step forward.

If, on the other hand, the groups of underdeveloped countries, lured by the siren song of the interests of the developed powers who profit from their backwardness, compete futilely among themselves for crumbs from the tables of the world's mighty, and break the unity of numerically superior forces; or if they are not capable of insisting on clear agreements, without escape clauses open to capricious misinterpretations; or if they rest content with agreements that can simply be violated at will by the powerful, then our efforts will have been to no avail and the lengthy deliberations at this conference will result in nothing more than innocuous documents and files for the international bureaucracy to guard zealously: tons of printed paper and kilometers of magnetic tape recording the opinions expressed by the participants. And the world will stay as it is.

Such is the nature of this conference. It will have to deal not only with the problems involved in the domination of markets and the deterioration in the terms of trade but also with the main cause of this state of world affairs: the subordination of the national economies of the dependent countries to other more developed countries that, through investments, hold sway over the main sectors of each economy.

It must be clearly understood, and we say it in all frankness, that the only way to solve the problems now besetting humanity is to eliminate completely the exploitation of dependent countries by developed capitalist countries, with all the consequences that implies. We have come here fully aware that what is involved is a discussion among the representatives of countries that have put an end to the exploitation of man by man, representatives of countries that maintain such exploitation as their guiding philosophy, and representatives of the majority group of the exploited countries. We must begin our discussion by affirming the truth of these statements.

But though our convictions are so firm that no arguments can change them, we are ready to join in constructive debate in the framework of peaceful coexistence between countries with different political, economic and social systems. The difficulty lies in making sure that we all know how much we can hope to get without having to take it by force, and where to yield a privilege before it is inevitably wrung from us by force. The conference has to proceed along this narrow, difficult path. If we stray, we shall find ourselves on barren ground.

We announced at the beginning of this statement that Cuba would speak here also as a country under attack. The latest developments, which have made our country the target of imperialist wrath and the object of every conceivable kind of repression and violation of international law, from before Playa Girón until now, are known to all. It was no accident that Cuba was the main scene of one of the acts that have most seriously endangered world peace, as a result of a legitimate action taken by Cuba in exercise of its right to adopt its own principles for its people's development.

Acts of aggression by the United States against Cuba began virtually as soon as the revolution triumphed. In the first stage, they took the form of direct attacks on Cuban centers of production.

Later, these acts took the form of measures aimed at paralyzing the Cuban economy. About the middle of 1960 an attempt was made to deprive Cuba of the fuel needed to operate its industries, transport and power stations. Under pressure from the State Department, the independent U.S. oil companies refused to sell petroleum to Cuba or to provide Cuba with tankers to ship it in. Shortly afterward, efforts were made to deprive Cuba of the foreign exchange needed for its foreign trade. A cut of 700,000 tons in the Cuban sugar quota the United States was made by then President Eisenhower on July 6, 1960, and the quota was abolished altogether on March 31, 1961, a few days after the announcement of the Alliance for Progress and a few days before Playa Girón. In an effort to paralyze Cuban industry by cutting off its supplies of raw materials and spare machine parts, the U.S. Commerce Department issued an order on October 19, 1960, prohibiting the shipment of a large number of products to our island. This ban on trade with Cuba was progressively intensified until, on February 3, 1962, the late President Kennedy placed an embargo on all U.S. trade with Cuba.

After all these acts of aggression had failed, the United States went on to subject our country to an economic blockade whose purpose was to stop trade between other countries and our own. First, on January 24, 1962, the U.S. Treasury Department announced a ban on the importation into the United States of any article made in whole or in part from products of Cuban origin, even if it was manufactured in another country. A further step, equivalent to setting up a virtual economic blockade, was taken on February 6, 1963, when the White House issued a statement announcing that goods bought with U.S. Government funds would not be shipped in vessels flying the flag of foreign countries that had traded with Cuba after January 1 of that year. This was the beginning of the blacklist, which now includes more than 150 ships belonging to countries that have not yielded to the illegal Yankee blockade. A further measure to obstruct Cuba's trade was taken on July 8, 1963, when the U.S. Treasury Department froze all Cuban property in the United States and prohibited the transfer of dollars to or from Cuba, together with any other kind of dollar transaction carried out through third countries.

— Mr. President, would it not be possible to ask that the disturbance be stopped, which is making it difficult to hear? —

Obsessed with the desire to attack us, the United States specifically excluded our country from the supposed benefits of the Trade Expansion Act.

Acts of aggression have continued this year. On February 18, 1964, the United States announced the suspension of its aid to Great Britain, France and Yugoslavia because these countries were still trading with Cuba. Dean Rusk, the Secretary of State, said, according to the text that appeared in the U.S. newspapers: "At the same time there can be no improvement in relations with Communist China as long as that country incites and supports acts of aggression in Southeast Asia, or in those with Cuba as long as it represents a threat to the Western Hemisphere. That threat can be ended to Washington's satisfaction only with the overthrow of the Castro regime by the Cuban people. We regard that regime as temporary."

Cuba calls on the delegation of the U.S. Government to say whether the actions foreshadowed by this statement and others like it, and the incidents we have described, are or are not at odds with coexistence in the world today, and whether, in the opinion of that delegation, the series of acts of economic aggression committed against our island and against other countries that trade with us are legitimate. I ask whether that attitude is or is not at odds with the principle of the organization that brings us together — that of practicing tolerance among states — and with the obligation imposed by that organization on countries that have ratified its charter to settle their disputes by peaceful means. I ask whether that attitude is or is not at odds with the spirit of this meeting in favor of abandoning all forms of discrimination and removing the barriers between countries with different social systems and at different stages of development. And we ask this conference to pass judgment on any explanation the U.S. delegation ventures to make. We, for our part, maintain the only position we have ever taken in the matter: we are ready to join in discussions provided that no prior conditions are imposed.

The period that has elapsed since the Havana Charter was signed has been marked by events of undeniable importance in the field of trade and economic development. In the first place, we have to note the expansion of the socialist camp and the collapse of the colonial system. Many countries, covering an area of more than 30 million square kilometers and with one-third of the world's population, have chosen as their system of development the construction of the communist society and, as their guiding philosophy, Marxism-Leninism. Others, without directly embracing the Marxist-Leninist philosophy, have stated their intention of laying the foundations on which to build socialism. Europe, Asia, and now Africa and Latin America are continents shaken by the new ideas abroad in the world.

The socialist camp has developed uninterruptedly at rates of growth much faster than those of the capitalist countries despite having started out, as a general rule, from fairly low levels of development and of having had to withstand wars of extermination and rigorous blockades.

In contrast to the rapid rate of growth of the countries in the socialist camp and to the development taking place, albeit much more slowly, in the majority of the capitalist countries, the unquestionable fact is that a large proportion of the so-called underdeveloped countries are in total stagnation, and in some of them the rate of economic growth is lower than that of its population increase.

These characteristics are not accidental. They are strictly in keeping with the nature of the developed capitalist system in the process of expansion, which transfers to the dependent countries the most abusive and naked forms of exploitation.

Since the end of the last century, this aggressive expansionist trend has been manifested in countless attacks on various countries in the more backward continents. Today, however, it mainly takes the form of control exercised by the developed powers over the production of and trade in raw materials in the dependent countries. In general, it is shown by the dependence of a given country on a single primary commodity, which sells only in a specific market in quantities restricted to the needs of that market.

The penetration of capital from the developed countries is the essential condition for this economic dependence. This penetration takes various forms: loans granted on onerous terms; investments that place a given country under the power of the investors; almost total technological subordination of the dependent country to the developed country; control of a country's foreign trade by the big international monopolies; and in extreme cases, the use of force as an economic power to reinforce the other forms of exploitation.

Sometimes this penetration of capital takes very subtle forms, such as the use of international financial, credit, and other types of organizations. The International Monetary Fund, the International Bank for Reconstruction and Development, GATT, and in Latin America, the Inter-American Development Bank are examples of international organizations placed at the service of the great capitalist colonialist powers — fundamentally, U.S. imperialism. These organizations inject themselves into domestic economic policy, foreign trade policy, and all kinds of internal financial relations as well as financial relations among different nations.

The International Monetary Fund is the watchdog of the dollar in the capitalist camp; the International Bank for Reconstruction and Development is the instrument for the penetration of U.S. capital into the underdeveloped world; and the Inter-American Development Bank performs the same sorry function in Latin America. All these organizations are governed by rules and principles that are represented as safeguards of fairness and reciprocity in international economic relations. In reality, however, they are merely fetishes behind which hide the most subtle instruments for the perpetuation of backwardness and exploitation. The International Monetary Fund, which is supposed to watch over the stability of exchange rates and the liberalization of international payments, merely denies the underdeveloped countries even the slightest measures of defense against competition and penetration by foreign monopolies.

The IMF imposes so-called austerity programs and opposes the forms of payment necessary for the expansion of trade between countries facing a balance-of-payments crisis and suffering from severe discriminatory measures in international trade. At the same time it strives desperately to rescue the dollar from its precarious situation without going to the heart of the structural problems afflicting the international monetary system, which block a more rapid expansion of world trade.

GATT, for its part, by establishing equal treatment and reciprocal concessions between developed and underdeveloped countries, helps to maintain the status quo and serves the interests of the former group of countries. Its machinery fails to provide the necessary means for eliminating agricultural protectionism, subsidies, tariffs and other obstacles to the expansion of exports from the dependent countries. For all that, it now has its so-called Program of Action and, by a rather suspicious coincidence, the "Kennedy round" is just about to begin.

In order to strengthen imperialist domination, the establishment of preferential areas has been adopted as a means of exploitation and neo-colonial control. We are well-acquainted with this, for we ourselves have suffered the effects of Cuban-U.S. preferential agreements, which shackled our trade and placed it at the disposal of the U.S. monopolies.

There is no better way to show what those preferences meant for Cuba than to quote the views of Sumner Welles, the U.S. ambassador [to Cuba], on the Reciprocal Trade Agreement, which was negotiated in 1933 and signed in 1934:

> The Cuban Government in turn would grant us a practical monopoly of the Cuban market for American imports, the sole reservation being that, in view of the fact that Great Britain was Cuba's chief customer for that portion of sugar exports which did not go to the United States, the Cuban Government would desire to concede certain advantages to a limited category of imports from Great Britain...
>
> Finally, the negotiation at this time of a reciprocal trade agreement with Cuba along the lines above-indicated, will not only revivify Cuba but will give us practical control of a market we have been steadily losing for the past 10 years not only for our manufactured products but for our agricultural exports as well, notably in such categories as wheat, animal fats, meat products, rice and potatoes.

This is a telegram from Ambassador Welles to the U.S. secretary of state, sent May 13, 1933, and published on pages 289 and 290 of volume V of the official publication, *Foreign Relations of the United States*, from 1933.

The results of the so-called Reciprocal Trade Agreement confirmed the view of Ambassador Welles.

Our country had to try to sell its main product, sugar, all over the world in order to obtain foreign currency with which to achieve a balance of payments with the United States. The special tariffs that were imposed prevented producers in European countries, as well as our own national producers, from competing with those of the United States.

It is necessary to quote only a few figures to prove that it was Cuba's function to seek foreign currency all over the world for the United States. During the period 1948–57, Cuba had a consistently unfavorable balance of trade with the United States, totaling 382.7 million pesos, whereas its trade balance with the rest of the world was consistently favorable, totaling 1.2746 billion pesos.

The balance of payments for the period 1948–58 tells the story even more eloquently: Cuba had a positive balance of 543.9 million pesos with countries other than the United States, but lost this to its rich neighbor, with whom it had a negative balance of 952.1 million pesos, with the result that its foreign currency reserves were reduced by 408.2 million pesos.

The so-called Alliance for Progress is another clear demonstration of the fraudulent methods used by the United States to maintain false hopes among nations while exploitation grows worse.

When Fidel Castro, our prime minister, pointed out at Buenos Aires in 1959 that a minimum of $3 billion a year of additional outside income was needed to finance a rate of development that would really reduce the enormous gap separating Latin America from the developed countries, many thought that the figure was exaggerated. At Punta del Este, however, $2 billion a year was promised. Today, it is recognized that merely to offset the loss caused by the deterioration in the terms of trade in 1961 (the last year for which figures are available), 30 percent a year more than the hypothetical funds promised will be required. The paradoxical situation now is that while the loans are either not forthcoming or are made for projects that contribute little or nothing to the industrial development of the region, increased amounts of foreign exchange are being transferred to the industrialized countries. This means that the wealth created by the labor of peoples who live for the most part in conditions of backwardness, hunger and poverty is enjoyed by the capitalist circles.

In 1961, for instance, according to figures given by the [United Nations] Economic Commission for Latin America, $1.735 billion left Latin America in the form of interest on foreign investments and similar payments, and $1.456 billion left in payments on foreign short-term and long-term loans. If we add to this the indirect loss of purchasing power of exports (or deterioration in the terms of trade), which amounted to $2.66 billion in 1961, and $349 million for the flight of capital, we arrive at a total of $6.2 billion, or more than three Alliances for Progress a year. Thus, assuming that the situation has not deteriorated further in 1964, the Latin American countries participating in the Alliance for Progress will lose, directly or indirectly, during the three months of this conference, almost $1.6 billion of the wealth created by the labor of their peoples. On the other hand, of the $2 billion pledged for the entire year, barely half can expected, at an optimistic estimate, to be forthcoming.

Latin America's experience with the real results of this type of "aid," which is represented as the surest and most effective means of increasing foreign earnings — better than doing it directly by increasing the volume and value of exports, and modifying their structure — has been a sad one. For this very reason it may serve as a lesson for other regions and for the underdeveloped world in general. At present our region is virtually at a standstill so far as growth is concerned. Moreover, it is devastated by inflation and unemployment, it is caught up in the vicious circle of foreign indebtedness, and it is racked with tensions that are sometimes resolved by armed conflict.

Cuba has exposed these facts as they emerged, and has predicted the outcome, while rejecting any implications in doing so other than those flowing from our example and our moral support. The development of events has proven us to be correct. The [1962] Second Declaration of Havana is proving its historical validity.

These phenomena, which we have analyzed in relation to Latin America but which are valid for the whole of the dependent world, have the effect of enabling the developed powers to maintain trade conditions that lead to a deterioration in the terms of trade between the dependent countries and the developed countries.

This aspect — one of the more obvious ones, which the capitalist propaganda machinery has been unable to conceal — is another of the factors that have led to the convening of this conference.

The deterioration in the terms of trade is quite simple in its practical effect: the underdeveloped countries must export more raw materials and primary commodities in order to import the same amount of industrial goods. The problem is particularly serious in the case of the machinery and equipment that are essential to agricultural and industrial development.

Many underdeveloped countries, on analyzing their troubles, arrive at what seems a logical conclusion. They say that if the deterioration of the terms of trade is an objective reality and the cause of most of their problems, and if it is attributable to the fall in the prices of raw materials that they export and the rise in the prices of manufactured goods that they import on the world market, then, in the case of trade relations with the socialist countries based on existing market prices, the latter will also benefit from the situation since they are, in general, exporters of manufactured goods and importers of raw materials.

We should honestly and bravely answer that this is true, but with the same honesty we must also recognize that the socialist countries have not caused the present situation. They absorb barely 10 percent of the underdeveloped countries' primary commodity exports to the rest of the world. For historical reasons they have been compelled to trade under the conditions prevailing in the world market, which is the outcome of imperialist domination over the internal economy and external markets of the dependent countries. This is not the basis on which the socialist countries establish their long-term trade with the underdeveloped countries. There are many examples to bear this out, Cuba in particular. When our social status changed and our relations with the socialist camp attained a new level of mutual trust, we did not cease to be underdeveloped, but we established a new type of relationship with the countries in that camp. The highest expression of this new relationship is the sugar price agreements we have concluded with the Soviet Union, under which that sister nation has undertaken to purchase increasing amounts of our main product at fair and stable prices until the year 1970.

Furthermore, we must not forget that there are underdeveloped countries in different circumstances and that they maintain different policies toward the socialist camp. There are some, such as Cuba, that have chosen the path of socialism; there are some that are developing in a more or less capitalist manner and are beginning to produce manufactured goods for export; there are some that have neocolonial ties; there are some that have a virtually feudal structure; and there are others that, unfortunately, do not participate in conferences of this type because the developed countries have not granted the independence to which their peoples aspire. Such is the case of British Guiana, Puerto Rico, and other countries in Latin America, Africa and Asia. Except for the first of these categories, foreign capital has made its way into these countries in one way or another.

The demands that are today being directed to the socialist countries should be dealt with on a real basis of dialogue. In some cases this means a dialogue between underdeveloped and developed country. Almost always, however, it means a dialogue between one country subject to discrimination and another in the same situation. On many occasions, these same countries demand unilateral preferential treatment from all the developed countries without exception, including the socialist countries in this category and putting all kinds of obstacles in the way of direct trade with them. There is a danger that, by seeking to trade through their national subsidiaries, companies from the imperialist powers could be given the opportunity to make spectacular profits by claiming that a given country is underdeveloped and therefore entitled to unilateral preferences.

If we do not want to wreck this conference, we must abide strictly by principles. As an underdeveloped country we must speak about right being on our side. In our case, as a socialist country, we can also speak of the discrimination that is practiced against us not only by some developed capitalist countries but also by underdeveloped countries that, consciously or otherwise, are serving the interests of monopoly capital, which has taken over basic control of their economies.

We do not regard the existing price relationships in the world as just, as fair, but this is not the only injustice that exists. There is direct exploitation of some countries by others. There is discrimination against countries because they have different economic structures. And, as we have already pointed out, there is the invasion of foreign capital to the point where it controls a country's economy for its own ends. To be consistent, when we address requests to the developed socialist countries we should also specify what we are going to do to end discrimination, and at least to end the most obvious and dangerous forms of imperialist penetration.

We all know about the trade discrimination practiced by the imperialist countries against the socialist countries with the aim of blocking their development. At times, it has been tantamount to a real blockade, such as the almost absolute blockade maintained by U.S. imperialism against the German Democratic Republic, the People's Republic of China, the Democratic Republic of Korea, the Democratic Republic of Vietnam and the Republic of Cuba. Everyone knows that this policy has failed, and that other powers that originally followed the lead of the United States have gradually parted company from it in order to secure their own profits. The failure of this policy is by now only too obvious.

Trade discrimination has also been practiced against dependent countries and socialist countries, with the ultimate aim of ensuring that the monopolies do not lose their fields of exploitation and at the same time strengthening the blockade of the socialist camp. This policy, too, is failing, and the question arises whether there is any point in remaining bound to historically doomed foreign interests, or whether the time has come to break through all the obstacles to trade and expand markets in the socialist area.

The various forms of discrimination that hamper trade, and that make it easier for the imperialists to manipulate a range of primary commodities and a number of countries producing those commodities, are still being maintained. In the nuclear age, it is simply absurd to classify products such as copper and other minerals as strategic materials and to prevent trade in them. Yet this policy has been maintained and is maintained to this day. There is also talk of so-called incompatibilities between state monopoly of foreign trade and the forms of trading adopted by the capitalist countries. Using that pretext, discriminatory relations, quotas, etc., are established — maneuvers in which GATT has played a dominant role under the official guise of combating unfair trade practices. Discrimination against state trading not only serves as a weapon against the socialist countries but is also designed to prevent the underdeveloped countries from adopting any of the most urgent measures needed to strengthen their negotiating position on the international market and to counteract the actions of the monopolies.

The suspension of economic aid by international agencies to countries adopting the socialist system of government is a further variation on the same theme. A common practice of the International Monetary Fund in recent years has been to attack bilateral payment agreements with socialist countries and to impose on its weaker members a policy of opposing this type of relations between peoples.

As we have already pointed out, all these discriminatory measures imposed by imperialism have the dual object of blockading the socialist camp and strengthening the exploitation of the underdeveloped countries.

It is undeniable that present-day prices are unfair. It is equally true that those prices are conditioned by monopoly restriction of markets and by the establishment of political relationships that make free competition a term applied one-sidedly: free competition for the monopolies — a free fox among free chickens.

Quite apart from the agreements that may emanate from this conference, opening up the large and growing markets of the socialist camp would help to raise raw material prices. The world has plenty of hunger, but not enough money to buy food. And paradoxically in the underdeveloped world, in the world of hunger, projects for increasing food production — that is, to be able to eat — are actually discouraged in order to maintain present prices. This is the inexorable law of the philosophy of plunder, which must cease to be the rule in relations between peoples.

Furthermore, it would be feasible for some underdeveloped countries to export manufactured goods to the socialist countries and even make long-term agreements so as to enable some nations to make better use of their natural wealth and specialize in certain branches of industry that would enable them to participate in world trade as producers of manufactured products. All this can be complemented by the supplying of long-term credits for the development of the industries, or branches of industry, we are considering. It must always be borne in mind, however, that certain measures with respect to relations between socialist countries and underdeveloped countries cannot be taken unilaterally.

It is a strange paradox that while in its reports the United Nations is forecasting adverse trends in the foreign trade of the underdeveloped countries, and while Dr. Prebisch, the secretary-general of the conference, is stressing the dangers that will arise if this state of affairs persists, there is still talk of the feasibility — and in some cases the necessity, as with the so-called strategic materials — of discriminating against certain states because they belong to the socialist camp.

All these anomalies are possible because of the incontrovertible fact that at the present stage of human history the underdeveloped countries are the battleground of economic systems that belong to different historical eras. In some of these countries feudalism still exists; in others a nascent, still weak bourgeoisie has to withstand the dual pressure of imperialist interests and of its own proletariat, which is fighting for a more just distribution of income. In the face of this dilemma, some national bourgeoisies have maintained their independence or adopted some forms of joint action with the proletariat, while others have made common cause with imperialism; they have become its appendages, its agents, and have transmitted this same quality to the governments representing them.

We must sound a warning that this type of dependence, skillfully used, may endanger the possibility of solid progress at the conference. But we must also point out that whatever advantages these governments may gain today, as the price of disunity, will be repaid with interest tomorrow, when in addition to facing the hostility of their own peoples they will have to stand up alone to the sudden attack of the monopolies, for whom the only law is maximum profit.

We have made a brief analysis of the causes and results of the contradictions between the socialist camp and the imperialist camp and between the camp of the exploited and that of the exploiting countries. Here are two clear dangers to world peace.

It must also be pointed out, however, that the growing boom in some capitalist countries, and their inevitable expansion in search of new markets, has led to changes in the balance of forces among them and given rise to tensions that must be taken into account if world peace is to be preserved. Do not forget that the last two world conflagrations were sparked by clashes between developed powers that could find no solution to their problems other than the use of force. We observe a series of phenomena that clearly demonstrate the growing acuteness of this struggle. This situation may involve real dangers to world peace in the future, but it is exceedingly dangerous to the smooth progress of this conference here today. There is a clear distribution of spheres of influence between the United States and other developed capitalist powers, embracing the backward continents and parts of Europe as well. If these influences are strong enough to turn the exploited countries into fields of battle for the profits of the imperialist powers, this conference will have failed.

Cuba believes, as is pointed out in the joint statement of the underdeveloped countries, that the trade problems of our countries are well known and that what is required is the adoption of clear principles and a specific action program to usher in a new era for the world. We also believe that the statement of principles submitted by the Soviet Union and other socialist countries forms the correct basis on which to begin discussion, and we endorse it fully. Our country also supports the measures formulated at the meeting of experts at Brasilia, which would give coherent effect to the principles we advocate and will now explain.

Cuba wishes to make one point clear at the outset: we are not begging for aid. We are demanding justice; but not a justice subject to the fallacious interpretations we have so often seen prevail at international meetings. We are demanding a justice that, perhaps, the people cannot define in legal terms but for which the desire is deeply rooted in the spirit of the people, oppressed by generations of exploitation.

Cuba affirms that out of this conference should come a definition of international trade as an appropriate tool for the more rapid economic development of the underdeveloped peoples and of those subject to discrimination. This definition must provide for the elimination of all forms of discrimination and all differences, even those arising from so-called equal treatment. Treatment must be fair, and fairness, in this context, is not equality; fairness is the inequality needed to enable the exploited peoples to attain an acceptable standard of living. Our task here is to lay a foundation on which a new international division of labor can be instituted. This can be done by making full use of a country's natural resources and by steadily raising its level of production until it has achieved the most complex forms of manufacturing.

In addition, the new division of labor must be achieved by restoring to the underdeveloped countries the traditional export markets that have been seized from them by artificial measures of protectionism and subsidization of production in the developed countries, and by a fair participation in future consumption increases.

This conference should recommend specific regulations on the use of surplus primary commodities to prevent them from being turned into a form of subsidized exports of developed countries, to the detriment of the traditional exports of the underdeveloped countries, or from being turned into instruments of penetration by foreign capital of an underdeveloped country.

It is unthinkable for the underdeveloped countries to have to bear the growing burden of the foreign debt while their just demands are ignored. These countries are already sustaining huge losses from the deterioration of the terms of trade. Moreover, through the steady drain of interest payments they have already more than repaid the value of the imperialists' investments. The Cuban delegation proposes that until such time as the export prices of the underdeveloped countries reach a level sufficient to reimburse them for the losses of the past decade, all payments of dividends, interest and principal should be suspended.

It must be made crystal clear that the domination of any country's economy by foreign capital investment, the deterioration in terms of trade, the control of one country's markets by another, discriminatory relations and the use of force as an instrument of persuasion, are dangers to world trade and world peace.

This conference should also clearly establish the right of all nations to unrestricted freedom of trade, and the obligation of all states signing the agreement emanating from this conference to refrain from restraining trade in any manner, directly or indirectly.

The right of all countries to freely arrange the shipment of their goods by sea or air and to move them freely throughout the world without hindrance should be clearly set forth.

The conference should condemn any application or instigation of economic measures by one state to infringe the sovereign freedom of another state and to obtain from it advantages of any kind whatsoever, or to bring about the collapse of its economy.

In order to achieve the foregoing, the principle of self-determination embodied in the United Nations Charter must be fully implemented. The conference should reaffirm the right of states to dispose of their own resources, to adopt the form of political and economic organization that suits them best, and to choose their own avenues of development and specialization in economic activity, without incurring reprisals of any kind whatsoever. The conference should adopt measures for the establishment of financial, credit and tariff organizations, with rules based on absolute equality and on justice and fairness, to replace the existing organizations, which are obsolete from the functional point of view and reprehensible from the standpoint of their specific aims.

In order to guarantee to a people the full use of its own resources, it is necessary to condemn the existence of foreign bases, the presence — temporary or otherwise — of foreign troops in a country without its consent, and the maintenance of colonial rule by some developed capitalist powers.

For all these purposes, the conference needs to reach agreement and lay a firm foundation for the establishment of an international trade organization, to be governed by the principle of the equality and universality of membership, and to possess sufficient authority to make decisions binding on all signatory states. The practice of barring from such forums countries that have won their liberation since the establishment of the United Nations, and/or that have social systems not to the liking of some of the world's powers, must be abolished.

The authority to make decisions that will be respected can come only from an organization of the kind I have described — one that will replace the existing organizations, which perpetuate the status quo and current discrimination in trade. Such authority cannot come from unenforceable formulas that lead only to endless discussions of what we already know all too well. This new type of organization is what can guarantee respect for new norms in international relations and the achievement of economic security.

Precise time periods for the establishment of each of these measures need to be set.

These are, distinguished delegates, the most important points that the Cuban delegation wished to bring to the attention of the conference. It should be pointed out that many of the ideas that are now gaining currency through being expressed by international bodies, by the precise analysis of the present situation of the developing countries submitted by Dr. Prebisch, the secretary-general of the conference, and many of the measures approved by other states — trading with socialist countries, obtaining credits from them, the need of basic social reforms for economic development, etc. — have been formulated and put into practice by Cuba during the five years of revolutionary government. Moreover, the adoption of these measures has caused our country to be subjected to unjust condemnation and to acts of economic and military aggression approved by some of the countries that now endorse those ideas.

Suffice it to recall the criticism and condemnation of Cuba for having established trade relations and cooperation with countries outside our hemisphere, and its de facto exclusion, to this day, from the Latin American regional group, organized under the auspices of the Charter of Alta Gracia, that is, of the Organization of American States, from which Cuba is excluded.[12]

We have dealt with the basic points concerning foreign trade, the need for changes in the foreign policy of the developed countries in their relations with the underdeveloped countries, and the need to restructure all international credit, financial, and similar bodies. We must emphasize, however, that these measures are not sufficient to guarantee economic development. Other measures — which Cuba, an underdeveloped country, has put into practice — are needed as well.

As a minimum, exchange controls must be established, prohibiting remittances of funds abroad or restricting them to a significant degree; there must be state control of foreign trade; there must be agrarian reform; all natural resources must be restored to the nation; technological education must be encouraged. And other measures of internal reorganization essential to a faster rate of development must be taken.

Out of respect for the wishes of the governments represented here, Cuba has not included among the irreducible minimum measures the taking over by the state of all the means of production. But we believe that this measure would contribute to a more efficient and quicker solution to the serious problems under discussion.

And the imperialists? Will they sit with arms folded? No!

Their system is the cause of the evils from which we are suffering, but they will try to obscure the facts with twisted statements; of this they are masters. They will try to render this conference powerless and sow disunity in the camp of the exploited countries by offering them crumbs.

They will try everything to keep in place the old international bodies that serve their ends so well. They will offer reforms, but not basic ones. They will seek a way to lead the conference into a blind alley, so that it will be suspended or adjourned. They will try to rob it of importance by counterposing other meetings convened by themselves, or to see that the conference ends without achieving any tangible results.

They will not accept a new international trade organization; they will threaten to boycott it and will probably do so. They will try to show that the existing international division of labor is beneficial to all, and will refer to industrialization as a dangerous and excessive ambition.

Lastly, they will allege that the blame for underdevelopment rests with the underdeveloped. To this we can reply that to a certain extent they are right, and that they will be even more right if we show ourselves incapable of uniting, in wholehearted determination, to form a united front of victims of discrimination and exploitation.

The questions we wish to ask this assembly are these: Will we be able to carry out the task history demands of us? Will the developed capitalist countries have the political acumen to accede to the minimum demands?

If the measures stated here cannot be adopted by this conference; if all that emerges once again is a hybrid document crammed with vague statements and escape clauses; and unless, at the very least, the economic and political barriers to trade among all regions of the world and to international cooperation are removed, then the underdeveloped countries will continue to face increasingly difficult economic situations, and world tension may mount dangerously. A world conflagration may be sparked at any moment by the ambition of some imperialist country to destroy the socialist camp, or, in the not-too-distant future, by insoluble contradictions between the capitalist countries. In addition, rebelliousness will grow stronger every day among the peoples subjected to various conditions of exploitation, and they will take up arms to gain by force the rights that reason alone has not won them.

This is happening today with the peoples of so-called Portuguese Guinea and Angola, who are fighting to free themselves from the colonial yoke, and with the people of South Vietnam who, weapons in hand, stand ready to shake off the yoke of imperialism and its puppets.

Let it be known that Cuba supports and applauds those peoples who, having exhausted all possibilities of a peaceful solution, have said "Enough!" to exploitation, and that their magnificent demonstration of rebellion has won our militant solidarity.

Having stated the essential points on which our analysis of the present situation is based, having put forward the recommendations we consider relevant to this conference and our views on what the future holds if no progress is made in trade relations between countries — an appropriate means of reducing tension and contributing to development — we wish to place on record our hope that the constructive discussion we spoke of will take place. The aim of our efforts is to bring about such a discussion, from which everyone will gain, and to rally the underdeveloped countries of the world to unity, so as to present a cohesive front. We place our hopes also in the success of this conference, and we join in friendship with the poor of this world and the countries in the socialist camp, putting all our powers to work for its success.

Thank you.

At the United Nations

(December 11, 1964)

This address was delivered to the 19th General Assembly of the United Nations in New York.

Mr. President;
Distinguished delegates:

he delegation of Cuba to this Assembly, first of all, is pleased to fulfill the agreeable duty of welcoming the addition of three new nations to the important number of those that discuss the problems of the world here. We therefore greet, in the persons of their presidents and prime ministers, the peoples of Zambia, Malawi and Malta, and express the hope that from the outset these countries will be added to the group of Nonaligned countries that struggle against imperialism, colonialism and neocolonialism.

We also wish to convey our congratulations to the president of this Assembly [Alex Quaison-Sackey of Ghana], whose elevation to so high a post is of special significance since it reflects this new historic stage of resounding triumphs for the peoples of Africa, who up until recently were subject to the colonial system of imperialism. Today, in their immense majority these peoples have become sovereign states through the legitimate exercise of their self-determination. The final hour of colonialism has struck, and millions of inhabitants of Africa, Asia and Latin America rise to meet a new life and demand their unrestricted right to self-determination and to the independent development of their nations.

We wish you, Mr. President, the greatest success in the tasks entrusted to you by the member states.

Cuba comes here to state its position on the most important points of controversy and will do so with the full sense of responsibility that the use of this rostrum implies, while at the same time fulfilling the unavoidable duty of speaking clearly and frankly.

We would like to see this Assembly shake itself out of complacency and move forward. We would like to see the committees begin their work and not stop at the first confrontation. Imperialism wants to turn this meeting into a pointless oratorical tournament, instead of solving the serious problems of the world. We must prevent it from doing so. This session of the Assembly should not be remembered in the future solely by the number 19 that identifies it. Our efforts are directed to that end.

We feel that we have the right and the obligation to do so, because our country is one of the most constant points of friction. It is one of the places where the principles upholding the right of small countries to sovereignty are put to the test day by day, minute by minute. At the same time our country is one of the trenches of freedom in the world, situated a few steps away from U.S. imperialism, showing by its actions, its daily example, that in the present conditions of humanity the peoples can liberate themselves and can keep themselves free.

Of course, there now exists a socialist camp that becomes stronger day by day and has more powerful weapons of struggle. But additional conditions are required for survival: the maintenance of internal unity, faith in one's own destiny, and the irrevocable decision to fight to the death for the defense of one's country and revolution. These conditions, distinguished delegates, exist in Cuba.

Of all the burning problems to be dealt with by this Assembly, one of special significance for us, and one whose solution we feel must be found first — so as to leave no doubt in the minds of anyone — is that of peaceful coexistence among states with different economic and social systems. Much progress has been made in the world in this field. But imperialism, particularly U.S. imperialism, has attempted to make the world believe that peaceful coexistence is the exclusive right of the earth's great powers. We say here what our president said in Cairo, and what later was expressed in the declaration of the Second Conference of Heads of State or Government of Nonaligned Countries: that peaceful coexistence cannot be limited to the powerful countries if we want to ensure world peace.[13] Peaceful coexistence must be exercised among all states, regardless of size, regardless of the previous historical relations that linked them, and regardless of the problems that may arise among some of them at a given moment.

At present, the type of peaceful coexistence to which we aspire is often violated. Merely because the Kingdom of Cambodia maintained a neutral attitude and did not bow to the machinations of U.S. imperialism, it has been subjected to all kinds of treacherous and brutal attacks from the Yankee bases in South Vietnam.

Laos, a divided country, has also been the object of imperialist aggression of every kind. Its people have been massacred from the air. The conventions concluded at Geneva have been violated, and part of its territory is in constant danger of cowardly attacks by imperialist forces.

The Democratic Republic of Vietnam knows all these histories of aggression as do few nations on earth. It has once again seen its frontier violated, has seen enemy bombers and fighter planes attack its installations and U.S. warships, violating territorial waters, attack its naval posts. At this time, the threat hangs over the Democratic Republic of Vietnam that the U.S. war makers may openly extend into its territory the war that for many years they have been waging against the people of South Vietnam. The Soviet Union and the People's Republic of China have given serious warnings to the United States. We are faced with a case in which world peace is in danger and, moreover, the lives of millions of human beings in this part of Asia are constantly threatened and subjected to the whim of the U.S. invader.

Peaceful coexistence has also been brutally put to the test in Cyprus, due to pressures from the Turkish Government and NATO, compelling the people and the government of Cyprus to make a heroic and firm stand in defense of their sovereignty.

In all these parts of the world, imperialism attempts to impose its version of what coexistence should be. It is the oppressed peoples in alliance with the socialist camp that must show them what true coexistence is, and it is the obligation of the United Nations to support them.

We must also state that it is not only in relations among sovereign states that the concept of peaceful coexistence needs to be precisely defined. As Marxists we have maintained that peaceful coexistence among nations does not encompass coexistence between the exploiters and the exploited, between the oppressors and the oppressed. Furthermore, the right to full independence from all forms of colonial oppression is a fundamental principle of this organization. That is why we express our solidarity with the colonial peoples of so-called Portuguese Guinea, Angola and Mozambique, who have been massacred for the crime of demanding their freedom. And we are prepared to help them to the extent of our ability in accordance with the Cairo declaration.

We express our solidarity with the people of Puerto Rico and their great leader, Pedro Albizu Campos, who, in another act of hypocrisy, has been set free at the age of 72, almost unable to speak, paralyzed, after spending a lifetime in jail. Albizu Campos is a symbol of the as yet unfree but indomitable Latin America. Years and years of prison, almost unbearable pressures in jail, mental torture, solitude, total isolation from his people and his family, the insolence of the conqueror and its lackeys in the land of his birth — nothing broke his will. The delegation of Cuba, on behalf of its people, pays a tribute of admiration and gratitude to a patriot who confers honor upon our America.

The United States for many years has tried to convert Puerto Rico into a model of hybrid culture: the Spanish language with English inflections, the Spanish language with hinges on its backbone — the better to bow down before the Yankee soldier. Puerto Rican soldiers have been used as cannon fodder in imperialist wars, as in Korea, and have even been made to fire at their own brothers, as in the massacre perpetrated by the U.S. Army a few months ago against the unarmed people of Panama — one of the most recent crimes carried out by Yankee imperialism.[14] And yet, despite this assault on their will and their historical destiny, the people of Puerto Rico have preserved their culture, their Latin character, their national feelings, which in themselves give proof of the implacable desire for independence lying within the masses on that Latin American island.

We must also warn that the principle of peaceful coexistence does not encompass the right to mock the will of the peoples, as is happening in the case of so-called British Guiana. There the government of Prime Minister Cheddi Jagan has been the victim of every kind of pressure and maneuver, and independence has been delayed to gain time to find ways to flout the people's will and guarantee the docility of a new government, placed in power by covert means, in order to grant a castrated freedom to this country of the Americas. Whatever roads Guiana may be compelled to follow to obtain independence, the moral and militant support of Cuba goes to its people.[15]

Furthermore, we must point out that the islands of Guadaloupe and Martinique have been fighting for a long time for self-government without obtaining it. This state of affairs must not continue.

Once again we speak out to put the world on guard against what is happening in South Africa. The brutal policy of apartheid is applied before the eyes of the nations of the world. The peoples of Africa are compelled to endure the fact that on the African continent the superiority of one race over another remains official policy, and that in the name of this racial superiority murder is committed with impunity. Can the United Nations do nothing to stop this?

I would like to refer specifically to the painful case of the Congo, unique in the history of the modern world, which shows how, with absolute impunity, with the most insolent cynicism, the rights of peoples can be flouted. The direct reason for all this is the enormous wealth of the Congo, which the imperialist countries want to keep under their control. In the speech he made during his first visit to the United Nations, *compañero* Fidel Castro observed that the whole problem of coexistence among peoples boils down to the wrongful appropriation of other peoples' wealth. He made the following statement: "End the philosophy of plunder and the philosophy of war will be ended as well."

But the philosophy of plunder has not only not been ended, it is stronger than ever. And that is why those who used the name of the United Nations to commit the murder of Lumumba are today, in the name of the defense of the white race, murdering thousands of Congolese. How can we forget the betrayal of the hope that Patrice Lumumba placed in the United Nations? How can we forget the machinations and maneuvers that followed in the wake of the occupation of that country by UN troops, under whose auspices the assassins of this great African patriot acted with impunity? How can we forget, distinguished delegates, that the one who flouted the authority of the UN in the Congo — and not exactly for patriotic reasons, but rather by virtue of conflicts between imperialists — was Moise Tshombe, who initiated the secession of Katanga with Belgian support? And how can one justify, how can one explain, that at the end of all the United Nations' activities there, Tshombe, dislodged from Katanga, should return as lord and master of the Congo? Who can deny the sad role that the imperialists compelled the United Nations to play?[16]

To sum up: dramatic mobilizations were carried out to avoid the secession of Katanga, but today Tshombe is in power, the wealth of the Congo is in imperialist hands — and the expenses have to be paid by the honorable nations. The merchants of war certainly do good business! That is why the government of Cuba supports the just stance of the Soviet Union in refusing to pay the expenses for this crime.

And as if this were not enough, we now have flung in our faces these latest acts that have filled the world with indignation. Who are the perpetrators? Belgian paratroopers, carried by U.S. planes, who took off from British bases. We remember as if it were yesterday that we saw a small country in Europe, a civilized and industrious country, the Kingdom of Belgium, invaded by Hitler's hordes. We were embittered by the knowledge that this small nation was massacred by German imperialism, and we felt affection for its people. But this other side of the imperialist coin was the one that many of us did not see. Perhaps the sons of Belgian patriots who died defending their country's liberty are now murdering in cold blood thousands of Congolese in the name of the white race, just as they suffered under the

German heel because their blood was not sufficiently Aryan.

Our free eyes open now on new horizons and can see what yesterday, in our condition as colonial slaves, we could not observe: that "Western Civilization" disguises behind its showy facade a picture of hyenas and jackals. That is the only name that can be applied to those who have gone to fulfill such "humanitarian" tasks in the Congo. A carnivorous animal that feeds on unarmed peoples. That is what imperialism does to men. That is what distinguishes the imperial "white man."

All free men of the world must be prepared to avenge the crime of the Congo. Perhaps many of those soldiers, who were turned into sub-humans by imperialist machinery, believe in good faith that they are defending the rights of a superior race. In this Assembly, however, those peoples whose skins are darkened by a different sun, colored by different pigments, constitute the majority. And they fully and clearly understand that the difference between men does not lie in the color of their skin, but in the forms of ownership of the means of production, in the relations of production.

The Cuban delegation extends greetings to the peoples of Southern Rhodesia and South-West Africa, oppressed by white colonialist minorities; to the peoples of Basutoland, Bechuanaland, Swaziland, French Somaliland, the Arabs of Palestine, Aden and the Protectorates, Oman; and to all peoples in conflict with imperialism and colonialism. We reaffirm our support to them.

I express also the hope that there will be a just solution to the conflict facing our sister republic of Indonesia in its relations with Malaysia.

Mr. President: One of the fundamental themes of this conference is general and complete disarmament. We express our support for general and complete disarmament. Furthermore, we advocate the complete destruction of all thermonuclear devices and we support the holding of a conference of all the nations of the world to make this aspiration of all people a reality. In his statement before this assembly, our prime minister warned that arms races have always led to war. There are new nuclear powers in the world, and the possibilities of a confrontation are growing.

We believe that such a conference is necessary to obtain the total destruction of thermonuclear weapons and, as a first step, the total prohibition of tests. At the same time, we have to establish clearly the duty of all countries to respect the present borders of other states and to refrain from engaging in any aggression, even with conventional weapons.

In adding our voice to that of all the peoples of the world who ask for general and complete disarmament, the destruction of all nuclear arsenals, the complete halt to the building of new thermonuclear devices and of nuclear tests of any kind, we believe it necessary to also stress that the territorial integrity of nations must be respected and the armed hand of imperialism held back, for it is no less dangerous when it uses only conventional weapons. Those who murdered thousands of defenseless citizens of the Congo did not use the atomic bomb. They used conventional weapons. Conventional weapons have also been used by imperialism, causing so many deaths.

Even if the measures advocated here were to become effective and make it unnecessary to mention it, we must point out that we cannot adhere to any regional pact for denuclearization so long as the United States maintains aggressive bases on our own territory, in Puerto Rico, Panama and in other Latin American states where it feels it has the right to place both conventional and nuclear weapons without any restrictions. We feel that we must be able to provide for our own defense in the light of the recent resolution of the Organization of American States against Cuba, on the basis of which an attack may be carried out invoking the Rio Treaty.[17]

If the conference to which we have just referred were to achieve all these objectives — which, unfortunately, would be difficult — we believe it would be the most important one in the history of humanity. To ensure this it would be necessary for the People's Republic of China to be represented, and that is why a conference of this type must be held. But it would be much simpler for the peoples of the world to recognize the undeniable truth of the existence of the People's Republic of China, whose government is the sole representative of its people, and to give it the seat it deserves, which is, at present, usurped by the gang that controls the province of Taiwan, with U.S. support.

The problem of the representation of China in the United Nations cannot in any way be considered as a case of a new admission to the organization, but rather as the restoration of the legitimate rights of the People's Republic of China.

We must repudiate energetically the "two Chinas" plot. The Chiang Kai-shek gang of Taiwan cannot remain in the United Nations. What we are dealing with, we repeat, is the expulsion of the usurper and the installation of the legitimate representative of the Chinese people.

We also warn against the U.S. Government's insistence on presenting the problem of the legitimate representation of China in the UN as an "important question," in order to impose a requirement of a two-thirds majority of members present and voting. The admission of the People's Republic of China to the United Nations is, in fact, an important question for the entire world, but not for the machinery of the United Nations, where it must constitute a mere question of procedure. In this way justice will be done. Almost as important as attaining justice, however, would be the demonstration, once and for all, that this august Assembly has eyes to see, ears to hear, tongues to speak with and sound criteria for making its decisions.

The proliferation of nuclear weapons among the member states of NATO, and especially the possession of these devices of mass destruction by the Federal Republic of Germany, would make the possibility of an agreement on disarmament even more remote, and linked to such an agreement is the problem of the peaceful reunification of Germany. So long as there is no clear understanding, the existence of two Germanys must be recognized: that of the German Democratic Republic and the Federal Republic. The German problem can be solved only with the direct participation in negotiations of the German Democratic Republic with full rights.

We shall only touch on the questions of economic development and international trade that are broadly represented in the agenda. In this very year of 1964 the Geneva conference was held at which a multitude of matters related to these aspects of international relations were dealt with. The warnings and forecasts of our delegation were fully confirmed, to the misfortune of the economically dependent countries.

We wish only to point out that insofar as Cuba is concerned, the United States of America has not implemented the explicit recommendations of that conference, and recently the U.S. Government also prohibited the sale of medicines to Cuba. By doing so it divested itself, once and for all, of the mask of humanitarianism with which it attempted to disguise the aggressive nature of its blockade against the people of Cuba.

Furthermore, we state once more that the scars left by colonialism that impede the development of the peoples are expressed not only in political relations. The so-called deterioration of the terms of trade is nothing but the result of the unequal exchange between countries producing raw materials and industrial countries, which dominate markets and impose the illusory justice of equal exchange of values.

So long as the economically dependent peoples do not free themselves from the capitalist markets and, in a firm bloc with the socialist countries, impose new relations between the exploited and the exploiters, there will be no solid economic development. In certain cases there will be retrogression, in which the weak countries will fall under the political domination of the imperialists and colonialists.

Finally, distinguished delegates, it must be made clear that in the area of the Caribbean, maneuvers and preparations for aggression against Cuba are taking place, on the coasts of Nicaragua above all, in Costa Rica as well, in the Panama Canal Zone, on Vieques Island in Puerto Rico, in Florida and possibly in other parts of U.S. territory and perhaps also in Honduras. In these places Cuban mercenaries are training, as well as mercenaries of other nationalities, with a purpose that cannot be the most peaceful one.

After a big scandal, the government of Costa Rica — it is said — has ordered the elimination of all training camps of Cuban exiles in that country. No-one knows whether this position is sincere, or whether it is a simple alibi because the mercenaries training there were about to commit some misdeed. We hope that full cognizance will be taken of the real existence of bases for aggression, which we denounced long ago, and that the world will ponder the international responsibility of the government of a country that authorizes and facilitates the training of mercenaries to attack Cuba.

We should note that news of the training of mercenaries in different parts in the Caribbean and the participation of the U.S. Government in such acts is presented as completely natural in the newspapers in the United States. We know of no Latin American voice that has officially protested this. This shows the cynicism with which the U.S. Government moves its pawns.

The sharp foreign ministers of the OAS had eyes to see Cuban emblems and to find "irrefutable" proof in the weapons that the Yankees exhibited in Venezuela, but they do not see the preparations for aggression in the United States, just as they did not hear the voice of President Kennedy, who explicitly declared himself the aggressor against Cuba at Playa Girón [Bay of Pigs invasion of April 1961]. In some cases, it is a blindness provoked by the hatred against our revolution by the ruling classes of the Latin American countries. In others — and these are sadder and more deplorable — it is the product of the dazzling glitter of mammon.

As is well known, after the tremendous commotion of the so-called Caribbean crisis, the United States undertook certain commitments with the Soviet Union. These culminated in the withdrawal of certain types of weapons that the continued acts of aggression of the United States — such as the mercenary attack at Playa Girón and threats of invasion against our homeland — had compelled us to install in Cuba as an act of legitimate and essential defense.

The United States, furthermore, tried to get the UN to inspect our territory. But we emphatically refuse, since Cuba does not recognize the right of the United States, or of anyone else in the world, to determine the type of weapons Cuba may have within its borders.

In this connection, we would abide only by multilateral agreements, with equal obligations for all the parties concerned. As Fidel Castro has said: "So long as the concept of sovereignty exists as the prerogative of nations and of independent peoples, as a right of all peoples, we will not accept the exclusion of our people from that right. So long as the world is governed by these principles, so long as the world is governed by those concepts that have universal validity because they are universally accepted and recognized by the peoples, we will not accept the attempt to deprive us of any of those rights, and we will renounce none of those rights."

The Secretary-General of the United Nations, U Thant, understood our reasons. Nevertheless, the United States attempted to establish a new prerogative, an arbitrary and illegal one: that of violating the airspace of a small country. Thus, we see flying over our country U-2 aircraft and other types of spy planes that, with complete impunity, fly over our airspace. We have made all the necessary warnings for the violations of our airspace to cease, as well as for a halt to the provocations of the U.S. Navy against our sentry posts in the zone of Guantánamo, the buzzing by aircraft of our ships or the ships of other nationalities in international waters, the pirate attacks against ships sailing under different flags, and the infiltration of spies, saboteurs and weapons onto our island.

We want to build socialism. We have declared that we are supporters of those who strive for peace. We have declared ourselves to be within the group of Nonaligned countries, although we are Marxist-Leninists, because the Nonaligned countries, like ourselves, fight imperialism. We want peace. We want to build a better life for our people. That is why we avoid, insofar as possible, falling into the provocations manufactured by the Yankees. But we know the mentality of those who govern them. They want to make us pay a very high price for that peace. We reply that the price cannot go beyond the bounds of dignity.

And Cuba reaffirms once again the right to maintain on its territory the weapons it deems appropriate, and its refusal to recognize the right of any power on earth — no matter how powerful — to violate our soil, our territorial waters, or our airspace.

If in any assembly Cuba assumes obligations of a collective nature, it will fulfill them to the letter. So long as this does not happen, Cuba maintains all its rights, just as any other nation. In the face of the demands of imperialism, our prime minister laid out the five points necessary for the existence of a secure peace in the Caribbean. They are:

1. A halt to the economic blockade and all economic and trade pressures by the United States, in all parts of the world, against our country.
2. A halt to all subversive activities, launching and landing of weap-

ons and explosives by air and sea, organization of mercenary invasions, infiltration of spies and saboteurs, acts all carried out from the territory of the United States and some accomplice countries.
3. A halt to pirate attacks carried out from existing bases in the United States and Puerto Rico.
4. A halt to all the violations of our airspace and our territorial waters by U.S. aircraft and warships.
5. Withdrawal from the Guantánamo naval base and return of the Cuban territory occupied by the United States."

None of these elementary demands has been met, and our forces are still being provoked from the naval base at Guantánamo. That base has become a nest of thieves and a launching pad for them into our territory. We would tire this Assembly were we to give a detailed account of the large number of provocations of all kinds. Suffice it to say that including the first days of December, the number amounts to 1,323 in 1964 alone. The list covers minor provocations such as violation of the boundary line, launching of objects from the territory controlled by the United States, the commission of acts of sexual exhibitionism by U.S. personnel of both sexes, and verbal insults. It includes others that are more serious, such as shooting off small caliber weapons, aiming weapons at our territory, and offenses against our national flag. Extremely serious provocations include those of crossing the boundary line and starting fires in installations on the Cuban side, as well as rifle fire. There have been 78 rifle shots this year, with the sorrowful toll of one death: that of Ramón López Peña, a soldier, killed by two shots fired from the U.S. post three and a half kilometers from the coast on the northern boundary. This extremely grave provocation took place at 7:07 p.m. on July 19, 1964, and the prime minister of our government publicly stated on July 26 that if the event were to recur he would give orders for our troops to repel the aggression. At the same time orders were given for the withdrawal of the forward line of Cuban forces to positions farther away from the boundary line and construction of the necessary fortified positions.

One thousand three hundred and twenty-three provocations in 340 days amount to approximately four per day. Only a perfectly disciplined army with a morale such as ours could resist so many hostile acts without losing its self-control.

Forty-seven countries meeting at the Second Conference of Heads of State or Government of Nonaligned Countries in Cairo unanimously agreed:

> Noting with concern that foreign military bases are in practice a means of bringing pressure on nations and retarding their emancipation and development, based on their own ideological, political,

economic and cultural ideas, the conference declares its unreserved support to the countries that are seeking to secure the elimination of foreign bases from their territory and calls upon all states maintaining troops and bases in other countries to remove them immediately.

The conference considers that the maintenance at Guantánamo (Cuba) of a military base of the United States of America, in defiance of the will of the government and people of Cuba and in defiance of the provisions embodied in the declaration of the Belgrade conference, constitutes a violation of Cuba's sovereignty and territorial integrity.

Noting that the Cuban Government expresses its readiness to settle its dispute over the base at Guantánamo with the United States of America on an equal footing, the conference urges the U.S. Government to open negotiations with the Cuban Government to evacuate their base.

The government of the United States has not responded to this request of the Cairo conference and is attempting to maintain indefinitely by force its occupation of a piece of our territory, from which it carries out acts of aggression such as those detailed earlier.

The Organization of American States — which the people also call the U.S. Ministry of Colonies — condemned us "energetically," even though it had just excluded us from its midst, ordering its members to break off diplomatic and trade relations with Cuba. The OAS authorized aggression against our country at any time and under any pretext, violating the most fundamental international laws, completely disregarding the United Nations. Uruguay, Bolivia, Chile and Mexico opposed that measure, and the government of the United States of Mexico refused to comply with the sanctions that had been approved. Since then we have had no relations with any Latin American countries except Mexico, and this fulfills one of the necessary conditions for direct aggression by imperialism.

We want to make clear once again that our concern for Latin America is based on the ties that unite us: the language we speak, the culture we maintain, and the common master we had. We have no other reason for desiring the liberation of Latin America from the U.S. colonial yoke. If any of the Latin American countries here decide to reestablish relations with Cuba, we would be willing to do so on the basis of equality, and without viewing that recognition of Cuba as a free country in the world to be a gift to our government. We won that recognition with our blood in the days of the liberation struggle. We acquired it with our blood in the defense of our shores against the Yankee invasion.

Although we reject any accusations against us of interference in the internal affairs of other countries, we cannot deny that we sympathize with those people who strive for their freedom. We must fulfill the obligation of our government and people to state clearly and categorically to the world that we morally support and stand in solidarity with peoples who struggle anywhere in the world to make a reality of the rights of full sovereignty proclaimed in the UN Charter.

It is the United States that intervenes. It has done so historically in Latin America. Since the end of the last century Cuba has experienced this truth; but it has been experienced, too, by Venezuela, Nicaragua, Central America in general, Mexico, Haiti and the Dominican Republic. In recent years, apart from our people, Panama has experienced direct aggression, where the marines in the Canal Zone opened fire in cold blood against the defenseless people; the Dominican Republic, whose coast was violated by the Yankee fleet to avoid an outbreak of the just fury of the people after the death of Trujillo; and Colombia, whose capital was taken by assault as a result of a rebellion provoked by the assassination of Gaitán.[18]

Covert interventions are carried out through military missions that participate in internal repression, organizing forces designed for that purpose in many countries, and also in coups d'état, which have been repeated so frequently on the Latin American continent during recent years. Concretely, U.S. forces intervened in the repression of the peoples of Venezuela, Colombia and Guatemala, who fought with weapons for their freedom. In Venezuela, not only do U.S. forces advise the army and the police, but they also direct acts of genocide carried out from the air against the peasant population in vast insurgent areas. And the Yankee companies operating there exert pressures of every kind to increase direct interference. The imperialists are preparing to repress the peoples of the Americas and are establishing an International of Crime.

The United States intervenes in Latin America invoking the defense of free institutions. The time will come when this Assembly will acquire greater maturity and demand of the U.S. Government guarantees for the life of the blacks and Latin Americans who live in that country, most of them U.S. citizens by origin or adoption.

Those who kill their own children and discriminate daily against them because of the color of their skin; those who let the murderers of blacks remain free, protecting them, and furthermore punishing the black population because they demand their legitimate rights as free men — how can those who do this consider themselves guardians of freedom? We understand that today the Assembly is not in a position to ask for explanations of these acts. It must be clearly established, however, that the government of the

United States is not the champion of freedom, but rather the perpetrator of exploitation and oppression against the peoples of the world and against a large part of its own population.

To the ambiguous language with which some delegates have described the case of Cuba and the OAS, we reply with clear-cut words and we proclaim that the peoples of Latin America will make those servile, sell-out governments pay for their treason.

Cuba, distinguished delegates, a free and sovereign state with no chains binding it to anyone, with no foreign investments on its territory, with no proconsuls directing its policy, can speak with its head held high in this Assembly and can demonstrate the justice of the phrase by which it has been baptized: "Free Territory of the Americas."

Our example will bear fruit in the continent, as it is already doing to a certain extent in Guatemala, Colombia and Venezuela.

There is no small enemy nor insignificant force, because no longer are there isolated peoples. As the Second Declaration of Havana states:

> No nation in Latin America is weak — because each forms part of a family of 200 million brothers, who suffer the same miseries, who harbor the same sentiments, who have the same enemy, who dream about the same better future, and who count upon the solidarity of all honest men and women throughout the world...
>
> This epic before us is going to be written by the hungry Indian masses, the peasants without land, the exploited workers. It is going to be written by the progressive masses, the honest and brilliant intellectuals, who so greatly abound in our suffering Latin American lands. Struggles of masses and ideas. An epic that will be carried forward by our peoples, mistreated and scorned by imperialism; our people, unreckoned with until today, who are now beginning to shake off their slumber. Imperialism considered us a weak and submissive flock; and now it begins to be terrified of that flock; a gigantic flock of 200 million Latin Americans in whom Yankee monopoly capitalism now sees its gravediggers...
>
> But now from one end of the continent to the other they are signaling with clarity that the hour has come — the hour of their vindication. Now this anonymous mass, this America of color, somber, taciturn America, which all over the continent sings with the same sadness and disillusionment, now this mass is beginning to enter definitively into its own history, is beginning to write it with its own blood, is beginning to suffer and die for it.
>
> Because now in the mountains and fields of America, on its flatlands and in its jungles, in the wilderness or in the traffic of

cities, on the banks of its great oceans or rivers, this world is begin ning to tremble. Anxious hands are stretched forth, ready to die for what is theirs, to win those rights that were laughed at by one and all for 500 years. Yes, now history will have to take the poor of America into account, the exploited and spurned of America, who have decided to begin writing their history for themselves for all time. Already they can be seen on the roads, on foot, day after day, in endless march of hundreds of kilometers to the governmental "eminences," there to obtain their rights.

Already they can be seen armed with stones, sticks, machetes, in one direction and another, each day, occupying lands, sinking hooks into the land that belongs to them and defending it with their lives. They can be seen carrying signs, slogans, flags; letting them flap in the mountain or prairie winds. And the wave of anger, of demands for justice, of claims for rights trampled underfoot, which is beginning to sweep the lands of Latin America, will not stop. That wave will swell with every passing day. For that wave is composed of the greatest number, the majorities in every respect, those whose labor amasses the wealth and turns the wheels of history. Now they are awakening from the long, brutalizing sleep to which they had been subjected,

For this great mass of humanity has said, "Enough!" and has begun to march. And their march of giants will not be halted until they conquer true independence — for which they have vainly died more than once. Today, however, those who die will die like the Cubans at Playa Girón. They will die for their own true and never-to-be-surrendered independence.

All this, distinguished delegates, this new will of a whole continent, of Latin America, is made manifest in the cry proclaimed daily by our masses as the irrefutable expression of their decision to fight and to paralyze the armed hand of the invader. It is a cry that has the understanding and support of all the peoples of the world and especially of the socialist camp, headed by the Soviet Union.

That cry is: *Patria o muerte!* [Homeland or death]

At the Afro-Asian Conference in Algeria

(February 24, 1965)

This speech was delivered at the Second Economic Seminar of Afro-Asian Solidarity. The conference, held in Algiers, Algeria, was attended by representatives from 63 African and Asian governments, as well as 19 national liberation movements. The meeting was opened by Algerian President Ahmed Ben Bella. Cuba was invited as an observer to the conference, and Guevara served on its presiding committee.

 uba is here at this conference to speak on behalf of the peoples of Latin America.[19] As we have emphasized on other occasions, Cuba also speaks as an underdeveloped country as well as one that is building socialism.

It is not by accident that our delegation is permitted to give its opinion here, in the circle of the peoples of Asia and Africa.[20] A common aspiration unites us in our march toward the future: the defeat of imperialism. A common past of struggle against the same enemy has united us along the road.

This is an assembly of peoples in struggle, and the struggle is developing on two equally important fronts that require all our efforts. The struggle against imperialism, for liberation from colonial or neocolonial shackles, which is being carried out by means of political weapons, arms, or a combination of the two, is not separate from the struggle against backwardness and poverty. Both are stages on the same road leading toward the creation of a new society of justice and plenty.

It is imperative to take political power and to get rid of the oppressor classes. But then the second stage of the struggle, which may be even more difficult than the first, must be faced.

Ever since monopoly capital took over the world, it has kept the greater part of humanity in poverty, dividing all the profits among the group of the most powerful countries. The standard of living in those countries is based on the extreme poverty of our countries. To raise the living standards of the underdeveloped nations, therefore, we must fight against imperialism. And each time a country is torn away from the imperialist tree, it is not only a partial battle won against the main enemy but it also contributes to the real weakening of that enemy, and is one more step toward the final victory.

There are no borders in this struggle to the death. We cannot be indifferent to what happens anywhere in the world, because a victory by any country over imperialism is our victory, just as any country's defeat is a defeat for all of us. The practice of proletarian internationalism is not only a duty for the peoples struggling for a better future, it is also an inescapable necessity. If the imperialist enemy, the United States or any other, carries out its attack against the underdeveloped peoples and the socialist countries, elementary logic determines the need for an alliance between the underdeveloped peoples and the socialist countries. If there were no other uniting factor, the common enemy should be enough.[21]

Of course, these alliances cannot be made spontaneously, without discussions, without birth pangs, which sometimes can be painful.

We said that each time a country is liberated it is a defeat for the world imperialist system. But we must agree that the break is not achieved by the mere act of proclaiming independence or winning an armed victory in a revolution. It is achieved when imperialist economic domination over a people is brought to an end. Therefore, it is a matter of vital interest to the socialist countries for a real break to take place. And it is our international duty, a duty determined by our guiding ideology, to contribute our efforts to make this liberation as rapid and deep-going as possible.

A conclusion must be drawn from all this: the socialist countries must help pay for the development of countries now starting out on the road to liberation. We state it this way with no intention whatsoever of blackmail or dramatics, nor are we looking for an easy way to get closer to the Afro-Asian peoples; it is our profound conviction. Socialism cannot exist without a change in consciousness resulting in a new fraternal attitude toward humanity, both at an individual level, within the societies where socialism is being built or has been built, and on a world scale, with regard to all peoples suffering from imperialist oppression.

We believe the responsibility of aiding dependent countries must be approached in such a spirit. There should be no more talk about developing mutually beneficial trade based on prices forced on the backward countries by the law of value and the international relations of unequal exchange that result from the law of value.[22]

How can it be "mutually beneficial" to sell at world market prices the raw materials that cost the underdeveloped countries immeasurable sweat and suffering, and to buy at world market prices the machinery produced in today's big automated factories?

If we establish that kind of relation between the two groups of nations, we must agree that the socialist countries are, in a certain way, accomplices of imperialist exploitation. It can be argued that the amount of exchange with the underdeveloped countries is an insignificant part of the foreign trade of the socialist countries. That is very true, but it does not eliminate the immoral character of that exchange.

The socialist countries have the moral duty to put an end to their tacit complicity with the exploiting countries of the West. The fact that the trade today is small means nothing. In 1959 Cuba only occasionally sold sugar to some socialist bloc countries, usually through English brokers or brokers of other nationalities. Today 80 percent of Cuba's trade is with that area. All its vital supplies come from the socialist camp, and in fact it has joined that camp. We cannot say that this entrance into the socialist camp was brought about merely by the increase in trade. Nor was the increase in trade brought about by the destruction of the old structures and the adoption of the socialist form of development. Both sides of the question intersect and are interrelated.

We did not start out on the road that ends in communism foreseeing all steps as logically predetermined by an ideology advancing toward a fixed goal. The truths of socialism, plus the raw truths of imperialism, forged our people and showed them the path that we have now taken consciously. To advance toward their own complete liberation, the peoples of Asia and Africa must take the same path. They will follow it sooner or later, regardless of what modifying adjective their socialism may take today.

For us there is no valid definition of socialism other than the abolition of the exploitation of one human being by another. As long as this has not been achieved, if we think we are in the stage of building socialism but instead of ending exploitation the work of suppressing it comes to a halt — or worse, is reversed — then we cannot even speak of building socialism.[23]

We have to prepare conditions so that our brothers and sisters can directly and consciously take the path of the complete abolition of exploitation, but we cannot ask them to take that path if we ourselves are accomplices in that exploitation. If we were asked what methods are used to establish fair prices, we could not answer because we do not know the full scope of the practical problems involved. All we know is that, after political discussions, the Soviet Union and Cuba have signed agreements advantageous to us, by means of which we will sell five million tons of sugar at prices set above those of the so-called free world sugar market. The People's Republic of

China also pays those prices in buying from us.

This is only a beginning. The real task consists of setting prices that will permit development. A great shift in ideas will be involved in changing the order of international relations. Foreign trade should not determine policy, but should, on the contrary, be subordinated to a fraternal policy toward the peoples.

Let us briefly analyze the problem of long-term credits for developing basic industries. Frequently we find that beneficiary countries attempt to establish an industrial base disproportionate to their present capacity. The products will not be consumed domestically and the country's reserves will be risked in the undertaking.

Our thinking is as follows: The investments of the socialist states in their own territory come directly out of the state budget, and are recovered only by use of the products throughout the entire manufacturing process, down to the finished goods. We propose that some thought be given to the possibility of making these kinds of investments in the underdeveloped countries. In this way we could unleash an immense force, hidden in our continents, which have been exploited miserably but never aided in their development. We could begin a new stage of a real international division of labor, based not on the history of what has been done up to now but rather on the future history of what can be done.

The states in whose territories the new investments are to be made would have all the inherent rights of sovereign property over them with no payment or credit involved. But they would be obligated to supply agreed-upon quantities of products to the investor countries for a certain number of years at set prices.

The method for financing the local portion of expenses incurred by a country receiving investments of this kind also deserves study. The supply of marketable goods on long-term credits to the governments of underdeveloped countries could be one form of aid not requiring the contribution of freely convertible hard currency.

Another difficult problem that must be solved is the mastering of technology.[24] The shortage of technicians in underdeveloped countries is well known to us all. Educational institutions and teachers are lacking. Sometimes we lack a real understanding of our needs and have not made the decision to carry out a top-priority policy of technical, cultural and ideological development.

The socialist countries should supply the aid to organize institutions for technical education. They should insist on the great importance of this and should supply technical cadres to fill the present need.

It is necessary to further emphasize this last point. The technicians who come to our countries must be exemplary. They are comrades who will face a strange environment, often one hostile to technology, with a different language and totally different customs. The technicians who take on this difficult task must be, first of all, communists in the most profound and noble sense of the word. With this single quality, plus a modicum of flexibility and organization, wonders can be achieved.

We know this can be done. Fraternal countries have sent us a certain number of technicians who have done more for the development of our country than 10 institutes, and have contributed more to our friendship than 10 ambassadors or 100 diplomatic receptions.

If we could achieve the above-listed points — and if all the technology of the advanced countries could be placed within reach of the underdeveloped countries, unhampered by the present system of patents, which prevents the spread of inventions of different countries — we would progress a great deal in our common task.

Imperialism has been defeated in many partial battles. But it remains a considerable force in the world. We cannot expect its final defeat save through effort and sacrifice on the part of us all.

The proposed set of measures, however, cannot be implemented unilaterally. The socialist countries should help pay for the development of the underdeveloped countries, we agree. But the underdeveloped countries must also steel their forces to embark resolutely on the road of building a new society — whatever name one gives it — where the machine, an instrument of labor, is no longer an instrument for the exploitation of one human being by another. Nor can the confidence of the socialist countries be expected by those who play at balancing between capitalism and socialism, trying to use each force as a counterweight in order to derive certain advantages from such competition. A new policy of absolute seriousness should govern the relations between the two groups of societies. It is worth emphasizing once again that the means of production should preferably be in the hands of the state, so that the marks of exploitation may gradually disappear.

Furthermore, development cannot be left to complete improvisation. It is necessary to plan the construction of the new society. Planning is one of the laws of socialism, and without it, socialism would not exist. Without correct planning there can be no adequate guarantee that all the various sectors of a country's economy will combine harmoniously to take the leaps forward that our epoch demands.

Planning cannot be left as an isolated problem of each of our small countries, distorted in their development, possessors of some raw materials or producers of some manufactured or semimanufactured goods, but lacking in most others.[25] From the outset, planning should take on a certain regional dimension in order to intermix the various national economies, and thus bring about integration on a basis that is truly of mutual benefit.

We believe the road ahead is full of dangers, not dangers conjured up or foreseen in the distant future by some superior mind but palpable dangers deriving from the realities besetting us. The fight against colonialism has reached its final stages, but in the present era colonial status is only a consequence of imperialist domination. As long as imperialism exists it will, by definition, exert its domination over other countries. Today that domination is called neocolonialism.

Neocolonialism developed first in South America, throughout a whole continent, and today it begins to be felt with increasing intensity in Africa and Asia. Its forms of penetration and development have different characteristics. One is the brutal form we have seen in the Congo. Brute force, without any respect or concealment whatsoever, is its extreme weapon. There is another more subtle form: penetration into countries that win political independence, linking up with the nascent local bourgeoisies, development of a parasitic bourgeois class closely allied to the interests of the former colonizers. This development is based on a certain temporary rise in the people's standard of living, because in a very backward country the simple step from feudal to capitalist relations marks a big advance, regardless of the dire consequences for the workers in the long run.

Neocolonialism has bared its claws in the Congo. That is not a sign of strength but of weakness. It had to resort to force, its extreme weapon, as an economic argument, which has generated very intense opposing reactions. But at the same time a much more subtle form of neocolonialism is being practiced in other countries of Africa and Asia. It is rapidly bringing about what some have called the South Americanization of these continents; that is, the development of a parasitic bourgeoisie that adds nothing to the national wealth of their countries but rather deposits its huge ill-gotten profits in capitalist banks abroad, and makes deals with foreign countries to reap more profits with absolute disregard for the welfare of the people.

There are also other dangers, such as competition between fraternal countries, which are politically friendly and sometimes neighbors, as both try to develop the same investments simultaneously to produce for markets that often cannot absorb the increased volume. This competition has the disadvantage of wasting energies that could be used to achieve much greater economic coordination; furthermore, it gives the imperialist monopolies room to maneuver.

When it has been impossible to carry out a given investment project with the aid of the socialist camp, there have been occasions when the project has been accomplished by signing agreements with the capitalists. Such capitalist investments have the disadvantage not only of the terms of the loans but other, much more important disadvantages as well, such as the establishment of joint ventures with a dangerous neighbor. Since these investments in general parallel those made in other states, they tend to cause divisions between friendly countries by creating economic rivalries. Furthermore, they create the dangers of corruption flowing from the constant presence of capitalism, which is very skillful in conjuring up visions of advancement and well-being to fog the minds of many people.

Some time later, prices drop in the market saturated by similar products. The affected countries are obliged to seek new loans, or to permit additional investments in order to compete. The final consequences of such a policy are the fall of the economy into the hands of the monopolies, and a slow but sure return to the past. As we see it, the only safe method for investments is direct participation by the state as the sole purchaser of the goods, limiting imperialist activity to contracts for supplies and not letting them set one foot inside our house. And here it is just and proper to take advantage of interimperialist contradictions in order to secure the least burdensome terms.

We have to watch out for "disinterested" economic, cultural and other aid that imperialism grants directly or through puppet states, which gets a better reception in some parts of the world.

If all of these dangers are not seen in time, some countries that began their task of national liberation with faith and enthusiasm may find themselves on the neocolonial road, as monopoly domination is subtly established step by step so that its effects are difficult to discern until they brutally make themselves felt.

There is a big job to be done. Immense problems confront our two worlds — that of the socialist countries and that called the Third World — problems directly concerning human beings and their welfare, and related to the struggle against the main force that bears the responsibility for our backwardness. In the face of these problems, all countries and peoples conscious of their duties, of the dangers involved in the situation, of the sacrifices required by development, must take concrete steps to cement our friendship in the two fields that can never be separated: the economic and the political. We should organize a great solid bloc that, in its turn, helps new countries to free themselves not only from the political power of imperialism but also from its economic power.

The question of liberation by armed struggle from an oppressor political power should be dealt with in accordance with the rules of proletarian internationalism. In a socialist country at war, it would be absurd to conceive of a factory manager demanding guaranteed payment before shipping to the front the tanks produced by his factory. It ought to seem no less absurd to inquire of a people fighting for liberation, or needing arms to defend its freedom, whether or not they can guarantee payment.

Arms cannot be commodities in our world. They must be delivered to the peoples asking for them to use against the common enemy, with no charge and in the quantities needed and available. That is the spirit in which the Soviet Union and the People's Republic of China have offered us their military aid. We are socialists; we constitute a guarantee of the proper utilization of those arms. But we are not the only ones, and all of us should receive the same treatment.

The reply to the ominous attacks by U.S. imperialism against Vietnam or the Congo should be to supply those sister countries with all the defense equipment they need, and to offer them our full solidarity without any conditions whatsoever.

In the economic field we must conquer the road to development with the most advanced technology possible. We cannot set out to follow the long ascending steps from feudalism to the nuclear and automated era. That would be a road of immense and largely useless sacrifice. We have to start from technology at its current level. We have to make the great technological leap forward that will reduce the current gap between the more developed countries and ourselves. Technology must be applied to the large factories and also to a properly developed agriculture. Above all, its foundation must be technological and ideological education, with a sufficient mass base and strength to sustain the research institutes and organizations that have to be created in each country, as well as the men and women who will use the existing technology and be capable of adapting themselves to the newly mastered technology.

These cadres must have a clear awareness of their duty to the society in which they live. There cannot be adequate technological education if it is not complemented by ideological education; without technological education, in most of our countries, there cannot be an adequate foundation for industrial development, which is what determines the development of a modern society, or the most basic consumer goods and adequate schooling.

A good part of the national revenues must be spent on so-called unproductive investment in education. And priority must be given to the development of agricultural productivity. The latter has reached truly incredible levels in many capitalist countries, producing the senseless crisis of over-production and a surplus of grain and other food products or industrial raw materials in the developed countries. While the rest of the world goes hungry, these countries have enough land and labor to produce several times over what is needed to feed the entire world.

Agriculture must be considered a fundamental pillar of our development. Therefore, a fundamental aspect of our work should be changes in the agrarian structure, and adaptation to the new technological possibilities and to the new obligations of eliminating the exploitation of human beings.

Before making costly decisions that could cause irreparable damage, a careful survey of the national territory is needed. This is one of the preliminary steps in economic research and a basic prerequisite for correct planning.

We warmly support Algeria's proposal for institutionalizing our relations. We would just like to make some supplementary suggestions:

First: in order for the union to be an instrument in the struggle against imperialism, the cooperation of Latin American countries and an alliance with the socialist countries is necessary.

Second: we should be vigilant in preserving the revolutionary character of the union, preventing the admission into it of governments or movements not identified with the general aspirations of the people, and creating mechanisms that would permit the separation from it of any government or popular movement diverging from the just road.

Third: we must advocate the establishment of new relations on an equal footing between our countries and the capitalist ones, creating a revolutionary jurisprudence to defend ourselves in case of conflict, and to give new meaning to the relations between ourselves and the rest of the world.

We speak a revolutionary language and we fight honestly for the victory of that cause. But frequently we entangle ourselves in the nets of an international law created as the result of confrontations between the imperialist powers, and not by the free peoples, the just peoples, in the course of their struggles.

For example, our peoples suffer the painful pressure of foreign bases established on their territories, or they have to carry the heavy burden of massive foreign debts. The story of these throwbacks is well known to all of us. Puppet governments, governments weakened by long struggles for liberation or the operation of the laws of the capitalist market, have allowed treaties that threaten our internal stability and jeopardize our future. Now is the time to throw off the yoke, to force renegotiation of oppressive foreign debts, and to force the imperialists to abandon their bases of aggression.

I would not want to conclude these remarks, this recitation of concepts you all know, without calling the attention of this gathering to the fact that Cuba is not the only Latin American country; it is simply the only one that has the opportunity of speaking before you today. Other peoples are shedding their blood to win the rights we have. When we send our greetings from here, and from all the conferences and the places where they may be held, to the heroic peoples of Vietnam, Laos, so-called Portuguese Guinea, South Africa, or Palestine — to all exploited countries fighting for their emancipation — we must simultaneously extend our voice of friendship, our hand and our encouragement, to our fraternal peoples in Venezuela, Guatemala and Colombia, who today, arms in hand, are resolutely saying "No!" to the imperialist enemy.

Few settings from which to make this declaration are as symbolic as Algiers, one of the most heroic capitals of freedom. May the magnificent Algerian people schooled as few others in sufferings for independence, under the decisive leadership of its party, headed by our dear *compañero* Ahmed Ben Bella — serve as an inspiration to us in this fight without quarter against world imperialism.

Create two, three, many Vietnams (Message to the Tricontinental)[26]

(April 1967)

In April 1965, Che Guevara left Cuba to lend his leadership abilities as a guerrilla commander to revolutionary struggles in other parts of the world — from the Congo to Bolivia. The following undated message was addressed to the Organization of Solidarity with the Peoples of Asia, Africa and Latin America (OSPAAAL, also referred to as the Tricontinental), which was established following a January 1966 conference in Havana. It was published on April 16, 1967, in a special inaugural edition of Tricontinental *magazine, published by the Executive Secretariat of OSPAAAL. It appeared there under Guevara's title, "Create two, three... many Vietnams, that is the watchword."*

> "It is the hour of the furnace,
> and the light is all that can be seen."
>
> JOSÉ MARTÍ

 wenty-one years have elapsed since the end of the last world conflagration, and various publications in every language are celebrating this event, symbolized by the defeat of Japan. A climate of optimism is apparent in many sectors of the different camps into which the world is divided.

Twenty-one years without a world war in these days of heightened confrontation, violent clashes and abrupt turns, appears to be a very large number. All of us declare our readiness to fight for this peace; but without analyzing its practical results (poverty, degradation, constantly increasing exploitation of enormous sectors of humanity), it is appropriate to ask whether this peace is real.

The purpose of these notes is not to write the history of the various conflicts of a local character that have followed one after another since Japan's surrender. Nor is it our task to recount the numerous and growing instances of civilian strife that have occurred in these years of supposed peace. It is enough to point to the wars in Korea and Vietnam as examples to counter the boundless optimism.[27]

In Korea, after years of ferocious struggle, the northern part of the country was left submerged in the most terrible devastation in the annals of modern war: riddled with bombs; without factories, schools or hospitals and without any kind of housing to shelter 10 million inhabitants.

Dozens of countries intervened in that war, led militarily by the United States under the false banner of the United Nations, with the massive participation of U.S. troops and the use of the conscripted South Korean people as cannon fodder. On the other side, the army and people of Korea and volunteers from the People's Republic of China received supplies and advice from the Soviet military apparatus. The United States carried out all kinds of tests of weapons of destruction, excluding thermonuclear ones, but including bacteriological and chemical weapons on a limited scale.

In Vietnam a war has been waged almost without interruption by the patriotic forces of that country against three imperialist powers: Japan, whose might plummeted after the bombings of Hiroshima and Nagasaki; France, which recovered its Indochinese colonies from that defeated country, disregarding the promises made at a time of duress; and the United States, in the latest phase of the conflict.

There have been limited confrontations on all continents, although on the Latin American continent there were for a long time only attempts at freedom struggles and military coups d'état. This was until the Cuban Revolution sounded its clarion call, signaling the importance of this region and attracting the wrath of the imperialists, compelling Cuba to defend its coasts first at the Bay of Pigs and then during the October [1962 missile] crisis. The latter incident could have touched off a war of incalculable proportions if a U.S.-Soviet clash had occurred over the Cuban question.

Right now, however, the contradictions are clearly centered on the territories of the Indochinese peninsula and the neighboring countries. Laos and Vietnam were shaken by conflicts that ceased to be civil wars when U.S. imperialism intervened with all its power, and the whole region became a lit fuse leading to a powder keg. In Vietnam the confrontation has taken on an extremely sharp character. It is not our intention to go into the history of this war. We will just point out some milestones.

In 1954, after the crushing defeat [of the French forces] at Dien Bien Phu, the Geneva Accords were signed, dividing Vietnam into two zones with the stipulation that elections would be held in 18 months to determine who would govern the country and how it would be reunified. The United States did not sign that document but began maneuvering to replace Emperor

Bao Dai, a French puppet, with a man who suited their aims. He turned out to be Ngo Dinh Diem, whose tragic end — that of an orange squeezed dry by imperialism — is known to everyone.[28]

In the months following the signing of the accords, optimism reigned in the camp of the popular forces. They dismantled military positions of the anti-French struggle in the southern part of the country and waited for the agreement to be carried out. But the patriots soon realized that there would be no elections unless the United States felt capable of imposing its will at the ballot box, something it could not do even with all its methods of electoral fraud.

The struggles in the southern part of the country began once again, and these have been gaining in intensity. Today the U.S. Army has grown to almost half a million invaders, while the puppet forces decline in number and, above all, have totally lost the will to fight.

It has been about two years since the United States began the systematic bombing of the Democratic Republic of Vietnam in yet another attempt to halt the fighting spirit in the south and to impose peace negotiations from a position of strength. At the beginning, the bombings were more or less isolated occurrences, carried out in the guise of reprisals for alleged provocations from the north. Then the intensity and regularity of the bombing increased, until it became one gigantic onslaught by the U.S. Air Force carried out day after day, with the purpose of destroying every vestige of civilization in the northern zone of the country. It is only one episode in the sadly notorious escalation.

The material aims of the Yankee world have been achieved in good part despite the valiant defense put up by the Vietnamese anti-aircraft batteries, the more than 1,700 planes brought down and the aid in military supplies from the socialist camp.

This is the painful reality: Vietnam, a nation representing the aspirations and hopes for victory of the disinherited of the world, is tragically alone. This people must endure the pounding of U.S. technology — in the south almost without defenses, in the north with some possibilities of defense — but always alone.

The solidarity of the progressive world with the Vietnamese people has something of the bitter irony of the plebeians cheering on the gladiators in the Roman Circus. To wish the victim success is not enough; one must share his or her fate. One must join that victim in death or in victory.

When we analyze the isolation of the Vietnamese we are overcome by anguish at this illogical moment in the history of humanity.[29] U.S. imperialism is guilty of aggression. Its crimes are immense, extending over the whole world. We know this, gentlemen! But also guilty are those who, at the decisive moment, hesitated to make Vietnam an inviolable part of socialist territory — yes, at the risk of a war of global scale, but also compelling the U.S. imperialists to make a decision. Also guilty are those who persist in a war of insults and maneuvers, begun quite some time ago by the representatives of the two biggest powers in the socialist camp.[30]

Let us ask, seeking an honest answer: Is Vietnam isolated or not, as it tries to maintain a dangerous balancing act between the two quarrelling powers? What greatness has been shown by this people! What a stoic and courageous people! And what a lesson for the world their struggle holds.

It will be a long time before we know if President Johnson ever seriously intended to initiate some of the reforms needed by his people — to paper over the class contradictions that are appearing with explosive force and mounting frequency.[31] What is certain is that the improvements announced under the pompous title of the Great Society have gone down the drain in Vietnam. The greatest of the imperialist powers is feeling in its own bowels the bleeding inflicted by a poor, backward country; its fabulous economy is strained by the war effort. Killing has ceased to be the most comfortable business for the monopolies.

Defensive weapons, and not in sufficient number, are all these marvelous Vietnamese soldiers have besides love for their country, for their society, and an unsurpassed courage. Imperialism is bogged down in Vietnam. It sees no way out and is searching desperately for one that will permit it to emerge with dignity from the dangerous situation in which it finds itself. Furthermore, the "four points" put forward by the north and the "five" by the south have it caught in a vise, making the confrontation still more decisive.

Everything seems to indicate that peace, the precarious peace that bears that name only because no global conflagration has occurred, is again in danger of being broken by some irreversible and unacceptable step taken by the United States.

What is the role that we, the exploited of the world, must play?

The peoples of three continents are watching and learning a lesson for themselves in Vietnam. Since the imperialists are using the threat of war to blackmail humanity, the correct response is not to fear war. Attack hard and without let-up at every point of confrontation — that must be the general tactic of the peoples.[32]

But in those places where this miserable peace that we endure has not been broken, what should our task be?

To liberate ourselves at any price.

The world panorama is one of great complexity. The task of winning liberation still lies ahead, even for some countries of old Europe sufficiently developed to experience all the contradictions of capitalism but so weak that they can no longer follow the course of imperialism or embark on that road. In those countries the contradictions will become explosive in the coming years. But their problems, and hence their solutions, are different from those facing our dependent and economically backward peoples.

The fundamental field of imperialist exploitation covers the three backward continents — Latin America, Asia and Africa. Each country has its own characteristics, but the continents, as a whole, have their own features as well.

Latin America constitutes a more or less homogeneous whole, and in almost its entire territory U.S. monopoly capital holds absolute primacy.[33] The puppet or — in the best of cases — weak and timid governments are unable to resist the orders of the Yankee master. The United States has reached virtually the pinnacle of its political and economic domination. There is little room left for it to advance; any change in the situation could turn into a step backward from its dominance. Its policy is to maintain its conquests. The course of action is reduced at the present time to the brutal use of force to prevent liberation movements of any kind.

Behind the slogan "We will not permit another Cuba" hides the possibility of cowardly acts of aggression they can get away with, such as the aggression against the Dominican Republic;[34] or before that, the massacre in Panama and the clear warning that Yankee troops are ready to intervene anywhere in Latin America where a change in the established order endangers their interests. This policy enjoys almost absolute impunity. Despite its lack of credibility, the OAS is a convenient mask. The ineffectiveness of the UN borders on the ridiculous or the tragic. The armies of all the countries of Latin America are ready to intervene to crush their own people. What has been formed, in fact, is the International of Crime and Betrayal.

On the other hand, the indigenous bourgeoisies have lost all capacity to oppose imperialism — if they ever had any — and are only dragged along behind it like a caboose.[35] There are no other alternatives: either a socialist revolution or a caricature of revolution.

Asia is a continent with different characteristics. The liberation struggles against a series of European colonial powers resulted in the establishment of more or less progressive governments, whose subsequent evolution has in some cases deepened the main objectives of national liberation and, in others, reverted toward pro-imperialist positions.

From the economic point of view, the United States had little to lose and much to gain in Asia. Changes work in its favor; it is struggling to displace other neocolonial powers, to penetrate new spheres of activity in the economic field, sometimes directly, sometimes utilizing Japan.

But special political conditions exist there, above all in the Indochinese peninsula, that give Asia characteristics of major importance and that play an important role in the global military strategy of U.S. imperialism. The latter is imposing a blockade around China utilizing at least South Korea, Japan, Taiwan, South Vietnam and Thailand.[36] This dual situation — a strategic interest as important as the military blockade of the People's Republic of China, and the ambition of U.S. capital to penetrate those big markets it does not yet dominate — makes Asia one of the most explosive places in the world today, despite the apparent stability outside of the Vietnamese area.

Belonging geographically to the Asian continent, but with its own contradictions, the Middle East is at boiling point. It is not possible to foresee what will be the outcome of the Cold War between Israel, which is backed by the imperialists, and the progressive countries of this region. It is another one of the threatening volcanoes in the world.

Africa appears almost like virgin territory for neocolonial invasion. Changes have occurred that, to a certain degree, have compelled the neocolonial powers to give up their former absolute prerogatives. But when these changes are carried out easily and without interruption, colonialism gives way to neocolonialism, with the same consequences in regard to economic domination.

The United States did not have colonies in this region and is now struggling to penetrate its partners' old private preserves. It can be said with certainty that Africa constitutes a long-term reservoir in the strategic plans of U.S. imperialism. Its current investments there are of importance only in the Union of South Africa, and it is beginning its penetration of the Congo, Nigeria and other countries, where competition between the imperialist powers that had previously been peaceful is now becoming violent. It does not yet have big interests to defend except its alleged right to intervene any place on the globe where its monopolies smell good profits or the existence of large reserves of raw materials. All this background makes it legitimate to pose the question about the possibilities for the liberation of the peoples in the short or medium term.

If we analyze Africa, we see that there are struggles of some intensity in the Portuguese colonies of Guinea, Mozambique and Angola, with particular success in Guinea and varying successes in the other two. We are also still witnessing a struggle between Lumumba's successors and the old accomplices of [Moise] Tshombe in the Congo, a struggle that appears at the moment to be leaning in favor of the latter, who have "pacified" a big part of the country for their benefit, although war is still latent.

In Rhodesia the problem is different: British imperialism used all the means at its disposal to hand over power to the white minority, which now rules the country. The conflict, from Britain's point of view, is absolutely unofficial. This Western power, with its usual diplomatic cleverness — in plain language also called hypocrisy — presents a facade of displeasure with the measures adopted by the government of Ian Smith. It is supported in this sly attitude by some Commonwealth countries that follow it, but is attacked by a good number of the countries of black Africa, even those that are docile economic vassals of British imperialism.

In Rhodesia the situation could become highly explosive if the efforts of the black patriots to rise up in arms were to crystallize, and if this movement were effectively supported by the neighboring African nations. But for now all these problems are being aired in bodies as innocuous as the UN, the Commonwealth or the Organization of African Unity.

Nevertheless, the political and social evolution of Africa does not lead us to foresee a continental revolutionary situation. The liberation struggles against the Portuguese must end victoriously, but Portugal signifies nothing on the imperialist roster. The confrontations of revolutionary importance are those that put the whole imperialist apparatus in check, although we will not for that reason cease struggling for the liberation of the three Portuguese colonies and for the deepening of their revolutions.

When the black masses of South Africa or Rhodesia begin their genuine revolutionary struggle, or when the impoverished masses of a country set out against the ruling oligarchies to conquer their right to a decent life, a new era will have opened in Africa. Up to now there has been a succession of barracks coups, in which one group of officers replaces another or replaces a ruler who no longer serves their caste interests and those of the powers that control them behind the scenes. But there have been no popular upheavals. In the Congo these characteristics were fleetingly present, inspired by the memory of Lumumba, but they have been losing strength in recent months.

In Asia, as we have seen, the situation is explosive. Vietnam and Laos, where the struggle is now going on, are not the only points of friction. The same holds true for Cambodia, where at any moment the United States might launch a direct attack.[37] We should add Thailand, Malaysia and, of course, Indonesia, where we cannot believe that the final word has been spoken despite the annihilation of the Communist Party of that country after the reactionaries took power.[38] And, of course, there is the Middle East.

In Latin America, the struggle is going on arms in hand in Guatemala, Colombia, Venezuela and Bolivia, and the first outbreaks are already beginning in Brazil. Other centers of resistance have appeared and been extinguished. But almost all the countries of this continent are ripe for a struggle of the kind that, to be triumphant, cannot settle for anything less than the establishment of a government of a socialist nature. In this continent virtually only one language is spoken save for the exceptional case of Brazil, with whose people Spanish-speakers can communicate in view of the similarity between the two languages. There is such a similarity between the classes in these countries that they have an "international American" type of identification, much more so than in other continents. Language, customs, religion, a common master, unite them. The degree and forms of exploitation are similar in their effects for exploiters and exploited in a good number of countries of our America. And within it rebellion is ripening at an accelerated rate.

We may ask: This rebellion, how will it bear fruit? What kind of rebellion will it be? We have maintained for some time that given its similar characteristics, the struggle in Latin America will in due time acquire continental dimensions. It will be the scene of many great battles waged by humanity for its own liberation.

In the framework of this struggle of continental scope, those that are currently being carried on in an active way are only episodes. But they have already provided martyrs who will figure in the history of the Americas as having given their necessary quota of blood for this final stage in the struggle for the full freedom of humanity. There are the names of Commander Turcios Lima, the priest Camilo Torres, Commander Fabricio Ojeda, the Commanders Lobatón and Luis de la Puente Uceda, central figures in the revolutionary movements of Guatemala, Colombia, Venezuela and Peru.

But the active mobilization of the people creates its new leaders — César Montes and Yon Sosa are raising the banner in Guatemala; Fabio Vázquez and Marulanda are doing it in Colombia; Douglas Bravo in the western part of the country and Américo Martín in El Bachiller are leading their respective fronts in Venezuela.

New outbreaks of war will appear in these and other Latin American countries, as have already occurred in Bolivia. And they will continue to grow, with all the vicissitudes involved in this dangerous occupation of the modern revolutionary. Many will die, victims of their own errors; others will fall in the difficult combat to come; new fighters and new leaders will arise in the heat of the revolutionary struggle. The people will create their fighters and their leaders along the way in the selective framework of the war itself.

The Yankee agents of repression will increase in number. Today there are advisers in all countries where armed struggle is going on. It seems that the Peruvian Army, also advised and trained by the Yankees, carried out a successful attack on the revolutionaries of that country. But if the guerrilla centers are led with sufficient political and military skill, they will become practically unbeatable and will make new Yankee reinforcements necessary. In Peru itself, with tenacity and firmness, new figures, although not yet fully known, are reorganizing the guerrilla struggle.

Little by little, the obsolete weapons that suffice to repress the small armed bands will turn into modern weapons, and the groups of advisers into U.S. combatants, until at a certain point they find themselves obliged to send growing numbers of regular troops to secure the relative stability of a power whose national puppet army is disintegrating in the face of the guerrillas' struggles.

This is the road of Vietnam. It is the road that the peoples must follow. It is the road that Latin America will follow, with the special feature that the armed groups might establish something such as coordinating committees to make the repressive tasks of Yankee imperialism more difficult and to help their own cause.

Latin America, a continent forgotten in the recent political struggles for liberation, is beginning to make itself heard through the Tricontinental in the voice of the vanguard of its peoples: the Cuban Revolution. Latin America will have a much more important task: the creation of the world's second or third Vietnam, or second *and* third Vietnam.

We must definitely keep in mind that imperialism is a world system, the final stage of capitalism, and that it must be beaten in a great worldwide confrontation. The strategic objective of that struggle must be the destruction of imperialism.

The contribution that falls to us, the exploited and backward of the world, is to eliminate the foundations sustaining imperialism: our oppressed nations, from which capital, raw materials and cheap labor (both workers and technicians) are extracted, and to which new capital (tools of domination), arms and all kinds of goods are exported, sinking us into absolute dependence. The fundamental element of this strategic objective, then, will be the real liberation of the peoples, a liberation that will be the result of armed struggle in the majority of cases, and that, in Latin America, will almost unfailingly turn into a socialist revolution.

In focusing on the destruction of imperialism, it is necessary to identify its head, which is none other than the United States of North America. We must carry out a task of a general kind, the tactical aim of which is to draw the enemy out of their environment, compelling them to fight in places where their living habits clash with existing conditions. The adversary must not be underestimated; the U.S. soldiers have technical ability and are backed by means of such magnitude as to make them formidable. What they lack essentially is the ideological motivation, which their most hated rivals of today — the Vietnamese soldiers — have to the highest degree. We will be able to triumph over this army only to the extent that we succeed in undermining its morale. And this is done by inflicting defeats on it and causing it repeated suffering.

This brief outline for victories, however, entails immense sacrifices by the peoples — sacrifices that must be demanded starting right now, in the light of day, and that perhaps will be less painful than those they would have to endure if we constantly avoided battle in an effort to get others to pull the chestnuts out of the fire for us.

Clearly, the last country to free itself very probably will do so without an armed struggle, and its people will be spared the suffering of a long war as cruel as imperialist wars are. But it may be impossible to avoid this struggle or its effects in a conflict of worldwide character, and that country might still suffer the same or even more. We cannot predict the future, but we must never give way to the cowardly temptation to be the standard-bearers of a people who yearn for freedom but renounce the struggle that goes with it, and who wait as if expecting it to come as a crumb of victory.

It is absolutely correct to avoid any needless sacrifice. That is why it is so important to be clear on the real possibilities that dependent Latin America has to free itself in a peaceful way. For us the answer to this question is clear: now may or may not be the right moment to start the struggle, but we can have no illusions, nor do we have a right to believe, that freedom can be won without a fight.

Moreover, the battles will not be mere street fights with stones against tear gas, or peaceful general strikes. Nor will it be the struggle of an infuriated people that destroys the repressive apparatus of the ruling oligarchies in two or three days. It will be a long, bloody struggle in which the battlefronts will be in guerrilla refuges in the cities, in the homes of the combatants (where the repression will go seeking easy victims among their families), among the massacred peasant population, in the towns or cities destroyed by the enemy's bombs. We are being pushed into this struggle. It cannot be remedied other than by preparing for it and deciding to undertake it.

The beginning will not be easy; it will be extremely difficult. All the oligarchies' repressive capacity, all its capacity for demagogy and brutality will be placed in the service of its cause.

Our mission, in the first hour, is to survive; then, to act, the perennial example of the guerrilla carrying on armed propaganda in the Vietnamese meaning of the term — that is, the propaganda of bullets, of battles waged against the enemy that are won or lost.

The great lesson of the guerrillas' invincibility is taking hold among the masses of the dispossessed, the galvanization of the national spirit, the preparation for more difficult tasks, for resistance to more violent repression. Hate as a factor in the struggle, intransigent hatred for the enemy that takes one beyond the natural limitations of a human being and converts one into an effective, violent, selective, cold, killing machine — our soldiers must be like that; a people without hate cannot triumph over a brutal enemy.

We must carry the war as far as the enemy carries it: into our enemy's home and places of recreation, making it total war. Our enemy must be prevented from having a moment's peace, a moment's quiet outside the barracks and even inside them. Attack them wherever they may be; make them feel like hunted animals wherever they go. Then their morale will begin to decline. They will become even more bestial, but the signs of the imminent decline will appear.

Let us develop genuine proletarian internationalism, with international proletarian armies.[39] Let the flag under which we fight be the sacred cause of the liberation of humanity, so that to die under the colors of Vietnam, Venezuela, Guatemala, Laos, Guinea, Colombia, Bolivia, Brazil — to mention only the current scenes of armed struggle — will be equally glorious and desirable for a Latin American, an Asian, an African and even a European.

Every drop of blood spilled in a land under whose flag one was not born is experience gathered by the survivor to be applied later in the struggle for the liberation of one's own country. And every people that liberates itself is a step forward in the battle for the liberation of one's own people.

It is time to moderate our disputes and place everything at the service of the struggle. We all know that big controversies are agitating the world that is struggling for freedom; we cannot hide that. We also know that these controversies have acquired a character and a sharpness that make dialogue and reconciliation appear extremely difficult, if not impossible. It is useless to seek ways to initiate a dialogue that those in dispute have avoided.

But the enemy is there, it strikes day after day and threatens new blows, and these blows will unite us today, tomorrow or the next day. Whoever understands this first and prepares this necessary unity will win the peoples' gratitude.

In view of the virulence and intransigence with which each side argues its case, we, the dispossessed, cannot agree with the way these differences are expressed, even when we agree with some of the positions of one or the other side, or when we agree more with the positions of one or the other side. In this time of struggle, the way in which the current differences have been aired is a weakness; but given the situation, it is an illusion to think that the matter can be resolved through words. History will either sweep away these disputes or pass its final judgment on them.

In our world in struggle, everything related to disputes around tactics and methods of action for the attainment of limited objectives must be analyzed with the respect due to the opinions of others. As for the great strategic objective — the total destruction of imperialism by means of struggle — on that we must be intransigent.

Let us sum up as follows our aspirations for victory. Destruction of imperialism by means of eliminating its strongest bulwark: the imperialist domination of the United States of North America. To take as a tactical line the gradual liberation of the peoples, one by one or in groups, involving the enemy in a difficult struggle outside his terrain; destroying his bases of support, that is, his dependent territories.

This means a long war. And, we repeat once again, a cruel war. Let no-one deceive himself or herself when setting out on this course, and let no-one hesitate to begin out of fear of the results it can bring upon one's own people. It is almost the only hope for victory.

We cannot evade the call of the hour. Vietnam teaches us this with its permanent lesson in heroism, its tragic daily lesson of struggle and death in order to gain the final victory.

Over there, the soldiers of imperialism encounter the discomforts of those who, accustomed to the standard of living that the United States boasts, have to confront a hostile land; the insecurity of those who cannot move without feeling that they are stepping on enemy territory; death for those who go outside their fortified compounds; the permanent hostility of the entire population. All this is provoking repercussions inside the United States. It is leading to the appearance of a factor that was attenuated by imperialism at full strength: the class struggle inside its own territory.

How close and bright would the future appear if two, three, many Vietnams flowered on the face of the globe, with their quota of death and their immense tragedies, with their daily heroism, with their repeated blows against imperialism, forcing it to disperse its forces under the lash of the growing hatred of the peoples of the world!

And if we were all capable of uniting in order to give our blows greater strength and certainty, so that the aid of all kinds to the peoples in struggle was even more effective — how great the future would be, and how near!

If we, on a small point on the map of the world, fulfill our duty and place at the disposal of the struggle whatever little we are able to give — our lives, our sacrifice — it can happen that one of these days we will draw our last breath on a bit of earth not our own, yet already ours, watered with our blood. Let it be known that we have measured the scope of our actions and that we consider ourselves no more than a part of the great army of the proletariat. But we feel proud at having learned from the Cuban Revolution and from its central leader the great lesson to be drawn from its position in this part of the world: "Of what difference are the dangers to a human being or a people, or the sacrifices they make, when what is at stake is the destiny of humanity?"

Our every action is a battle cry against imperialism and a call for the unity of the peoples against the great enemy of the human race: the United States of North America.

Wherever death may surprise us, let it be welcome if our battle cry has reached even one receptive ear, if another hand reaches out to take up our arms, and others come forward to join in our funeral dirge with the rattling of machine guns and with new cries of battle and victory.

PART 4

LETTERS

"If imperialism is finished, you, Camilo and I will take a vacation to the moon..."

To José E. Martí Leyva

Havana, February 5, 1959

Sr. José E. Martí Leyva
Mártires No. 180
Holguín, Oriente

Dear Friend,

I read with real pleasure your generous offer to fight for the freedom of our neighbors, the people of Santo Domingo.

Having taken into account the full value of this disinterested and noble offer, I urge you to keep alive your enthusiasm for the future, when an opportunity will arise. Meanwhile, take advantage of your years in school and make of yourself a useful man, something we have great need of in Cuba. I am sure that you will be one of them. Devote yourself to drawing. Promise me.

My cordial greetings,

Dr. Ernesto Che Guevara
Commander in Chief,
Military Dept. of La Cabaña

To José Tiquet

Havana, May 17, 1960

Sr. José Tiquet
Publicaciones Continente, S.A.
Pasco de la Reforma 95
México, D.F.

Dear Friend,

I implore you to forgive me for the delay in answering your letter. It was due not so much to negligence on my part but to lack of time. It would give me great pleasure to bear the cost of your trip to Cuba but I do not possess the means to do it. My income is limited to my salary as major of the Rebel Army which, in accordance with the austerity policy of our revolutionary government, consists only of the amount necessary to maintain a decent standard of living.

Your letter was no bother at all; on the contrary I was glad to receive it.

Affectionately,

Commander Ernesto Che Guevara

To Dr. Fernando Barral

Havana, February 15, 1961
"Year of Education"

Dr. Fernando Barral
Ujpest, Hungary

Dear Fernando,

It is truly a pity that we have not been able to see each other for even a few minutes. I write with the haste and brevity imposed by my many diverse pursuits. I hope you will understand. To come to the point, though you did not speak of it in your last letter as you had in the one before that, I assume that you want to come to work in these parts. I can tell you now that there is work here for you and your wife; that the salary will be adequate but will not suffice for luxuries; that the experience of the Cuban Revolution is something I deem to be highly interesting for people such as you, who must someday begin to work again in their native land. Of course you could bring your mother; all necessary personal facilities for your work would be available. The University is being reorganized and there is room for you there if you are interested.

Naturally you will find more irrational things here than there, since a revolution upsets and disarranges everything; little by little everybody must be placed in the job he is best suited to. The only important thing is not to hamper anyone's work.

To sum up, *aquí está tu casa*. If you want to come, let me know in the way you consider advisable, and explain to me the steps that would have to be taken, if any, in order to bring your wife.

Since we have followed such different paths for many years, I can tell you as a matter of personal information that I am married and have two daughters. I had some news of old friends from Mamá who visited me a few months ago.

A fraternal embrace from your friend,

Commander Ernesto Che Guevara

To Carlos Franqui

This letter was written in response to the publication by *Revolución* of a special photo supplement entitled "Che in the Escambray: Diary of an Invasion" in its December 24, 1962, issue. This letter was published in the December 29, 1962 *Revolución*.

Compañero Carlos Franqui
Editor, *Revolución*
Havana

Compañero Franqui,

I did not like the photo supplement published the other day. Allow me to tell you this very frankly and to explain why, hoping that these lines will be published as my "outburst."

Leaving aside small things that do not speak well of the newspaper's seriousness, such as those photos with a group of soldiers aiming at a supposed enemy with their eyes turned to the camera, there are fundamental errors:

1. That extract from the diary is not entirely authentic. The thing was like this: I was asked (during the war) if I had kept a diary of the invasion [by Guevara's column from Oriente to Las Villas]. I had, but in the form of very bare notes, for my personal use; and at the time I had no opportunity to develop it. A gentleman from Santa Clara took charge of doing that (I don't remember now under what circumstances); he turned out to be quite "flamboyant" and felt like adding feats by means of adjectives.

What little value those four notes might have is destroyed when they lose authenticity.

2. It is false that the war for me took second place to meeting the needs of the peasantry. At that time winning the war was the important thing, and I believe I devoted myself to that task with all the dogged determination I was capable of. After entering the Escambray Mountains I gave two days' rest to a troop that had been on the march for 45 days under extremely difficult conditions, and resumed operations, seizing Güinía de Miranda. If a mistake was made it was in the opposite sense: little attention to the difficult task of dealing with all the "cattle rustlers" who had taken up arms in

those cursed hills. Gutiérrez Menoyo and his crew vexed me to no end and I had to put up with it to be able to devote myself to the central task: the war.

3. It is false to say that Ramiro Valdés was a "close collaborator of Che's in organizational matters." I don't know how that could have gotten by you, as editor, knowing him as well as you do.

Ramirito was at Moncada, he was imprisoned on the Isle of Pines, he came on the *Granma* as a lieutenant, rose to captain when I was made a commander, he led a column as a commander, he was the second chief of the invasion, and then he led the operations in the eastern sector while I marched toward Santa Clara.

I believe that the historical truth must be respected: to fabricate it at whim does not lead to any good results. For that reason, and because I was an actor in that part of the drama, I made up my mind to write you these critical lines, which try to be constructive. It seems to me that if you had checked the text the errors could have been avoided.

I wish you happy holidays and a coming year without many big headlines (because of what they bring).

Che

To Guillermo Lorentzen

Havana, May 4, 1963
"Year of Organization"

Compañero Guillermo Lorentzen
Havana

Compañero,

I have received your letters and I thank you for them.

I was born in Argentina, I fought in Cuba, and I began to be a revolution-ary in Guatemala.

This autobiographical synthesis will perhaps serve as some justification for my interference in your affairs.

In Guatemala the guerrillas are fighting. The people have to some extent taken up arms. There is only one possibility of slowing the development of a struggle that shows all signs of developing toward a Cuban- or Algerian-type revolution.

Imperialism has that possibility, although I am not sure if they will bother to use it: "free elections" with Arévalo.

That is how we see the matter. Can you think it is otherwise?

A revolutionary greeting,

Patria o Muerte
Venceremos

Commander Ernesto Che Guevara

To Peter Marucci

Havana, May 4, 1963
"Year of Organization"

Mr. Peter Marucci
Wire Editor
The Daily Mercury
Guelph, Canada

Compañero,

First of all, allow me to confess that in our country bureaucracy is strong and well entrenched; into its immense bosom it absorbs papers, incubates them, and in time sees to it that they reach their destination. That is why I am only now answering your kind letter.

Cuba is a socialist country: tropical, unpolished, ingenuous and gay. It is socialist, without relinquishing even one of its own characteristics while it adds to its people's maturity. It is worth getting acquainted with. We hope you will come, whenever you like.

Sincerely,

Patria o muerte
Venceremos

Commander Ernesto Che Guevara

To Dr. Aleida Coto Martínez

May 23, 1963
"Year of Organization"

Dr. Aleida Coto Martínez
Asst. Director of Primary Regional Education
Puerto Regla — Guanabacoa
Ministry of Education
City

Dear *Compañera*,

Thank you for your letter.

Sometimes we revolutionaries are lonely. Even our children look on us as strangers. They see less of us than of the soldier on sentry duty, whom they call "uncle."

The compositions you sent me took me back for a moment to the composition that we wrote for a president's visit to our town, when I was in the second or third grade. The difference between what those children expressed and what these children of today's revolution express makes us confident of the future.

A revolutionary greeting,

Patria o muerte
Venceremos

Commander Ernesto Che Guevara

To the *compañeros* of the
Motorcycle Assembly Plant

Havana, May 31, 1963

Compañeros of the Motorcycle Assembly Plant
Santiago de Cuba

Compañeros,

There is an error in your proposals. Workers responsible for the production of any article have no right over it. Bakers have no right to more bread, cement workers have no right to more bags of cement, nor do you have any right to motorcycles.

The day of my visit, I saw that one of the three-wheelers was being used as a kind of little bus. Just as I was criticizing that, a member of the Communist Youth was leaving on a motorcycle to do some work for that organization, which I was doubly critical of, given the improper use of the vehicle and the incorrect attitude of using time paid for by society for tasks that are supposed to represent an extra contribution of time to society, of an absolutely voluntary nature. In the course of the conversation I said I would look into the question of the conditions of payment and whether or not it would be possible to give vehicles to some workers and technicians.

Since responsibility for all the tasks of distribution and sale of vehicles has been turned over to the Ministry of Transportation, I don't see the possibility of that happening.

With revolutionary greetings,

Patria o muerte
Venceremos

Commander Ernesto Che Guevara

To Pablo Díaz González

Havana, October 28, 1963
"Year of Organization"

Compañero Pablo Díaz González,
Administrator
Camagüey

Pablo,

I read your article. I must thank you for how well you portray me; too well, I think. Furthermore, it seems to me you portray yourself pretty well, too.

The first thing a revolutionary who writes history has to do is stick to the truth like a finger inside a glove. You did that, but it was a boxing glove, and that's not fair.

My advice to you: reread the article, eliminate everything you know is not true and be careful with everything you don't know for certain is the truth.

A revolutionary greeting,

Patria o muerte
Venceremos

Commander Ernesto Che Guevara

To Lydia Ares Rodríguez

Havana, October 30, 1963

Sra. Lydia Ares Rodríguez
Calle Cárdenas 69
Havana

Compañera,

Your letter has been forwarded to the Ministry of the Interior, since that is the agency responsible for solving such problems.

In any case, I appreciate your attitude toward work and toward the revolution; but I must tell you that, in my personal opinion, your son must serve his sentence because the commission of a crime against socialist property is the gravest offense, independently of any extenuating circumstances.

I am sorry to tell you this, and I regret the suffering it will cause you, but I would not be fulfilling my revolutionary duty were I not to do so frankly.

A revolutionary greeting,

Patria o muerte
Venceremos

Commander Ernesto Che Guevara

376 ■ CHE GUEVARA READER

To María Rosario Guevara

Havana, February 20, 1964
"Year of the Economy"

Sra. María Rosario Guevara
36, rue d'Annam
(Maarif) Casablanca
Morocco

Compañera,

Truthfully speaking, I don't know what part of Spain my family came from. Of course, my ancestors left there a long time ago, with one hand in front and another behind;[1] and if I don't keep mine in the same place, it is only because of the discomfort of the position.

I don't think you and I are very closely related, but if you are capable of trembling with indignation each time that an injustice is committed in the world, we are comrades, and that is more important.

A revolutionary greeting,

Patria o muerte
Venceremos

Commander Ernesto Che Guevara

To José Medero Mestre

Havana, February 26, 1964
"Year of the Economy"

Mr. José Medero Mestre
Havana

Compañero,

Thank you for your interest and your comments. In order to convince me, you have touched a sore spot; you quote my adversaries. Unfortunately, because of the time involved I cannot continue this polemic by mail. Future issues of *Nuestra Industria Económica* will be carrying articles by a select number of Soviet technicians showing their concern with similar questions.

Just one statement for you to think about: counterposing socialist efficiency to capitalist inefficiency in factory management is to confuse wishes with reality. It is in distribution that socialism achieves unquestionable advantages, and it is in centralized planning that it has been able to overcome its technological and organizational disadvantages with respect to capitalism. With the break up of the old society, an attempt has been made to establish the new one with a hybrid. Man as a wolf, the society of wolves, is being replaced by another genus that no longer has the desperate urge to rob his fellow man, since the exploitation of man by man has disappeared. But he still does have some urges of that type (although quantitatively fewer), due to the fact that the lever of material interest is still the arbiter of the well-being of the individual and of the small collectivity (factories, for example). And that is where I see the root of the evil. Conquering capitalism with its own fetishes, having removed their most magical quality, profit, seems like a tricky business.

If this is very obscure (my watch says it's past midnight), perhaps another simile will make it clearer: the lever of material interest under socialism is like Pastorita's lottery;[2] it can neither light up the eyes of the most ambitious nor budge the others' indifference.

I don't pretend to have exhausted this theme, much less to have given the papal "amen" to these and other contradictions. Unfortunately, in the eyes of most of our people, and in mine as well, apologetics for a system can have more impact than scientific analysis of it. This does not help us in the task of clarification, and our whole effort is aimed at inviting people to think, to treat Marxism with the seriousness this towering doctrine deserves.

Because of this, because you think, I thank you for your letter; least important is the fact that we do not agree.

If you ever have to tell me anything else, remember, I am not a teacher; I am just one of many men struggling today to build a new Cuba, but who had the good fortune to be at Fidel's side during the most difficult moments of the Cuban Revolution and some of the most tragic and glorious moments in the history of the worldwide struggle for freedom. That is why you know who I am, while I don't remember your name. It might have been the other way around, except that in that case I would have had to write you from some remote part of the world, wherever my wandering bones might have taken me, since I was not born here.

That is all.

A revolutionary greeting,

Patria o muerte
Venceremos

Commander Ernesto Che Guevara

To Dr. Eduardo B. Ordaz Ducungé

May 26, 1964
"Year of the Economy"

Dr. Eduardo B. Ordaz Ducungé
Director, Psychiatric Hospital
Havana

Dear Ordaz,

I acknowledge receipt of the journal. Although I am very short of time, the topics look very interesting and I will try to read it.

I am curious about something else: How can 6,300 copies of a specialized journal be published when there are not even that many doctors in Cuba?

Something keeps gnawing away at my mind and it is driving me to the verge of a neuro-economic psychosis: Are the rats using the journal to deepen their understanding of psychiatry or to satisfy their stomachs? Or perhaps each patient has a copy of the publication at his bedside?

At any rate, there are 3,000 copies too many in the run. I beg you to think about this.

Seriously, the journal is good, the size of the run is intolerable. Believe me, because madmen always tell the truth.

A revolutionary greeting,

Patria o muerte
Venceremos

Commander Ernesto Che Guevara

To Haydée Santamaría

June 12, 1964
"Year of the Economy"

Compañera Haydée Santamaría
Director, Casa de las Américas
Havana

Dear Haydée,

I instructed the Writer's Union to put that money at your disposal as a compromise measure, so as not to let this trifle become a struggle over principles that are much more far-reaching.

The only important thing is that I cannot accept a cent from a book that does nothing more than narrate incidents from the war. Do whatever you wish with the money.[3]

A revolutionary greeting,

Patria o muerte
Venceremos

Commander Ernesto Che Guevara

To Dr. Regino G. Boti

June 12, 1964
"Year of the Economy"

Dr. Regino G. Boti
Minister and Technical Secretary
Central Planning Board
City

Re: Request to increase the number of copies of the journal, *Confederación Médica Panamericana*

Dear Minister,

We shall carry out the Board's orders fully. Backed by my limited and scarcely edifying experience as a doctor, I must tell you that the journal is hogwash; and it is my opinion that hogwash does not fulfill political functions which, probably, you are attempting to do.

Let that remain for the other history — the large-scale one.

Yours respectfully,

Patria o muerte
Venceremos

Commander Ernesto Che Guevara

To Elías Entralgo

August 31, 1964
"Year of the Economy"

Elías Entralgo
President, University Extension
University of Havana

Dear *Compañero*,

I have received your kind invitation, which demonstrates to me — without your intending it, I am sure — the radical differences of opinion that separate us on the question of what is a leader.

I cannot undertake to give the lecture to which you invite me; if I were to do so, it would be on the basis of giving all my available time to working for the revolution. For me it is inconceivable that a monetary remuneration be offered to a leader of the government and the party for any work of any kind.

Among the many recompenses I have received, the most important is that of being considered part of the Cuban people; I could not evaluate this in *pesos* and *centavos*.

I am sorry to have to write to you in this way; I urge you to give it no other importance than that of an expression of hurt feelings caused by what I consider to be a gratuitous affront, none the less painful for being unintentional.

Patria o muerte
Venceremos

Commander Ernesto Che Guevara

To my children (1965)

Dear Hildita, Aleidita, Camilo, Celia, and Ernesto,

If you ever have to read this letter, it will be because I am no longer with you. You practically will not remember me, and the smaller ones will not remember at all.

Your father has been a man who acted on his beliefs and has certainly been loyal to his convictions.

Grow up as good revolutionaries. Study hard so that you can master technology, which allows us to master nature. Remember that the revolution is what is important, and each one of us, alone, is worth nothing.

Above all, always be capable of feeling deeply any injustice committed against anyone, anywhere in the world. This is the most beautiful quality in a revolutionary.

Until forever, my children. I still hope to see you. A great big kiss and a big hug from

Papá

To my parents (1965)

Dear old folks,

Once again I feel beneath my heels the ribs of Rocinante. Once more, I'm on the road with my shield on my arm. Almost 10 years ago, I wrote you another farewell letter. As I recall, I lamented not being a better soldier and a better doctor. The latter no longer interests me; I am not such a bad soldier.

Nothing has changed in essence, except that I am much more conscious. My Marxism has taken root and become purified. I believe in armed struggle as the only solution for those peoples who fight to free themselves, and I am consistent with my beliefs. Many will call me an adventurer, and that I am — only one of a different sort: one who risks his skin to prove his truths.

It is possible that this may be the end. I don't seek it, but it's within the logical realm of probabilities. If it should be so, I send you a final embrace. I have loved you very much, only I have not known how to express my affection. I am extremely rigid in my actions, and I think that sometimes you did not understand me. It was not easy to understand me. Nevertheless, please believe me today.

Now a willpower that I have polished with an artist's delight will sustain some shaky legs and some weary lungs. I will do it.

Give a thought once in a while to this little soldier of fortune of the 20th century.

A kiss to Celia, to Roberto, Juan Martín and Patotín, to Beatriz, to everybody. For you, a big hug from your obstinate and prodigal son,

Ernesto

To Hildita

The following letter was sent to Guevara's oldest daughter Hildita on her 10th birthday.

February 15, 1966

Dearest Hildita,

I am writing you now, although you'll receive this letter much later. But I want you to know I am thinking about you and I hope you're having a very happy birthday. You are almost a woman now, and I cannot write to you the way I do to the little ones, telling them silly things or little fibs.

You must know I am still far away and will be gone for quite some time, doing what I can to fight against our enemies. Not that it is a great thing, but I am doing something, and I think you will always be able to be proud of your father, as I am of you.

Remember, there are still many years of struggle ahead, and even when you are a woman, you will have to do your part in the struggle. Meanwhile, you have to prepare yourself, be very revolutionary — which at your age means to learn a lot, as much as possible, and always be ready to support just causes. Also, obey your mother and don't think you know it all too soon. That will come with time.

You should fight to be among the best in school. The best in every sense, and you already know what that means: study and revolutionary attitude. In other words: good conduct, seriousness, love for the revolution, comradeship, etc.

I was not that way at your age, but I lived in a different society, where man was an enemy of man. Now you have the privilege of living in another era and you must be worthy of it.

Don't forget to go by the house to keep an eye on the other kids and advise them to study and behave themselves. Especially Aleidita, who pays a lot of attention to you as her older sister.

All right, old lady. Again I hope you are very happy on your birthday. Give a hug to your mother and to Gina. I give you a great big strong one to last as long as we don't see each other.

Your Papá

To Fidel Castro (1965)

This letter was read by Fidel Castro on October 3, 1965, at a public ceremony presenting the Central Committee of the newly created Communist Party of Cuba. In the presence of Guevara's wife and children, Castro stated: "I am going to read a letter, handwritten and later typed, from compañero Ernesto Guevara, which is self-explanatory... It reads as follows: 'Havana' — It has no date, as the letter was to have been read at the most opportune moment, but was actually delivered on April 1 of this year." The reading of this letter was the first public explanation of the circumstances of Guevara's absence from Cuba.

Havana

Fidel,

At this moment I remember many things — when I met you in María Antonia's house, when you proposed I come along, all the tensions involved in the preparations. One day they came by and asked who should be notified in case of death, and the real possibility of that fact struck us all. Later we knew that it was true, that in a revolution one wins or dies (if it is a real one). Many comrades fell along the way to victory.

Today everything has a less dramatic tone, because we are more mature. But the event repeats itself. I feel that I have fulfilled the part of my duty that tied me to the Cuban Revolution in its territory, and I say goodbye to you, to the comrades, to your people, who now are mine.

I formally resign my positions in the leadership of the Party, my post as minister, my rank of commander, and my Cuban citizenship. Nothing legal binds me to Cuba. The only ties are of another nature — those that cannot be broken as can appointments to a post.

Recalling my past life, I believe I have worked with sufficient honesty and dedication to consolidate the revolutionary triumph. My only serious failing was not having had more confidence in you from the first moments in the Sierra Maestra, and not having understood quickly enough your qualities as a leader and a revolutionary.

I have lived magnificent days, and at your side I felt the pride of belonging to our people in the brilliant yet sad days of the Caribbean crisis. Seldom has a statesman been more brilliant than you in those days. I am also proud of having followed you without hesitation, identified with your way of thinking and of seeing and appraising dangers and principles.

Other nations of the world call for my modest efforts. I can do that which is denied you because of your responsibility at the head of Cuba, and the time has come for us to part.

I want it known that I do so with a mixture of joy and sorrow. I leave here the purest of my hopes as a builder and the dearest of my loved ones. And I leave a people who received me as a son. That wounds a part of my spirit. I carry to new battlefronts the faith that you taught me, the revolutionary spirit of my people, the feeling of fulfilling the most sacred of duties: to fight against imperialism wherever it may be. This comforts and heals the deepest wounds.

I state once more that I free Cuba from any responsibility, except that which stems from its example. If my final hour finds me under other skies, my last thought will be of this people and especially of you. I am thankful for your teaching, your example, and I will try to be faithful up to the final consequences of my acts.

I have always been identified with the foreign policy of our revolution, and I continue to be. Wherever I am, I will feel the responsibility of being a Cuban revolutionary, and I shall behave as such. I am not ashamed that I leave nothing material to my children and my wife; I am happy it is that way. I ask nothing for them, as the state will provide them with enough to live on and have an education.

I would have a lot of things to say to you and to our people, but I feel they are unnecessary. Words cannot express what I would want them to, and I don't think it's worthwhile to keep scribbling pages.

> Hasta la victoria siempre! Patria o muerte!
> I embrace you with all my revolutionary fervor.

> Che

Letter to My Children

Somewhere in Bolivia, 1966

My dearest Aliusha, Camilo, Celita and Tatico,

I write to you from far away and in great haste, which means I can't tell you about my latest adventures. It's a pity, because I've met some very interesting friends through Pepe the Crocodile.[4] Another time…

Right now I want to tell you that I love you all very much and I remember you always, along with mama, although the younger ones I almost only know through photos, as they were very tiny when I left. In a minute I'm going to get a photo taken so that you know how I look these days — a little bit older and uglier.

This letter should arrive about the time Aliusha has her sixth birthday, so may it serve to congratulate her and hope that she has a very happy birthday.

Aliusha, you should study hard and help your mother in everything you can. Remember, you are the oldest.

Camilo, you should swear less as in school you shouldn't speak like that and you have to learn what is appropriate. Celita, help your grandmother around the house as much as you can and continue being as sweet as when we said goodbye — do you remember? How could you not. Tatico, you should grow and become a man so that later we'll see what you make of yourself. If imperialism still exists, we'll set out to fight it. If it is finished, you, Camilo and I will take a vacation on the moon.

Give a kiss from me to your grandparents, to Miriam and her baby, to Estela and Carmita, and here's an elephant-sized kiss from…

Papa

Note in the margin:
To Hildita [Che's oldest daughter], another elephant-sized kiss and tell her I'll write soon, but now I don't have time.

Notes to Part 1

1. In the midst of the 1933 revolutionary upsurge against Cuban dictator Gerardo Machado, Sumner Welles was sent as ambassador by Washington to help install a pro-U.S. regime to replace Machado and thereby forestall a revolutionary triumph.

    The Platt Amendment of 1901 was imposed by the U.S. Congress on the Cuban constitution during the U.S. military occupation. It granted Washington the right to intervene in Cuban affairs at any time and gave it the right to establish military bases on Cuban soil. It was abrogated in 1934.

    Narciso López, a former Spanish officer, organized an expedition that landed in Cuba in 1850 with the backing of the United States. López was taken prisoner by Spanish forces and executed. He is viewed as a hero of Cuba's fight for independence from Spain.

2. On July 26, 1953, Fidel Castro led an attack on the Moncada army garrison in Santiago de Cuba that marked the beginning of the revolutionary armed struggle against the Batista regime. After the attack's failure, Batista's forces massacred more than 50 of the captured revolutionaries. Castro and others were taken prisoner, tried, and sentenced to prison. They were released in May 1955 after a public defense campaign forced Batista's regime to issue an amnesty.

3. Guevara had been separated from the main column for about a month. Following the Rebel Army victory at El Uvero on May 27–28, 1957, Guevara was assigned to stay back, together with a small troop, and care for the wounded. The El Uvero victory marked a decisive turning point in the war against the Batista dictatorship. In this chapter, he has just rejoined the main troop.

4. The Miami Pact was endorsed on November 30, 1957, by a number of opposition forces, including Felipe Pazos, who signed the agreement in the name of the July 26 Movement without authorization. The document was designed to ensure that a pro-U.S. regime would emerge following Batista's downfall. Castro denounced the agreement in an open letter and publicly disassociated the July 26 Movement from it. The Caracas Pact, broadcast over Radio Rebelde on July 20, 1958, was signed by many of the same forces that had backed the Miami Pact, plus Fidel Castro on behalf of the July 26 Movement and Rebel Army. This document opposed any military coup and called for an end to U.S. support for Batista, reflecting the shift in the relationship of forces within the opposition since the time of the Miami Pact.

5. The July 26 Movement had two wings at the time. These became known as the *Sierra* (mountain) and the *Llano*. Although *Llano* means "plain," it referred to the urban areas, where the July 26 Movement maintained an underground

organization. Throughout this period there was an ongoing debate between the two groupings on fundamental questions of strategy.

6. The "M-26" was an improvised mortar devised by the Rebel Army. It consisted of tin cans (often empty condensed milk cans) filled with explosives and fired from a makeshift spear gun or a rifle, specially rigged for the purpose. The name M-26 was derived from the name of the July 26 Movement, which was often abbreviated "M-26-7."

7. Law No. 3 of the Sierra Maestra was proclaimed by the Rebel Army on October 10, 1958. It granted tenant farmers, squatters and sharecroppers the ownership of the land they worked, providing its total area was less than two *caballerías* (67 acres). The law was a precursor to the even more sweeping agrarian reform proclaimed by the revolutionary government on May 17, 1959.

Notes to Part 2

1. Mexico nationalized British- and U.S.-owned oil companies in 1938.

2. This is a reference to the "Associated Free State of Puerto Rico," a U.S. possession.

3. Egypt was attacked in October-November 1956 by British, French, and Israeli troops following its nationalization of the Suez Canal. In July 1958, Washington landed 15,000 marines in Lebanon to bolster the pro-U.S. regime there in the face of popular opposition.

4. On August 12, 1933, dictator Gerardo Machado was deposed in a massive popular revolt. On February 24, 1895, the final Cuban independence war against Spain began. October 10, 1868, was the beginning of the first independence war.

5. The 1809 uprising in Upper Peru (now Bolivia), led by Pedro Domingo Murillo, was one of the first revolts against Spanish rule. It was defeated and Murillo was hanged. In 1810 an autonomous government was established in Buenos Aires by the Cabildo Abierto (Open Council).

6. Valeriano Weyler y Nicolau was commander in chief of Spanish forces in Cuba during the 1895-98 independence war. He gained notoriety for torturing and murdering captured independence fighters.

7. The term *mambí* refers to Cuba's fighters in the independence wars against Spain.

8. The revolutionary upsurge of 1933-35, although successful in ousting dictator Gerardo Machado, was not able to end Cuba's status as a U.S. semicolony. The person who emerged as Cuba's strongman following these events was Fulgencio Batista.

9. The Tenth Congress of the Confederation of Cuban Workers (CTC) in November 1959 voted to encourage workers to donate four percent of their wages to a fund to promote Cuba's industrialization.

10. The agrarian reform law of May 17, 1959, set a limit of 30 *caballerías*

(approximately 1,000 acres) on individual landholdings. Implementation of the law resulted in the confiscation of the vast estates in Cuba — many of them owned by U.S. companies. These lands passed into the hands of the new government. The law also granted sharecroppers, tenant farmers and squatters a deed to the land they tilled. Another provision of the law established the National Institute of Agrarian Reform (INRA).

11. Nicolás Guillén was a leading member of the Communist Party, then known as the Popular Socialist Party.

12. V.I. Lenin, "What Is To Be Done," in Lenin, Collected Works (Moscow: Progress Publishers, 1973), vol. 5, 369.

13. "History Will Absolve Me" was Fidel Castro's reconstruction of his 1953 courtroom speech at the trial following the Moncada attack. It subsequently became the program of the July 26 Movement.

14. In November 1959 the revolutionary government approved a law authorizing the Ministry of Labor to "intervene" in an enterprise, assuming control of its management without changing its ownership. The private owners of "intervened" enterprises were still entitled to receive profits. In practice, however, most owners of these companies left the country. This procedure continued to be used by the revolutionary government until late 1960, when it nationalized the major branches of the economy.

15. At the time this article was written, the United Party of the Socialist Revolution (PURS) was in the process of being formed. In March 1962, its predecessor, the Integrated Revolutionary Organizations (ORI) — formed through the fusion of the July 26 Movement, the Popular Socialist Party and the Revolutionary Directorate — had begun to undergo a process of reorganization leading, by the latter half of 1963, to the consolidation of the new party. At the heart of this reorganization were assemblies held in thousands of workplaces throughout Cuba. Each meeting discussed and selected who from that workplace should be considered an exemplary worker. Those selected were in turn considered for party membership.

16. Located in the Sierra Maestra, Turquino is the highest mountain in Cuba.

17. On April 17, 1961, 1,500 Cuban-born mercenaries invaded Cuba at the Bay of Pigs on the southern coast in Las Villas Province. The action, organized directly by Washington, aimed to establish a "provisional government" to appeal for direct U.S. intervention. The invaders were defeated within 72 hours by the militia and the Revolutionary Armed Forces. On April 19, the last invaders surrendered at Playa Girón (Girón Beach), which has come to be the name Cubans use to designate the battle.

18. From late 1960 through 1961, the revolutionary government undertook a literacy campaign to teach one million Cubans to read and write. Central to this effort was the mobilization of 100,000 young people to go to the countryside, where they lived with peasants whom they were teaching. As a result of this drive, Cuba virtually eliminated illiteracy.

19. Karl Marx, "Economic and Philosophic Manuscripts of 1844," in Karl Marx and Frederick Engels, Collected Works, vol. 3, 296-97. In the last phrase, the

English edition of the *Collected Works* reads "knows itself to be." The word "conscious" has been substituted in accordance with the version Guevara quoted in Spanish and which he elaborates on subsequently.

20. Marx, "Critique of the Gotha Program," in Marx and Engels, *Selected Works* (Moscow: Progress Publishers, 1977), 17.
21. V.I. Lenin, "On the Slogan for a United States of Europe," in Lenin, *Collected Works,* vol. 21, 342-43.
22. Joseph Stalin, "The Foundations of Leninism," in Stalin, *Works* (Moscow: Foreign Languages Publishing House, 1953), vol. 6, 75-76.
23. Lenin, "Five Years of the Russian Revolution and the Prospects of the World Revolution," in Lenin, *Collected Works,* vol. 33, 419-22.
24. Oscar Lange (1904-1965) was a Polish economist and government official of the Polish People's Republic. Documents from the Soviet Union and the Eastern European countries were frequently referred to during the 1963-64 discussion in Cuba. Among the others cited in this article by Guevara are the writings of Soviet economist E.G. Liberman (1897-1983), whose views advocating greater financial self-management of industrial enterprises influenced the new management system adopted by the government of the Soviet Union in 1965.
25. Lenin, "Our Revolution," in Lenin, *Collected Works,* vol. 33, 477-79.
26. Marx, "Critique of the Gotha Program," in Marx and Engels, *Selected Works,* vol. 3, 16-17.
27. *The Manual of Political Economy* was issued by the Institute of Economics of the Academy of Sciences of the USSR.
28. Karl Marx, *Capital,* (New York: Vintage Books, 1977), vol. 1, 899.
29. This letter was sent to Carlos Quijano, director of the Uruguayan weekly publication, *Marcha.* It was published on March 12, 1965, under the title, "From Algiers, for *Marcha.* The Cuban Revolution Today." In the original edition the following editor's note was added: "Che Guevara sent this letter to *Marcha* from Algiers. This document is of the utmost importance, especially in order to understand the aims and goals of the Cuban Revolution as seen by one of the main actors in that process. The thesis presented is intended to provoke debate and, at the same time, give a new perspective on some of the foundations of current socialist thought." On November 5, 1965, the letter was republished and presented as "Exclusive: A Special Note from Che Guevara." A memo explained that *Marcha's* readers in Argentina had not been able to read the original publication, because the week that it was first published the magazine was banned in Buenos Aires. Subheadings are based on those used in the original Cuban edition. They have been added by the publisher.
30. When Che sent the letter to Quijano, he had been touring Africa since December 1964. During this African tour, Che held many meetings with African revolutionary leaders.
31. Che's concept of the man or woman of the future, as first evident in the consciousness of the combatants in Cuba's revolutionary war, was explored by

his article, "Social Ideals of the Rebel Army" (1959). These ideas were further developed in a speech, "The Revolutionary Doctor" (1960), where he described how Cuba was creating "a new type of individual" as a result of the revolution, because "there is nothing that can educate a person... like living through a revolution." These first ideas were deepened as part of Che's concept of the individual as a direct and conscious actor in the process of constructing socialism. This article presents a synthesis of his ideas on this question.

32. These two events in the early years of the revolution seriously tested the valor of the Cuban people in the face of disaster: first, the October [Missile] Crisis of 1962, during which the U.S. actions aimed at overthrowing the Cuban Revolution brought the world to the brink of crisis; and second, Hurricane Flora, which battered the eastern region of Cuba on October 4, 1963, resulting in over a thousand deaths. Nevertheless, Che believed that if, in fact, a new society was to be created, the masses needed to apply the same kind of consciousness in everyday activities as they had heroically displayed in such special circumstances.

33. The revolutionary victory of January 1, 1959, meant that for the first time in their history, the Cuban people attained a genuine level of popular participation in power. At first, the government was made up of figures from traditional political parties that had in one way or another supported the revolution. As measures were adopted that affected the ruling classes, some dissent emerged that became the germ of the future counterrevolution, which was subsequently supported and funded by the U.S. Government. In this early confrontation, President Manuel Urrutia was forced to resign due to public pressure when it became clear that he was presenting obstacles to measures that would benefit the population as a whole. It was at this time, with the full backing of the Cuban people, that Fidel assumed government leadership and became Prime Minister.

34. The Agrarian Reform Law of May 17, 1959, after only four months of taking power, was seen as the decisive step in fulfilling the revolutionary program proposed at Moncada in 1953. Che participated in the drafting of this new law along with other comrades proposed by the revolutionary leadership.

35. On April 17, 1961, mercenary troops that were trained and financed by the U.S. Government, along with exile counterrevolutionary groups, invaded Cuba at the Bay of Pigs. This was part of the U.S. plan to destabilize and ultimately overthrow the revolution. In these circumstances, the Cuban masses, who felt that they were the participants in a genuine process of social transformation, showed they were ready to defend the gains of the revolution and were able to defeat any attempt to destroy it.

36. The manifestations of sectarianism, which emerged in Cuba in the 1960s, forced the revolutionary leadership to take measures that would impede any tendency toward separating the government from the masses. As part of that leadership, Che participated in this process and analyzed on many occasions the grave consequences of such a separation. He expressed these

views, for example, in the prolog he wrote for the book, *The Marxist-Leninist Party*, published in 1963, where he explained: "Mistakes were made in the leadership; the party lost those essential qualities that linked them with the masses, the exercise of democratic centralism and the spirit of sacrifice... the function of the driving force of ideology is lost... [F]ortunately the old bases for this type of sectarianism have been destroyed."

37. The debate over the role of the law of value within the construction of socialism formed part of Che's outline of an economic framework and his initial ideas for the Budgetary Finance System. Due to his revolutionary humanist perspective, Che rejected any notion that included using capitalist tools or fetishes. These ideas were widely discussed in his article, "On the Concept of Value," published in the magazine *Our Industry* in October 1963. Here we see the beginning of the economic debate that Che initiated in those years and which had international significance. This polemic was conducted in his typically rigorous style. Outlining the guidelines to be followed, Che wrote: "We want to make it clear that the debate we have initiated can be invaluable for our development only if we are capable of conducting it with a strictly scientific approach and with the greatest equanimity."

38. Nelson Rockefeller, who became one of the wealthiest people in the United States, acquired his capital by a "stroke of luck," so the story goes, when his family discovered oil. Rockefeller's economic power brought him great political influence for many years — especially with regard to Latin America policy — irrespective of who was in the White House.

39. For Che, socialism could not exist if economics was not combined with social and political consciousness. Without an awareness of rights and duties, it would be impossible to construct a new society. This attitude would be the mechanism of socialist transition and the essential form of expressing this would be through consciousness. In this work, Che analyzed the decisive role of consciousness as opposed to the distortions produced by "real existing socialism," based on the separation of the material base of society from its superstructure. Unfortunately, historical events proved Che right, when a moral and political crisis brought about the collapse of the socialist system. Among Che's writings on this question are: "Collective Discussion: Decisions and Sole Responsibilities" (1961), "On the Construction of the Party" (1963), "Awarding Certificates for Communist Work" (1964) and "A New Attitude to Work" (1964).

40. From early on Che studied the concept of underdevelopment as he tried to define the realities of the Third World. In his article, "Cuba: Historical Exception or Vanguard in the Anticolonial Struggle?" (1961), Che asked: "What is 'underdevelopment'? A dwarf with an enormous head and swollen chest is 'underdeveloped,' insofar as his fragile legs and short arms do not match the rest of his anatomy. He is the product of an abnormal and distorted development. That is what we are in reality — we, who are politely referred to as 'underdeveloped.' In truth, we are colonial, semicolonial or dependent countries, whose economies have been deformed by imperialism, which has

peculiarly developed only those branches of industry or agriculture needed to complement its own complex economy."

41. Che argued that the full liberation of humankind is reached when work becomes a social duty carried out with complete satisfaction and sustained by a value system that contributes to the realization of conscious action in performing tasks. This could only be achieved by systematic education, acquired by passing through various stages in which collective action is increased. Che recognized that this would be difficult and would take time. In his desire to speed up this process, however, he developed methods of mobilizing people, bringing together their collective and individual interests. Among the most significant of these instruments were moral and material incentives, while deepening consciousness as a way of developing toward socialism. See Che's speeches: "Homage to Emulation Prize Winners" (1962) and "A New Attitude to Work" (1964).

42. In the process of creating the new man and woman, Che considered that education should be directly related to production and that it should be conducted on a daily basis as the only way for individuals to better themselves. This should also be undertaken in a collective spirit, so that it contributes to the development of consciousness and has a greater impact. On a practical level he developed an education system within the Ministry of Industry that guaranteed a minimum level of training for workers, so that they could meet the new scientific and technolgical challenges Cuba faced.

43. Che discussed the role of the vanguard at key points. First, he defined the vanguard as a necessary element in leading the struggle and within the first line of defense. After the revolution, Che saw the vanguard as providing the real impulse for the masses to participate actively in the construction of a new society; at the head of the vanguard being the party. For this reason, Che occasionally insisted that the revolution was an accelerated process wherein those who play an active role have the right to become tired but not to become tired of being the vanguard.

44. In the period when Che was a leader, the Cuban Revolution had not yet reached a level of institutionalization so that old power structures had been completely eliminated. Nevertheless, Che argued that such institutionalization was important as a means of formalizing the integration of the masses and the vanguard. Years later in 1976, after the First Congress of the Cuban Communist Party, this task of institutionalization was codified, as an expression of the power structures created by the revolution.

45. It was Che's view that work played a crucial role in the construction of a new society. He analyzed the differences between work undertaken within a capitalist society and that which was free of alienation in a socialist society. He was aware of what was required so that workers would give their utmost and put duty and sacrifice ahead of individual gain. In a speech in 1961, Che referred to daily work as, "the most difficult, constant task that demands neither an instant violent sacrifice nor a single minute in a comrade's life in order to defend the revolution, but demands long hours ever day..."

46. In order to understand the construction of socialism as a process that would eliminate the persistent roots of the previous society, Che examined the inherited relations of production. He insisted that two fundamental changes must occur as the only way to put an end to the exploitation of one human being by another and to achieve a socialist society: an increase in production and a deepening of consciousness.

47. An article such as *Socialism and Man in Cuba* could not avoid a discussion of culture, given the enormous changes that were taking place in Cuban society and power structures at the time. It was not an easy task to reflect on the concept of socialist culture in a country that was just emerging from underdevelopment and was still characterized by a neocolonial culture, imposed by a dominant class. There was a constant struggle between the values of the past and the attempt to construct an all-encompassing culture based on solidarity between people and real social justice. The struggle was made more difficult, not only by the persistence of the past culture but also by dogmatic and authoritarian tendencies of so-called "socialist realism" in socialist countries. The antidote was to defend the best and most unique aspects of Cuban culture, avoiding excesses, and by trying to construct a culture that would express the feelings of the majority without vulgarity and schemas. This is the perspective that has been maintained in the development of revolutionary culture in Cuba, and neither neoliberalism nor globalization has been able to impede the genuine process of popular culture. This is the expression of a truly socialist society.

48. The role of the party and revolutionary youth in the construction of a new society was broadly analyzed by Che: "On the Construction of the Party," "The Marxist-Leninist Party," "To be a Young Communist" and "Youth and Revolution."

49. The harmony established between Fidel and Che from their first meeting in Mexico in 1955 represented a coming together of common ideals and a common approach to the liberation of Latin America and the building of a new society. Che referred to Fidel on many occasions in his writings and speeches, evaluating his qualities as a leader and statesman with sincere admiration and respect. Fidel reciprocated these feelings countless times. Their relationship should be investigated more deeply in order to gain a greater understanding of a transcendental historical era. For further reference see Che's *Episodes of a Revolutionary War, Guerrilla Warfare*, "Cuba: Historical Exception or Vanguard in the Anticolonial Struggle?", "Political Sovereignty and Economic Independence" and "The Marxist-Leninist Party."

50. The study of the different stages of the Cuban Revolution — from guerrilla warfare to the achievement of revolutionary power — is systematically reflected in all Che's writings and speeches. He always highlighted the significance of Cuba's example for the rest of the Third World, as a symbol of freedom and showing the fruits of the initial stages of constructing socialism in an underdeveloped country. Aside from those already cited, see: "Farewell to the International Brigades for Voluntary Work" (1960) and "The Cuban

Revolution's Influence in Latin America" (1962).

51. Che's conclusions here summarized some of the most important concepts permeating his works, which are beautifully synthesized in this volume. These ideas provide a complete spectrum that encompasses philosophy, ethics and politics, spanning a range of complex questions.

Notes to Part 3

1. José Enrique Rodó was an Uruguayan writer. His work *Ariel* was published in 1900.
2. Guevara is referring to the speech of C. Douglas Dillon.
3. In his address to the Punta del Este conference, Felipe Herrera, President of the Inter-American Development Bank, had referred to the International Monetary Commission meeting held in 1891 in Washington, D.C. That gathering included government representatives from the United States and Latin America.
4. The U.S. State Department White Paper on Cuba was written by Arthur Schlesinger, Jr., an adviser to President Kennedy. Schlesinger was part of the U.S. delegation to the Punta del Este conference. The White Paper was released on April 3, 1961, two weeks before the Bay of Pigs invasion.
5. On May 17, 1961, Fidel Castro had proposed that the U.S. exchange 500 tractors for the 1,179 mercenaries captured at the Bay of Pigs as indemnification for the damage Cuba suffered in that invasion. Ultimately Washington agreed to deliver $53 million in food, medicines, and medical equipment, in exchange for the prisoners.
6. Isla del Cisne (Swan Island) had been Honduran territory since 1861. In 1893, a U.S. sailor "discovered" the island and took possession of it on behalf of the United States. Using this as a legal basis, the U.S. government established a radio station on the island, which after 1961 was used by the Central Intelligence Agency to broadcast to Cuba. In 1974 Washington agreed to recognize Honduran sovereignty over the island, although the U.S. maintained its radio station.
7. Cuba was expelled from the Organization of American States (OAS) in January 1962.
8. A UN Conference on Trade and Employment was held in Havana from November 1947 to March 1948. It adopted the Havana Charter, which was to be the charter of a new international body to be known as the International Trade Organization. This organization never came into being, however, largely as the result of the U.S. government's refusal to become part of it. Instead, many of its anticipated functions were assumed by the General Agreement on Tariffs and Trade (GATT), which had been established in October 1947 at a conference in Geneva.
9. At the time, China's UN seat was occupied by the government of Taiwan. In

1971, the Taiwan regime was expelled and the People's Republic of China assumed the seat.

10. This is a reference to Namibia (South-West Africa), which had been a South African colony since 1920, under the authorization of the League of Nations. In 1946 the United Nations called for South Africa to submit a new trusteeship agreement. This request was rejected by South Africa, which maintained that the UN had no right to challenge its occupation of Namibia. In 1966 the UN General Assembly voted to strip South Africa of its mandate.

11. Shortly after the Congo obtained its independence in June 1960, an uprising broke out in Katanga Province (today Shaba), led by Moise Tshombe. The government of Congolese Prime Minister Patrice Lumumba appealed to the United Nations for help, and UN troops were sent as a peacekeeping force. The UN forces stood aside while Lumumba's government was toppled in December 1960. Lumumba was taken prisoner by Congolese rightists and murdered.

12. The Inter-American Economic and Social Council, a commission of the Organization of American States, sponsored a meeting in February 1964 in Alta Gracia, Argentina. This gathering issued a charter constituting the Special Committee for Latin American Coordination, an organization designed to facilitate trade negotiations.

13. Cuban President Osvaldo Dorticós attended the October 1964 Nonaligned summit conference in Cairo.

14. In January 1964 U.S. forces opened fire on Panamanian students demonstrating in the U.S.-occupied Canal Zone, sparking several days of street fighting. More than 20 Panamanians were killed and 300 were wounded.

15. Cheddi Jagan had become Prime Minister of British Guiana after the People's Progressive Party won the 1953 elections; shortly thereafter Britain suspended the constitution. Jagan was reelected in 1957 and 1961. In 1964 he was defeated in an election by Forbes Burnham. In 1966 Guiana won its independence.

16. In mid-1964, a revolt broke out in the Congo led by followers of murdered Prime Minister Patrice Lumumba. In an effort to crush the uprising, during November U.S. planes ferried Belgian troops and mercenaries to rebel-held territory. These forces carried out a massacre of thousands of Congolese.

17. An OAS conference in July 1964 called on all its members to break diplomatic relations and suspend trade with Cuba. The meeting charged Cuba with following a "policy of aggression" for allegedly smuggling arms to Venezuelan guerrillas. The Rio Treaty, invoked as justification for this action, was the OAS Inter-American Treaty of Reciprocal Assistance, signed September 2, 1947, in Rio de Janeiro. It declared that aggression against any treaty member state would be considered an attack on all of them.

18. Dominican dictator Rafael Trujillo was assassinated on May 30, 1961. In November 1961, in the context of a growing rebellion by the Dominican people triggered by the return to Santo Domingo of two of Trujillo's brothers, Washington sent warships off the Dominican coast. In April 1948 the assassination of Colombian Liberal Party leader Jorge E. Gaitán sparked a rebellion

that became known as the *Bogotazo*.

19. Che Guevara delivered this speech at the Second Economic Seminar of Afro-Asian Solidarity, February 24, 1965. He had been touring Africa since December, after addressing the United Nations General Assembly on December 11, 1964. At this crucial time Che was preparing for his involvement in the liberation movement in the Congo, which began in April 1965. This edition of the speech incorporates for the first time corrections made by Che Guevara to the original published version of the Algiers speech. The corrections were made available from the personal archive of Che Guevara held at the Che Guevara Studies Center, Havana.

20. Che's participation in the Algiers conference reflects the relationship of Cuba to the Third World. In 1959, following the triumph of the revolution, from June to September, Che embarked on a tour of the countries involved in the Bandung Pact. The Bandung Pact was the precursor to what later became the Movement of Nonaligned Nations. At the First Seminar on Planning in Algeria on July 16, 1963, Che had outlined the experiences of the Cuban Revolution, explaining that he had accepted the invitation to attend "only in order to offer a little history of our economic development, of our mistakes and successes, which might prove useful to you some time in the near future..."

21. In this speech Che defined very precisely his revolutionary thesis for the Third World and the integration of the struggle for national liberation with socialist ideas. Che's call in Algeria on the socialist countries to give unconditional and radical support to the Third World provoked much debate. Nevertheless, history would prove him correct.

22. This definition of unequal exchange was part of Che's profound appeal made in Geneva on March 25, 1964, at the UN World Conference on Economics and Development in the Third World: "It is our duty to... draw to the attention of those present that while the status quo is maintained and justice is determined by powerful interests... it will be difficult to eliminate the prevailing tensions that endanger humankind."

23. For Che, socialism inherently meant overcoming exploitation as an essential step toward a just and humane society. Che was outspoken on this issue in debates and was often misunderstood, as was his emphasis on the need for international unity in the struggle for socialism. Che's idea was that the international socialist forces would contribute to the economic and social development of the peoples that liberated themselves.

24. Che's direct participation from 1959 to 1965 in the construction of a technological and material basis for Cuban society is strongly linked to his idea of creating the new man and woman. This is a question that he constantly returned to, considering it one of the two main pillars on which a new society would be constructed. His strategy was not only to solve immediate problems but to put in place certain structures that would secure Cuba's future scientific and technological development. He was able to advance this strategy during his time as head of the Ministry of Industry. For further

reading on this topic, see his speeches: "May the Universities be Filled with Negroes, Mulattos, Workers and Peasants" (1960) and "Youth and Revolution" (1964).

25. In his efforts to understand fully the tasks in the transition to a socialist economy, Che came to see the vital role of economic planning, especially in the construction of a socialist economy in an underdeveloped country that retained elements of capitalism. Planning is necessary because it represents the first human attempt to control economic forces and characterizes this transitional period. He warned also of the trend within socialism to reform the economic system by strengthening the market, material interests and the law of value. To counter this trend, Che advocated centralized, antibureaucratic planning that enriched consciousness. His idea was to use conscious and organized action as the fundamental driving force of planning. For further reading see his article "The Significance of Socialist Planning" (1964).

26. In January 1966, the Tricontinental Conference of Solidarity with the People of Asia, Africa and Latin America took place in Cuba; it was agreed that an organization with a permanent Executive Secretariat would be created. At the time of the conference, Che Guevara was in Tanzania having left the Congo. The Cuban leader Manual Piñeiro, in charge of Cuba's relationship with revolutionaries in the Third World at the time, explained in 1997 that the "Message" was written by Che in a training camp in Pinar del Río in Cuba before setting out for Bolivia in 1966. Che's "Message" was published for the first time on April 16, 1967, in a special supplement which later became *Tricontinental* magazine. It was published under the title "Create Two, Three, Many Vietnams, That is the Slogan."

27. Che's first analyses of the wars in Korea and Vietnam were written in 1954 during his stay in Guatemala, which was also invaded by imperialist forces. In very different circumstances, after the triumph of the Cuban Revolution, he again discussed events in Asia. See, for example, "Solidarity with South Vietnam" (1963), the prolog of the book *War of the People, People's Army* (1964) and Che's UN speech (1964).

28. South Vietnamese dictator Ngo Dinh Diem was assassinated on November 1, 1963, at the instigation of Washington, which was dissatisfied at the inability of his regime to counter the military and political successes of the Vietnamese National Liberation Front.

29. For a more detailed understanding of these ideas, see Che's speech at the UN and his Algerian speech in this volume, where he proclaimed: "The ominous attack of U.S. imperialism on Vietnam or in the Congo must be met by a show of unity, gathering all our defenses to give our sister countries our unconditional solidarity."

30. On many occasions, Che referred to the differences that beset the international revolutionary movement — particularly the conflict between China and the Soviet Union — and the need to resolve those differences within the movement itself, in order to avoid damage on a wider scale. Following this line of thought, Che's theses on the Third World tried to avoid dogma and

schemas. The works in this volume are an expression of Che's position on this issue.

31. President Lyndon B. Johnson was Vice-President when John F. Kennedy was assassinated on November 22, 1963. Johnson escalated U.S. involvement in the Vietnam War and increased the level of open aggression against Cuba, providing unconditional support for counterrevolutionary organizations.

32. Che's ideas about tactics and strategy reflect a dialectical development in terms of content and objectives, tracing his experience in the Cuban revolutionary struggle up to the point where he joined the struggles in Africa and Latin America. The following works are key references: *Guerrilla Warfare*, "Guerrilla Warfare: A Method," *Episodes of the Revolutionary War*, "Tactics and Strategy of Latin American Revolution" and *Episodes of the Revolutionary War in the Congo*.

33. The involvement of U.S. capital in Latin America was a major concern for Che throughout his life and was reflected in his writings. In many of his writings and reflections Che made the connection between economics and politics and the way they function in each Latin American country. A very detailed analysis of this is found in his article "Tactics and Strategies..."

34. In April 1965 tens of thousands of U.S. troops invaded the Dominican Republic to crush a popular uprising.

35. Following his experience in the Congo, Che wrote *Episodes of the Revolutionary War in the Congo*, in which he detailed the most important lessons of that struggle. In the epilogue he outlined aspects of the economic, social and political realities of the region, as well as the possibilities for struggle. He described the national bourgeoisie and their dependent position within the power structures; and concluded they were a spent force, politically speaking.

36. Che's analysis about the essential realities of the Third World is fundamental to understanding his participation in the liberation struggles of different peoples. Che's "Message," written before he left for Bolivia, firmly established his political approach and the criteria on which his decision was based, echoing the views he expressed publicly at the United Nations. The content of Che's UN speech, especially his remarks about the crisis in the Middle East and Israel, is surprisingly relevant today.

37. Under President Nixon, the United States began blanket bombing in Cambodia in 1970.

38. On September 30, 1965, Indonesian General Suharto seized power and proceeded to carry out a massacre of members and supporters of the once-powerful Indonesian Communist Party. In the next several months, nearly one million people were killed.

39. The idea of internationalism on a global scale outlined by Che in his "Message" represents a synthesis of his thought and political praxis. It is this synthesis that brings us closer to the essential revolutionary, who supports the construction of a new order beginning with the taking of power through armed struggle. Che recognized that the world had reached a crossroads

and that the national bourgeoisie was incapable of standing up to imperialism. Under these circumstances, the only way to liberation would be through prolonged people's war.

Notes to Part 4

1. A saying in Spanish indicating severe poverty.
2. Pastorita's lottery was a national lottery run by a government agency headed by Pastora Núñez.
3. This letter relates to the publication of Guevara's *Episodes of the Revolutionary War*.
4. Pepe the Crocodile is a playful reference to Uncle Sam.

Glossary

Agramonte, Ignacio (1841–1873) — a leader of Cuba's first independence war; major general in Army of Liberation; killed in battle.

Albentosa, Emilio — participant in preparations for Moncada attack; *Granma* expeditionary.

Albizu Campos, Pedro (1891–1965) — leader of Puerto Rican Nationalist Party; imprisoned by U.S. Government for pro-independence activities, 1937–43, 1950–53, 1954–64; paralyzed by stroke in 1956; released from prison just prior to death.

Alegría de Pío — site of Batista army's attack on *Granma* expeditionaries in Oriente Province on December 5, 1956; majority of Rebels were killed or captured.

Almeida, Juan (1927–) — participant in Moncada attack and imprisoned subsequently; *Granma* expeditionary; became Rebel commander February 1958 and headed Third Front of Oriente; currently member of Central Committee and Political Bureau of Communist Party of Cuba; headed Commission to Perpetuate the Memory of Commander Ernesto Guevara.

Arbenz, Jacobo (1914–1971) — President of Guatemala, 1951–54; overthrown by CIA-backed coup in 1954.

Authentic Organization — part of bourgeois opposition to Batista regime formed by members of Authentic Party; after 1959 its leaders opposed revolution and left Cuba.

Authentic Party (Partido Revolucionario Cubano [Cuban Revolutionary Party]) — founded 1934; took name used by José Martí's party; formed government 1944–52; opposed Batista; opposed revolutionary government.

Barquín, Ramón — army officer under Batista; part of Montecristi Group; took command of army in attempted coup following Batista's flight on January 1, 1959.

Barrón, Arnaldo — headed Patriotic Club, a pro-July 26 Movement organization of Cuban exiles in New York.

Batista, Fulgencio (1901–1973) — army sergeant who seized control of Cuban Government in 1934; left office, 1944; on March 10, 1952, led coup overthrowing government of Carlos Prío; fled Cuba on January 1, 1959.

Bayo, Alberto (1892–1967) — fought against fascists in Spanish civil war (1936–39); provided military training in Mexico to future *Granma* expeditionaries; moved to Cuba after 1959 and worked for Revolutionary Armed Forces.

Bay of Pigs — location of U.S.-backed invasion on April 17, 1961; last invaders surrendered at Playa Girón [Girón Beach] on April 19.

Ben Bella, Ahmed (1918–) — leader of Algerian liberation forces; following independence served as prime minister (1962–63), and president (1963–65); deposed by coup in 1965.

Benítez, Reynaldo — participant in Moncada attack and imprisoned subsequently; *Granma* expeditionary.

Bolívar, Simón (1783–1830) — led armed rebellion that helped win independence from Spain for much of Latin America; known as the Liberator.

Borrego, Orlando — fighter in Rebel Army; leading cadre in Ministry of Industry following revolution.

Buch, Luis (d. 2002) — active in July 26 Movement in Santiago de Cuba and abroad; served in cabinet after revolution.

Cantillo, Eulogio — Cuban general under Batista; imprisoned by revolutionary government; later went to United States.

Cárdenas, Lázaro (1895–1970) — President of Mexico, 1934–40; carried out nationalization of petroleum industry.

Carrillo, Justo — founded Montecristi Group in 1956; fled to U.S. after revolution and helped organize counterrevolutionary activities.

Casillas, Joaquín (d. 1959) — army official notorious for brutality; tried and executed after revolution.

Castillo Armas, Carlos (1914–1957) — Guatemalan colonel; installed as dictator by U.S.-backed coup in 1954.

Castro, Fidel (1926–) — led attack on Moncada garrison; imprisoned subsequently; released in 1955 as result of public defense campaign; organized July 26 Movement; went to Mexico to organize Rebel forces; *Granma* expeditionary; commander in chief of Rebel Army; Cuban Prime Minister from February 1959 until December 1976, since then president of Council of State and Council of Ministers; first secretary of ORI, PURS and Communist Party.

Castro, Raúl (1931–) — participant in Moncada attack and imprisoned subsequently; *Granma* expeditionary; commander of Rebel Army's Second Front of Oriente; minister of Revolutionary Armed Forces, 1959–present; Vice-Premier, 1959–76; in 1976 became first vice-president of Council of State and Council of Ministers; second secretary of Communist Party since 1965; brother of Fidel Castro.

Central Planning Board (Junta Central de Planificación [JUCEPLAN]) — founded March 1960; state institution responsible for coordinating Cuban economy.

Céspedes, Carlos Manuel de (1819–1874) — central leader of Cuba's first independence war; on October 10, 1868, issued *Grito de Yara* [Cry of Yara], proclaiming Cuba's independence; killed by Spanish troops in ambush.

Chao, Rafael (1916–) — veteran of Spanish civil war (1936–39); *Granma* expeditionary and Rebel Army combatant.

Chibás, Eduardo (1907–1951) — founded Orthodox Party in 1947; elected senator in 1950; committed suicide in 1951 at conclusion of radio address as protest against government corruption.

Chibás, Raúl (1914–) — Orthodox Party leader; brother of Eduardo Chibás; signed Sierra Manifesto in 1957; subsequently treasurer of July 26 Movement Committee in Exile; fled to U.S. after revolution.

Chomón, Faure (1929–) — a founding leader of Revolutionary Directorate; participated in March 13, 1957, attack on Presidential Palace; Directorate's general secretary from 1957; led guerrilla column in Escambray Mountains; member of ORI National Directorate; member of Communist Party Central Committee since its founding.

Cienfuegos, Camilo (1932–1959) — *Granma* expeditionary; became Rebel commander and headed Antonio Maceo Column No. 2, leading march westward from Sierra Maestra to Las Villas Province; became Rebel Army chief of staff in January 1959; plane lost at sea on October 28, 1959.

Committees for the Defense of the Revolution (CDRs) — formed September 1960 as network of neighborhood committees organized for vigilance against counterrevolutionary activities; have also assumed wide variety of functions including public health campaigns, neighborhood repairs, education activities and mobilization for voluntary work.

Communist Party of Cuba — founded in 1965; predecessors were Integrated Revolutionary Organizations and United Party of the Socialist Revolution.

Crespo, Luis (1923–2002) — participant in Moncada attack; *Granma* expeditionary; became commander in Rebel Army.

CTC — founded in 1939 as Confederación de Trabajadores de Cuba [Confederation of Cuban Workers] with Lázaro Peña as general secretary; in 1947 right-wing forces led by Eusebio Mujal gained dominance; supported Batista dictatorship after 1952; reorganized after revolution and known as CTC-Revolutionary for several years; in 1961 changed name to Central de Trabajadores de Cuba [Central Organization of Cuban Trade Unions].

Cuba Socialista [Socialist Cuba] — monthly journal launched October 1961; editorial board composed of Fidel Castro, Osvaldo Dorticós, Blas Roca, Carlos Rafael Rodríguez, and Fabio Grobart; ceased publication in 1967; resumed in 1981 as quarterly journal of Communist Party Central Committee.

Cubela, Rolando (1933–) — a leader of Revolutionary Directorate's guerrilla column in Escambray Mountains; imprisoned in 1966 for involvement in CIA conspiracy to assassinate Fidel Castro; went to United States after release.

del Valle, Sergio (1927–) — joined guerrillas in Sierra Maestra in 1957 as combatant and physician, becoming captain in Guevara's column; long-time member of Communist Party Central Committee.

Diario de la Marina — right-wing Cuban daily; closed by revolutionary government May 13, 1960.

Díaz, Julio (1929–1957) — participant in Moncada attack and *Granma* expedition; killed May 28, 1957.

Díaz González, Pablo — *Granma* expeditionary; escaped capture after battle of Alegría de Pío and went to United States; headed Cuban Exiles' Democratic Workers Committee in New York; returned to Cuba after 1959.

Dorticós, Osvaldo (1919–1983) — regional coordinator of July 26 Movement in Cienfuegos; expelled by Batista from Cuba in 1958; became president of Cuba in July 1959, holding that position until 1976; member of Communist Party Central Committee and Political Bureau at time of death.

Dubois, Jules (1910–1966) — former U.S. Army colonel attached to State Department; Havana correspondent for *Chicago Tribune* during revolutionary war.

Dulles, John Foster (1888–1959) — partner in law firm representing United Fruit Co.; U.S. secretary of state, 1953–59.

Echeverría, José Antonio (1932–1957) — elected president of Federation of University Students in 1954; central leader of Revolutionary Directorate; killed by government forces in events surrounding March 13, 1957, attack on Presidential Palace.

El Uvero — site of May 27–28, 1957, battle in Oriente Province during revolutionary war; Rebel Army overran well-fortified army outpost.

Escalante, Aníbal (1909–1977) — longtime leader of PSP and editor of *Hoy;* ORI organizational secretary until March 1962.

Espín, Vilma (1930–) — helped organize November 1956 Santiago de Cuba uprising; leader of July 26 Movement in Oriente Province and member of its National Directorate; fighter in Rebel Army; president, Federation of Cuban Women since 1960 founding; currently member of Communist Party Central Committee and Political Bureau.

Fajardo, Manuel — one of first peasants to join Rebel Army; became commander; later served on Communist Party Central Committee.

Fajardo, Piti (1930–1960) — joined Rebel Army in 1958 as doctor and combatant; killed in combat against counterrevolutionary forces in Escambray Mountains.

Fernández, Marcelo (1932–) — national coordinator of July 26 Movement from 1958 until early 1960; later head of National Bank.

FONU. See United National Workers Front.

Franqui, Carlos (1921–) — active in July 26 Movement in Havana; worked on Radio Rebelde in Sierra Maestra in 1958; editor of *Revolución* until 1963; left Cuba in 1968 as opponent of revolution.

García, Calixto (1839–1898) — a central leader of Cuba's wars for independence against Spain; lieutenant general in Army of Liberation.

García, Calixto (1931–) — participated in July 26, 1953, attack on Bayamo garrison; *Granma* expeditionary; Rebel Army commander; served as member of Communist Party Central Committee for many years.

Gómez, Juan Gualberto (1854–1930) — Cuban fighter during independence war; leading member of Cuban Revolutionary Party formed by José Martí.

Gómez, Máximo (1836–1905) — native of Santo Domingo; leader of Cuban revolutionary armies during 1868–78 and 1895–98 independence wars; became commander in chief of Cuban independence forces in 1870.

Gómez Ochoa, Delio — Rebel Army commander; became head of July 26 Movement in Havana after April 1958 general strike attempt.

Granma — yacht used by revolutionaries to travel from Mexico to Cuba, November–December 1956; taken as name of daily newspaper of Communist Party of Cuba in 1965.

Guillén, Nicolás — noted Cuban poet; member of PSP National Committee; lived in exile during revolutionary war; returned early 1959; became president of Union of Writers and Artists in 1961; winner of numerous national and international prizes for artistic work; member of Communist Party Central Committee at time of death.

Guiteras, Antonio (1906–1935) — student leader in 1920s and 1930s; interior minister in government brought to power by 1933 revolutionary upsurge; ousted by Batista in 1934; later assassinated.

Gutiérrez Menoyo, Eloy — leader of "Second National Front of Escambray" guerrilla group; refused to collaborate with Rebel Army; after revolution left Cuba; returned with counterrevolutionary band; captured and imprisoned in January 1965; released in 1987 and went to Spain.

Hernández, Melba (1922–) — lawyer; participant in Moncada attack, imprisoned; member of National Directorate of July 26 Movement and leader of underground movement; joined Rebel Army in Sierra Maestra; founder and president of Committee in Solidarity with Vietnam and the Peoples of Indochina; member of Central Committee of Communist Party of Cuba.

Hoy [Today] — founded in 1938; newspaper of PSP; following 1961 fusion was published by ORI; published until founding of *Granma* in October 1965.

Iglesias, Joel (1941–) — member of Guevara's guerrilla column; became commander; first president of Association of Young Rebels in 1960.

INRA. See National Institute of Agrarian Reform.

Integrated Revolutionary Organizations (Organizaciones Revolucionarios Integrados [ORI]) — formed in 1961 from fusion of July 26 Movement, PSP and Revolutionary Directorate; became United Party of the Socialist Revolution (PURS) in 1963 and Communist Party of Cuba in 1965.

July 26 Movement (Movimiento 26 de Julio [M-26-7]) — founded in 1955 by veterans of Moncada attack, youth activists from left wing of Orthodox Party, and others; broke officially with Orthodox Party in March 1956; during revolutionary war was composed of Rebel Army in mountains (*Sierra*) and urban underground network (*Llano*); published newspaper *Revolución;* fused in 1961 with PSP and Revolutionary Directorate to found ORI and later Communist Party of Cuba.

Lamothe, Humberto (1919–1956) — *Granma* expeditionary; killed at Alegría de Pío.

La Plata — site in Oriente Province of first Rebel Army victory, January 17, 1957.

Larrazábal, Wolfgang (1911–) — headed government of Venezuela, January–November 1958.

Las Coloradas — beach in southern Oriente Province where *Granma* landed, December 2, 1956.

Llano. See July 26 Movement.

Llerena, Mario (1913–) — chairman and public relations director of July 26 Movement Committee in Exile; quit July 26 Movement, August 1958; opposed revolution's measures and went to United States in June 1960.

López, Narciso (1798–1851) — headed armed expedition to Cuba in 1851 to fight Spanish rule; captured and executed.

Lumumba, Patrice (1925–1961) — founder and president of Congolese National Movement; first prime minister of Congo after independence from Belgium in June 1960; overthrown and imprisoned three months later in U.S.-backed coup; murdered by captors in February 1961.

Maceo, Antonio (1845–1896) — prominent military leader and strategist in the three Cuban independence wars; opposed 1878 treaty that ended first war; led march from eastern to western ends of island in 1895–96; killed in battle.

Machado, Gerardo (1871–1939) — Cuban dictator, 1925–33; deposed by revolutionary upsurge.

March 13 Revolutionary Directorate. See Revolutionary Directorate.

Martí, José (1853–1895) — Cuban national hero; noted poet, writer, speaker and journalist; founded Cuban Revolutionary Party in 1892 to fight Spanish rule and oppose U.S. plans; launched 1895 independence war; killed in battle.

Masetti, Jorge Ricardo (1929–1964) — Argentine journalist; traveled to Sierra Maestra in January 1958 and joined Rebel movement; founding director of Prensa Latina, Cuba's press service; killed while organizing guerrilla movement in Argentina.

Matos, Huber (1919–) — commander in Rebel Army; in October 1959 attempted to organize counterrevolutionary rebellion in Camagüey Province; arrested and imprisoned until 1979.

Mella, Julio Antonio (1903–1929) — leader of university reform movement in 1923; a founding leader of first Communist Party of Cuba in 1925; assassinated in Mexico by agents of Machado dictatorship.

Miró Cardona, José (1902–1974) — a leader of bourgeois opposition to Batista; prime minister of Cuba, January–February 1959; left for U.S. in 1960; served as president of counterrevolutionary Cuban Revolutionary Council in exile.

Mobutu Sese Seko (1930–) — organized coup against Lumumba Government in 1960; president of Congo (renamed Zaire) from 1965 until 1997, when he was himself deposed.

Moncada, Guillermo (1841–1895) — fought in Cuba's independence wars against Spain as leader in Oriente region.

Montané, Jesús (1923–1999) — participant in Moncada attack; member of National Directorate of July 26 Movement; *Granma* expeditionary; captured after Alegría de Pío; held prisoner during entire course of war; currently member of Communist Party Central Committee.

Montecristi Group — group including officers in Batista army, formed in 1956 by Justo Carrillo with goal of encouraging military coup against Batista.

Morales, Calixto — *Granma* expeditionary and Rebel Army combatant.

Mujal, Eusebio (1915–1985) — right-wing head of CTC, 1947–59; supporter of Batista; fled to United States after revolution's triumph.

Murillo, Pedro Domingo (1757–1810) — led 1809 uprising against Spanish rule in Upper Peru (today Bolivia); captured and hanged by Spanish authorities.

National Institute of Agrarian Reform (INRA) — created May 17, 1959, to implement agrarian reform law; coordinated Cuban factory production until formation of Ministry of Industry in 1961; dissolved in 1976.

Núñez Jiménez, Antonio (1923–) — Cuban geographer; combatant in Rebel Army under Guevara, becoming captain; served as executive director of INRA.

Organization of American States (OAS) — founded on Washington's initiative in 1948 as regional organization of Western Hemisphere governments; expelled Cuba in 1962.

ORI. See Integrated Revolutionary Organizations.

Orthodox Party (Partido del Pueblo Cubano [Cuban People's Party]) — formed in 1947 by Eduardo Chibás; main plank was honesty in government; after Chibás's death in 1951, members of youth wing under Fidel Castro's leadership provided initial cadres of July 26 Movement; official leadership moved rightward and fragmented.

País, Frank (1934–1957) — central leader of July 26 Movement in Oriente Province; led November 30, 1956, uprising; member of July 26 Movement National Directorate; organized supplying of Rebel Army; head of *Llano* [urban underground] until murdered by Batista forces in July 1957.

Pazos, Felipe (b. 1912) — signed Sierra Manifesto in 1957; president of National Bank, January–October 1959, replaced by Guevara; opposed revolutionary measures and fled to United States.

Peña, Lázaro (1911–1974) — joined first Communist Party in 1929; member of PSP; general secretary of CTC, 1939–49, 1961–66, 1973–74; member of Communist Party Central Committee at time of death.

Pérez, Cresencio — one of first peasants to join Rebel Army; became commander.

Pérez, Faustino — anti-Batista activist; joined July 26 Movement; *Granma* expeditionary; headed *Llano* following death of Frank País; member of Communist Party Central Committee at time of death.

Pérez Vidal, Ángel — headed Civic Action Committee, a pro-July 26 Movement organization of Cuban exiles in New York.

Playa Girón (Girón Beach) — beach near Bay of Pigs where last mercenary troops surrendered April 19, 1961; Cubans use this name to refer to entire battle.

Ponce, José (1926–2001) — participant in Moncada attack and imprisoned subsequently; *Granma* expeditionary; captured and imprisoned following Alegría de Pío.

Popular Socialist Party (Partido Socialista Popular [PSP]) — founded in 1925 as first Communist Party of Cuba; changed name to PSP in 1944; after revolution's victory fused with July 26 Movement and Revolutionary Directorate to form ORI, and later Communist Party of Cuba in 1965.

Prío Socarrás, Carlos (1903–1977) — leader of Authentic Party; Cuban Minister of Labor, 1944–48; elected president in 1948; overthrown by Batista in 1952; opposed revolution; went to United States in 1961.

PSP. See Popular Socialist Party.

PURS. See United Party of the Socialist Revolution.

Ramos Latour, René (1932–1958) — close collaborator of Frank País; became July 26 Movement national action coordinator after País's death; Rebel Army commander after May 1958; killed in action.

Ray, Manuel — member of July 26 Movement; minister of public works in 1959; emigrated to United States; later participated in clandestine counterrevolutionary activities in Cuba.

Rebel Army — armed force of July 26 Movement in revolutionary war against Batista; became Revolutionary Armed Forces in 1959.

Redondo, Ciro (1931–1957) — participant in Moncada attack and imprisoned subsequently; *Granma* expeditionary; captain in Rebel Army; killed in action.

Revolución — founded as underground organ of July 26 Movement; following 1961 fusion was published by ORI; published until founding of *Granma* in October 1965.

Revolutionary Directorate — formed in 1955 by José Antonio Echeverría and other leaders of Federation of University Students; led March 13, 1957, attack on Presidential Palace, later adding that date to its name; organized guerrilla column in Escambray Mountains in February 1958; fused with July 26 Movement and PSP to form ORI.

Rodríguez, Roberto (1935–1958) — Rebel Army captain; headed Suicide Squad in Guevara's column; died in combat.

Salvador, David (1923–) — headed workers' section of July 26 Movement, 1957–58; general secretary of CTC, 1959–60; imprisoned in 1960 for organizing counterrevolutionary activities.

Sánchez, Celia (1920–1980) — a founding leader of July 26 Movement in southern Oriente Province; organized Rebel Army's urban underground supply network in the cities; first woman fighter to join Rebel Army; member of Communist Party Central Committee at time of death.

Sánchez, Universo — *Granma* expeditionary; became Rebel Army commander.

Sánchez Mosquera, Ángel — colonel in Batista's army; notorious for brutality against peasants.

Santamaría, Haydée (1925–1980) — participant in Moncada attack and jailed subsequently; participated in November 1956 Santiago de Cuba uprising; founding member of July 26 Movement's National Directorate; fighter in Rebel Army; member of Communist Party Central Committee at time of death.

Santos Ríos, Eduardo — economist; worked with Guevara in National Bank.

Sardiñas, Lalo — peasant recruit to Rebel Army; became captain.

Sierra. See July 26 Movement.

Somoza — family of dictators that ruled Nicaragua, 1933–79; overthrown by 1979 Sandinista revolution.

Suárez, Raúl (d. 1956) — helped organize July 26 Movement in Las Villas Province; *Granma* expeditionary; captured following Alegría de Pío and murdered.

Tabernilla, Francisco (b. 1888) — military leader who participated in Batista's 1952 coup, subsequently becoming chief of general staff; fled Cuba January 1, 1959.

Torres, Ñico — railroad worker; leader of July 26 Movement's National Workers Front and of FONU.

Torres, Félix — led PSP guerrilla column in northern Las Villas, which put itself under command of Camilo Cienfuegos.

Trujillo, Rafael (1891–1961) — dictator in Dominican Republic from 1930 until his assassination.

Tshombe, Moise (1919–1969) — led attempted breakaway of Katanga (now Shaba) Province after Congo won independence in 1960; helped arrange murder of Lumumba in 1961; Congolese Prime Minister, 1964–65.

Union of Young Communists (Unión de Jóvenes Comunistas [UJC]) — founded in 1960 as Association of Young Rebels; changed name to UJC on April 4, 1962.

United National Workers Front (Frente Obrero Nacional Unido [FONU]) — founded November 10, 1958, by National Workers Front of July 26 Movement, and by forces from the PSP, Revolutionary Directorate and Orthodox Party; played central role in organizing January 1959 general strike.

United Party of the Socialist Revolution (Partido Unido de la Revolución Socialista [PURS]) — formed in 1962–63 as part of ORI restructuring; became Communist Party of Cuba in 1965.

Urrutia, Manuel (1902?–1981) — a judge at trial of captured *Granma* expeditionaries, where he publicly criticized Batista regime; became Cuban President in January 1959; resigned in July and went to United States.

Valdés, Ramiro — participant in Moncada attack and *Granma* expedition; commander in Rebel Army; currently a member of Communist Party Central Committee.

Verde Olivo [Olive Green] — weekly magazine of Cuban Revolutionary Armed Forces.

Welles, Sumner (1892–1961) — sent to Cuba in 1934 as U.S. ambassador; served as U.S. Undersecretary of State, 1937–42.

Yabur, Alfredo — revolutionary combatant; minister of justice after triumph of revolution; served on Communist Party Central Committee.

Bibliography of Writings and Speeches by Ernesto Che Guevara

The following listing of published articles, speeches, interviews and letters by Guevara was compiled by the José Martí Foreign Languages Publishing House in Havana. An important source in preparing this list was the "Bibliografía del Comandante Ernesto Che Guevara," published in Revista de la Biblioteca José Martí *[Journal of the José Martí Library], July–December 1967.*

A nine-volume selection of Guevara's works, Escritos y discursos *[Writings and Speeches] was published in 1977 by Editorial Ciencias Sociales [Social Sciences Publishing House] in Havana. A two-volume* Obras escogidas *[Selected Works] was published by Casa de las Américas in 1970.*

Unless otherwise indicated, all of the publications listed here are Cuban.

1. ARTICLES AND BOOKS

"Machu-Picchu: Enigma of Stone in America"
 (*Siete* [Panama], December 12, 1953)

"What We Have Learned and What We Have Taught," December 1958
 (*La Patria,* January 1, 1959)

"What Is a Guerrilla?" (*Revolución,* February 19, 1959)

"War and the Peasant Population" (*Lunes de Revolución,* July 26, 1959)

"Latin America as Seen from the Afro-Asian Balcony"
 (*Humanismo* [Mexico], September–October 1959)

"The United Arab Republic: An Example" (*Verde Olivo,* October 5, 1959)

"India: A Country of Great Contrasts" (*Verde Olivo,* October 12, 1959)

"Japan Recovers from the Atomic Tragedy" (*Verde Olivo,* October 19, 1959)

"Indonesia and the Solid Unity of Its People" (*Verde Olivo,* October 26, 1959)

"Commercial Trade and Friendship with Ceylon and Pakistan"
 (*Verde Olivo,* November 16, 1959)

"Yugoslavia: A People that Fights for Its Ideals"
 (*Verde Olivo,* November 23, 1959)

"Opinions about *Lunes de Revolución* on Its First Anniversary"
 (*Lunes de Revolución,* March 28, 1960)

"Notes for the Study of the Ideology of the Cuban Revolution"
 (*Verde Olivo,* October 8, 1960)

"Comments on the Cuban Revolution" (*Kuba Istoriko-etnograficheskye Ocherki*, Moscow, 1961)

"Cuba: Historical Exception or Vanguard of the Anti-colonialist Struggle?" (*Verde Olivo*, April 9, 1961)

"Collective Discussion; One-Person Decision-Making and Responsibility" (*Trabajo*, July 1961)

Guerrilla Warfare, (*Humanismo* [Mexico], March–June 1960, July–October 1960, November 1960–February 1961)

"The Influence of the Cuban Revolution in Latin America" (Havana: Partido Unido de la Revolución Socialista, 1962)

"Industrial Tasks of the Revolution in the Coming Years" (*Cuba Socialista*, March 1962)

"Editorial" (*Nuestra Industria, Revista Económica*, May 1962)

"War Industry" (*Revolución*, August 29, 1962)

"The Cadres: Backbone of the Revolution" (*Cuba Socialista*, September 1962)

"Strategy and Tactics of the Latin American Revolution" October–November 1962 (*Verde Olivo*, October 6, 1968)

"Against Bureaucratism" (*Cuba Socialista*, February 1963)

"First Impressions on Meeting Fidel Castro" (*Revolución*, May 8, 1963)

"Considerations on the Costs of Production as the Basis for Economic Analysis of the Enterprises Subject to the Budgetary System" (*Nuestra Industria, Revista Económica*, June 1963)

"Guerrilla Warfare: A Method" (*Cuba Socialista*, September 1963)

"On the Concept of Value" (*Nuestra Industria, Revista Económica*, October 1963)

"On the Budgetary Finance System" (*Nuestra Industria, Revista Económica*, February 1964)

"The Bank, Credit, and Socialism" (*Cuba Socialista*, March 1964)

"The Trade and Development Conference in Geneva" (*Nuestra Industria, Revista Económica*, June 1964)

"Socialist Planning, Its Significance" (*Cuba Socialista*, June 1964)

"Cuba, Its Economy, Its Foreign Trade, Its Significance in Today's World" (*Nuestra Industria, Revista Económica*, December 1964)

"Socialism and Man in Cuba" (*Marcha* [Uruguay], March 12, 1965)

"Message to the Peoples of the World via the Tricontinental" (*Tricontinental*, special supplement, April 16, 1967)

The Diary of Che in Bolivia, (Havana: Book Institute, 1968)

Prefaces

To Alberto Bayo, *My Contribution to the Cuban Revolution* (Havana: Rebel Army Publications, 1960)

To Gaspar Jorge García Galló, *Biography of the Havana Cigar*
(Havana: National Tobacco Commission, 1961)

To *The Marxist-Leninist Party* (Havana: National Directorate of the United
Party of the Socialist Revolution, vol. 1, 1963)

To *Geology of Cuba* (Havana: ICRM Scientific Department of Geology, 1964)

To Vo Nguyen Giap, *People's War, People's Army*
(Havana: Political Publishers, 1964)

Episodes of the Revolutionary War

*Many of the following articles, listed here chronologically by original publication date,
were subsequently included in* Pasajes de la guerra revolucionaria *[Episodes of the
Revolutionary War], first published in book form by* Verde Olivo *in 1963.*

"Lidia and Clodomira" (*Humanismo,* January–April 1959)

"A Revolution Begins" (*0 Cruzeiro* [Brazil], June 16, July 1, July 16, 1959)

"The Murdered Puppy" (*Humanismo* [Mexico],
November 1959–February 1960)

"A Sin of the Revolution" (*Verde Olivo,* February 12, 1961)

"Alegría de Pío" (*Verde Olivo,* February 26, 1961)

"The Battle of La Plata" (*Revolución,* March 9, 1961)

"The Battle of Arroyo del Infierno" (*Verde Olivo,* November 18, 1961)

"Air Attack" (*Verde Olivo,* April 16, 1961)

"Surprise Attack at Altos de Espinosa" (*Verde Olivo,* June 25, 1961)

"Death of a Traitor" (*Verde Olivo,* July 9, 1961)

"Bitter Days" (*Verde Olivo,* July 23, 1961)

"Reinforcements" (*Verde Olivo,* August 13, 1961)

"Our Men are Toughened" (*Verde Olivo,* October 1, 1961)

"A Famous Interview" (*Verde Olivo,* October 15, 1961)

"On the March" (*Verde Olivo,* December 24, 1961)

"The Weapons Arrive" (*Verde Olivo,* January 7, 1962)

"The Battle of El Uvero" (*Verde Olivo,* February 4, 1962)

"Caring for the Wounded" (*Verde Olivo,* April 29, 1962)

"Our Return" (*Verde Olivo,* June 10, 1962)

"A Betrayal in the Making" (*Verde Olivo,* August 5, 1962)

"El Patojo" (*Verde Olivo,* August 19, 1962)

"The Attack on Bueycito" (*Revolución,* August 24, 1962)

"The Battle of El Hombrito" (*Verde Olivo,* November 18, 1962)

"The First Battle of Pino del Agua" (*Verde Olivo,* March 17, 1963)

"An Unpleasant Episode" (*Verde Olivo,* April 28, 1963)

"Struggle Against Banditry" (*Verde Olivo,* June 9, 1963)

"The Battle of Mar Verde" (*Verde Olivo,* September 8, 1963)

"Altos de Conrado" (*Verde Olivo,* October 6, 1963)

"Adrift" (*Hoy,* December 1, 1963)

"One Year of Armed Struggle" (*Verde Olivo,* January 5, 1964)

"The Second Battle of Pino del Agua" (*Verde Olivo,* January 19, 1964)

"Interlude" (*Verde Olivo,* August 23, 1964)

"A Decisive Meeting" (*Verde Olivo,* November 22, 1964)

Articles Published Under Pseudonyms

The following articles appeared in a column Guevara wrote in the weekly Verde Olivo *under the pseudonym "Sharpshooter."*

"The Macabre Clown and Other Treacheries" (April 10, 1960)

"The Most Dangerous Enemy and Other Silly Things" (April 17, 1960)

"Continental Disarmament and Other Waverings" (April 24, 1960)

"Don't Be a Fool, Pal and Other Capitulations" (May 2, 1960)

"South Korean Representative Democracy and Other Lies" (May 8, 1960)

"Cackling, Argentine Votes and Other Rhinoceroses" (May 15, 1960)

"The Two Great Dangers, Private Planes and Other Violations" (May 22, 1960)

"Frog Jumps, International Bodies and Other Genuflections" (May 29, 1960)

"Istanbul, Puerto Rico, Caimanera and Other 'Bases for Discussion'"
    (June 5, 1960)

"Ydígoras, Somoza and Other Tests of Friendship" (June 12, 1960)

"The Marshall Plan, the Eisenhower Plan and Other Plans" (June 19, 1960)

"Nixon, Eisenhower, Hagerty and Other Warnings" (June 26, 1960)

"Accusations Before the OAS, the United Nations and Other Feints"
    (July 10, 1960)

"Submarine Bases, Missile Bases and Other Monsters" (July 17, 1960)

"Beltrán, Frondizi and Other Weighty Reason$" (July 24, 1960)

"The 'Court of Miracles' and Other OAS Nicknames" (July 31, 1960)

"It Only Takes a Small Sample and Other Short Stories" (August 7, 1960)

"Once Upon a Time There Was a Sugar Mill and Other Popular Legends"
    (August 14, 1960)

The following articles by Guevara appeared in Verde Olivo *under the heading "Advice to Combatants."*

"Morale and Discipline of Revolutionary Combatants" (March 17, 1960)

"Discipline Under Fire in Combat" (May 8, 1960)

"Solidarity in Combat" (May 15, 1960)

"Taking Advantage of the Terrain" (May 22, May 29, June 5, 1960)

"The Counterattack" (June 26, July 17, 1960)

"Machine Guns in Defensive Combat" (July 24, July 31, August 7, 1960)

"Pocket Artillery" (September 24, October 8, October 22, 1960)

2. SPEECHES AND INTERVIEWS

1958

Interview with Jorge Ricardo Masetti, April 1958 (*Granma,* October 16, 1967)

War Bulletin over Radio Rebelde, December 16, 1958
   (*Revolución,* December 16, 1961)

1959

Answer to journalists on assuming command of La Cabaña fortress, January
   2, 1959 (*Granma,* October 17, 1975)

Press interview (*El Mundo,* January 5, 1959)

Telephone interview with Argentine *Correo de la Tarde*
   (*Revolución,* January 5, 1959)

Declaration to the press, January 5, 1959 (*Hoy,* January 6, 1959)

Declaration that he will not accept posts (*El Mundo,* January 8, 1959)

Speech at meeting in his honor, January 13, 1959 (*Revolución,* January 16, 1959)

Speech at meeting in his honor organized by Cuban workers,
   January 19, 1959 (*El Mundo,* January 20, 1959)

Talk given at *Nuestro Tiempo* Society on the Social Projections of the Rebel
   Army, January 27, 1959 (*Revolución,* January 29, 1959)

Speech at El Pedrero, February 8, 1959 (*Islas,* July–September 1968)

Television appearance on "Economic Commentary" program,
   February 11, 1959 (*Revolución,* February 12, 1959)

Opening words at Nicolás Guillén poetry reading February 20, 1959
   (*Hoy,* February 21, 1959)

Remarks in support of Movement of National Unity, April 4, 1959
   (*Hoy,* April 7, 1959)

Remarks at Tobacco Forum (*Hoy,* April 11, 1959)

Speech at conference of Union of Revolutionary Women, April 11, 1959
   (*Hoy,* April 12, 1959)

Remarks to Cuban Industries Exposition, April 17, 1959 (*Hoy,* April 19, 1959)

Interview with Chinese journalist, April 18, 1959
   (*Shih-chieh Chih-shih* [China], June 5, 1959)

Speech acknowledging gift of $30,000 for agrarian reform
(*Revolución*, April 27, 1959)

Speech at graduation of soldiers completing military training, April 28, 1959
(*Hoy*, April 29, 1959)

Television appearance on "Telemundo pregunta," April 28, 1959
(*Revolución*, April 29, 1959)

Speech at May Day rally in Santiago de Cuba, May 1, 1959 (*Hoy*, May 3, 1959)

Speech to militia members, May 3, 1959 (*Hoy*, May 7, 1959)

Remarks at University of Havana, May 11, 1959 (*Hoy*, May 12, 1959)

Speech to architecture students at University of Havana, May 25, 1959
(*Revolución*, May 26, 1959)

Remarks to journalists on trip to Egypt (*Revolución*, June 6, 1959)

Declaration to press in Egypt, June 19, 1959 (*Hoy*, June 20, 1959)

Press conference in Egypt, June 30, 1959 (*Hoy*, July 1, 1959)

Interview with J. Nehru in New Delhi, India, July 1, 1959
(*Revolución*, July 2, 1959)

Press conference in Jakarta, Indonesia, July 30, 1959 (*Revolución*, July 31, 1959)

Press conference in Ceylon (*El Mundo*, August 9, 1959)

Press conference in Belgrade, Yugoslavia, August 15, 1959
(*El Mundo*, August 16, 1959)

Press conference on return to Cuba, September 8, 1959
(*Hoy*, September 9, 1959)

Interview with Mexican journalist Gerardo Anzueta, September 1959 (*Alma Mater*, June 28–30, 1973)

Television appearance on "Economic Commentary" program,
September 14, 1959 (*Revolución*, September 15, 1959)

Interview with foreign students visiting Havana, September 17, 1959
(*Revolución*, September 18, 1959)

Remarks at burial of combatants, September 25, 1959
(*Revolución*, September 26, 1959)

Speech at National Academy of Revolutionary Police, September 30, 1959
(*Revolución*, October 1, 1959)

Interview with Mexican *Siempre*, October 1959 (*Moncada*, October 15–19, 1969)

Speech on education and popular culture, October 8, 1959
(*Hoy*, October 9, 1959)

Speech commemorating Cuban independence war, October 10, 1959
(*Hoy*, October 18, 1959)

Speech at meeting initiating a campaign of honor and honesty,
October 14, 1959 (*Hoy*, October 15, 1959)

Speech on university reform and revolution, October 17, 1959
(*Sierra Maestra,* October 18, 1959)

Speech on reestablishment of Revolutionary Tribunals, October 26, 1959
(*Revolución,* October 27, 1959)

Interview with *Revolución,* October 28, 1959 (*Revolución,* October 29, 1959)

Interview transmitted by Radio Rivadavia of Buenos Aires
(*Revolución,* November 3, 1959)

Interview with Carlos Franqui on becoming head of National Bank,
November 26, 1959 (*Revolución,* November 27, 1959)

Interview with Guatemalan *Prensa Libre,* November 26, 1959
(*Revolución,* December 1, 1959)

Speech commemorating 1871 shooting of medical students,
November 27, 1959 (*Hoy,* November 28, 1959)

Speech at meeting with United Civic Youth (*Hoy,* December 2, 1959)

Speech at inauguration of guano fertilizer plant
(*Revolución,* December 17, 1959)

Speech in Santa Clara on Rebel Army Day, December 28, 1959
(*Revolución,* December 29, 1959)

Speech at University of Las Villas, December 28, 1959
(*Revolución,* December 31, 1959)

1960

Speech honoring José Martí, January 28, 1960 (*Revolución,* February 1, 1960)

Speech at National Bank supporting industrialization, January 29, 1960
(*Revolución,* January 30, 1960)

Television appearance on "Ante la Prensa" (Meet the Press), February 4, 1960
(*Revolución,* February 5, 1960)

Speech to textile workers, February 7, 1960 (*Hoy,* February 9, 1960)

Remarks at meeting honoring outstanding workers, February 22, 1960
(*Revolución,* February 23, 1960)

Speech at ceremony converting Holguín military fortress into school,
February 24, 1960 (*Hoy,* February 26, 1960)

Remarks at National Assembly of Tenant Farmers, February 26, 1960
(*El Mundo,* February 27, 1960)

Speech on role of the university in Cuba's economic development,
March 2, 1960 (*Revolución,* March 3, 1960)

Television talk on political sovereignty and economic independence,
March 20, 1960 (*Revolución,* March 21, 1960)

Speech at May Day rally in Santiago de Cuba, May 1, 1960
(*El Mundo,* May 3, 1960)

Speech at opening of railroad industry exposition, May 20, 1960
  (*Revolución*, May 21, 1960)

Television talk on role of the working class, June 18, 1960
  (*Revolución*, June 19, 1960)

Speech at technical school, July 1, 1960 (*Revolución*, July 2, 1960)

Speech at rally supporting revolutionary government, July 10, 1960
  (*Revolución*, July 11, 1960)

Speech at opening of First Congress of Latin American Youth, July 28, 1960
  (*Revolución*, July 29, 1960)

Speech at inauguration of training course organized by Ministry of Public
  Health, August 20, 1960 (*Hoy*, August 21, 1960)

Speech in Sierra Maestra commemorating anniversary of Rebel Army
  invasion column, August 28, 1960 (*Revolución*, August 29, 1960)

Speech at National Tobacco Plenary meeting, September 17, 1960
  (*El Mundo*, September 18, 1960)

Speech at rally in Camagüey supporting First Declaration of Havana,
  September 18, 1960 (*Hoy*, September 20, 1960)

Declaration on nationalization of three U.S. banks, September 19, 1960
  (*Hoy*, September 20, 1960)

Speech at send-off of International Voluntary Work Brigades,
  September 30, 1960 (*Revolución*, October 1, 1960)

Remarks at armed forces training school graduation
  (*Verde Olivo*, October 15, 1960)

Television appearance on "Ante la Prensa" (Meet the Press), October 20, 1960
  (*Revolución*, October 21, 1960)

Declaration on arrival in Czechoslovakia, October 23, 1960
  (*Revolución*, October 24, 1960)

Television appearance in Prague, October 27, 1960
  (*Revolución*, October 27, 1960)

Interview in Moscow with *Sovietskaya Rossya*, November 1, 1960
  (*Revolución*, November 2, 1960)

Interview in Moscow with Dennis Ogden of London *Daily Worker*
  (*Daily Worker*, November 3, 1960)

Interview with Laura Berquist (*Look* [United States], November 8, 1960)

Remarks on arrival in Peking, November 17, 1960
  (*Revolución*, November 18, 1960)

Remarks at meeting in his honor in Peking, November 22, 1960
  (*Hoy*, November 23, 1960)

Remarks during visit to Foreign Languages Publishing House in Moscow
  (*Revolución*, November 23, 1960)

Remarks at welcoming ceremony in Shanghai, November 28, 1960
  (*El Mundo*, November 29, 1960)

Remarks in Pyongyang, Korea, December 3, 1960 (*Hoy*, December 4, 1960)

Speech to Chinese people over Radio Peking, December 8, 1960
  (*Revolución*, December 9, 1960)

Speech in Moscow at Soviet-Cuban friendship meeting, December 10, 1960
  (*Hoy*, December 11, 1960)

1961

Televised speech informing Cuban people of economic aid by socialist
  countries, January 6, 1961 (*Revolución*, January 7, 1961)

Remarks at memorial for Osvaldo Sánchez and other combatants,
  January 10, 1961 (*Revolución*, January 11, 1961)

Speech at Nícaro nickel plant, January 20, 1961 (*Revolución*, January 21, 1961)

Speech to militias in Cabañas, Pinar del Río, January 22, 1961
  (*Revolución*, January 23, 1961)

Speech at national convention of Technical Advisory Committees,
  February 11, 1961 (*Hoy*, February 12, 1961)

Speech honoring outstanding workers, February 22, 1961
  (*Revolución*, February 23, 1961)

Interview with *Revolución* on being named minister of industry,
  February 26, 1961 (*Revolución*, February 27, 1961)

Speech on the role of foreign aid in Cuba's development, March 9, 1961
  (*Verde Olivo*, March 19, 1961)

Remarks to Argentine daily *Noticias Gráficas* (*El Mundo*, March 18, 1961)

Speech at First National Sugar Meeting in Santa Clara, March 28, 1961
  (*Revolución*, March 29, 1961)

Speech at inauguration of pencil factory in Batabanó, March 30, 1961
  (*El Mundo*, March 31, 1961)

Speech to leaders of Ministry of Industry on problems of spare parts,
  April 8, 1961 (*Revolución*, April 10, 1961)

Remarks at closing of China exposition, April 11, 1961 (*Hoy*, April 12,1961)

Speech in Santiago de Cuba on bombing of Ciudad Libertad, April 15, 1961
  (*Granma*, March 31, 1968)

Televised talk on the economy and planning, April 30, 1961
  (*Hoy*, May 3, 1961)

Speech on anniversary of death of Antonio Guiteras, May 8, 1961
  (*Revolución*, May 9, 1961)

Speech on occasion of General Lister's visit, June 2, 1961
  (*Revolución*, June 3, 1961)

Speech at closing of international work camp, June 4, 1961
(*Revolución*, June 5, 1961)

Remarks honoring outstanding workers, June 22, 1961
(*Revolución*, June 23, 1961)

Remarks to Ministry of Industry functionaries, June 23, 1961
(*Revolución*, June 24, 1961)

Address to OAS Inter-American Economic and Social Conference in Punta del
Este, Uruguay, August 8, 1961 (*Hoy*, August 9, 1961)

Press conference in Punta del Este, August 9, 1961
(*Revolución*, August 11, 1961)

Speech at Punta del Este conference explaining Cuba's refusal to sign
conference document, August 16, 1961 (*Revolución*, August 18, 1961)

Speech at University of Montevideo, August 17, 1961
(*Revolución*, August 19, 1961)

Interview with *El Popular* of Montevideo on Punta del Este conference,
August 17, 1961 (*Hoy*, August 19, 1961)

Televised speech on results of Punta del Este conference, August 23, 1961
(*Revolución*, August 24, 1961)

Speech at First National Production Meeting, August 27, 1961
(*Hoy*, August 29, 1961)

Interview with Maurice Zeitlin, September 14, 1961
(*Root and Branch* [United States], January 1962)

Speech at First Production Assembly of Greater Havana, September 24, 1961
(*Revolución*, September 25, 1961)

Talk with workers from Ministry of Industry, October 6, 1961
(*El Mundo*, October 7, 1961)

Remarks at Ministry of Industry on 1962 economic plan, October 25, 1961
(*Revolución*, October 26, 1961)

Speech at inauguration of Patrice Lumumba metal sulphates plant in Pinar
del Río, October 29, 1961 (*Hoy*, October 31, 1961)

Message sent to meeting on National Economic Development Plan
(*El Mundo*, November 5, 1961)

Remarks to students leaving to study in socialist countries, November 6, 1961
(*Revolución*, November 7, 1961)

Speech honoring factories that won literacy emulation, November 15, 1961
(*El Mundo*, November 16, 196 1)

Speech at paint factory, November 15, 1961 (Ministry of Education, 1961)

Speech to participants in workers' congresses, November 25, 1961
(*Hoy*, November 26, 1961)

Speech on anniversary of 1871 shooting of medical students,
November 27, 1961 (*Hoy*, November 28, 1961)

Speech at 11th Congress of CTC, November 28, 1961
(*Revolución,* November 29, 1961)

1962

Speech at inauguration of biscuit factory in Guanabacoa, January 3, 1962
(*Revolución,* January 4, 1962)

Speech to general assembly of Havana dock workers, January 6, 1962
(*Hoy,* January 7, 1962)

Declaration to factory administrators on basic technical course,
January 10, 1962 (*Hoy,* January 11, 1962)

Televised talk on sugar harvest, January 27, 1962 (*Hoy,* January 28, 1962)

Remarks to winners of Ministry of Industry study circle emulation,
January 31, 1962 (*Revolución,* February 1, 1962)

Remarks at inauguration of workers' training school in Santa Clara,
February 1, 1962 (*Revolución,* February 2, 1962)

Speech at Central University of Las Villas, February 2, 1962
(*Hoy,* February 3, 1962)

Declaration to Buenos Aires weekly *Principios,* March 3, 1962
(*El Mundo,* March 4, 1962)

Speech to meeting of administrators and trade union leaders, March 16, 1962
(*Hoy,* March 20, 1962)

Speech at National Sugar Plenary meeting in Santa Clara,
April 13, 1962 (*Revolución,* April 14, 1962)

Speech at CTC National Council, April 15, 1962 (*Revolución,* April 16, 1962)

Remarks after completing voluntary work at farm cooperative, April 16, 1962
(*Diario de la Tarde,* April 17, 1962)

Speech honoring outstanding workers in industry, April 30, 1962
(*Revolución,* May 4, 1962)

Talk to foreign workers who attended May Day celebration, May 4, 1962
(*Revolución,* May 5, 1962)

Speech to technology students, May 11, 1962 (*Revolución,* May 12, 1962)

Remarks on anniversary of Argentina's independence, May 25, 1962
(*Revolución,* May 26, 1962)

Speech honoring outstanding technicians and workers, June 8, 1962
(*Revolución,* June 9, 1962)

Remarks to sugar refinery workers in Regla, June 11, 1962
(*Revolución,* June 12, 1962)

Speech honoring outstanding workers, June 20, 1962
(*Revolución,* June 29, 1962)

Interview with Vladimir Listov for Soviet *New Times,* July 4, 1962
(*Revolución,* July 10, 1962)

Remarks at flour mill in Regla, July 30, 1962 (*El Mundo*, August 1, 1962)

Remarks at inauguration of shipyards, August 15, 1962
(*Revolución*, August 16, 1962)

Speech honoring outstanding workers, August 21, 1962
(*Revolución*, August 22, 1962)

Remarks after completing voluntary work at Camilo Cienfuegos textile
factory in Güines, September 9, 1962 (*Hoy*, September 11, 1962)

Speech honoring outstanding workers and technicians, September 14, 1962
(*El Mundo*, September 15, 1962)

Speech commemorating second anniversary of fusion of youth organizations,
October 20, 1962 (*El Mundo*, October 21, 1962)

Interview with Sam Russell for London *Daily Worker* on "missile crisis"
(*Daily Worker*, December 4, 1962)

Speech commemorating death of Antonio Maceo, December 7, 1962
(*Diario de la Tarde*, December 8, 1962)

Speech at workers' improvement school graduation, December 14, 1962
(*Revolución*, December 15, 1962)

Remarks honoring outstanding workers and technicians, December 15, 1962
(*El Mundo*, December 16, 1962)

Speech at National Sugar Plenary meeting, December 19, 1962
(*El Mundo*, December 20, 1962)

Speech at graduation ceremony of Patrice Lumumba School for
Administrators, December 21, 1962 (*El Mundo*, December 22, 1962)

1963

Speech at final assembly of first People's School, January 26, 1963
(*Hoy*, January 27, 1963)

Speech honoring outstanding technicians and workers, January 27, 1963
(*Revolución*, January 28, 1963)

Speech honoring outstanding technicians and workers of Ministry of
Industry, February 1, 1963 (*Revolución*, February 2, 1963)

Speech at National Sugar Plenary meeting in Camagüey, February 9, 1963
(*Hoy*, February 10, 1963)

Interview filmed for Canadian TV in Camagüey cane fields, February 9, 1963
(*Revolución*, February 12, 1963)

Speech at inauguration of barbed wire factory in Nuevitas, February 10, 1963
(*Revolución*, February 11, 1963)

Speech at meeting of workers presenting nominees for PURS membership at
textile factory, March 24, 1963 (*Revolución*, March 25, 1963)

Remarks at inauguration of cocao processing plant in Baracoa, April 1, 1963
(*Revolución*, April 2, 1963)

Speech at Minas del Frío, April 3, 1963 (*Escritos y discursos,* vol. 7)

Speech on sugar harvest in Santa Clara, April 6, 1963 (*Hoy,* April 7, 1963)

Interview with Laura Berquist (*Look* [United States], April 9, 1963)

Speech honoring outstanding workers and technicians, April 30, 1963
(*Hoy,* May 2, 1963)

Speech at luncheon celebrating 25th anniversary of *Hoy,* May 16, 1963
(*Hoy,* May 21, 1963)

Farewell remarks to delegation of People's National Army of Algeria,
May 20, 1963 (*Hoy,* May 21, 1963)

Interview with Victor Rico Galán for Mexican magazine *Siempre*
(*Hoy,* June 19, 1963)

Declarations in Algeria (*Hoy,* July 11, 12, 1963)

Interview in Algeria with *Revolution Africaine* (*Revolución,* July 13, 1963)

Remarks at seminar on planning in Algeria, July 13, 1963
(*Revolución,* July 15, 1963)

Interview with journalists in Algeria, July 23, 1963 (*Revolución,* July 24, 1963)

Interview with Jean Daniel (*L'Express* [France], July 25, 1963)

Interview with U.S. students visiting Cuba, August 1, 1963
(*Revolución,* August 2, 1963)

Interview with visiting Latin Americans (*Revolución,* August 21, 1963)

Remarks at opening of chess tournament, August 25, 1963
(*Revolución,* August 26, 1963)

Remarks after completing voluntary work at wood factory, August 25, 1963
(*Revolución,* August 26, 1963)

Speech at meeting of architecture teachers and students, September 29, 1963
(*Revolución,* September 30, 1963)

Remarks honoring vanguard workers, October 16, 1963
(*El Mundo,* October 27, 1963)

Interview with *Revolución's* Siquitrilla column
(*Diario de la Tarde,* November 11, 1963)

Speech at closing of Ministry of Industry seminar, November 17, 1963
(*Revolución,* November 18, 1963)

Speech at Electrical Energy Forum, November 24, 1963
(*Revolución,* November 25, 1963)

Speech at People's Schools of Statistics and Mechanical Drawing graduation,
December 16, 1963 (*Diario de la Tarde,* December 17, 1963)

Speech at closing meeting of Solidarity Week with the People of South
Vietnam, December 20, 1963 (*Revolución,* December 21, 1963)

Televised appearance on establishment of work norms and wage scale,
December 26, 1963 (*Revolución,* December 27, 1963)

Speech at inauguration of Havana plastics plant, December 29, 1963
(*Revolución*, December 30, 1963)

1964

Remarks at Thermoelectric Power Station in Mariel, January 3, 1964
(*Hoy*, January 4, 1964)

Speech at ceremony awarding Certificates of Communist Work,
January 11, 1964 (*Hoy*, January 12, 1964)

Interview for Siquitrilla column of *Revolución* (*Revolución*, February 4, 1964)

Televised talk on need for developing Cuban industry,
February 25, 1964 (*Revolución*, February 26, 1964)

Remarks honoring vanguard workers, March 4, 1964
(*Revolución*, March 5, 1964)

Talk with workers at cement factory, March 11, 1964
(*Revolución*, March 12, 1964)

Speech honoring winners of national emulation, March 14, 1964
(*Hoy*, March 15, 1964)

Speech at UN conference on Trade and Development in Geneva, Switzerland,
March 25, 1964 (*Hoy*, March 26, 1964)

Press conference in Geneva, March 31, 1964 (*Revolución*, April 1, 1964)

Interview on Swiss television, April 11, 1964 (*Hoy*, April 12, 1964)

Declaration in Algeria to Algerian press and Prensa Latina, April 15, 1964
(*Revolución*, April 16, 1964)

Speech at meeting of Cuban Academy of Sciences, April 24, 1964
(*Granma*, November 25, 1967)

Speech at machinery plant in Santa Clara, May 3, 1964
(*Revolución*, May 4, 1964)

Speech at seminar on Youth and Revolution, May 9, 1964 (*Hoy*, May 10, 1964)

Speech at inauguration of kaolin processing plant on the Isle of Pines,
May 10, 1964 (*Revolución*, May 11, 1964)

Speech at inauguration of candle factory in Sagua la Grande, May 17, 1964
(*Revolución*, May 18, 1964)

Remarks in Camagüey to military units participating in sugar harvest,
May 26, 1964 (*Hoy*, May 27, 1964)

Speech at CTC meeting in Camagüey, June 12, 1964 (*Revolución*, June 12, 1964)

Speech honoring emulation winners, June 26, 1964 (*Revolución*, June 27, 1964)

Speech at inauguration of barbed wire factory in Nuevitas, July 12, 1964
(*Hoy*, July 14, 1964)

Speech at inauguration of pencil factory in Batabanó, July 18, 1964
(*Hoy*, July 19, 1964)

Speech at inauguration of bicycle factory in Caibarién, July 19, 1964
(*Revolución,* July 20, 1964)

Speech at inauguration of National Industry for Producing Domestic Utensils
in Santa Clara, July 24, 1964 (*Revolución,* July 25, 1964)

Speech at Patrice Lumumba School for Administrators graduation,
August 2, 1964 (*Escritos y discursos,* vol. 8)

Speech at ceremony awarding Certificates for Communist Work,
August 15, 1964 (*Hoy,* August 16, 1964)

Remarks celebrating sixth anniversary of invasion by Rebel Army columns,
August 20, 1964 (*Verde Olivo,* September 13, 1964)

Speech honoring winners of socialist emulation, October 22, 1964
(*Revolución,* October 23, 1964)

Speech at meeting presenting PURS members at sugar refinery,
October 23, 1964 (*Hoy,* October 24, 1964)

Speech at inauguration of tack factory, October 28, 1964
(*Revolución,* October 29, 1964)

Speech in tribute to Camilo Cienfuegos, October 28, 1964
(*Hoy,* October 29, 1964)

Remarks in Moscow at founding of Soviet-Cuban Friendship Society,
November 11, 1964 (*Hoy,* November 12, 1964)

Interview in Moscow with Uruguayan *El Popular,* November 12, 1964
(*Revolución,* November 13, 1964)

Interview in Moscow with Soviet journalists (*Hoy,* November 18, 1964)

Speech at administrators' plenary meeting in Oriente,
(*Hoy,* December 1, 1964)

Speech commemorating eighth anniversary of Santiago de Cuba uprising,
November 30, 1964 (*Revolución,* December 1, 1964)

Interview with Soviet *New Times* (*Hoy,* December 3, 1964)

Remarks at University of Oriente, December 2, 1964
(*Revolución,* December 3, 1964)

Address to United Nations General Assembly, December 11, 1964
(*Revolución,* December 12, 1964)

Reply to discussion at UN General Assembly, December 11, 1964
(*Revolución,* December 12, 1964)

Appearance on CBS "Face the Nation," in New York, December 14, 1964
(*Revolución,* December 15, 1964)

Interview in Algeria by Josie Fanon for *Revolution Africaine,*
December 22, 1964 (*Revolución,* December 23, 1964)

Remarks in Algeria to *Jeunesse,* December 23, 1964
(*Revolución,* December 26, 1964)

Interview in Algeria with Serge Michel of *Alger Ce Soir*
(*Revolución*, December 28, 1964)

1965

Declaration on visit to Republic of Mali, January 1, 1965
(*Revolución*, January 2, 1965)

Speech to Ghanian journalists and writers on "Neocolonialist activity in Latin
America and some considerations on the necessary unity between Africa,
Asia and Latin America," January 16, 1965 (*Hoy*, January 19, 1965)

Interview with *L'Etincel* of Accra, Ghana, and Prensa Latina, January 18, 1965
(*Revolución*, January 19, 1965)

Remarks to Ghanian trade union leaders, January 19, 1965
(*Revolución*, January 20, 1965)

Speech at Kwame Nkrumah Ideological Institute in Ghana, January 21, 1965
(*Revolución*, January 22, 1965)

Remarks on Algerian radio and television on UN, January 27, 1965
(*Revolución*, January 28, 1965)

Interview in Algeria with *Alger Ce Soir*, January 30, 1965
(*Hoy*, January 31, 1965)

Declaration to Prensa Latina in Tanzania, February 18, 1965
(*Revolución*, February 19, 1965)

Address to Second Economic Seminar of Afro-Asian Solidarity in Algeria,
February 24, 1965 (*Revolución*, February 25, 1965)

Declaration at meeting in United Arab Republic, March 10, 1965
(*Revolución*, March 11, 1965)

Interview with African weekly *Liberation* (*Revolución*, March 25, 1965)

Interview with *Al-Tali-'ah* [Egypt] (No. 4, April 1965)

3. LETTERS

To his parents from prison, July 6, 1956 (*OCLAE*, November 1977)

To Fidel Castro, December 1, 1957 (*Granma*, November 29, 1967)

To Fidel Castro, December 9, 1957 (*Granma*, October 16, 1967)

To Fidel Castro, January 6, 1958 (*Granma*, October 16, 1967)

To Fidel Castro, February 19, 1958 (*Verde Olivo*, January 19, 1964)

To Camilo Cienfuegos, April 2, 1958 (*Juventud Rebelde*, October 20, 1967)

To Camilo Cienfuegos, April 3, 1958 (*Juventud Rebelde*, October 20, 1967)

To Camilo Cienfuegos, April 5, 1958 (*Juventud Rebelde*, October 20, 1967)

To Camilo Cienfuegos, April 12, 1958 (*Juventud Rebelde*, October 20, 1967)

To Camilo Cienfuegos, September 7, 1958 (*Juventud Rebelde*, October 20, 1967)

To Camilo Cienfuegos, October 19, 1958 (*Juventud Rebelde*, October 20, 1967)

To Fidel Castro, October 23, 1958 (*Escritos y discursos*, vol. 2)

To Faure Chomón, October 25, 1958 (*Escritos y discursos*, vol. 2)

To Enrique Oltuski, November 3, 1958 (*Escritos y discursos*, vol. 2)

To Faure Chomón, November 7, 1958 (*Escritos y discursos*, vol. 2)

To Faure Chomón, December 1958 (*Escritos y discursos*, vol. 2)

To the Red Cross, December 18, 1958 (*Granma*, December 21, 1968)

To the people of Las Villas, January 2, 1959
(*El Mundo del Domingo*, December 30, 1962)

To Sergia Cordoví, January 14, 1959 (*Escritos y discursos*, vol. 9)

To José E. Martí Leyva, February 5, 1959 (*Juventud Rebelde*, October 19, 1967)

To Juan Hehong Quintana, February 5, 1959 (*Obras escogidas*, vol. 2)

To Carlos Franqui, March 10, 1959 (*Revolución*, March 11, 1959)

To Alberto Granados, Military Department of La Cabaña, March 11, 1959
(*Granma*, October 16, 1967)

To William Morris, February 5, 1959 (*Verde Olivo*, October 6, 1968)

To Miguel Angel Quevado, May 23, 1959 (*Hoy*, June 6, 1959)

To Valentina González Bravo, May 25, 1959
(*Obra Revolucionaria*, [Mexico City: Ediciones ERA, 1967])

To José Ricardo Gómez, June 7, 1959 (*Reminiscences of the Cuban Revolutionary War*, [New York: Monthly Review Press, 1968])

To Alfredo Guevara, July 26, 1959 (*CIN CUBA*, 1979)

Telegram to Conrado Rodríguez, January 5, 1960 (*Revolución*, January 8, 1960)

To Nelson Mesa López, April 5, 1960 (*Escritos y discursos*, vol. 9)

To Ernesto Sábato, April 12, 1960 (*Casa de las Américas*,
November 1968–February 1969)

To José Tisquet, May 5, 1960 (*Juventud Rebelde*, October 19, 1967)

To Fernando Barral, February 15, 1961 (*Reminiscences*)

Autographed opinions in China exposition album (*Hoy*, March 16, 1961)

Circular to heads of consolidated enterprises
(*Diario de la Tarde*, January 11, 1962)

Agreement No. 6 of the Leadership Council of the Ministry of Industry
(*Orientador Revolucionario*, April 1, 1962)

To Anna Louise Strong, November 19, 1962 (*Reminiscences*)

To Carlos Franqui (*Revolución*, December 29, 1962)

To Guillermo Lorentzen, May 4, 1963 (*Reminiscences*)

To Peter Marucci, May 4, 1963 (*Reminiscences*)

To Aleida Coto Martínez, May 23, 1963 (*Juventud Rebelde,* October 19, 1967)

To the *compañeros* of the motorcycle assembly plant, May 31, 1963
(*Boletín Provincial Habana del PCC,* No. 10, February 15, 1967)

Circular to the heads of the Ministry of Industry, June 7, 1963
(*Nuestra Industria, Revista Económica,* August 1963)

To Pablo Díaz González, October 28, 1963 (*Escritos y discursos,* vol. 9)

To Arturo Don Varona, October 28, 1963 (*Cuba,* November 1967)

To Carlos Rafael Rodríguez, October 28, 1963 (*Reminiscences*)

To Lydia Ares Rodríguez, October 30, 1963 (*Cuba,* November 1967)

To Juan Angel Cardi, November 11, 1963 (*Reminiscences*)

To Luis Amado Blanco, February 15, 1964 (*Reminiscences*)

To María Rosario Guevara, February 20, 1964
(*Juventud Rebelde,* October 17, 1967)

To Roberto las Casas, February 21, 1964 (*Reminiscences*)

To José Medero Mestre, February 26, 1964 (*Granma,* October 8, 1968)

To Luis Corvea, March 14, 1964 (*Escritos y discursos,* vol. 9)

To Eduardo B. Ordaz Ducungé, May 26, 1964 (*Escritos y discursos,* vol. 9)

To Haydée Santamaría, June 12, 1964 (*Obras Escogidas,* vol. 2)

To Regino G. Boti, June 12, 1964 (*Reminiscences*)

To Ezequiel Vieta, June 16, 1964 (*Vida Universitaria,* July–August 1968)

To the Ministry of Foreign Trade, June 25, 1964 (*Reminiscences*)

To León Felipe, August 21, 1964 (*Obras escogidas,* vol. 2)

To Elías Entralgo, August 31, 1964 (*Cuba,* November 1967)

To Manuel Moreno Fraginals, October 6, 1964 (*Obras escogidas,* vol. 2)

To Charles Bettelheim, October 26, 1964 (*Obras escogidas,* vol. 2)

To Hildita, February 1965 (*Pensamiento Crítico,* October 1967)

To Pepe (José Aguilar), 1965 (*Granma,* October 16, 1967)

To Alberto Granados, 1965 (*Granma,* October 16, 1967)

To my parents, 1965 (*Casa de las Américas,* September 1967)

To my children, 1965 (*Tricontinental,* October 1968)

To Fidel Castro, April 1, 1965 (*El Mundo, October* 5, 1965)

To Hildita, February 15, 1966 (*El Mundo,* October 16, 1967)

To Don Tomás Roig Mesa, undated (*Granma,* January 6, 1968)

Index

(GATT), 306, 312-13, 318
General strike, 37, 44, 46, 89, 125, 172, 359
German Democratic Republic, 143, 264, 307, 317, 332
Germany, West, 130, 186, 307, 332
Gómez Ochoa, Delio, 44
Gómez, Juan Gualberto, 101
Gómez, Máximo, 101
Granma expedition, 22, 61, 87, 102, 116, 123, 133, 369, 140, 153
Guadaloupe, 328
Guantánamo base, 145, 249
Guatemala, 20, 57-58, 60, 97, 113, 231, 240, 252, 286, 298, 337, 357, 360, 370
Guerrilla warfare, 64, 66, 69, 70
Guerrillaism, 178
Guiana, 252
Guillén, Nicolás, 118
Guiteras, Antonio, 52, 101
Gutiérrez Menoyo, Eloy, 52, 368

Haedo, Eduardo, 242
Haiti, 112, 239, 268, 337
Havana Charter, 306, 311
Hegel, George Wilhelm Friedrich, 191
Hijacking, 251
Hiroshima, 351
History Will Absolve Me, 124
Hitler, Adolf, 98, 329
Ho Chi Minh, 67
Honduras, 252, 269, 333
Housing, 105, 254, 264, 351
Hunger, 50, 91, 112, 116, 135, 247, 262, 300, 308, 314, 318
Hurricane Flora, 213

Ibañez, Roberto, 254
Iglesias, Joel, 162
Imperialism, 72, 78, 83, 128, 132, 137, 145, 170, 187, 216, 226, 238, 253, 262, 275, 286, 291, 299, 312, 317, 324, 338, 349, 351, 358, 361, 387
Imports, 110, 246, 313
Individual, role of, 114, 120, 147, 155, 160, 179, 185, 208, 210, 218, 225-27
Individualism, 102, 113, 115, 141, 193, 197, 201, 214-16, 221
Indonesia, 330, 356
Industrialization, 32, 93, 104, 110, 255, 299, 323

Infante, Enso, 42
INRA. See National Institute of Agrarian Reform
Institutionalization, 138, 219
Inter-American Development Bank, 243, 254, 312
Interest payments, 321
Integrated Revolutionary Organizations (ORI), 157, 162, 165, 170, 174
Inter-imperialist conflicts, 134, 346
International Monetary Fund (IMF), 237, 312, 318
Iran, 108
Iraq, 108
Isla del Cisne (Swan Island), 252
Israel, 355

Jagan, Cheddi, 328
Japan, 67, 256, 350-51, 355
Johnson, Lyndon B., 353
July 26 Movement, 20, 31, 37, 42, 44, 57, 61, 87, 89, 91, 127, 153, 171, 174, 282

Katanga Province, 329
Kennedy, John F., 244-45, 248-49, 310, 333
Khrushchev, Nikita, 273
Korea, 245, 306, 317, 328, 351, 355

La Cabaña fortress, 56
La Coubre, 246
La Plata, battle of, 26-27, 123
Lamothe, Humberto, 24
Landowners, 27, 50, 56, 91, 102, 105, 138, 235, 280
Lange, Oskar, 189-90
Laos, 245, 327, 349, 351, 357, 360
Larrazábal, Wolfgang, 45
Las Coloradas, 23, 128
Las Villas invasion, 48, 50-51, 53, 55, 89, 91, 124, 127
Latin American Free Trade Association, 260
Law of value, 199, 200-02, 215, 222, 341
Lenin, V. I., 74, 77, 121, 123, 176, 186-87, 189, 196, 216, 294
Liberman, E.G., 195, 204
Literacy, 32, 160, 247, 253, 265
Llano, 34, 42-43, 172
Llerena, Mario, 45, 46